To my dear ... ist.
I pray that you ...
daily with the Lord.

A Special Gift

Presented to:

Vicky Bamford

From:

Linda Llaguno

Date:

6/23/02

The very best friends are the ones
who simply inspire us to be more like Jesus.
—Twila Paris

Alone With God

The Women's Devotional Series

Among Friends

The Listening Heart

A Gift of Love

A Moment of Peace

Close to Home

From the Heart

This Quiet Place

In God's Garden

Fabric of Faith

Alone With God

Alone With God

Ardis Dick Stenbakken, Editor

REVIEW AND HERALD® PUBLISHING ASSOCIATION
HAGERSTOWN, MD 21740

The authors assume full responsibility for the accuracy of all facts and quotations as cited in this book.

This book was
Edited by Jeannette R. Johnson
Copyedited by Jocelyn Fay and Lori Halvorsen
Designed by Patricia Wegh
Electronic makeup by Shirley M. Bolivar
Cover jacket illustration by Lee Christiansen
Typeset: 11/13.5 Minion

PRINTED IN U.S.A.
05 04 03 02 01 5 4 3 2 1

R&H Cataloging Service
Stenbakken, Ardis Dick, 1939- , ed.
Alone with God, edited by Ardis Dick Stenbakken.

1. Devotional calendars—SDA. 2. Devotional calendars—women.
3. Women—religious life. 4. Devotional literature—SDA. I. Title.

242.643

ISBN 0-8280-1587-2

Be still,

and know that

I am God.

—Psalm 46:10

Sunrise Commitment, Sunset Praise

Commit thy way unto the Lord; trust also in him; and he shall bring it to pass. Ps. 37:5.

LONG AGO A FRIEND who knew I was a worrier gave me a bookmark. The woven bookmark was a poem explaining how to give God my best and how to receive His best by beginning and ending each day with Him. A book later reinforced this message, reminding me to pause at sunrise and sunset to remember my Creator.

The same message is still being given in many forms—in puffy white clouds and blue sky, gentle murmuring streams, a bird's song, and quiet moments between tasks. I rediscover that each day is an adventure; I find joy and excitement in God's fingerprints on my daily schedule. I have begun to look for them. They are divine appointments, even when I don't recognize them.

Upon opening my eyes each morning, I have two options: I can use my own judgment, or I can give God permission to arrange my day according to His wisdom. Within moments a schedule of some kind quickly begins to dictate my use of time and resources. When I commit myself and all that concerns me to God early in the day, I can better hear His still small voice offering to guide my choices. With my consent, God whispers at each turn, "This is the way." The beauty of sunrise, private moments created by rain, encounters with the right people to meet my daily responsibilities, and unexpected trails leading to new understanding are divine adventures.

I am frequently amazed by the paths God chooses for these adventures, trails I would have missed on my own. With God as tour guide, the path is exciting and purposeful, whether limping along winding creekbeds of pain and loss, struggling up narrow trails to glorious peaks, or quietly ambling through a serene environment. The best part of each day's walk is the companionship of God and angels and quiet conversations addressing my concerns, my needs, and my dreams. Frequently I find surprise gifts along the way, always wrapped appropriately and timed perfectly, each designed to produce character, to reduce pride, to strengthen courage and peace, to polish faith, and always to reveal God's love.

STELLA THOMPSON

Covered With Snow

Take away my sin, and I will be clean. Wash me, and I will be whiter than snow. Ps. 51:7, NCV.

RIDING ALONG THE INTERSTATE, I see debris on the shoulders of the road. Riding through the city, I see trash along the curbs. Beautiful green lawns are now brown. Lovely blossoming flowers droop with the cold morning dew. High winds have stripped trees of every leaf. Yes, it is winter.

Suddenly it happens. During the wee hours of the night the quiet tiny flakes of snow begin falling. Quickly showers of big flakes come. By morning everything is under a white blanket. However, when the cars, buses, and trucks begin moving again and the snowplows do their work, the white blanket becomes an ugly, grimy, dirty, slushy mess. Just one step in the snow will leave its mark.

So it is with our lives. When we awaken each morning we begin with a clean white page of life. But before the day is over that page is soiled so quickly and quietly with ugly words, thoughts, and actions. The debris of sin has spoiled our snowlike blanket.

I cannot explain how one can take red, mix it with dirt, and it becomes white. Only through the chemistry of the blood of Jesus is this possible. We use a machineful of water with detergent to clean clothes. If a dark color accidentally falls in the washer with the white clothes, the white will come out dingy. However, just a drop of Jesus' blood will make our lives white.

In Isaiah 1:18 we read "Though your heart is stained with sin, it can be washed as white as snow. Though your heart is stained the deepest red, it can be made as white as wool" (Clear Word). I thank God for this comforting promise. Each morning is a new beginning. We need the cleansing power of the blood of Jesus to keep us from the trash and debris that Satan throws our way. "Oh! precious is the flow that makes me white as snow; no other fount I know, nothing but the blood of Jesus." Unlike some cleaning agents, the blood of Jesus will never lose its power. His robe of righteousness cleans us whiter than snow.

Here is my life—my soiled, dirty life. I need Your blood to be applied to it. I need the cleaning, covering power of Your righteousness. And oh, how I do thank You for this miracle applied today. MARIE H. SEARD

Hidden Treasure

Where your treasure is, there will your heart be also. Luke 12:34.

IT WAS A COLD DAY, as January days in Utah usually are. Jim and I had been spending every minute of every day occupied at work, busy with church responsibilities, and taking care of guests. When our daughter called, inviting us to go with her family on a weekend of birding and searching for precious stones, Topaz Mountain sounded wonderful. For decades scores of rockhounds at Topaz Mountain have chipped the precious crystals out of the rock. Our favorite spot to set up camp is on the back side. No one goes there anymore, since the crystals are now so small it is hardly worth the effort.

Almost before the cars had stopped, each person was on his or her way to a favorite spot—some to climb to the highest peak, and others with their hammers in hand to break out the topaz crystals. Our two granddaughters and I headed to the dry creekbed, where we hoped some of the topaz had washed under rocks and into the sand. It is still startling to me to catch sight of those little bits of shining crystal hiding in the most remote places. When the sun comes out from behind the clouds, they are much easier to spot. Most of the crystals are clear and glasslike, but their natural color is a transparent amber. To find even one of those tiny treasures is a real treat.

After a couple hours the girls walked me back to the car, where I could rest and look at my pocketful of beauty. My mind began to wander to other interesting sites where we had found utterly fascinating displays of underground treasure. How restful to ponder our Creator and His ways of hiding the beauty for those who desperately want to search for them. On our nature trips we have searched for gold, silver, and copper, but are happy with just a humble little crystal. I dozed off in the warm sunlight, thinking about the challenge of finding treasure underground.

What a God we have! He undoubtedly understood our need for beauty. But He hid more of that beauty than we can ever find in a lifetime, making each discovery a truly exciting experience. In our heavenly home we will uncover something new and impressive every day. He has shared a little bit of heaven with us just so we can anticipate the things that He has prepared for us.

JEAN REIFFENSTEIN-ROTHGEB

Focus

Let the words of my mouth, and the meditation of my heart, be acceptable in thy sight, O Lord, my strength, and my redeemer. Ps. 19:14.

I NEED TO SPEND MEANINGFUL, quality time with Jesus each morning. But I haven't formed the habit yet of really focusing wholly on Him and experiencing a balanced prayer and spiritual life. I get caught up majoring in minor things," wrote a freshman college student in a recent letter.

After rereading her words several times, I thanked God for this Christian young woman who longs for a quiet half hour to focus on Jesus. The cares of life whisk me, too, into perpetual motion. *Dishes need doing—then I'll have my devotions,* I think. Then the phone rings—a friend needs to talk . . . checks written for unpaid bills . . . and so it goes, if I allow it. To stay focused on Jesus and His goodness is a daily challenge. Even if I try to set aside a special time, something—or someone—interrupts.

One time I completely lost focus when a friend accused me of something that wasn't true. As hard as I tried to stay focused, I repeatedly discovered those accusations plowing through my mind. Finally I prayed the prayer in our text for today—again and again. I prayed for wisdom to receive insight into her error. At last my prayer seemed to be answered, and our relationship improved.

Enoch and Elijah must have made the words of today's text their constant prayer. These men discovered how to remain truly focused and thus built an intimate relationship with Jesus. Enoch daily walked with God, and God took him, we're told. Neither Enoch nor Elijah experienced death. Was this because they daily kept their focus on Jesus? Often I've asked myself this question.

Lord, help me, in spite of each day's turmoil, to keep focused on You. "Let the words of my mouth, and the meditation of my heart, be acceptable in thy sight, O Lord, my strength, and my Redeemer." Give me wisdom, words, and ways to encourage my young college friend to keep focused on You, Jesus!

NATHALIE LADNER-BISCHOFF

A Path Through the Snow

Even the wind and the waves obey him! Mark 4:41, NIV.

OUR GIRLS' DOUBLE TRIO was returning to boarding school from a weekend singing tour. We had gotten a late start, and even though we knew we would be going through the mountains on the cold wintery night, we had asked for God's protection, and we trusted our driver. Exhausted, we had soon drifted off to sleep.

Suddenly we were awakened by our driver. "Girls," she was saying, "could you please wake up and have special prayer? We are in a terrible snowstorm, and I can't even see the road. I think we're still on the road, but for all I know we may be out driving through a cow pasture."

We were awake in an instant. When we looked out the windows, not only was it snowing, but the wind was blowing the snow horizontally across the windows, making visibility practically zero. We immediately began to pray for guidance. This was in the days before cell phones, and we were running low on fuel. The situation was serious.

As we prayed, the driver gasped. There, right in front of the car, was a clear path through the snow. There was snow on each side and behind us, but directly in front it was clear enough that we could slowly go on to the next town. We were so excited we could hardly believe our eyes! When we arrived in town, we bought gas.

We then remembered that one of our classmates lived in that town and knew that her parents would be happy to put us up for the night. We made a quick phone call, and they gave us directions to their home. All the way there we continued to have a clear path, though it was snowing hard all around us.

Even though it was very late, those kind people indeed made us welcome. With a quick call to the school, warm food in our stomachs, and comfortable beds for all of us, we were soon sound asleep, secure in the knowledge that God had delivered us from the storm.

I have often thought about that night and wondered why we were so surprised when God answered our prayers and gave us a clear path through the snow.

ANNA MAY RADKE WATERS

Standing on the Train

I have learned the secret of being content in any and every situation. . . . I can do everything through him who gives me strength. Phil. 4:12, 13, NIV.

AS SOON AS I STEPPED onto the station platform, I realized a train had been canceled. Twice as many commuters huddled in the drafty winter cold. It was only a short ride into London, but I prayed hard that I would be able to find a seat. Because I was recovering from chronic fatigue syndrome, standing was still very tiring for me.

By the time I got inside the crowded train every seat had been taken. Discouraged, I found a place to stand. Standing for even 10 minutes could make me feel very ill. But I had to take the tube across London to attend an important meeting. I had to feel and be at my best. I put my bag on the floor and leaned against the partition in the carriage. One of the biggest problems for CFS sufferers is that they don't always look ill or disabled. I knew no one would give up their seat for me.

I took a deep breath and prayed that I would be able to cope. Almost immediately I realized that I was much more comfortable standing, with plenty of space around me, than sitting in the crowded car, squashed between businesspeople trying to read newspapers and working on their laptops. Leaning against the partition took the weight off my feet. A small open window washed me with refreshingly cool air. I saw interesting sights that I'd never noticed when sitting down. I needed a handkerchief, and it was easy to reach my pocket without bumping the person next to me. During the next few minutes I counted all the positive things about having to stand on the train. I smiled at the miserable-looking commuters and thanked God that I had to do this trip only a few times a year, not every day.

Standing there, I felt wrapped in God's love. Concentrating on the positive things in my situation—however small or unusual—lifted my heart. In a situation that could have crushed me, I felt content and able to cope, knowing God was there, giving me strength and providing for my needs in the most unexpected ways. When I finally stepped off that train, I felt refreshed and energized, ready to face the day ahead with God.

KAREN HOLFORD

A New Creature in Christ

Therefore if any person is [ingrafted] in Christ (the Messiah), he is a new creation (a new creature altogether); the old [previous moral and spiritual condition] has passed away. Behold, the fresh and new has come! 2 Cor. 5:17, Amplified.

EARLY EVERY MORNING I spend my devotional time with God in my special room, in my special chair. I get up earlier than the rest of my family, so the house is unusually quiet as I pray and read my Bible. I have a wonderful time in those early hours!

One morning as I was praying in my chair, the door to my room opened. Soon I felt a gentle thud as my cat joined me in my chair. Without a sound, Misty twisted around and curled up in my lap and began to purr.

I focused my attention on the furry body in wonder. Under normal circumstances, having a cat sitting in one's lap and purring is no miracle, but for Misty it was. Misty came to me several years ago, an abandoned city cat who had been horribly abused. My veterinarian told me that Misty would be put to sleep if I didn't take her into my home. So Misty became a member of our family.

As you would expect, Misty was very frightened of human contact. It took a long time for her even to eat in front of me. Over time she consented to being touched, but only in short spurts. After several years she got to where she would actually sit in a lap, consent to being petted, and finally would actually purr.

I love to hold, pet, and play with cats, so it was difficult for me to have a frightened and unsociable cat in the house. There were many times I wished I had never taken Misty into our house. But as I looked at her that morning, I was so glad I had.

As I continued to ponder the change in Misty, I realized that when God had found me, I was wounded, emotionally and spiritually. I was destined for death unless God took me in. Over time, through the continual love of Jesus, my fear was overcome. I was healed and became a new person in Christ.

Father, thank You for taking me in, for not giving up on me, for showering me with Your love, and for making me into a new person.

SHARON DALTON WILLIAMS

January 8

Greater Love

My command is this: Love each other as I have loved you. Greater love has no one than this, that he lay down his life for his friends. You are my friends if you do what I command. John 15:12-14, NIV.

SHE SAID IT SO FAST that I almost didn't catch the significance of her words.

Ann Marie and I had been friends for many years and shared food and fun together. Now we were catching up after a few years' separation. We spoke of the happiness of mutual friends, Sue and Marvin, who had recently married. Sue had been alone for a long time after tragically losing her husband of many years. Some time earlier she had begun mentioning Marvin, a friend of hers who had lost his wife. I was delighted when Sue told me the two hurting hearts were lonely no longer, that they were happily married. I had seen them occasionally since and was pleased to note how happy they were together.

Now Ann Marie added a dimension to the love story such as my wildest imagination would not have conceived.

"He looked at me first," Ann Marie said. "But I told him Sue needed him more, having lost her husband and all."

"You mean," I said, "you thought of how lonely Sue was, how much she missed her husband, and gave away your opportunity for a comfortable, happy home of your own?"

"Well, yes, if you want to put it that way. You know, I've been single all my life, and I'm used to it. It's no big deal for me to be alone. Sue was so lonesome."

I marveled at the unselfishness of this precious friend. I knew how much she enjoyed her nieces and nephews and thrilled with their progress and their families, something she had never experienced herself as a single person. Now she had had a chance to marry and have a home of her own and had given away the opportunity to a bereaved and lonely friend. What unselfishness! What love!

I remembered Someone who gave an infinitely greater gift to heal hurting and lonely hearts. He gave Himself to die in our place. Greater love has no one than this!

RUTH WATSON

A Balm in Gilead

Is there no balm in Gilead; is there no physician there? Jer. 8:22.

TO UNDERSTAND HOW MUCH my cat Gilead means to me, you would have to know what a mess my life was before he was born.

My emotional problems started with a broken romance. Then the job that I had once enjoyed became hateful to me when the promotion I had been promised went to someone else. Things continued to go downhill for me when a speeding car crashed into mine. I was fine, but my car spent weeks in the shop. Shortly after that my hours at work were cut back, and I was plunged into debt.

As a 12-year-old I had suffered from anorexia, starving myself in an effort to stay skinny. Since then I had put on weight. Now I decided that since a low-fat diet and exercise didn't help, I would just stop eating, and I set off once more down the path of self-destruction. I counted every calorie to make sure I didn't go over 200 a day. I was living mostly on water and fruit juice. I obsessed continually over the breakup—what he said, what I said, why I hadn't seen it coming.

It was into this world that Gilead was born. I found a litter of feral kittens living under my house. They were a scruffy lot, and Gilley was the obvious runt. He was crawling with fleas and had an infection on his neck where some larger animal had bitten him. Finding the kittens was like finding hope for me. Suddenly I was needed. My life had a purpose. I started feeding the kittens and was able to catch two before the mother moved them.

I found a home for the little female, but no one wanted the sickly little male. Six weeks later, after yet another potential home for him had fallen through, I thought maybe God meant for me to keep him.

All this happened 12 years ago. Gilley is sitting on the couch with me now. I named him Gilead after the old hymn "Balm in Gilead." To other people, he's just a cat; but to me, he's a miracle. He came along at just the right time to soothe my soul. Taking care of him got me back on the track of taking care of myself—eating properly, exercising, and sleeping. I thank God every day for sending him to me.

GINA LEE

Prayer Ministry

Before they call I will answer; and while they are still speaking, I will hear. Isa. 65:24, NKJV.

I HAVE A NEW FRIEND, but not just any friend. She is a new Christian friend who has a prayer ministry for those in our church, for those outside our church, and for all those who need the Lord—which really includes everyone. My friend is not without personal problems. She has an inoperable brain tumor that the Lord has chosen, for now, to keep from growing. Some women would choose to dwell on this type of problem and become very depressed. But not my friend! I wonder, would I be as cheerful in the same circumstances, or would I choose to dwell on my own problems and ignore the needs of others?

I try to call her every day or so and send a card once a month, just to let her know I remember and I care. She is always cheerful, always ready to pray for whatever problem or concern I may have. And I have seen the Lord respond to her prayers and answer them in a positive way.

I teach nutrition classes from time to time. I try, in these classes, to convey the philosophy that we are placed on this earth to be of service to others. I also try to convey that God has a plan for each one of us, and that He will show us that plan if we ask for His guidance. One can teach much about God when teaching about health and nutrition. I often ask my friend to pray for those who come to my classes, and she willingly does so. Perhaps that's why I have such a diverse group—some are young, some are middle-aged, some are older, some are male, and some are female. But all are interested in nutrition and health and ask intelligent questions. This gives me further opportunity to teach more about God's design for our bodies.

Sometimes I find myself saying things I had not planned to talk about, and I am often amazed at this. I believe that my friend's ministry of prayer for me and those I teach has everything to do with what I say. The Lord knows just what each person in my class needs to hear so much more than I do.

If you have a prayer ministry in your church, put it to the test. And if you don't already have one, maybe the Lord is calling you to start one. When we work with the Lord, He provides amazing results!

LORAINE F. SWEETLAND

Laundry Day

Joshua's clothing was filthy as he stood before the Angel of the Lord. Then the Angel said to the others standing there, "Remove his filthy clothing." And turning to Joshua he said, "See, I have taken away your sins, and now I am giving you these fine new clothes." Zech. 3:3, 4, TLB.

I CURLED UP ON MY PARENTS' BED, a 5-year-old bundle of fear, my face stained with tears. Minutes earlier I had been watching my mother iron my father's white baker pants. Little did I know that the experiment I was planning when she finished would plummet me into an abyss so deep I would despair of ever climbing out.

"There. That's done," she sighed, walking out of the room.

Quickly I moved a stool over to the ironing board, climbed atop, and reached into my pocket for a pencil. With a flourish I swiped the lead across the pants. Next I brandished an eraser. "The black mark will disappear like magic!" I hypothesized. But the harder I rubbed, the more the mark smeared. Soon it became a sinister, mocking grin. I stared in horror. After what seemed like an eternity I sneaked into my parents' bedroom and flung myself across the bed.

After another eternity my mother entered the room, knelt beside me, and asked why I was crying. "Daddy's— Daddy's—" were the only words I could utter.

She patted my shoulders. "I know. It'll be OK," she replied. "I can get the stain out. Just remember what you learned here today." Then she walked out to where my father's pants were, marred and ugly, lifted them from the ironing board, went back to the laundry room, and started the process all over again. By the time she had finished, the clock had struck 8:00, and I lay in bed.

It wasn't until 40 years later, one starless, moonless adult night, that I really understood what I had learned from that incident. I was contemplating yet another sinister stain, this time on my heavenly Father's white garment. Suddenly, through another veil of tears, I saw again my mother kneeling beside me. I heard once more her reassuring words that she could remove the spot, and I thought about the energy she had sacrificed to right the wrong I had committed. Only then did I realize that everything I could possibly need to know about God's grace, I had learned late one afternoon on a long-ago faraway laundry day.

LYNDELLE CHIOMENTI

Train Station Prayer

They that know thy name will put their trust in thee: for thou, Lord, hast not forsaken them that seek thee. Ps. 9:10.

WINTER VACATION HAD ENDED for my daughter, Cynthia, who was 12 years old. I traveled with her that morning to Roorkee, Uttar Pradesh, where she was enrolled in a Christian boarding school. As soon as I got her settled I started back, hoping to reach home the same evening. I had to report to work the next morning at the school where I taught.

I couldn't get a direct train or bus home, but by changing my train twice I hoped I could somehow reach home that same evening. It had started raining, and there was a cold wind that would not stop. It was a miserable evening, and I longed to be home.

At last the train reached my destination, and I hurried to the door, as I knew the train would stop for only two minutes at the station. I pulled and pushed on the door, but it would not open. I found the door on the opposite side open, so I jumped down. This put me where I would have to cross another set of rails before climbing up to the platform on the other side.

I crossed the tracks and looked up just in time to see a train rapidly approaching on that line. I threw my bags onto the platform, then tried to pull myself up onto the high platform as well, but couldn't. The train was almost upon me. I fell to the ground below and pressed my body as flat as it would go in the narrow space between the steel rail and the cement wall of the platform. I hoped the train would pass over me, but I expected that I would die.

I felt parts of the locomotive hit my back. The vacuum pipes pounded me. The pain was terrible. As I lay there I cried out to God, "Lord, save me!"

Suddenly the train stopped. I lifted my hand to feel where I was, and touched the joints of the train. It had stopped in the only place possible that would allow me to lift myself out of my position. I held on to some train parts and raised myself to the platform. The locomotive and four cars had passed over me.

I examined myself, surprised that I was all in one piece. I was certainly bruised and battered, but nothing was broken. God had saved me when I called on His name.

BALKIS RAJAN

Hope Can Die With a Mirror

[Her] work will be shown for what it is, because the Day will bring it to light. 1 Cor. 3:13, NIV.

ONE FRIDAY I POPPED INTO a beauty school's salon for a quick shampoo and style. I wanted to look especially good for Sabbath. Before I could register, a student stylist came toward me and ushered me to her chair. I hoped she was not the one who had recently styled my daughter's hair, because my child had not been pleased with the result.

Covering me with a plastic cape, she asked, "Didn't I style your daughter's hair?"

"I don't think so," I replied, still hoping. "My daughter doesn't live here."

"But wasn't she here at Christmas?"

My worst fears were realized. I could do nothing but submit to her ministrations. I reassured myself with the notion that she certainly must have learned a lot in the four months since my daughter's last visit.

When the curlers started falling out while I was still under the dryer, I knew that the hoped-for improvement was definitely not to be. "Don't worry," the stylist consoled, collecting the pink cylinders that were rolling on the floor. "I'll use a curling iron on those strands." A half hour later she handed me the bill, and I left. She had not used the curling iron. I had not used the mirror.

When I picked up my granddaughter from kindergarten on the way home, she cried out, "Oh, Grandma! Your hair is a mess!" The little voice was despairing. Briana had not yet learned to soften unvarnished truth. Instinctively I glanced at the rearview mirror. She was right. My hair looked dreadful!

That experience made me wonder what others see when they look at my life each day. I resolved to use the mirror of God's law to examine myself constantly. Only through His grace can we come up to God's standard of perfection, which He made possible by His death on Calvary. Unlike my beauty school experience, in that final day of judgment perfect satisfaction is guaranteed.

I place myself in Your hands; I can trust You to do what is best for me. Today I not only want to look good, but be good because of what You do for me.

CAROL JOY GREENE

Be Still

Be still, and know that I am God. Ps. 46:10.

ONE COMMAND CHILDREN receive often—perhaps more often than they would like—is "Sit still!" or "Stand still!" or "Be still!" I am sure they believe the adults in their lives are unreasonable to expect them to be still all the time in church, in school, on the bus, in the waiting room, at the doctor's, the dentist's, the barber's, or during a shampoo. "Just don't wiggle! Keep still!"

Our world is restless. We are conditioned to be in a constant state of motion. Even when circumstances render us helpless we wish we could "do something," and when we can't, we pace.

It is not easy to be still. Ask the Israelites. Boxed in by the Red Sea and the Egyptian army, they panicked. Hysteria spread. Death seemed certain. Then God spoke through Moses: "Do not be afraid. Stand still, and see the salvation of the Lord, which He will accomplish for you today" (Ex. 14:13, NKJV). God invited them to rest and watch while He worked.

Jehoshaphat could also speak to this. When the combined military forces of the Ammonites and Moabites set up camp in an effort to intimidate Judah and the inhabitants of Jerusalem, he learned to stand back, keep still, and observe God at work. "You will not need to fight in this battle," the Lord promised. "Position yourselves, stand still and see the salvation of the Lord" (2 Chron. 20:17, NKJV). Then God delivered yet again. He worked while His children stood still.

Keeping still requires discipline, especially in a crisis. This accident victim can testify to that. I was trying to crawl out of a car wreck when the first emergency responder shouted down to me, "Lie still! Don't move! Lie still! Don't move!" He had concluded from the assessment of the impact that I might have sustained spinal injuries. He was right. I later discovered that if I had continued the struggle to free myself, I would have caused extensive spinal cord damage, resulting in permanent paralysis from the neck down.

If we crave equilibrium in our world of decadence, decay, and disorder, we would do well to listen to David. In his years as a fugitive he used whatever quiet moments he could snatch to record his thoughts. On one such occasion he recorded these words: "Meditate within your heart on your bed, and be still. . . . And put your trust in the Lord" (Ps. 4:4, 5, NJKV).

MARIA G. MCCLEAN

Live Wire

There shall no evil befall thee, neither shall any plague come nigh thy dwelling. For he shall give his angels charge over thee, to keep thee in all thy ways. Ps. 91:10, 11.

THE DAY AFTER MY ENGAGEMENT ceremony was a long day. My grandparents and other relatives had come for the occasion. Many of my friends were there. The entire following day we were busy making wedding plans and programs. It was a happy time, a festive time, with so many relatives and friends around. We were up late talking, and the lights were on in all the rooms.

My parents were in one room, and my friends and I were laughing together in another room. My mother came in to interrupt our conversation. "You should take your bath now, Sushama," she advised. Although I didn't like leaving my friends, I did as she asked. However, instead of going to the outside bath house we usually used, I decided to use the inside one. Since the light was off, I stepped inside and, in the semidarkness, reached for the switch.

In the excitement of the day I had forgotten that the electricity connection for this bathroom was under repair. As I reached for the switch, I touched the live wire, and a jolt of electricity shot through my body, knocking me to the bathroom floor.

My family heard me fall and ran to see what had happened. They found me unconscious on the bathroom floor and realized immediately what had happened. They administered first aid and took me to the hospital, where I was kept under observation for five days.

"Your daughter is very fortunate she is alive," the doctors told my parents. "Even in the fall she has not been seriously injured." I am very, very thankful to God that I had no permanent effect from that electric shock or the fall.

I believe that night God gave His angels charge over me and protected me. I often read Psalm 91 and remember that experience of the protecting hands of the angels.

Thank You, Father, for Your unseen messengers of love, the angels, who are always with us to protect us from harm and danger. I want their presence with me today, because I have no idea what evil I may have to face.

SUSHAMA JOSEPH

Beautiful Buffy

There will be no more death or mourning or crying or pain, for the old order of things has passed away. Rev. 21:4, NIV.

BUFFY, A BEAUTIFUL GOLDEN RETRIEVER, was a joy from the moment we got her at the age of 5 weeks. She was eager to please and so pleasing to us. When she ran she was as beautiful as the dogs you see on the dog food commercials. She would greet us with a smile that told us how much she enjoyed living in our home. (Yes, dogs *do* smile. They smile all over from their heads to the ends of their tails.) Buffy lived with us for 10 wonderful years. She was never sick, always happy, and she never met a stranger. She loved everyone and would let us do anything to her, trusting and loving unconditionally. Grandchildren climbed over her and pulled at her tail and she took it all—never snapping or growling. She accepted it as her role in our family. When morning came, she would wake up, eager to go for her walk. It was the high point of her day.

One day Buffy couldn't get up. Something was terribly wrong. She wouldn't eat and couldn't stand. She had to be carried into the vet's office, and the verdict was not good. Cancer had riddled her liver, and there was another large mass on her spleen. She probably wouldn't survive an operation, and because she couldn't eat, to take her home would mean she would starve to death. Facing this news was the most horrifying nightmare a dog lover can imagine. We held her paw as the drug was administered. Buffy's death left us with a gaping hole in our hearts that will never be filled.

This was not the work of God. This was the work of the enemy. Satan delights in watching us ache with grief. Disease, even in our pets, came into the world with sin. But God is victorious, and one day we will live with Him forever without sickness, disease, or death. No more tears! We were reminded by this heartbreaking incident that we live on borrowed time. Treat your loved ones with loving hearts and trusting souls, eager to spend time together, sharing God's beautiful world. None of us know when our last day will be, but very soon we will spend eternity with each other and with Him.

SUZANNE FRENCH

Come, Have Breakfast With Jesus

Early in the morning, Jesus stood on the shore, but the disciples did not realize it was Jesus. . . . When they landed, they saw a fire of burning coals there with fish on it, and some bread. . . . Jesus said to them, "Come and have breakfast." John 21:4-12, NIV.

EARLY-MORNING TIMES WITH JESUS are the best part of my day! One morning I began reading John 21 and soon became engrossed in the story.

Seven of Christ's disciples gathered on the shore of Galilee. The disturbing events of His crucifixion and the thrilling news of His coming forth alive from the tomb, but no longer to stay with them here on earth, had unsettled them. They seemed to have no leader.

Peter, ever restless, told the others, "I'm going fishing."

"We'll go with you," the other six responded.

Though all were experienced fishers and worked hard throughout the night (the best time to fish in Galilee), they caught nothing. As morning approached they turned disconsolately toward the beach.

A man on the shore called out, "Did you catch any fish?"

"No," they responded.

"Try throwing the net out on the other side of the boat," the man called again. Feeling it was hopeless, yet willing to try anything, the weary fishers obeyed. Immediately the net filled with fish—so many that they were unable to haul the catch on board and had to drag the net alongside.

The apostle John, remembering a similar experience early in their connection with Jesus, shouted above the tumult of the sea, "Peter, I think it's the Lord!"

Immediately Peter impulsively jumped out of the boat and waded through the breakers toward the beloved figure. Yes, it was Jesus! And the fish and bread He had braising on the fire perfumed the cool morning air.

"Come," Jesus called out to the weary men. "Have breakfast with Me."

I had read that story many times before, but this time Jesus' call to the men was also a call to me. Every morning He invites me to spend time with Him. And He already has the bread and fish prepared. The words of that call thrill me yet: "Come, have breakfast with Jesus!"

CARROL JOHNSON SHEWMAKE

Love in a Pot of Soup

Husbands, love your wives, even as Christ also loved the church, and gave himself for it. Eph. 5:25.

I HAD SPENT THREE DAYS WORRYING about a family problem. I had been so despondent that I was unable to carry out my home duties at my usual pace. I was scheduled to work at the hospital Thursday and Friday, so that left no time to do my usual cleaning for the weekend.

My dear husband had tried to reassure me that there was nothing I could do about the situation and that everything was going to be all right, but I resisted his efforts to restore my usually sunny disposition.

As I prepared for work on Friday, I dreaded entering the weekend with a not-so-tidy house. Things seem to go better when everything is neat and in order. All day at work I felt guilty for not cleaning the house as usual.

When I arrived home I opened the door to find a neat, clean laundry room. I proceeded into our bedroom and noticed that the bedroom and bathroom were also clean. After changing clothes I entered the den/kitchen area. They too were neat and clean.

Then I smelled the soup. In the middle of an immaculate kitchen, my smiling husband stood stirring a steaming pot of lentil soup. I ran to him and gave him a big hug. All I could say was "Thank you." At that time I felt very loved.

He said, "You always say I don't tell you I love you often enough. 'I love you' is very easy to say, but real love is shown by actions."

I knew he was right, and I loved him even more than ever for his kind actions at a time when I needed love and understanding.

Father in heaven, You have also told us, "Yea, I have loved thee with an everlasting love: therefore with lovingkindness have I drawn thee" (Jer. 31:3). Today I would like to show those around me that I have them in mind, and that I want to draw them close to You.

ROSE NEFF SIKORA

Unity in Diversity

The body is not made up of one part but of many. . . . If one part suffers, every part suffers with it. 1 Cor. 12:14-26, NIV.

ONE WEEK AGO MY STUDENT Melissa had been jumping up and down at the thought of a new girl enrolling in school. "There'll be nine of us now," she had told me, "and we can have our own softball game!" Today there was nothing about her body language that suggested happy.

Melissa explained that the new girl was so different. She spoke scarcely any English, her hair was braided, she was left-handed, and her name was Punella. I wanted to laugh, but Melissa was far too serious to appreciate the humor in this situation.

I mentally grasped at straws and pulled one out. "Remember when you named all the fingers on your right hand?" I asked her.

"Of course," Melissa responded, rolling her eyes and wondering what this had to do with the matter at hand. She rattled them off. "There's Tami Thumb, Patty Pointer, Laura Long, Sarah Straight, and Paula Pinky." (She had insisted on girls' names!)

Then I read aloud the section in 1 Corinthians about one body with many parts. We talked about how different Tami Thumb was from Paula Pinky but that how, together, there was unity in diversity. She was intrigued with that oxymoron.

"Let's think of ways in which Punella could contribute to your girls' group," I suggested as we moved into the kitchen to fix supper. As she got into the brainstorming mode, her laughter once again filled the house. And by the time her mother came to pick her up a couple hours later, we had come up with a long list that included writing on the left side of the blackboard that butted right up against the wall to teaching them to sing in a different language for the upcoming musical program.

"If we could think of this many things," Melissa said, wrapping her arms around me in a goodbye hug, "just wait until I brainstorm with the girls tomorrow!"

After Melissa left I thought about the Punellas in my life. I was 100 percent behind the concept of unity of diversity, but some practical applications would be improved.

ARLENE TAYLOR

January 20

Through the Valley

Yea, though I walk through the valley of the shadow of death, I will fear no evil: for thou art with me. Ps. 23:4.

YOU WILL HAVE TWINS!" the doctor announced after one of my prenatal examinations. I was so excited I immediately began to get everything I needed for two babies instead of one.

One morning the pain came, and I was rushed to the hospital, where I went through a very difficult labor and delivered twins, a boy and a girl. Sadly, the boy survived for only an hour.

Eight days later I was again rushed to the hospital with severe abdominal pain and heavy bleeding. I wondered if I would live to raise my new baby girl and my 6-year-old son. My family stood near my bed as I waited to go into the operating room. Once again I was facing the valley of the shadow, and I was afraid. Six-year-old Enoch began to cry. I wanted to comfort him, but my tongue felt so dry it would not form the words.

As they wheeled me into surgery I was crying, thinking of my children. I prayed, "Lord, please give me two more years of life to care for my son and my daughter. Don't let me die now. My children need me."

I thought of Enoch saying his nightly prayers. I knew that that night he would repeat Psalm 23 as he always did before he slept. I too began to whisper the psalm. Those words gave me peace as I submitted to the anesthesia.

After the operation they gave me a blood transfusion. Suddenly I felt very hot and itchy and had pain in my heart. Again I was frightened. My mother, who stood nearby, realized what was happening and quickly removed the needle and stopped the transfusion. They called the doctor, who verified that I had been given the wrong blood and was reacting to it.

I was very weak and ill, and the whole family gathered around again to pray for my recovery. As they prayed a peace settled over me, and I felt the Lord touch me and knew that all would be well. It has been 21 years since that experience. I asked God for two years, and He has given me more than 10 times that. What a marvelous, wonderful God He is! JEAN SUNDARAM

I'm Happy Today!

Hide me under the shadow of thy wings. Ps. 17:8.

I WAS NOT HAPPY THAT MORNING. Ron had just left on itinerary after being home for only one day. I was sick with a fever, and work was piling up on all sides. I felt sorry for myself because I was so far away from my children and grandchildren. That morning I decided to share all of my miserable feelings with the Lord.

Lord, this morning I feel like a pest coming to You with my miserable feelings, but I have to share with someone, and I have no one else to talk to right now. I know You will listen. I don't have the strength to pretend. I just feel too miserable to be the happy woman I want to be.

I then wrote two pages of complaints to the Lord. I named each feeling: sick, discouraged, hopeless, anxious, incapable, frustrated, worried, and fearful. I circled each feeling so that it stood out on the pages. I wrote a paragraph for each one, telling the Lord why I had that particular negative feeling. As I did, tears rolled down my cheeks.

So Lord, that is how I feel. I don't want to feel this way, but I don't know what to do about it. I don't have energy to even think rationally. I want to run away from all my problems, my responsibilities, my miserable feelings. I feel like hiding, Lord!

Then I looked at the bottom of the journal page (each page had a promise printed there), and I smiled when I read Psalm 17:8: "Hide me under the shadow of thy wings."

Lord, that is just how I feel! My miserable feelings are like hawks, foxes, weasels, and wolves ready to devour me. So like a baby chick, I run to You to hide under Your wings for protection, comfort, and peace. Hide me under the shadow of Your wings as a mother hen hides her little chicks.

That day an unheard-of thing happened on the busy Hosur campus where I work. Not even one person came near my house or office to talk to me. No one phoned. It was as if I were hidden and no one knew I was there! I marveled at how smoothly my day went. I felt energized.

I awoke the next morning singing, "I'm happy today!" My happiness was a miracle after the gloominess of the past two days. God had hidden me under His wing and rejuvenated my spirit. DOROTHY EATON WATTS

January 22

Lessons From the Snow

Cleanse me with hyssop, and I will be clean; wash me, and I will be whiter than snow. Ps. 51:7, NIV.

SNOW. WITH MORE THAN 40 inches of the white stuff in the past month, there is enough of it to admire or despise. And lessons to learn, as well.

The bald spots in the lawn are now gone. How beautifully the imperfections are disguised, even eliminated! My life needs that too. Christ has offered to cover me with His life, white and pure. *Gracious Lord, thank You!*

How it glistens in the bright sunlight. At night the snow even reflects the moonlight. How well does my life reflect the Sun of righteousness? *Thank You, Lord, for making me into a mirror of Your grace and beauty!*

David and Isaiah used snow to illustrate the cleanness and purity of a life purged from sin (Ps. 51:7; Isa. 1:18). While getting my mail yesterday, I considered how the pristine beauty of the snow had been marred by human hands. The snow is ugly where it has been plowed and driven on. How easily purity is tarnished! To stay white, snow on the ground has to receive fresh layers from above. *Thank You, Lord, for fresh mercies every day!*

Not knowing too much about Michigan winters, we asked whether we should uncover our yew bushes. "Oh, no," said our neighbor. "The snow protects them from freezing temperatures." *Thank You, Lord, for protecting me from the frostbite of sin and its effects.*

Indiana farmers are glad for all the snow after the drought last summer. Snow provides gentle moisture for the thirsty soil. My soul needs irrigation—water from above. *Thank You, Lord, for Your gentle watering, to satisfy my spiritual thirst.*

I come from a warmer climate. As beautiful as it may be, snow is still cold. I watch with envy as the children make snow angels in it! My fingers ache inside thick gloves. And I think of my life. It may be beautiful, helpful, and even shiny—just like the snow. But if it is cold, it is uncomfortable to me and to those around me. *Thank You, Lord, for warming my life with the fire of Your love and for helping me to pass on that warmth to others whose fingers are cold. Thank You, Lord, for the snow!* NANCY JEAN VYHMEISTER

Anticipation

We are looking forward to a new heaven and a new earth, the home of righteousness. 2 Peter 3:13, NIV.

I NEVER ASPIRED TO BE a career girl, probably because the kinds of things I really enjoy doing—writing, music, quilting—are not the kinds of things it is easy to earn a living at. But when our third and youngest son started parochial school, I reluctantly entered the work force.

After many years the stresses and frustrations of performing well in an area that did not utilize my natural abilities gradually led to burnout. My sixtieth birthday began my countdown to early retirement. I hung a string of 24 safety pins on my calendar and removed one each month. The shorter my string of safety pins, the greater my anticipation of retirement!

When the alarm jolted me out of a fitful sleep and I wearily faced another day, I could almost taste the luxury of sleeping till I woke up naturally. When I attempted to cope with the stress of working in an office in which finances dictated trying to do more work with less help, I imagined the peace of starting the day with a leisurely breakfast and devotions, and of walking meditatively around the nearby lake and enjoying the natural beauties of the Northwest. Likewise, when I came home exhausted from a long day of work and took care of the "have-to's" instead of the "want-to's," I dreamed of when I would have time for all the fun things I longed to do.

R-Day finally came. I soon made some sobering discoveries. Workaholic habits, whether part of your personality or developed out of necessity, are not easily overcome. I had so many expectations of what I would be able to get done once I retired that at first I attempted far too much. Recovery from burnout is a slow process.

Things are getting better. My expectations are more realistic, my demands on myself are lower, and I am enjoying some of those rewards I dreamed of for so long. Increased time for thoughtful reflection has also led me to compare my anticipation of retirement with my anticipation of Jesus' coming. I have resolved to focus my desire and my life on something far more wonderful than retirement—something that will not only live up to my expectations, but far exceed them: the joy of being with my Best Friend forever.

Carrol Grady

January 24

On the Inside

"Blessed forever are all who . . . have the right to enter in through the gates of the city and to eat the fruit from the Tree of Life. Outside the city are those who have strayed away from God." Rev. 22:14, 15, TLB.

IT WAS 12:55, AND THE EMPLOYEE cafeteria closed at 1:00! As I hadn't packed a lunch, I hurried toward the cafeteria entrance. Oh, no! The gate was already closed one third of the way. *I've got to get lunch,* I thought, and quickly ducked under the bottom of the gate. Another employee, who was right behind me, ducked under also.

"Whew! Just made it," he said. Then, chuckling, he added, "Sure glad it wasn't the gate to heaven we were trying to get through at the last second."

"You're right about that," I agreed wholeheartedly.

As I made my food selections, I noticed the gate was now halfway down. At least seven more employees dashed into the cafeteria and had to duck even farther down than I had.

I've often thought about how many of us had just made it in that day, how we almost had an unplanned fast. Was it because we were too lazy to prepare something for ourselves at home, weren't hungry enough, lost track of the time while we were engrossed in our work, or because we were too busy to be concerned with eating? I guess it actually doesn't matter—we were on the inside (by just a few seconds) only through the grace extended to us from the cafeteria manager.

Oh, friends, how close are we to missing out on eternal life? How often we forget the importance, the necessity, of feeding on the spiritual food that has been lovingly prepared for us as our souls are slowly dying. Life happens—and in the midst of all the business, we ignore the One who can give us all that we ever need. In mercy He has extended an extra measure of His grace to us—time to make it in. But heaven's gate will close one day, leaving many who choose not to eat from the bounties in God's storehouse.

Lord, help me today to hunger for the spiritual nourishment that only You can give. Let me take all the time I need and feed on Your Word. When the gates of heaven close one day soon, may I be safe and secure on the inside—eating from Your tree of life—blessed forever.

IRIS L. STOVALL

Holding the Seed

If you have faith as small as a mustard seed, you can say to this mountain, "Move from here to there," and it will move. Nothing will be impossible for you. Matt. 17:20, NIV.

I'M SURE WE'VE ALL HEARD about faith, a mustard seed, and the moving of mountains. I'm trying to hold on to that mustard seed.

Has this ever happened to you? You're walking tall and strong, then *wham!* Knocked down by a breeze. Or you've just taken two important steps forward when all of a sudden you feel a jerk—that's five steps you've just been yanked back! But that's OK, because you're getting up and starting to walk again when—you guessed it! You feel that tap on your shoulder that tells you "Go directly to jail—do not pass go!" Sad day!

Want to know the truth? You've just slipped again on that little seed you've dropped. Funny how something so tiny can make you fall so hard. Or, should I say, how the lack of something so tiny will make you fall.

There are days when I can't seem to make it without a five- to 10-minute respite in our prayer chapel. I just sit there and stare at the stained glass mural. I don't even need to put my feelings into thoughts, much less words. God is the only one who can enter into the deepest corners of my mind and appreciate every aspect of my being. He's more than willing to heal and reconstruct my heart, my soul. I keep slipping because at times I'm not brave enough or strong enough to hold on to the seed. So I have to let God pick me up, dust me off, and reach down to pick up that elusive seed and place it in my hand once again.

Yet even if my faith tends sometimes to be smaller than a mustard seed, it's the ability and the desire to allow God that counts. I refuse to give it up. I once read, "You may have no remarkable evidence at the time that the face of your Redeemer is bending over you in compassion and love, but this is even so" (Ellen White, *Testimonies for the Church,* vol. 3, p. 323). I say Amen! I pray that God will always bend over and pick me up, because I intend to make that seed grow into a huge and vibrant tree.

Strange how we usually think that we must ask for big things, big changes. I simply try to ask for the seed. How about you? Keep holding on!

LUDI LEITO

My New Suit

Come now, and let us reason together, saith the Lord: though your sins be as scarlet, they shall be white as snow; though they be red like crimson, they shall be as wool. Isa. 1:18.

WE RECEIVED AN INVITATION to attend a celebration at a church that we had attended some years before. It was a beautiful day, so I put on my new suit.

After the worship services a lunch was served. I went over to the salad section and, as I love coleslaw, I asked the woman in charge to put a helping on my paper plate. The next thing I knew, salad dressing was running right down the front of my new suit and onto my shoes. I was horrified! My suit was spoiled. My day was spoiled. I just wanted to go home. I felt miserable!

I washed the suit, but as soon as it was dry I could see the stains from the dressing. The next day I phoned a dear friend and told her about my experience.

"Don't worry; just send it to me, and I'll get it clean for you," she offered.

I told her of my attempt to clean the suit myself and how the marks were still there.

When she returned the suit, every stain was gone! It looked as good as new. She was a friend indeed.

Jesus, my Saviour, is also a friend indeed. He says, "Now, let's settle the matter. You are stained red with sin, but I will wash you as clean as snow. Although your stains are deep red, you will be as white as wool" (Isa. 1:18, TEV).

If I had not sent the suit to my friend, I would not have gotten it clean. I could not clean it on my own. Likewise, I am helpless in my sinful condition. My friend used a special solution to remove the stains; Jesus used His blood to cleanse me from the stain of sin. My friend did not charge me for cleaning my suit; Jesus paid the price on Calvary. My friend helped me because she loves me; Jesus died for me because He loves me.

Thank You, Friend, for showing Your love to me. May I show Your love to others, too, day by day.

PRISCILLA ADONIS

Hope for Tomorrow

Hope is vital for our restoration. If God answered all our prayers and gave us everything we asked for, we would not long for anything better. If we had everything, there would be nothing to hope for. Rom. 8:24, Clear Word.

WHEN I WAS ATTENDING a university for my graduate degree, I noticed a paper on the bulletin board that declared: "Due to lack of interest, tomorrow has been canceled." I was amused and bewildered. Obviously someone was calling attention to the fact that tomorrow did not hold much hope or promise for many on the campus. But that statement has stuck in my mind, and I've drawn a lesson from it.

Reading today's verse helps me realize that tomorrow has great hope for me, and I would not want it canceled. I have not lost my interest in it. Hope is vital as we look forward to our restoration.

When I sing the song "Great Is Thy Faithfulness," I really mean the words "bright hope for tomorrow" and "all I have needed Thy hand hath provided." Sometimes it may seem that my tomorrow has been canceled, but it's not because of my lack of interest. I remember that God is still there, and His faithfulness is still great. He has not lost His interest in me or my outcome, even if I sleep for a while. I just remember the great sacrifice Jesus made in my behalf.

My greatest hope is for the second coming of Jesus and my restoration to His kingdom that He has prepared for me. I need patience to watch and wait for it. That's my tomorrow, and I know it will not be canceled. Even though it seems there is such a general lack of interest in it and it is so slow coming, it will come. I read in Hebrews 10:37, "For yet a little while, and he that shall come will come, and will not tarry."

I will hang on to Your promises as I await that great tomorrow. I know it will not be canceled! I believe in that hope for tomorrow because my hope is in You, my Saviour. There is much to look forward to. BESSIE SIEMENS LOBSIEN

Double Blessing

Now unto him that is able to do exceeding abundantly above all that we ask or think, according to the power that worketh in us. Eph. 3:20.

ON A VISIT WITH MY SON and daughter-in-law I noticed that they were not happy. "What is wrong?" I wanted to know. "Don't you like your work? Are you homesick?"

At that time they were working in Nepal, and we lived in the southern part of India. They were working in a different culture and had to learn a new language. But the problem was none of these things. Instead, Reena confided to me that she and Alwyn were sad because she had not been able to get pregnant.

I understood their concern. In India it is expected that every woman will give birth to a child in the first year after marriage. If not, people look down on her. The pressure becomes great to have a child. When people asked about their children, they were embarrassed and felt as though something was wrong with them. They became tense and unhappy.

We didn't know what to do except to pray. For seven weeks my husband and I fasted and prayed each Saturday. On the Monday after the seventh Saturday Alwyn called to say that Reena was pregnant. We were all so happy!

Then I had a very strange dream. In my dream I saw a tomato plant in my garden. On it were two huge tomatoes, ripe and ready to pluck. I used both hands to pick them and place them on a large tray. It was a strange dream, and I didn't know the significance until one day Reena told me she was carrying twins.

What a blessing! We asked God for one child, and He gave us, as we say in India, "two two." When God gives, He gives abundantly above all that we can ask or think. We were very happy and celebrated a day of thanksgiving for the good news.

I used to think that miracles and wonderful things happen only to others, not to me or my family. My grandsons showed me that God is willing to do miracles in our family as well. He is willing to hear and answer our prayers, giving us even more than we could dream about.

WINIFRED DEVARAJ

Daniel's God

Be not far from me, O God; come quickly, O my God, to help me. Ps. 71:12, NIV.

I WAS HURRYING TOWARD MY OFFICE, my arms full of books and papers, when another staff member caught up with me and offered to carry my load. He was always like that, helpful and invariably cheerful, so as I looked at him I asked what had wiped the smile from his face.

"I need your help," he said. "Could you spare me a few minutes?"

"Sure! Come into my office," I invited.

Laying down my books and papers, John sat on the proffered chair and leaned forward. "I need you to pray for me. Will you do that? I know that when you pray, God answers, and do I need an answer ASAP!"

"Oh! Oh!" I exclaimed, smiling at him as my mind began to whirl. "What do you want us to pray about?"

"It's a case of my folder for my senior class. I have looked for weeks. I've looked carefully, sporadically, and now frantically. But I can't find it. Next week I have to start teaching that unit. I'm desperate. I've prayed," he said, catching my eye, "but I can't find it. Then I thought that if I asked you to pray, I'd find it."

Dear God, I silently prayed in half-horror, *I'm not Daniel. I am not given visions, but I sure need You now. Help me!* John was waiting expectantly as I said, "I'd be happy to pray, John. Let's do it now."

After we prayed, I prayed again. *Dear Father, please answer this prayer so that John's faith may be strengthened. I know that I am just Your disciple who happens to be John's friend.*

The bell rang for the end of break, and I hurried out of my office only to literally bump into John in the doorway. His whole face was lit by joy and relief, and I knew that my wonderful God, Daniel's wonderful God, had already answered my prayer.

"I knew it would work!" he exclaimed. "Isn't God wonderful?"

"He certainly is!" I grinned back, my legs a bit weak with relief and my mind telling me God had blessed my mustard seed of faith.

URSULA M. HEDGES

"Please, Ma'am, Baby"

Search me, O God, and know my heart; try me, and know my anxieties. Ps. 139:23, NKJV.

WITH ALMOST NO WARNING the young woman shoved the filthy little baby in my face. "Please, ma'am, baby. Please, baby!"

I had just walked out of the airport arrivals section of the Bangalore, India, airport and was walking toward the parking lot with friends who had come to pick me up. First there had been the intense heat that had slapped me in the face. Then there were the milling crowds around the doors, looking for friends, for handouts, for a job—something to carry, someone who would pay to have something done. The noise and the smells inundated and overwhelmed. And then there was the baby thrust in my face.

The baby was tiny, obviously sick, face plastered with flies and other unidentified matter. The eyes were sunken. I couldn't look. I wasn't sure whether the infant was dead or alive; I wasn't sure I wanted to know. I knew from experience that if I gave any money to the young woman, the baby would never get any of the help—the pitiful tyke was being used to get sympathy and money, simply being used.

I began to think of other situations. How often do we thrust our babies in someone's face to get sympathy? Perhaps they are the specter of past traumas, abuse, mistreatment by an employer, deception by a church member. Its form makes no difference. It is an ugly picture. They are useful to us for attention, for sympathy.

These things are serious and need to be cared for. There needs to be sympathy and help from someone who is able to make a difference. Is it possible that we are not really looking for help but for sympathy and acknowledgment, a handout rather than healing?

There is Someone who understands our needs, who can read our hearts, who knows our motives. We can bring our thoughts, our hurts, our pitiful conditions to Him for healing—He knows exactly what we need and how to administer it. We can be totally honest and open to Him. Furthermore, He will never look the other way.

Father, here is my baby. Take it and heal us, I pray.

ARDIS DICK STENBAKKEN

His Own Kind

We are God's masterpiece. He has created us anew in Christ Jesus, so that we can do the good things he planned for us long ago. Eph. 2:10, NLT.

WE WERE DISCUSSING WHY people don't sit in the front row at church. I told my sister in Christ why Sonny and I always sit in the front row. She said that I needed to share this story.

Every Sabbath my blessed little family sat in the pews in the back of the sanctuary: those reserved for parents with small children. But people would turn around in their seats and look at us when Sonny made noise. I saw the looks. Then Andrea, our daughter, or I would take Sonny back into the mothers' room.

We have dealt with those looks since Sonny's birth. He is severely retarded and can be disruptive or good as gold, the same as any normal child can be. Finally I made a vow to God that from then on, when I went to church, Sonny and I would always sit in the front row. No one would ever again have to turn around and look at us because they would be behind us! Should Sonny become disruptive, then all would see with their own eyes why I was taking him elsewhere. Sonny must learn there are fair and just consequences for undesirable behavior, and it was my duty to teach him that for his own sake.

Often people say to me, "I remember when you were pregnant with Sonny—most people would have never kept him. You and your husband have done a marvelous job caring for him."

People often tell me that Sonny's name perfectly suits him. They say that he has such a warm, glowing, sunny disposition, and that he makes others around him feel happy.

When I was pregnant, I felt the Holy Spirit impress me to name my child "Sonny," should I have a baby son. Later I reasoned that if He told me in advance what to name my child, then He would certainly take very good care of us. God made me and my baby feel very, very special to Him—this has kept me from being overwhelmed with grief and disappointments.

I hope it's in Jesus' plan to come soon. Nothing would please us more than to keep Sonny safe until then. He knows our hearts, and He knows our circumstances. *Please come quickly, Lord Jesus. Amen.*

DEBORAH SANDERS

The Barriers of Assumption

Let anyone with ears to hear listen! Luke 8:8, NRSV.

HOLA," I GREETED THE adorable 3-year-old, inching toward my seat by the window as we waited at gate 44 of the Orlando International Airport. It was one of the few Spanish words I knew.

His dark eyes sparkled as he looked away from a landing plane and turned to smile up at me. "Hi!" My ears did the proverbial doubletake. I was sure that I had heard him speaking Spanish to his mother not five minutes earlier. "Why don't those planes land in the lake?" He put his little hand on my shoulder as he directed my gaze to the issue in question.

I have no idea how I answered him. I was too floored by his ability to realize so immediately that English was my language of choice. I had spoken to no one else but him. Was that one Spanish word I spoke so obviously accented? Before I could ask his mother, our flight was called and my question got lost in the flurry of departure.

All the way to Chicago I mulled over the incident. Before we deplaned, however, I realized that the dynamics that cued my 3-year-old friend into selecting the appropriate medium for his discourse with me were also available to this fortysomething woman. How many times, I wondered, had I assumed, incorrectly, that I could not converse with my neighbor? How many times had I deprived myself of the blessings of meaningful communication?

All around us are tentative questions voiced by interested souls. Often we unwittingly erect barriers to block them out. With God's help, however, we can break down the roadblocks and hear the questions. We know the words, engendered from the wisdom-laden seeds of His gospel. He will help us use them. "If you have ears, then listen to what I'm telling you," our heavenly Brother exhorts us (Matt. 11:15, Clear Word).

Loving Lord, help us eradicate those assumptions that destroy our witness. Thank You for our marvelous brains and the often inexplicable dynamics of their controlling functions. Thank You that we have ears. Help us use them to truly listen to those around us. GLENDA-MAE GREENE

The Picture

Call to Me, and I will answer you, and show you great and mighty things, which you do not know. Jer. 33:3, NKJV.

MY HUSBAND WAS SCHEDULED for major surgery, and I was worried. There was a difference of opinion among his physicians as to where the surgery should be performed. We had decided on our local hospital, but I was still scared. One of his physicians was emphatically against this decision. I prayed frequently, asking God for assurance that we were doing the right thing. I even asked for some type of sign that would give me some peace.

The night before the surgery I awoke with severe nausea and vomiting. To allow my husband to get the sleep he needed, I went into the family room and made myself a bed on the couch. Almost overcome with fear and apprehension, I felt absolutely rotten. How could I go to the hospital in the morning to be with him when I was so sick?

I slept fitfully, praying for his safety each time I awoke. I had just finished claiming the promise in Psalm 86:7: "In the day of my trouble I will call upon You, for You will answer me" (NKJV). When I opened my eyes, I saw a beautiful sight—a picture of Jesus hanging on the guest closet door. It was the most beautiful portrait of Jesus I'd ever seen. My husband does scroll saw work as a hobby and frequently hangs his most recent creation on this door. I was surprised, because I'd not noticed this new picture before. As I gazed at it I felt a special peace come over me and felt sure that everything was going to be all right.

Sleep came quickly, and I didn't wake again until the alarm clock sounded. Although I was weak and my stomach still felt waves of nausea, the vomiting was over, and I was able to accompany my husband to the hospital. The surgery proceeded uneventfully, and when he was safely back in his room, I returned home.

Remembering the portrait and the comfort it had given me the night before, I went to look at it more closely. But there was no picture hanging on the closet door!

MARGIE PENKALA

February 3

Forgiveness

Forgive us as we have forgiven others. Matt. 6:12, Clear Word.

THE CLUTTER OF DISHES piled up as each family member dropped what he or she had used in the kitchen sink, ignoring the notice over the sink that read, "Thank you for washing whatever you use." Disgusted, I stood looking at the unsightly mess, then reluctantly and painstakingly started to remove each piece until the sink was empty. Then I filled it with soap and water and began the cleanup job.

As I held each dish or glass in my hand I contemplated my relationship with God. The task completed, I took a few minutes to think about my Christian experience. The stack of dirty dishes could very well represent unconfessed sins in my life, sins that pile up and clutter my spiritual survival.

"If we confess our sins," John tells us, "He is faithful and just to forgive our sins . . . and purify us from all unrighteousness" (1 John 1:9, Clear Word). Why stockpile these sins when they can be easily forgiven by a loving and willing Father?

There are unconfessed sins of harbored hurt, lust, envy, and selfishness. We cannot truly ask forgiveness of our heavenly Father if we are not willing to forgive others. Unconfessed sins block the connection between God and us by blurring our vision of a compassionate Father and Friend. These sins interfere with our relationship between us and our colleagues and family members. We spend so much time brooding over our hurt or our guilt instead of giving it to God that we can't even see how our behavior is negatively affecting others.

Today you can begin the healing process. First, ask God to forgive you of the unconfessed sins, the harbored hurt, whatever stands between you and your God. Then ask Him to show you how your behavior is affecting someone else. Go ahead. God is waiting, and you will feel so much better.

Lord God, thank You for the promise of forgiveness that You have given. Give me the love and grace I need this day to extend this same forgiveness to others. GLORIA GREGORY

After 13 Years

Casting all your care upon him; for he careth for you. 1 Peter 5:7.

NEENA STOOD BEFORE ME, her eyes downcast. Her friend Shalini, from fifth grade, stood beside her, an arm around her waist. I read concern in Shalini's eyes. "What's wrong?" I asked.

Neena bit her lip and sighed. Shalini spoke. "Teacher, we've come to ask you to pray for Seema."

At those words tears spilled from under Neena's eyelids and trickled down her cheeks. She used one hand to brush them away.

I hugged Neena. "Tell me what is wrong with your sister," I said. "We will surely pray for her, and I know Jesus will hear our prayers. Is she sick?"

Neena nodded her head.

"Then let's pray for her," I said, kneeling. Neena and Shalini knelt beside me. After asking Jesus to touch Seema and heal her, if it was His will, we got up. Neena and Shalini were both smiling now. The burden of just moments before had been rolled away.

"My father cries at every meal," Neena said. "My sister never moves from her bed. She has been in a coma for 13 years. She was like that even before I was born. Why does my family have to go through such a terrible experience?"

"I don't know," I admitted, "but I do know God loves you. Pray to Jesus every day. I know He has a plan and a purpose for your family, and He will help you understand someday."

Although I was at that school for only a few days for a Week of Prayer, I couldn't get Neena and her sister out of my mind. Neena and Seema were the burden of many of my prayers during that time. Four months later I visited the school again and asked one of the teachers about Neena.

"You won't believe what happened!" Mr. Paulraj told me. "Seema is out of danger. It has been several weeks now since she came out of the coma."

Thank You, Father, for caring so much for Neena and her family. Thank You for being willing to take all of my burdens today, whatever they may be. Help me to remember that nothing is too hard for You to do, if it is Your will.

AHALYA BAI PHILIPS

God's Two Gifts

Give ear to my words, O Lord. . . . Hearken unto the voice of my cry, my King, and my God: for unto thee will I pray. Ps. 5:1, 2.

I WAS PREGNANT, AND MY husband and I were so excited. He insisted I go to my parents until it was time to deliver the baby so I would have good care. At that time we were working far from any relatives and from proper medical care. My parents and I rented a small house near Giffard Memorial Hospital in Nuzvid, Andhra Pradesh, and there we waited for the birth of my first child.

One morning I said to my mother, "I think something is wrong with the baby. It doesn't feel right somehow."

"Come; we'll go see the doctor right now," Mother urged. "She will know what to do. There is no use sitting around here and worrying about it."

The doctor confirmed that there was something wrong. We had lost the baby. I was in shock. It couldn't be! My husband and I had prayed over this baby. It would be our first, and we had such wonderful plans for it. Now there would be no baby, and my heart could not take it. The hospital sent a telegram to my husband, and he came immediately.

Then the doctor told us, "I don't have good news for you. I'm afraid you will never be able to have children again. Even if you should get pregnant, the baby will not survive. I think you should give up the idea of even trying. Perhaps you should adopt."

I shook my head. My loss just then was so great that I couldn't even consider it. Surely, if we prayed, God would give us a child. My husband and I prayed earnestly for one year. God heard our prayers and gave us a healthy baby boy and, the following year, a healthy baby girl.

God gave us two very precious gifts in answer to our cries for help. Our children are grown now and have been such a joy to us. We still feel they are God's special gifts that He gave us after our great sorrow of losing our first child.

The doctors said it was impossible for me to have those children. But God can do what doctors cannot do. We praise Him for His goodness every day.

MERCY SAMSON

He Grabbed Them From Me

It is good for me to draw near to God: I have put my trust in the Lord God. Ps. 73:28.

I WAS PASSING THROUGH OUR office hallway when I heard Joanne talking about the invader. She had adopted some stray cats that she visited and fed every day. Everyone was happy with the arrangement. Then came the invader.

As usual, Joanne had had some food on the ground for her cats, and they quietly ate. Then a man, with half a tin of fish cake, sat on the opposite bench and started calling the cats. The cats smelled the fish and ran over to him. Joanne was heartbroken; the invader had spoiled the day.

"How could he just grab them from me?" she asked, hurt and amazed.

While standing there in the hallway, the thought struck me: Jesus must feel sad and heartbroken just like that every time I heed Satan's voice. After all, He died to save me from Satan's grip. But the world has many things to allure me so that I forget that my life is secure in Jesus only if I stay on His side.

When the tin of fish was finished, the cats returned to Joanne and continued eating the daily food that she had given them. You see, the man gave the cats only a piece of fish. They did not know if he would give them anything the next day. Joanne fed the cats every day, without fail. They had security with Joanne.

Can you see the parallelism? Satan may offer us the glitter of a good job, beautiful house, money, prestige, rank, or power. These are temporary; they will all pass away. In Jesus we have security; we have eternal life. Let's not break the heart of Jesus by heading to Satan. Let us pray always to be on Jesus' side.

Cover my eyes, Lord, that I may not see the allurement of Satan. Cover my ears, that I may not hear his temptation. Use my hands and my feet, that I may do things only for You. Finally, Lord, take my heart and make it wholly Thine. Lord, take my hand today—please help me to hold on tight to You.

JEMIMA D. ORILLOSA

Just for Me!

Eye hath not seen, nor ear heard . . . the things which God hath prepared for them that love him. 1 Cor. 2:9.

MY HUSBAND AND I HAD RECENTLY moved from New York to Glendale, California. We looked forward to the mild temperatures and balmy sunshine that southern California offered. We were delighted to see flowers blooming in midwinter, to be free from icy streets and frozen water pipes.

I worked as administrative secretary for H.M.S. Richards, the founder-director emeritus of a religious radio broadcast. My work required me to visit him several days each week in his library. What a privilege! I loved sitting at his feet, drinking in the truths he had to offer, enjoying his wit and wisdom, and exchanging necessary information to carry on his program. I savored the grandness and humility of this man of God. I was touched by his appreciation for little duties I performed, and for his thoughtfulness and understanding.

As I was leaving his library one afternoon Pastor Richards' eyes twinkled. "Miss Lorraine," he queried, "have you ever picked an orange right off the tree?"

"No, I never have," I replied.

"Well, I've been saving this one just for you to pick." And with that he moved the branch in my direction. Because the man I highly respected had designated that orange just for me, picking it was a very special experience.

A few months later, as I entered the library, I saw a large zucchini on the counter.

"Miss Lorraine," began my thoughtful boss, "do you like zucchini? I've been growing this one just for you." Again I was delighted by the thoughtful effort he had put into its nurturing.

I envision my Saviour one day leading me to the tree of life in that beautiful heavenly garden and saying, "My child, I've saved the fruit on this branch just for you to pick." I will see His nail-pierced hand directing it toward me. I will be unable to hold back tears, and I will fall at His feet in gratitude. I will cherish it because He prepared it for me at such cost. I will thank Him for paying the price, for rescuing me from this cold world, and for bringing me into the warm sunshine of His love to live forever in His presence.

Lord, thank You for loving me. LORRAINE HUDGINS

My Dream

In the day of my trouble I will call upon You, for You will answer me. Ps. 86:7, NKJV.

WHEN WILL YOU BE BACK?" was my inevitable question when my husband, Orm, was about to leave on "walkabout" into the wilds of Papua New Guinea.

"I really can't say," he replied. "I've no idea where Awoma is. They're calling for a teacher."

Kokoda was a week's very rugged hike from our mission. Orm had supplies for about two weeks. When the third week passed with no sign of him, I became concerned. (Is our faith sometimes deliberately tested?) By the fourth week I was more than concerned. My prayers became more persistent now.

Finally, with a surge of excitement and relief, I saw carriers bringing Orm's cargo down the hill toward our house one Sunday morning. But no husband followed! To my rather shrill questioning, the carriers simply shook their heads.

"He must be dead!" I concluded. Distressed, I rang the police.

"Mrs. Speck, if your husband is lost in that godforsaken jungle, who could find him? He's walked over that trail more than any other European. If you don't even know in which direction he's gone, where would we look?"

What should I do? What could I do? After much agonizing I dropped to my knees again that evening and asked God to show me what to do. I stayed there until I felt at peace.

That night I had a dream. In my dream it was Wednesday. I saw my husband walking down the hill, haggard and worn. When I ran up to greet him and embraced him with a big hug, he asked, "Is there any fruitcake in the cupboard?"

So I waited. Monday and Tuesday passed. Wednesday, as I was getting into the Jeep to collect the children, suddenly I saw my "dream" coming down the hill, thin, haggard, and weary.

Occasionally God still needs to place me in circumstances that will not only test my faith but remind me that I must be continually in contact with Him. But He never lets go of my hand unless I let go of His.

L. Winsome Speck

February 9

Witness

You will be his witness to all the world of what you have seen and heard. Acts 22:15, NRSV.

I'VE ALWAYS ENJOYED ATTENDING Christian women's retreats. It's great to go to the various sessions at which wonderful speakers feed our souls and encourage a strong devotional life with God. I had attended just such a seminar in the beautiful Tenaya Lodge, nestled in the California mountains, when I discovered that instead I could have attended an intercessory prayer group occurring at the same time.

Frustration over my lack of information was soon replaced by amazement at what happened next. A tall well-dressed Asian man walked into the banquet room where a number of us mingled in informal conversation. For some reason he walked up to me.

He was quite interested that this was a Christian group of women, all gathered to enhance their walk with the Creator God. Who is this God? he wanted to know. I sent silent prayers to the Lord that I would have the exact words to unfold what Jesus had done for me in my life. The man was all ears, all questions.

It thrilled me beyond words to describe the beauty of the plan of salvation to someone who had never before heard it but was thirsty to know! Amazing! Here was a man, probably in his mid-30s, living in the United States, who had never heard about how Jesus Christ came to earth—not just to live, but to die and rise again for him so that he could have eternal life. He was astounded, transfixed, by what he was hearing as I introduced him to my dearest friend, Jesus.

I discovered that someone had given him a gift Bible, but he had never read it. I offered practical suggestions on how to really make it his own. He showed a genuine eagerness to read his Bible, to treasure it as never before.

The man beamed with real joy as he exited the banquet room, as if he had just had another kind of banquet.

Some introductions are extra special, Lord, and I thank You for the opportunity I had. I hope to meet this man again when we all join You for the banquet in heaven.

JUDY COULSTON

Two Cents' Worth

Are not five sparrows sold for two pennies? Yet not one of them is forgotten by God. . . . Don't be afraid; you are worth more than many sparrows. Luke 12:6, 7, NIV.

TWO MONTHS BEFORE OUR wedding my fiancé, Lonnie, and I prepared for the graduation ceremony that marked the completion of my doctorate. That Friday, as he prepared to leave work, the CEO announced that the company had been sold. Lonnie and half his fellow employees were to clean out their offices that afternoon. Since we lived in neighboring states, he viewed his job loss as a sign that he should sell his house and move in with me after our marriage.

Our October wedding was lovely, but Lonnie's house had not sold, nor did he have another job. By November we were beginning to second-guess our interpretation of events. Then as we returned from a walk one afternoon and Lonnie unlocked the door, I heard rustling from within the hollow steel pillar supporting the porch roof.

The scratching and fluttering told us that it was a bird that had apparently fallen through a small hole at the top of the pillar. We wanted the bird to grab a cord until we could pull it up through the top. As Lonnie pulled gently on the rope, he felt the weight of the bird. Carefully he disentangled the bird and cupped a tiny male house sparrow in his hand. The bird did not appear hurt, so we released him. Twittering, he flew off with a flurry of tired brown wings.

Though we were thrilled at the chance to aid one of God's creatures, we also marveled at the way circumstances fell into place. No other wildlife had ever fallen into that pillar. If we had not walked by at that time of the day or if the bird had not rustled inside the post as we passed by, it would have frozen during the night.

Later that evening, when Lonnie looked up today's text, we stopped to compare God's feelings of concern for us to our compassion for a small trapped creature. We realized anew how much greater is God's love. He sent His Son to rescue us from the pillars of sin, even though it would cost Him His life.

We are still waiting for the solution to our concerns, but we are comforted by the knowledge that our Father cares for us as much as—or more than—He did for the sparrow.

JOAN ULLOTH

Love Notes and Love Plants

Take us the foxes, the little foxes that spoil the vines; for our vines have tender grapes, . . . Let us get up early to the vineyards; . . . there will I give thee my loves. S. of Sol. 2:15-7:12.

WHEN I WAS 7 YEARS OLD I dressed in my prettiest white blouse with the lace collar and my candy-cane red-and-white skirt (which looked plain red until I twirled around to unfurl the stripes). My mother snapped red seesawing bunny barrettes into my hair. I was excited because it was finally Valentine's Day. I had carefully chosen my snuggly bear Valentine cards two weeks before and had printed each of my 23 classmates' names in my proud scrawl. But best of all, my valentines were special. My mother had carefully sliced two notches in each stiff paper note with a razor blade, and I had slid the stick of a heart-shaped sucker through the slits.

Even as a married woman with children, I treasure the love notes that this season brings. I have a butterfly marker in my Bible from my daughter that reads "Be cheerful, Mom, and I love you." I also have two worn and watermarked notes saved in my cosmetics drawer. One is carefully sketched on binder paper in my husband's flowing script. It is a list of I-really-feel-loved-when things that I do that make my spouse soar.

The other is a frayed and yellowed index card that contains a quotation that was given to me as premarital advice nearly 20 years ago. It reads: "Live for the glory of God. Be tender, kind, and courteous to each other. The happiness of your life will consist in making God your trust, and in seeking to make each other happy. Practice self-control. It is so easy to speak thoughtlessly, words that grieve and wound. . . . Love is a delicate plant; rude blasts frequently bruise it if they do not uproot it entirely. . . . Live for God and for each other" (Ellen G. White to Edson and Emma White, October 1870).

All great advice and, despite the old English, still current more than 130 years later. This faded card reminds me that special relationships are indeed a delicate plant, a precious living thing. They can be nurtured by little acts of kindness and bruised by neglect or thoughtless words. Reading my well-worn card sets me to thinking: *What can I do today to remind my husband that I love him all year long? I think I'll start with a note tucked into his surgical scrubs and fix his favorite lasagna for lunch.*

MELINDA SKAU

Stuffy Muffy

Love one another with mutual affection. Rom. 12:10, NRSV.

IT WAS OBVIOUS FROM THE moment I brought them home—they were as different as night and day. Toby went to work on his milk as soon as his gray-and-black paws touched the floor. Muffy eyed his bowl suspiciously. Then, pink nose in the air, he walked away. The more I coaxed, the more he paid me no mind. After my attention was turned to something else, I caught sight of him leaning over the bowl. At 10 weeks he had decided who would be running this show and made it clear it wouldn't be me.

Plump and cuddly, Toby belonged to my then-12-year-old daughter, Dion. Muffy was my scrawny kitten, sullen and withdrawn. Whenever I attempted to stroke his fur, he moved away. If the older girls, Dana or Darla, picked him up, he squirmed and whined until deposited elsewhere. When I called to him, his tail would fly up, and he'd strut on by, ignoring me completely. Eventually he earned the name Stuffy Muffy.

Muffy's mood could shift without warning. One minute it would be as dark as his gray-and-black-striped fur; the next, he and Toby would be stalking houseplants and jetting off furniture like metal objects in a pinball machine. Every time Dana swung her yarn and Popsicle stick concoction, there were bound to be backward flips and flying somersaults. No longer amused with their typical antics, Toby would roll on his back, paws poised, waiting for a tummy rub. Not Muffy. He was back to his usual self, curled in a circle, shutting us out.

Still, I talked to him each morning, and the girls tried carrying him on their shoulders. Darla affectionately rubbed his forehead on hers. It seemed nothing could warm his heart.

Later that summer I was totally surprised by some unusual behavior. Stuffy Muffy climbed on my chest while I sat in the recliner, rubbed his forehead on mine, and purred softly.

"He loves you," my husband noted.

I choked back tears and whispered, "I know."

My encounter with Muffy helped me realize that people are a lot like my cat. They can be sullen and withdrawn, but when we reach out in God's love, it can melt the coldest heart. Ethel Footman Smothers

Prayer of a Single Woman

If you can find a truly good wife, she is worth more than precious gems! Prov. 31:10, TLB.

CHARLOTTE, YOU REALLY NEED to go away to college," Emily counseled me. "If you stay here, you will never find a nice husband."

Emily was my boss's wife, and indeed, she was giving me some good advice; but since money did not come easily and I had been out of school for two years, I had chosen to find a job to help my parents out a little. My parents hadn't asked me to stay home—they probably would have been thrilled to have a college graduate—but they didn't push me either. I had made my own choice. So I picked peaches, apples, and plums in the orchard that Emily's husband managed.

Four years later I was still living at home, working in a Laundromat my parents had purchased and doing odd jobs. I was content, but I decided I would like to have a home of my own. Get married. Be a wife, a truly good wife.

My mother purchased a book for me at the local bookstore called *Letters to Young Lovers* by a wonderful author named Ellen White. Besides counseling young people how to be good moral Christians, the book put the thought in my brain that prayer for a mate is very important. So I decided to pray for a mate—not just anyone, but one that God would sanction especially for me. And pray I did.

Not long after this a young man came into our Laundromat to wash his clothes. He and I struck up a conversation, and soon our conversation turned to religion. He told me he was not going to any certain church, but he believed in God. Yes, he was praying for God to let him meet the right woman for him.

After repeated visits to our Laundromat, David started attending church with me. Three months later I became an answer to his prayer.

It is exciting when God answers your prayer, but it is even more exciting when you find out that you are an answer to someone else's prayer. Fourteen years later I am still excited that God answered David's and my prayers in such a way.

CHARLOTTE ROBINSON

Only a Mother

For God so loved the world that he gave his one and only Son, that whoever believes in him shall not perish but have eternal life. John 3:16, NIV.

SIX-YEAR-OLD JOEL PICKED UP a handmade Valentine card I had sent to my husband, Bernie, a few years before. I had lightly gilded the handmade paper, pressed it into a terra-cotta mold to create a heart-shaped frame, and glued lace behind the center of the frame. When I had fixed the entire heart shape onto the card, I had filled the space behind the lace and frame with rosebud potpourri, and added a small ivory satin bow. The message inside the card said, "To my darling Bernie, with all my love. I am as happily in love with you as ever—happier, probably! It's so exciting to serve God together! I love you! I love you! From Guess Who?"

Joel read the message, then said a very surprising thing. "Granny must have sent this card to Daddy." I found it hard not to smile, as the card was so very obviously a Valentine card.

"That's interesting," I said. "What makes you think Granny could have sent a card like this to Daddy?"

"Well," he said very seriously, "only a mommy could love you this much." I gently explained that I had sent the card to Daddy because I loved him very much too. But the most profound love that Joel had experienced in his short life was that of a parent. Although Joel knew that Bernie and I were very much in love, he found it hard to relate to the love between a husband and a wife.

In the Bible there is a special love verse for each one of us. It could be rewritten like this: For God so loved me that He gave His one and only Son, that if I believe in Him I shall not perish but have eternal life." Whenever I read it, I think, *Only my Father could love me that much!*

Why not find or make a lovely card for yourself and write this verse inside? You could personalize the card with your own name. Then you will never forget just how much He loves you. Make cards like this for your friends, including their names, and scatter His love today!

KAREN HOLFORD

Driving Safely With God

Thou art with me. Ps. 23:4.

I DRIVE 25 MILES (40 kilometers) to work each day—not a terribly long distance, but one that takes me 35 to 40 minutes each way. It is time to myself to enjoy listening to favorite cassette music and talking to God as I drive. Always, as I leave home, I ask God for His protection—and have thanked Him again and again, for I have no doubt my guardian angel has been right there with me. "For he shall give his angels charge over thee, to keep thee in all thy ways" (Ps. 91:11).

There was the time tubes fell off the back of a truck passing in the opposite direction. The tubes flew over the guardrail in the center of the road and just missed my car. Another time several paint tins fell off a worker's pickup utility I was following—another near miss. Yet another time a car careened off an overpass bridge I had just passed.

I start my job early, so in the winter I am driving to and from work in the dark. Half the distance I travel daily is on a freeway on which a lot of heavy machinery is transported to the many gold, coal, nickel, copper, and phosphate mines in Queensland. The enormous trucks are ablaze with lights, each one accompanied by small pilot vehicles with flashing lights warning motorists that larger-than-normal loads are passing. The flashing lights really stand out in the darkness. And I think, and am thankful, that God is light, and in Him is no darkness at all (1 John 1:5).

We have subtropical storms here in Brisbane, storms that seem to come out of nowhere. The clouds are thick, black, and menacing, accompanied by rolling thunder and both forked and sheet lightning. Sometimes damaging hail comes with the storms, and sometimes the rain is so intense that visibility is practically zero within seconds. When the rain is pouring down, I keep my eyes on the guides on the center of the road (cat's eyes, we call them) as I inch my way along.

How thankful I am for a loving heavenly Father who directs my paths and keeps me safe from dangers, seen and unseen, on my daily drive.

LEONIE DONALD

Danger: Attitude in Progress!

The wrath of man worketh not the righteousness of God. James 1:20.

THE DAY STARTED OUT WELL, but it progressed into something awful. I was not sure what set me off, but before I knew it I had developed quite the attitude. The day continued on this destructive path, and it seemed as though no one was spared from my wrath. The damage included snapping at various people, not being able to focus on my work, not smiling as usual, and being just plain disappointed in myself.

Although I recognized my plight, I never stopped to ask God for His assistance, even though I contemplated going to Him in prayer several times. Looking back, it seems that I didn't want His help. I preferred to be miserable that day, and I was spreading the misery around.

On the way home I recalled the day's events. Interesting how a negative attitude could fester so much and how many people could be affected by one attitude! What made it worse was knowing that I was not a helpless victim. I had actually chosen to be miserable!

My next thought was that actions speak louder than words, and mine had been loud and clear. Not only did these actions speak about my character to my friends and coworkers, but, as a Christian, I was being disrespectful to God. Having a "bad day" appeared to be a little thing, but the implications were clear. If I am not working the righteousness of God, then I am working against Him. I began to ponder how the situation could change. I knew I could go to God, and He would remedy the situation. And He did. By that evening my "attitude" had been eliminated, so that my family was spared from my wrath. I went to bed knowing that I was loved by God and would have the opportunity to start a new day in the morning.

Now when I feel the twinge of a "tude" coming on, I think of verses such as Psalm 97:12: "Rejoice in the Lord, ye righteous; and give thanks at the remembrance of his holiness." I have found that not only does going to God immediately help eliminate the attitude in progress, it also gives me joy throughout the day. The joy is so easy to access. Psalm 33:21 reads "Our heart shall rejoice in him, because we have trusted in his holy name." What a difference attitude can make!

MARY WAGONER ANGELIN

February 17

Sister of My Heart

A [woman] who wants to have friends must be friendly; but there is one Friend who sticks closer than a brother. Prov. 18:24, Clear Word.

WE RECENTLY MOVED TO A new home on the opposite side of the large metropolitan area where we have resided for the past 20 years. The move was hard work and caused many changes in our daily life. One of the resultant changes was moving our church membership to a closer location, as our previous congregation was more than an hour's drive away. This was a rather traumatic event for my children, who had never known any another congregation.

But for me it was like coming back home. I had been a member in this church before I married and moved away and lost touch with some of my friends here. One of my best friends, my bridesmaid with whom I had spent many a happy time prior to our marriages, goes to church here, and I was so thrilled to be able to renew my friendship with her. She is the sister of my heart, as close as my biological sister, and we share and understand many things about each other that others never will.

We've both grown up since those carefree premarriage days, and we laugh about some of the predicaments we managed to get into back in those days. We both have children to whom we are trying to teach life's lessons. We've both celebrated 20-plus years of marriage and have learned to take the bad with the good. We've both lost a parent now and know the resulting sorrow from the loss. But we're both looking forward to the Lord's second coming and know the joy this brings to our lives.

I have a "Brother of the heart" also. Very soon we'll be moving again, and I'll see His face. He knows things about me that no one else knows. He knows what it's like to laugh and cry with me, knows my joy and sorrow. I'll learn why things happen the way they do and how He's always working things out for my good. I'll get to hear how my guardian angel has protected me, even when I didn't know I was in danger.

Just as I look forward to time with my "sister," so I am looking forward to my time with my big Brother. I know that He's looking forward to being with me, too.

FAUNA RANKIN DEAN

Emergency Call

Now go; I will help you speak and will teach you what to say. Ex. 4:12, NIV.

WHILE FINISHING MY LAST YEAR of seminary, I became very critical. I had my opinion about teachers, preachers, and students. I became an expert in searching for mistakes and faults in lectures, sermons, and lives.

Three months before graduation I was asked to teach a class of my former classmates in addition to my research work. Having no teaching experience, I studied teaching techniques, waking up at 4:00 a.m. and going to bed after midnight. However, that did not matter to the students. They disrupted my presentations, asked questions just for the sake of questions, and looked for possible and impossible contradictions. When the course was over I declared that it was my first—and last—teaching experience. Moreover, I would never again open my lips against anyone.

After a few weeks I was informed that I was to teach at an extension school in Asia. I hated even the thought of going there. I did not want to teach experienced pastors who were 10 to 20 years older than I was. In spite of my feelings, one day I found myself at the extension school and saying to the Lord, "Look, here I am. The equivalent of six months' salary was spent for me to fly here. I don't know how to teach and what to teach. I failed the first time, and I don't want that terrible experience again. You are the greatest teacher. Please give me Your counsel."

This was the first time that I had ever prayed about something, opened my Bible, and immediately found the answer. I read in Exodus 4:10-12 and 15 that Moses also had difficulty speaking and that the Lord promised to help him.

After a quick thank-you prayer, I rushed to class. Three hours of lecture went absolutely perfectly, and I gave a 60-page reading assignment with a promise for a quiz the next morning. That night I was speechless. While walking around campus, I noticed a number of students sitting on the grass, studying by moonlight because the electricity had been unexpectedly turned off.

That night my prayers were mingled with tears. *Thank You for the dedication of these students and for the truthfulness of Your Word.* He will tell you what to say also, if you ask Him! IRENA BOLOTNIKOVA

February 19

What a Place to Be!

The Lord Himself will descend from heaven with a shout, with the voice of the archangel and with the trumpet of God, and the dead in Christ will rise first. Then we who are alive and remain shall be caught up together with them in the clouds to meet the Lord in the air, and thus we shall always be with the Lord. 1 Thess. 4:16, 17, NASB.

FROM THE TIME OUR GRANDDAUGHTER, Brandy, was about 10 years old we began taking her on vacations with us. Because of our wanderlust, she has seen many interesting places. She still says that the best grilled cheese sandwich is in Murdo, South Dakota.

One year we headed north to Michigan. We first stopped at the sand dunes on the shore of Lake Michigan, then on to Mackinac Island, the locks at Sault Sainte Marie, and just into Canada so she could say she'd been there, then back down to Battle Creek.

We wanted to visit a very special cemetery in Battle Creek where many of the pioneers of our religious faith are buried. Since we hadn't stopped anywhere to obtain a map, we were delighted to see that the state of Michigan had erected a large sign telling of our church's history. Someone had even placed identifying flags on each appropriate grave site. Moving from flag to flag was like being on the world's greatest treasure hunt.

Brandy was in a state of awe, for it was quite a moving experience. She said, "Wouldn't it be wonderful to be right here when Jesus returns! We could watch all these people, who are so special to us, rise from their graves, and those of us here would be caught up with them."

Thank You, Lord, for the promise that my loved ones and I can be caught up with Your sleeping people, to spend eternity with You.

Help me to learn more from Your Word, Lord, so that I may be ready on Your great return. Teach me many ways to spread Your Word and Your love so that we may all come together in Your magnificent kingdom on that splendid day. I pray these things in devotion to You, amen.

JUDY HAUPT JAGITSCH

Reaching Out in Love

Each one should use whatever gift he has received to serve others, faithfully administering God's grace in its various forms. 1 Peter 4:10, NIV.

I WAS FORTUNATE TO HAVE HAD a wonderful Christian mother. All who knew her also loved her, and her life was a blessing to many people. Our family and many friends celebrated her ninetieth birthday with her with much fanfare and fun. Little did we know that less than four months later, after she fell and fractured her hip, we would lose her. In attending to many matters on her behalf, I had to be gone for a few days. Much to my sorrow, she passed away one day before my return. My heart was broken because I had not been there holding her hand when she went to sleep in Jesus.

Although she was attended to by many kind nurses, there was one person who was special to my spirit, and that person was Laura. The day before my mother died Laura visited my mother and read the Bible to her for an extended period of time. There were not words to express my thankfulness to her for this kind act. What a comfort to me to know that some of my mother's last thoughts were of a spiritual nature.

Laura's thoughtful act was also a lesson to me. Surely we can pass such a gesture of friendliness and love to someone else in need! I believe if we open our hearts and ask God to guide us He will present to us opportunities for our lives to touch lonely hearts.

Yes, we can read to a shut-in or someone in a nursing home. We can take an elderly person for a ride when they no longer drive. We can make soup for a friend who is ill. Think of neighbors or someone at church who is alone or lonely and befriend them. Invite a widow home for dinner. Include new church members into fellowship with your circle of friends. Or possibly God may ask you to make a phone call or take a loaf of bread or cookies to a friend or new neighbor. Open your heart to God's leading, and He will pour out a blessing to you as you, in turn, can be a blessing to others.

Lord, because of what You have done for me, help me find someone in need today, and give me the comforting words that they need.

GINGER SNARR

Touching Hearts

Dear friends, let us love one another, for love comes from God. 1 John 4:7, NIV.

MY GRANDFATHER WAS SKINNY, long-boned, and lived by himself in a one-room house behind his sister's place in Fort Worth, Texas. We lived in Dallas, a long, hot 25 miles away. Sometimes he took the bus to visit us for the weekend, but more often we went to see him. A bed, a trunk, a rocking chair, and a table filled his room. Hidden in the trunk, my sister and I found candy bars and tiny cotton tobacco bags filled with pennies. We'd give Papa a hug, and he'd fold us in his flabby old-man arms and say, "I don't know what people do who don't have grandbabies."

When we left, he'd stand in his weedy curving driveway, waving until our car turned out of sight. He must have been lonely, but as a child I didn't think about that. He had a TV, and his brother lived a few streets away.

Many years later I drove to Texas with our youngest daughter, Bronwen, and helped her move into an apartment plunked down on the flat prairie. And leaving her, I pondered the goodbyes I'd said in the past. Gerald and I and our kids leaving his mom—or my parents—to watch sadly as we drove away. Our own kids happily leaving for boarding school and college, on mission trips, and to study and work overseas. I vowed I'd never take another airport photo of my child's happy face next to my stressed face, trying to look cheerful.

But on this day I thought of Papa, shading his eyes and waving until he couldn't see us anymore. A teen has little understanding of an elderly grandparent, nor does a confident young woman of a mother's tears.

At best, communication is difficult in our shadowed world. Using fragile tools—a touch, a glance, mere words—we grope toward each other, trying to reach each other's hearts. And yet the wonder of it is that we do communicate. Parent to child, husband to wife, friend to friend. For there is One who specializes in building bridges across the abyss of years or culture or learning. It is rare, the intuitive knowing what the other feels or meant to say. But it happens. Saying goodbye, for example, and knowing that mere space can never separate you from the one you love. And when this happens, it is like touching the face of God. PENNY ESTES WHEELER

A Message in Snow

My God will meet all your needs according to his glorious riches in Christ Jesus. Phil. 4:19, NIV.

AS I STOOD AT THE KITCHEN sink washing dishes, I looked out the window, longing for spring. There was almost a foot of snow still on the ground, and the sky was a dreary gray. Winter sometimes lingers too long in Michigan and drags my spirits down.

Day after day I watched out the window as the snow began to melt, and before long, patches of earth appeared. This could be the last snow of the season, I hoped. Thoughts of springtime began to run through my mind as I continued to see more green grass every day.

Then the day came when most of the snow was gone except in shaded areas. Along the north side of our deck, just outside the kitchen window, I began to see a form taking shape in a patch of snow. I tried to guess what it might turn out to be. At first I didn't know, but then it became obvious. It seemed to me to be the perfect shape of a fawn lying on its side as though sunning itself.

Since deer typically give birth in the early spring, this snowy fawn was a sign of hope to my longing heart. *Warm weather is on the way,* I thought, and my spirits were lifted.

The Lord has so many ways of speaking to us in answer to our every need that we should never doubt His loving care for us. The desire for spring to arrive seems like such a minor thing in the light of all the needs in the world, yet I believe the Lord enjoys giving us even the smallest evidence of His love. We need only to be alert and not miss a message—even in the ever-changing shape of melting snow.

I long for messages of hope for the world, too, Lord. I want You to come back to get us soon. I'm watching signs of Your love in the world around me each day. Thank You for pointing me to those signs. DONNA MEYER VOTH

February 23

Stalker in the City

He orders his angels to protect you wherever you go. Ps. 91:11, NLT.

WHEN I WAS 18 YEARS OLD I moved back to New York City. I lived with my parents in an apartment uptown in Manhattan. I worked downtown at Times Square and rode the subway back and forth each day.

One Monday evening on my way home, when I exited the subway station, I noticed a man standing by the newsstand watching me. I looked the other way and continued walking the three blocks to our apartment.

For the next few days I saw the same man standing by the newsstand every evening as I returned home from work. Every day the man watched me as I passed by. As was my custom, I always prayed for God's protection as I traveled back and forth.

On Friday evening as I left the subway station I passed the man again. As I continued walking I sensed someone following me, so I started watching the reflections in the glass panes on the storefronts and saw the same man behind me. At first I told myself it was just a coincidence, but my heart was racing. I decided to speed up. So did he.

My heart was pounding as I continued praying for God's protection and claiming His promise to send His angels to keep me safe. I kept watching the man behind me in the window reflections. I wondered what to do when I had to take the elevator up to our apartment. What if the elevator door stayed open long enough for him to get in with me?

My mind was racing. I kept praying. Suddenly out of a doorway stepped a police officer. He fell into step with me and kept walking by my side—I could see him in the window reflections. He had a kind face and walked with confidence. As I passed the next storefront and looked for my stalker's reflection, he was gone! I was so thrilled that I quickly said, "Thank You, Jesus," and turned to see where the stalker was. He was walking the other way! I turned around to thank the police officer, but he was gone.

I know God sent me an angel in answer to my call for help. *Thank You, Lord, for keeping Your promises to send Your angels to protect us!*

CELIA MEJIA CRUZ

God Knows Best

We know that God causes all things to work together for good to those who love God, to those who are called according to His purpose. Rom. 8:28, NASB.

OUR OFFICE OPENING WILL BE delayed for two hours," said Terry, my office mate on the other line. I got ready to go to the office anyway, but it started to snow as I left the house. The road was becoming so slippery that I could drive only 20 miles per hour. When I reached the office, I was surprised to see my fellow workers walking back to their cars, heading for home.

"The office is closed for today because of the weather," one of them told me.

I was a little bit upset when I heard that. Had I been informed ahead of time, I could have been spared that one-hour hard drive to the office and stayed home instead. I went back to my car very worried. I imagined that driving back home would be even rougher and tougher. Sure enough, the snow was already picking up and hitting my car even harder and heavier. When I finally got home, I was greatly relieved and thanked God

That evening I tried to use my time wisely by calling a friend. In the middle of our conversation I smelled something burning. I cut our conversation off and jumped out of my bed to find out what was going on. I was shocked to see smoke filling the dining room. I felt my eyes becoming itchy and watery. Fortunately, my housemate was able to turn off the heater and called the fire marshals. The operator advised us to leave the house at once. Still wearing my pajamas, I found my self exposed to the deep coldness of the night that chilled me all the way through.

When the fire marshals came and checked on the fire, they found a short circuit. I was very thankful and praised God for His safekeeping.

When something like this happens, one has deep thoughts, provoking questions. What if the fire had happened in the middle of the night, or while all of us were at work that day? My resentment from earlier in the day suddenly slipped away. I realized that God had a message for me to accept things as they are and be ready for any unexpected incidents. I am thankful and grateful to God that He is in charge. I could now easily accept, adjust, and adapt to events without letting them jeopardize my relationship with God.

LANNY LYDIA PONGILATAN

Musically Challenged!

The Lord is my strength . . . therefore my heart greatly rejoiceth; and with my song will I praise him. Ps. 28:7.

ALTHOUGH THE LEAST IN talent among them, I come from a musical family. When my mother was 7 years old she sat down at the little pump organ for the first time and started playing hymns, complete with chords.

I began piano lessons at age 6, but what a contrast! The ivory on F above middle C on our piano had been broken off and glued on, leaving a dark line across the middle. By using that as a guide, I could find middle C, the first note of the little piece I was to play in a recital.

In those days in my small town there was always a large turnout for recitals. As one of the younger ones, I took my turn early in the program. In my frilly little dress, I marched confidently to the piano, clambered across the bench, and got ready to play. But where was middle C? All the keys were stark white. Not one to give up easily, I reasoned that everybody who knew anything about music was in the recital, so the audience would not know that I had a problem. With that, I banged both hands down on the keyboard, climbed back over the middle of the bench, curtsied, and walked off to thunderous applause! To her credit, my teacher let me live; however, that was my only time to appear in recital.

Through the years I took lessons rather sporadically, but when I started dating a ministerial student in college, it became important to learn to play hymns reasonably well. In due time I became the wife of that ministerial student.

One night at prayer meeting the organist was present, but no pianist, so I was drafted. One of the hymns was written in three or four sharps, and as we played, it was obvious even to my ear that something was wrong. Holding my breath, I transposed to flats, and that took care of it. Later the organist mentioned that she and the regular pianist always did that for more than two sharps!

When my life seems out of harmony and I can't transpose, I must remind myself that there is Someone ready to change the discordant notes to a beautiful melody, and it doesn't take musical talent on my part at all!

MARY JANE GRAVES

I Am Your Neighbor

But he, willing to justify himself, said unto Jesus, And who is my neighbour? Luke 10:29.

IT HAD SNOWED ALL DAY—a classic nor'easter, they called it. The next morning, after all precipitation ceased, my teenage daughter and I ventured out from the warmth of our home and started the long digging-out process. We lamented that her older brother was away in school and could not help us. She and I agreed that I would dig out the snow surrounding the car and parking space, and she would shovel the snow on the porch and walkway.

After my daughter had completed her assignment, it was my turn. So with shovel in hand, I began plowing through what seemed liked mountains of heavy snow. It wasn't long before I realized that lifting 18 inches of snow was more than I alone could handle. I silently prayed, *Lord, I am feeling really tired, and You know I need to get this job done, so please help me.*

Because I was facing in the direction of the house, I didn't hear her approaching. But I did hear the sound of snow being shoveled behind me. I turned around, and there she stood. "Are you an angel?" I asked, as our eyes met.

"No," she replied. "I'm your neighbor."

Not recognizing her as being one of the neighborhood regulars, I probed further. "And where do you live?" I asked.

She pointed to a group of houses near the end of the courtyard and returned to the task at hand, remarking, "You looked like you needed some help, so I'm here to help."

In the brief moments that followed, she and I worked fervently to clear the snow. Suddenly the task became considerably easier as she and I chatted about the neighborhood and other topics of interest. It wasn't long before we completed our work and my neighbor was on her way.

As she disappeared behind the snowbank that blocked my vision, I paused and thanked the Father for this woman, this woman called "Heidi," who looked beyond the differences in our ages and ethnicities and chose to be my neighbor.

Father, help me to seek out ways to be a good neighbor. Amen.

YVONNE LEONARD CURRY

February 27

Life's Cycles

We know that the whole creation groaneth and travaileth in pain together until now. Rom. 8:22; He hath made every thing beautiful in his time. Eccl. 3:11.

I REMEMBER THE WORDS OF A young artist I once interviewed: "You can't be afraid to make a mistake. Just go for it. If you make mistakes, you paint over them." Life is—and is not—like that. We cannot simply begin again, as an artist can, and repaint some original scene. But the Master Artist can touch up our mistakes, making something beautiful from them.

We groan for the fulfillment of our expectation, the day when all things will be made right. God has set eternity in our hearts, and He longs for us as well. But He is not inattentive to details of the present. He makes things beautiful while we wait. Like an artist touching up a spoiled painting, God's brushstrokes bring order out of chaos, beauty out of human error.

On gray winter mornings I long for the freshness of spring or the meditative loveliness of autumn or the warmth of summer or the brisker beauty of winter. The seasons repeat their cycles, each bearing a message of hope. Their cycles of cold and warmth, sun and rain, barren and flowered landscapes offer encouragement.

Life is also cyclical. There are cycles of success and failure, progress and regression, joy and sadness. We have days of richness and poverty. Unwittingly, we chart our inner weather. We paint landscapes of budding and earthy hope or damp fallen foliage. Our response to these cycles of our lives is a powerful influence. Our accounts of our surroundings, like paintings that captivate viewers, weave a corresponding mood. The lives we touch feel our sadness, defeat, or uncertainty; our courage, hope, and faith. We stir up for others an exhilarating breeze and a fragrance of peace, or an anxious chill of dread.

Hope is an essential element of human existence. We look out on a snowy world and enjoy the season's pleasures and inconveniences because we are patiently waiting for the timely return of other glories and joys. This hope is the fabric of our spirit. It marks the face of the clock and the turning of the calendar page. Hope is the tender of the hearth's fire and life's garden. It is the patient watcher at the lighted window on dark nights.

STELLA THOMPSON

My Hiding Place

Thou art my hiding place; thou shalt preserve me from trouble; thou shalt compass me about with songs of deliverance. Ps. 32:7.

SATURDAY EVENING, RIGHT AFTER the evening worship, my daughter and I headed straight to the kitchen to prepare a quick meal. I proceeded with the preparation of a simple lentil soup, while she started working on an Indian savory called pakoras. I put the soup in the pressure cooker to get it done quickly, and she set a pan of oil on the other burner of our gas stove to deep fry the pakoras. She had mixed the batter and was just waiting for the oil to get hot. I had already put the weight on the vent of the cooker, so we moved away from the stove.

As soon as we moved away there was a loud explosion. We were so shocked that we couldn't even scream. My daughter was first to react. She saw that the gas burners had gone out, so she quickly turned off the gas. The pressure cooker had fallen on the floor, and the pan of oil had changed places with the cooker. The handle of the pan was bent, and the cooker was dented. Soup was everywhere—ceiling, counter, walls, and on the clean dishes.

When I checked the cooker, I found that the safety valve was intact, the weight and the lid still on. Then how did the pressure get out? With the vent all blocked up with the soup, God had allowed the gasket to break, allowing space for the pressure to escape.

I have heard of two people whose bones were broken when such an accident with a pressure cooker took place. In our case the oil could have caught fire, but the Lord had put out the burners. The hot soup could have burned us, but we were spared because we had moved away. My daughter got only one small burn on her cheek.

How did it all happen? I then realized it was my fault. In my haste to get the cooking done, I had not checked to see if the steam was coming through the vent before placing the weight on it. Yet the Lord did not hold me responsible for it but protected us instead. He also saw to it that the children were not near. Truly the Lord is our hiding place, and we are compassed about with songs of deliverance.

BIRDIE PODDAR

Thanks, Lord, for Walking in My Skin

The Word was made flesh, and dwelt among us. John 1:14.

RECENTLY I ATTENDED A workshop at which I was rendered "disabled" in order to experience the frustrations of the elderly and physically challenged. First my glasses were removed, and I wore goggles that were blurred to simulate cataracts. Then five-pound weights were applied to my right ankle and left wrist. Plugs were placed in my ears and an inflated device was attached to my upper right arm. I was then given a cane and a list of tasks to complete in a half hour around a six-story building.

For the first time in my life, in a small way, I entered the world of those impaired by disease and/or trauma. I finished my tasks with great difficulty, but I came away with three powerful lessons: (1) a new appreciation of the obstacles that the elderly and physically challenged face not merely for a half hour, but every hour, every day, every year; (2) a determination to refrain from judging others, since God alone knows everyone's circumstances and motives; and (3) a renewed gratitude to the Saviour for His willingness to "walk in my skin" in order to save me forever.

The last lesson remains the most poignant, because my "disabling" experience was temporary. At the end of the experiment I removed the paraphernalia that had limited my movements and continued my regular activities unencumbered. Not so with Jesus. After His resurrection He did not abandon His human form but retained it, and will do so throughout eternity. Two angels confirmed this with Jesus' friends as they witnessed His ascension (Acts 1:11). This is an awesome thought!

"For verily he took not on him the nature of angels; but he took on him the seed of Abraham. Wherefore in all things it behooved him to be made like unto his brethren, that he might be a merciful and faithful high priest in things pertaining to God, to make reconciliation for the sins of the people" (Heb. 2:16, 17).

"Thanks be unto God for his unspeakable gift" (2 Cor. 9:15).

MARIA G. MCCLEAN

My Angel to the Rescue

There shall no evil befall thee. . . . He shall give His angel charge over thee. Ps. 91:10, 11.

I LIKE DRIVING, BUT I DON'T like driving in snow. I had just finished the night shift and was getting ready to go home when I looked through the window. Oh, no! It had snowed.

"I thought I should have let my husband drive me to work," I said to no one in particular. "I usually do if the weather forecasters predict snow, but they didn't. Now what am I going to do?"

I thought of calling my husband to come pick me up, but I didn't know how I would get my car home. I didn't want to leave my car parked on the road all day. I breathed a silent prayer and stepped outside. Horror of horrors! Not only had it snowed, but freezing rain was mixed into the snow. I walked slowly to the car, and after a little difficulty I got the door open. While waiting for the car to warm up, I prayed. *Lord, please take me home safely. I am scared. Help me to drive wisely, and keep me safe from other drivers. You know I don't like doing this.*

I put the car in drive and started for home. I didn't feel as scared. The drive up the hill went just fine. About five minutes from home I came to an intersection. A park was in front of me, so I could turn either right or left. I decided to turn left, as there seemed to be less ice there. I pulled slowly into the right lane, and suddenly I found myself facing oncoming traffic with a car coming straight toward me. I had turned onto a one-way street. I froze. When the car was a couple yards from me, my car miraculously moved into the other lane. The rest of the drive home was uneventful.

I have no doubt that the angel of the Lord turned that steering wheel.

Help me, Lord, to continue to trust You, allowing You to lead, knowing You are my helper always.

ENA THORPE

March 3

My Computer Cord

All power is given unto me in heaven and in earth. Matt. 28:18.

I STRUGGLED UP THE STEPS into the waiting airplane, lugging my heavy carry-on bag with me. It contained not only my computer but also my speaking notes and materials. The agent at the check-in counter had offered to check it in, but I had replied, "No way! This has my brains inside, and I can't afford to lose it!"

Later, at the hotel, I discovered we were up three flights of stairs and the elevator wasn't working. The bellboy took the larger luggage, but I insisted on carrying the one with my "brains" myself. I didn't want to risk its being dropped. I had brought along a lot of work to do in my spare time, as well as my daily e-mail hookups to keep in touch with my office.

Once settled in, I got out my computer to get to work. I found the telephone connecting cord. I found the adapter plug that I needed to accommodate my computer cord's square prongs to the round prongs of the room's outlet. But there was no electrical cord. I unpacked everything and searched everywhere. It was not there. In my rush to pack, I had left the cord on my office desk. "Oh, no!" I groaned. My battery would last only a short time.

Before the week was up I borrowed a cord from another speaker to get my 70 messages and read them, but I never did get them answered until I got back home. None of the writing I had planned got accomplished. All because in my haste I had left my power connection behind.

Fortunately, when it comes to plugging in to the power God offers me—"all power . . . in heaven and in earth"—I don't need an adapter. Nor am I dependent on a short-lived battery. I can "plug in" to heaven's power supply in the remotest villages of India. I can send my messages to heaven as I sit in an airplane and the flight attendant has just announced that all electrical devices must be turned off. There is nowhere on earth nor any circumstance where this power connection is unavailable to me. There is nothing that can stop me from making this contact with heaven.

Help me to remember, Lord, that whatever my need for Your power today, I can have it just for the asking. The moment I reach out my thoughts to You, that very moment the connection is made and Your power is mine. Thank You!

DOROTHY EATON WATTS

Boundaries

I know the plans I have for you, . . . plans to prosper you and not to harm you, plans to give you hope and a future. Jer. 29:11, NIV.

WHEN I WAS A SMALL CHILD my parents lived on a heavily traveled street in the city of Portland, Oregon, where my dad owned and operated a very busy service station. I must have been one of the most adventuresome, curious children ever born, causing my parents to have to take a lot of precautions for my safety.

Every time my mother took me to the large department stores in downtown Portland she had to put a leash on me so I would not take off and get lost. I had no idea that I was in any danger—I just wanted to see all the pretty things in the store and talk to all the people who paid attention to me. I was not a bit happy when she started putting me on that leash, because I thought she was trying to spoil all my fun.

Since we lived in a nice two-bedroom home that was attached to the service station, I spent a lot of time playing in the office of the station. As I got older I wanted to go outside more, and finally my parents built a big play yard for me that was enclosed by a very tall fence. Was I happy inside that enclosure? No way! I wanted to be outside, seeing everything I might be missing.

One day—no one knows how, not even I—I got over the top of that fence. The next thing my parents knew, horns were honking and brakes screeching out in the busy street. My dad's heart nearly stopped beating as he looked out and saw me sitting in the middle of the street, waving and smiling at the people in their cars. He ran out through all that traffic, picked me up, and ran back to safety. Somehow, as he sat and held me and hugged me, it got through my little mind that I had scared my daddy, and that I should not go out into the road anymore.

Were my folks trying to spoil my fun with high fences and leashes? No; they needed to give me boundaries so I could grow up and be safe. They wanted what was best for me. That is why God gives us boundaries too. He knows what is best and wants us to be safe in Him.

ANNA MAY RADKE WATERS

March 5

Your Gentleness Has Made Me Great

Your gentleness has made me great. Ps. 18:35, NKJV.

W*HAT'S A NICE GIRL LIKE ME doing in a place like this?* I asked myself for the hundredth time as I sat in the plush waiting room of a company in Marina Del Rey, California.

I already knew the answer. When you're your own boss, you have to do what the boss says. I needed to collect the money owed my growing traveling physical therapy company. I wasn't sure how to go about this, but I thought it might have something to do with Abigail. It was only this morning in my motel room that I had been directed to her story in the Bible.

Abigail was experienced in handling "snarly" men. Her husband had insulted David (the future king), and now David and his men of war were on their way to wipe out Abigail's family. Her meekness and gentleness were disarming. She took responsibility for the problem herself. "You wouldn't want this on your record when you come into the office, would you?" she had asked.

At length I was ushered into the president's office. "I'm Elizabeth Boyd with Traveling Medical Professionals, Mr. Italiano. I'm sure you know why I'm here." I extended my hand.

"You leave my office!" he shouted. "I don't owe you a thing. I didn't ask you here." He got up from his chair and stomped to the other side of his desk. "Get out!" he shouted again.

I presented copies of the invoices. He snatched them from my hand and continued shouting. "I don't owe you a thing." I leaned back in my chair and relaxed and began to pray. Mr. Italiano walked back to his chair. His tantrum subsided. I listened.

He opened his desk drawer and took out his checkbook. "I don't know why I'm doing this," he said, a little smile playing around the corners of his mouth.

I knew why. It was because of Abigail. Her humility, her gentleness.

The president placed a check in my hand. I have made the trip to California three more times now. Each time I have followed up the visit with an inspirational book.

As I left his office the last time, Mr. Italiano took my hand and said quietly, looking into my eyes, "I'm a committed Christian now too!"

ELIZABETH BOYD

Dirty Handkerchiefs

The King will reply, "I tell you the truth, whatever you did for one of the least of these brothers of mine, you did for me." Matt. 25:40, NIV.

I HAD TRIED EVERYTHING I KNEW to get rid of those marks. Even soaking in expensive stain removers had not worked. It looked as though those handkerchiefs would be stained forever. I had run out of solutions to the problem.

Of course, I had pointed out to my dear husband that handkerchiefs were designed for a specific purpose, but it never mattered to him. He had been using them for an amazing number of tasks for years and would probably continue to do so. Even the new ones eventually ended up sharing the same fate because they were so handy, even on Sabbaths, when crises arose such as helping someone with a car problem or (to the accompaniment of gasps from all the women in the congregation) wiping the board when he was teaching or preaching, if no eraser had been provided by the deacons.

To be perfectly honest, I had to admit that when he took out a handkerchief—no matter how clean it was, no matter how carefully I had ironed it—I felt a failure as a wife, especially when everyone present could see those stains. And then it dawned on me that really it was my pride at stake when I imagined everyone judging me by the stains on my husband's handkerchiefs.

However, one insight, painful though it was, was not all that God had in mind for me. In His love and wisdom He had another idea to plant in my brain. One day when I looked at those handkerchiefs I was ironing, it struck me what kind of man I had married—a caring man, a man who was always willing to help others, no matter how inconvenient it was to himself. Every stain could tell a tale of kindness and hard work.

And my pride, you might ask? It suddenly became redirected, for I was proud to be married to a man who was dedicated to showing Jesus to the world. Who am I to judge another harshly because of stained handkerchiefs when, indeed, the stains could be considered badges of honor?

As I meet people today, help me to look beyond the outward stains to what is in the heart. Thank You for doing that with me. URSULA M. HEDGES

Dead Ends

Trust in the Lord with all your heart, and lean not on your own understanding: in all your ways acknowledge Him, and He shall direct your paths. Prov. 3:5, NKJV.

THIS SHORTCUT WAS TURNING OUT to be a nightmare. My husband and I were traveling across Ontario from Thunder Bay to the 80 acres of land on which we planned to build. We'd already lost time that morning when an ice storm had forced us to abandon the northern route and backtrack to the southern one. Now the pressure was on to reach our destination. The private logging road had looked great on the map and would cut off many miles.

But that was more than an hour ago. Now my driving was alternating between crawling and braking. The road had started out very rough, then had become a sort of conglomerate of rocks and boulders. Two or three times the road had forked. Each time we strained to decide which path looked more traveled. And each time we came to a dead end, and I'd have to carefully wiggle the car around on the narrow trail between deep ditches. Then we'd backtrack and try the other road.

I voted to go back, though by now I was hopelessly lost. One more slow turnaround. The streaming light of the setting sun made it look as if we were on the surface of the moon. There was no sign of life, and great boulders cast ominous shadows. What an eerie feeling. Such total desolation. I couldn't wait to get out of there. Fortunately, my husband remembered every turn we'd made and kept us headed in the right direction.

At one point he said, "It's as if there's been a nuclear holocaust, and we're the only two people left alive on earth!" I shuddered and didn't look back until we reached the little village that had marked the entrance to the tomblike world.

We began to make our way back and around to where we would have been without the "shortcut." Falling snow delayed us further, and we finally booked into a costly motel.

Sometimes that day reminds me of my life. I forget to let God lead. And I always seem to have a shortcut for everything. But if I'm not allowing God to guide my paths, those shortcuts tend to lead me astray on some pretty rocky roads. I'm so glad that when I do finally turn around to go back, God always knows the way!

DAWNA BEAUSOLEIL

The Big Picture

Commit thy works unto the Lord, and thy thoughts shall be established. Prov. 16:3.

HAVE YOU HEARD THE SAYING "Life is like a puzzle with a thousand pieces gone"? If you enjoy putting together a jigsaw puzzle from beginning to end, you have been convinced that there have got to be a few pieces missing. Sometimes the right pieces lie just at hand, but at a glance they bear no features of the right piece. At other times the wrong piece is so convincing that if you're not careful, you'll spoil the shape of that piece by trying to make it fit in the wrong place. However, if you thought those were the greatest challenges in doing a puzzle, try putting one together without the cover, the whole picture, as a reference.

The irony is that we do this every day. We get a brand-new day with new pieces, but we have no idea what the whole picture looks like. Like an eager child, we rush to the challenge of putting the puzzle together. Sometimes we bend the pieces out of shape in frustration, trying to make the picture what we think it should be. Sometimes the wrong pieces do seem to hold together, but somewhere else is left void and incomplete. Yes, there are a few that accidentally get the right fit, but most times the picture is left unfinished, and the "fixer" is frustrated.

If this has been your experience, I have a solution. There's Someone who is looking just now at the whole picture. He knows exactly where each piece belongs. His instructions may not be in the order you had in mind, but then, you can't see the big picture.

Will you consult Him today before you touch even one piece? Lay all your plans and dreams before Him in prayer and wait for His directives. It will surprise you how fulfilling it will be to see the pieces fit together at the end of your day.

In her book *Steps to Christ,* Ellen White recommends, "Consecrate yourself to God in the morning; make this your very first work. Let your prayer be, 'Take me, O Lord, as wholly Thine. I lay all my plans at Thy feet. Use me today in Thy service. Abide with me, and let all my work be wrought in Thee' " (p. 70).

Life can be a puzzle. I want to give You all the pieces of my life right now. Please help me fit them into a beautiful picture for You.

PATRICE WILLIAMS-GORDON

March 9

My Oboe Teacher

The Lord is . . . tender and compassionate. . . . For he understands how weak we are. Ps. 103:13, 14, NLT.

AFTER CONDUCTING OUR CHURCH orchestra for several years, I was convinced by some of my friends to learn an instrument. I chose the oboe, and they sent me to a wonderful teacher.

However, when I go to my lesson I play the worst that I have played all week. Duets that I played with my friend on Sunday now won't connect. Notes that were all in perfect order yesterday now can't be found. Songs that I performed with the band at church suddenly dissolve in disarray. But it's OK, because my teacher accepts that and accepts me and gently corrects the problem. Then all week long I play better because of her help. And I feel validated that she is on my side; I don't have to impress her, because she is already pleased that I come to her to study and learn. Besides, she is such an expert and experienced player—so far beyond any aspirations that I might have—that she knows exactly what to tell me so that I can become the best I can be. We both revel in my progress. I look forward to my lessons all week long, and from the way she smiles to welcome me, I know she likes it too.

God is so much like my oboe teacher. He always greets me at the door with a smile and is genuinely glad to see me. He wants to hear about how my practicing is going and where I ran into snags. He wants to celebrate the victories—the times I played my part well and people were blessed. He knows my potential and helps me to be the best I can be without expecting me to live up to someone else's standard. He accepts my mistakes and uses them, ever so sweetly, to teach me what I need to know next. Even though I might play well enough in public that others are satisfied (after all, they are my friends), He knows and helps me see clearly the areas in which I need to grow.

Best of all, His approval is both the dearest to me and the most easily won. He is happy that I have chosen to study and practice. He congratulates and encourages me as I return, lesson after lesson, trying to do better. After each lesson I leave full of hope and fresh enthusiasm.

HELENE HUBBARD

God Knows Best

Your Father knoweth what things ye have need of, before ye ask him. Matt. 6:8.

I PRAYED FOR GOD'S GUIDANCE in changing my lifestyle to one of fewer responsibilities. My house sold before it was listed. Every transaction from selling my home to buying a suite in a brand-new condominium went without a hitch. Unbelievable!

Although I had moved several times over the years, this move would be a major undertaking. I had lived in my house for 25 years. Given time, it's amazing how much one can cram into a small space. Being a schoolteacher and traveler had added to my accumulation. You guessed it! I had more stuff than my new home could hold, so I decided to sell my excess household furnishings, souvenirs, and antique collection at an auction in a nearby hall. To speed up the process, I decided to rent a van, load it the day before, and transfer everything in one trip on sale day.

If my nephew could move his whole household—a family of five—in a 26-foot moving van, I figured a 14-foot van would be more than adequate for the items I planned to sell. The first truck rental company didn't have a 14-foot van and had no interest in accommodating me. They weren't in the business of short hauls. I was somewhat annoyed at their lack of service. The second rental firm was more obliging, but had only a 24-foot truck available. Again I was a bit frustrated. However, God had dealt kindly with me in every other aspect of my moving plans. Surely I could accept an oversized van!

In addition to a ramp, this truck had the added feature of a lift. I knew the five men I had conscripted to load the truck would be delighted, because one item was a heavy piano. But really, 24 feet of space seemed ridiculous! Having no other options, I signed up for the huge truck.

My helpers laughed at the monstrosity, and I was embarrassed. The one consoling factor was that the cost of the larger truck was little more than what a smaller van would have cost.

Within 100 minutes the truck was loaded and filled to the hilt. We all laughed again, but for a different reason. I thanked the Lord for making sure there were no 14- or 20-foot trucks available. He knew I needed a 24-foot truck. I need to always trust His wisdom.

EDITH FITCH

How to Be a Failure

You may make your plans, but God directs your actions. Prov. 16:9, TEV.

NOBODY SETS OUT TO BE A failure. Public speakers, TV shows, and magazines all make money by telling us how to be a success. But instant success cannot provide us with the valuable education that failure can.

I had this point made clear to me during a writers' workshop I was teaching. One of my students surprised me by saying that she had had a story published five years earlier. She had been paid $800 for her piece.

Eight hundred dollars is a good price for an experienced writer, but for a beginner to get that for her first story is almost unheard-of. Everything she wrote for me in class was excellent. But when I asked her what other stories she had sold, the answer was "None." After that one story she had never tried to sell another one. She explained that she knew if she kept sending out stories some of them would be rejected, and she didn't want to end up as a failure.

Fear of failure had prevented this talented person from realizing her dreams. When my students have their stories rejected, I tell them to stop feeling sorry for themselves and write more stories! Their little failures along the way can teach them to be better writers. Rejections show them what doesn't work.

We have no way of knowing, when we begin a project, just how it will end up. If we don't know how to accept failure along the way, our growth will be stunted. Failure is often the first step on the road to success.

I pray, *What are You trying to show me, God?* whenever I am confronted with my own failures. The most important thing that failure has taught me is that I still have so much left to learn!

Sometimes I can see clearly where I went wrong, and other times I am still confused and repeat the same mistakes. Teach me Your way. Let me learn from my mistakes and take those precautions the next time so that I won't hurt You again. Teacher, only You know the true life path for me. Lead me there, I pray.

GINA LEE

A Little Child Shall Lead Them

If the eagerness is there, the gift is acceptable according to what one has—not according to what one does not have. 2 Cor. 8:12, NRSV.

THE PIECE OF LUMBER WAS about four feet long, taller than she was. I watched in wonder as my 2½-year-old granddaughter, Whitney, picked up the wood and started up the steps with it.

We had a giant pine on the steep slope of our backyard. My son was building a playhouse in the tree, supporting it by posts set in concrete and by the strong limbs spreading out about 15 feet above the ground. Whitney was an extremely interested and enthusiastic supporter of this project and watched carefully everything her daddy did as he dug holes and poured concrete around the posts, then constructed the floor and side walls and cut the spaces for the windows. She observed that he used many pieces of lumber.

When she found this piece of lumber, she believed it would be useful. It was difficult for her just to negotiate the steps we had built up the hill to the foot of the ladder into the tree house. Now she had this additional burden to carry with her. But she managed.

"Daddy, here's a board for you," she triumphantly called out. Of course he accepted her offering with pleasure and thanked her for working hard to "help" with the construction. There was no place he could use it—it was just a scrap cut off the end of a plank for an earlier project. But she had done her best, and he was pleased and delighted with her attempts to help.

"Thank you, Whitney! Daddy loves to have you help him!"

As I watched her give this precious offering of love, I thought of another Father who is constructing mansions above for us. Sometimes we, His children, see something we would like to give Him as a token of love. Sometimes the offering is very small, such as that of the widow who gave her only two mites. Sometimes the offering is misunderstood and criticized, as was Mary's perfume that she poured on Jesus' feet. Sometimes we completely fail in our offering, as did John Mark in his first attempt to be a missionary with Paul and Barnabas. But let us remember that the gift is acceptable according to our love, not according to the success of our attempts.

RUTH WATSON

March 13

Firmness Amid Tantrum

As many as I love, I rebuke and chasten: be zealous therefore, and repent. Rev. 3:19.

I HAD HOPED FOR MONTHS that I would not have to take up a new job assignment at the head office 100 miles (160 kilometers) from home. I didn't relish the thought of traveling to the city on Mondays and back home on Fridays, so I prayed for a way out of what I saw as inevitable unless there was divine intervention.

My worst fears were realized when a movement order came for me to take up this new assignment. I mourned and questioned God. How could He allow such a thing to happen when He knew I was needed at home and at my church? When would I get to do choir practice? How would I get to work with the youth in their witnessing project? Surely everything could not be done on the weekend. These were the questions and points of reasoning I took to my heavenly Father.

After hours of complaining I decided to be rational and prayed that God would show me a sign that He was in the decision. Immediately after praying and without being conscious of what I was doing, I reached for the women's devotional and opened it. There was the reading for three months later entitled "Why Grow More?" It spoke of the selfishness displayed by persons who seek to develop themselves academically but then don't want to help to develop others.

I was shocked and surely not pleased with the answer, but as reality penetrated my thoughts and I became conscious of my position as a child of God, I was humbled that He was so direct and uncompromising in His answer. I had just completed a postgraduate degree, and my colleagues were expecting me to move into administration so I could help in promoting the cause of our profession in an organization in which our role was not clearly understood.

I still wish I were home, and often ask how the tasks I so want to do at church can be integrated into the available time. Each time I do, God has shown me that there are many other ways in which I can work for Him while on this assignment. My tantrums do not frighten Him; neither can I twist His arm with my excuses.

Lord, I feel like a stubborn child who tried to get You to allow me to have my way. Thank You for being fair and gentle yet firm with me.

DESMALEE NEVINS

Rediscovering God's Grace

God forbid that I should glory, save in the cross of our Lord Jesus Christ, by whom the world is crucified unto me, and I unto the world. Gal. 6:14.

WHILE WORKING IN HONG KONG, I was privileged to visit the neighboring peninsula, Macau. It was a short trip across the water on a hydrofoil boat. That was in 1980, long before Macau was returned to China, while it was still a Portuguese colony.

One of the most famous landmarks there is the ruins of St. Paul's cathedral. It was almost consumed by fire in a typhoon. All that remains is its splendid five-tiered Baroque facade. Its carvings and bas-reliefs are remarkably preserved for tourists even now. At the very top of its highest peak stands a cross, visible for miles around. It is said that the famous hymn "In the Cross of Christ I Glory" was written about that cross.

The author, John Bowring (1792-1872), was governor of British Hong Kong. He was said to be one of the most brilliant and versatile men England ever had. And he wrote hymns! Inspired by the words of the apostle Paul in Galatians 6:14, he wrote, "In the cross of Christ I glory, towering o'er the wrecks of time; all the light of sacred story, gathers round its head sublime."

John Bowring literally lived out the verse that inspired his hymn, learning that there is no glory in fame and power but only in the grace of God demonstrated on the cross of Christ.

And I too am inspired by that verse and the hymn. Every time I sing it I remember that cross I saw high on the top of that old ruined cathedral in Macau.

"The transforming power of Christ's grace molds the one who gives [herself] to God's service. . . . [She] realizes that every part of [her] being belongs to Christ, who has redeemed [her] from the slavery of sin; that every moment of [her] future has been bought with the precious lifeblood of God's only-begotten Son" (Ellen G. White, *Maranatha,* p. 100).

Dear Lord, just for today let me glory in Your cross that bought my pardon, while I turn from the attractions of this world and behold Your wonderful grace.

BESSIE SIEMENS LOBSIEN

Pure Joy

In everything I did, I showed you that by this kind of hard work we must help the weak, remembering the words the Lord Jesus himself said: "It is more blessed to give than to receive." Acts 20:35, NIV.

ONCE AGAIN I WAS BACK in the former U.S.S.R., to me a land of intrigue. In my pocket I held $1,000 to give away to needy people—dollars donated by a women's ministry group that meets in my home monthly.

Two of the Ukrainian women's ministries leaders gathered some of the neediest elderly together in a garden courtyard outside the rented church. Twenty-some people were brought to me, one by one. I asked a few questions about their need. Their stories of desperation unfolded before me through my translator.

One woman was shaking with fever, medical condition unknown. Two women supported her or she could not have walked. She nearly fainted several times. Igor was elderly, blind, but very pleasant. The KGB had blinded him years before because he wrote "propaganda against the government." He spent 19 years in prison. A smile never left his face. Yuri, who was 73, kept kissing my hands and telling me he loved me. He lives with his daughter on a pension of $5 a month. He loves to attend church but can't afford the 40 cents it costs to ride the trolley round trip. He shepherds geese for 10 cents a day to earn the 40 cents weekly for trolley fare. Another woman, 46, works for the government. She works faithfully, but she hasn't been paid in many months. Some get so desperate over their seemingly hopeless situations that they commit suicide.

Their stories were so touching that I bawled like a baby. "Don't cry," the woman I was talking to repeated again and again in Ukrainian.

To each one I doled out small sums—$30 to $40. No one became a millionaire that day, but hopefully each one's burdens were lifted slightly because a caring someone made it possible.

What joy it brings to me to become an instrument in God's hand to lift someone's load—if only for a few minutes. I thanked God for the many blessings I take for granted but enjoy daily. And once again I learned how much more blessed it is to give rather than to receive.

NANCY L. VAN PELT

Names Do Matter

But now this is the word of the Lord, the word of your creator, O Jacob, of him who fashioned you, Israel: have no fear; for I have paid your ransom; I have called you by name and you are my own. Isa. 43:1, NEB.

I HAVE NEVER REALLY LIKED the name my parents gave me. I would have preferred them to call me after my grandmother, Alexandra. I grew up and lived in countries in which my Finnish name, Hannele, sounded strange and acquired all kinds of pronunciations.

When I moved to Germany, though, where my name sounds perfectly normal, people would change it. Hannele is the diminutive form of Hanna, meaning little Hanna. The Germans also have the name Hannelore, which they connect with my name. So when I get official mail the correct-minded Germans often change Hannele to Hannelore, thinking that the first can't be my right name! I can't stand the name Hannelore, and so I get upset.

The first time I realized how upset I can get was at a service at which I was to play the piano part of a Bach concerto with two violinists. These orchestra transcriptions for the piano are often quite tricky. I think I could have managed quite well if we had not been announced by name before the performance: "So-and-so and so-and-so and *Hannelore*—"

"What did they do to my name? That's not me!" And so all through the concerto my heart was pounding in indignation at how they had treated my name, and I was not able to concentrate on my part, stumbling along and trying frantically to keep up with the violins.

Why was it so important to me to be called by my right name, even though I didn't even really like it? My name has become such an integral part of my being that when it is mistreated I feel abused myself. I feel that I don't exist and that people are talking about somebody else.

"Sticks and stones may break your bones, but names will never matter" is one of the first English phrases I was taught by my father. But I disagree. Names do matter. God knows that. And He knows each of us by name. God will never use the wrong name when He speaks to me. He sent His Son to redeem me. He wanted me on this earth, and He is going to see me through until one day on the new earth I will hear Him say, "Hannele, My dear daughter, welcome home!"

HANNELE OTTSCHOFSKI

Better Than Gold

He will sit as a refiner and purifier of silver; he will purify the Levites and refine them like gold and silver. Mal. 3:3, NIV.

MOM, WHY CAN'T WE WORK miracles the way the disciples did?" 11-year-old Jed asked as we finished a short bedtime worship from the Gospel of Matthew.

"I'm not sure, Jed. Maybe we just don't have enough faith," I said, tucking him into bed for the night. He wasn't much for kisses, but I squeezed his hand gently before I left.

I was used to the feel of the scars, but my heart still ached because of the injuries he had sustained in the flames that nearly cost him his life three years before. It was through no fault of his own he bore those scars, and my mother-heart was still clinging to the hope of a healing remedy that would renew his hands, face, and legs.

I lay down to read and rest, but my mind continued the familiar flashbacks—the explosion, the rescue, the long days and nights when Jed lay between life and death. We prayed constantly for his life.

Funny thing about spending long hours in hospitals—there was always someone who was worse off. There was Carol, who had lost her infant son in a gas explosion. There was Donald, an artist who was trapped in his studio when his paint rags spontaneously combusted. And there was Charlie, who was trapped in a mine-shaft fire while cleaning parts with chemical cleaners. Charlie had long since relearned his trade, and often the fingers he still had would bear gifts for Jed.

I closed my eyes and breathed a prayer of thanks for Jed's spared life and the many friends and acquaintances who had been there for us. Just as I did so, Jed called to me from his room.

"Mom! Know what I'd do if I could work a miracle?"

I knew what I would do. I would touch my son with healing, restoring his face, hands, and legs. I curbed my imagination and wiped away an unbidden tear. "What would you do, Jed?"

"I'd give Charlie back his hands."

And suddenly, through my tears, I thought I caught a glimpse of gold.

LINDA FRANKLIN

Sights on the Prize

Know ye not that they which run in a race run all, but one receiveth the prize? So run, that ye may obtain. 1 Cor. 9:24.

THROUGH LIFE I'VE HAD CERTAIN goals that I have worked toward accomplishing; some big, some small. Here's an example: I recall having been given a recipe from a friend for a delicious dish she had made. The first time I tried, it was a failure. I studied the recipe again, checked each ingredient, and decided to try the second time, thinking as I mixed the ingredients how delicious the finished product would be. Upon completion, to my surprise, the dish was indeed a prize dish, tasting oh, so delicious, just as my friend's had.

In school we set goals, and with prayer, study, hard work, and focusing on what we wished to achieve, whether it was becoming a lawyer, doctor, teacher, administrator, or whatever the chosen career, we kept on until our goal had been reached and we received our prized accomplishment.

In the field of sports, basketball, tennis, and football players work hard, and through sweat, strenuous exercises, setting their eyes on the prize, and teamwork they win the game.

I follow the Winter Olympics and listen to various ice skaters tell how many long, often tiring hours they practice. Because they keep their sight on the prize of winning the gold, silver, or bronze medal, they persevere and keep pushing on.

As I recall these famous sport events, my thoughts are focused on a prize we should keep in our sights. Never looking back at past mistakes and failures, but with prayer and faith in God who forgives, let's keep pressing on until we get to the finish line. There we receive the grand prize waiting for us: heaven in all its glory. It surpasses any gold, silver, or bronze medal.

We must keep our sights on the heavenly prize, keep our minds focused on the questions that the songwriter asks: "Are you ready for Jesus to come? Are you faithful in all that you do? Have you fought a good fight, have you stood for the right? Have others seen Jesus in you?" If so, then the grand prize, heaven in all its glory, will be ours to receive and enjoy.

Annie B. Best

March 19

I Could Do That

The spirit is willing, but the body is weak. Matt. 26:41, NIV.

I HATE EXERCISING. FOR ONE thing, I have to get out of bed earlier, and then I have to stop my devotional time. I would much rather read and enjoy time with the Lord. I usually read sitting on my bed or in a nice chair, and I hate moving from there. I don't like even putting on my exercise clothes and secretly hope no one sees me in them. When the weather is nice, my husband and I walk. But I don't like that either when the mornings are dark. If the weather is bad, I use our ski machine. That is awful. It's boring. It's tiring. It's hard. I listen to language tapes, but that only makes it barely tolerable. There is an aerobics class offered at noon where I work, but when I exercise, I sweat so badly my hair feels wet. So I don't want to do anything then, either.

In my mind, exercise seems so easy. I see women on TV, jogging. I think *I could do that.* Or I hear about a 10-kilometer run and think *I could do that.* But have I done either one? Not yet. I have lots of ideas, but putting them into practice is the hard part.

To do a 10-kilometer run or to jog or do any of the other activities that I think I could do, there must be preparation. Daily exercise. The spirit is willing, but the body is indeed weak.

I often see someone who has a powerful spiritual walk, or is obviously very knowledgeable about the Bible. I wish I were more that way. I know, however, that one does not get that way without spending quality time with the Bible and with the Lord. I think to myself *I could do that.* But it does not seem to have happened. The spirit is willing, but the flesh is weak.

Spiritually, to be the one we want to be, to have the spiritual walk that so many of us long for, requires daily contact with Christ. We must spend time in daily devotions. Fortunately, unlike exercise, it is neither boring, tiring, nor painful. But it does require discipline, a daily determination to do what will make me a better person.

So I think *I could do that.* I can, too, and I am determined to do what is necessary to do so. My flesh may be weak, but if my spirit is willing, I know that with His Spirit I can be a success every day. ARDIS DICK STENBAKKEN

To Love, Honor, and Obey

Behold, to obey is better than sacrifice. 1 Sam. 15:22.

I HAVE INSISTED ON MY OWN way on many occasions. This has made my life more difficult at times. I am forever grateful for the forgiveness of our heavenly Father and others whom my decisions affected.

On one March morning I awoke to a beautiful blanket of sleet and snow. Despite the fact that I enjoyed looking out on the peaceful scene, I realized that I had an appointment later that morning. I mentioned this to my husband, who promptly replied, "You're not going anywhere today."

Somehow that statement did not set well with this mature, independent woman. "Well, I'm going to walk out to the main road and see how slick it is," I said.

He remained silent.

I was clad in my long warm blue robe and a pair of old shoes. I opened the front door and walked down the sidewalk and up the driveway to the road. It was then that I realized I was standing on a frozen layer of sleet. I looked longingly toward the house and thought, *How am I ever going to get back down the driveway without slipping?* I decided to try walking sideways. It seemed like slow motion when my right leg slipped out from under me and I fell gently, landing on my right knee. I then began to slide rapidly back down the drive. As I was sliding, I thought, *Dear Lord, how many other times have You had to allow pain for me to look up and obey You?*

When I came to a rest at the bottom of the drive, I thought, *Well, that wasn't so bad.* I pulled up my robe to see what injury my right knee had sustained. To my dismay there was a three-inch abrasion that the cold had prevented me from feeling.

When I showed my injury to my husband, I would like to say that he didn't say "I told you so," but he did. He watched me as I cleansed and carefully dressed my wound. As I went about my duties for the next two weeks the discomfort frequently reminded me of making poor decisions. During my recovery my husband was kind and sympathetic, just as the dear Lord is when we have to suffer the consequences from making unwise decisions.

ROSE NEFF SIKORA

March 21

Walking Billboard

Look carefully then how you walk! Live purposefully and worthily and accurately, not as the unwise and witless, but as wise (sensible, intelligent people). Eph. 5:15, Amplified.

WALKING FROM THE PARKING lot to my office one morning, I noticed Steve carrying a large billboard. It didn't appear heavy or awkward to carry, and he wasn't having a problem carrying it. Still, he looked rather funny carrying the sign, because only the lower half of his legs, his feet, and a few fingers were showing. It was almost as if the sign was walking by itself. Fascinated, I watched him make his way toward the front of the building with the large and colorful sign. I hurried to catch up with him, then couldn't resist the urge to tease him.

"Walking billboard?" I questioned.

"Yes," Steve chuckled. "I had to bring this sign back to the office."

"Oh," I replied as we entered the door, "I just had to tell you—you look funny. Guess you already know that, though." We both chuckled as he went his way, and I went mine.

Months later I still remember the walking billboard. Whenever I see Steve I laugh to myself again. I even mentioned the billboard incident one day when passing him in the hallway. Such a simple thing made a big impression on me. Perhaps Steve didn't give it a lot of thought as he maneuvered his way across the parking lot. He was simply focused on getting the sign to its destination. But in my eyes he was a walking billboard.

Every day we carry signs that advertise who we are, what we believe in, or what we're offering. Making our way through life, we announce this to the world. Walking billboards. Yet more times than not our signs are dull-colored, crudely created, and poorly designed. Or our signs are too glitzy, outrageous, or offensive. No one is interested in approaching us to see what we're advertising.

Lord, help me to look carefully how I walk. May each step I take today be in the direction You would have me to go. Help me to live purposefully, worthily, and accurately so that I will advertise the Christian life simply. May I be a walking billboard that will point everyone I meet to You so they, too, can have the opportunity to enjoy the good life You offer.

IRIS L. STOVALL

Midnight Prowlers

The angel of the Lord encamps around those who fear him, and delivers them. Ps. 34:7, RSV.

IT WAS GOOD TO RELAX with my husband over a light supper after a hectic day at work. Rejuvenated, we decided to walk a short distance to visit my husband's parents. We knew a visit from us meant a lot to them. It was quite dark by the time we left them for the walk home.

By the time we had family worship together, it was 10:00 and time for my husband's favorite news program on TV. That over, I got ready for bed, while he decided to stay up and finish some work he had brought home from the office. I tried waiting up for him, but quickly dozed off.

Suddenly I heard my husband shouting, "Bahadur! Bahadur!" He sounded alarmed.

I opened my eyes—he was no longer at his study table. Something was wrong. I jumped out of bed and rushed to the living room. There I found my husband peeping through the curtains, shouting for the watchman, Bahadur.

Bahadur came running, and I grew even more alarmed as I listened to my husband tell Bahadur that five well-armed robbers had been trying to break into our home. They had run away at the sound of my husband's shout for help. However, this was not before he had seen them. They were armed with wooden bed legs, iron rods, and guns.

We discovered the back screen door, which had been locked, wide open. They had attempted to open the wooden door, but had run away before they succeeded in prying it open.

That night neither of us could go to sleep. We kept talking about what had happened and how close a call it had been. Had my husband gone to bed when I did, we would not have heard their attempts to enter the house. We shuddered to think of what might have happened had they entered the house and attacked us with their weapons.

We spent the rest of the night praying and reading promises from the Bible and thanking God for watching over us that night, protecting us from harm.

Lord, I thank You for being such a great God who does not forget Your people. Thank You for being with us in times of great danger and saving us from so much evil around us.

TARAMANI NOREEN SINGH

The Courtesy Bridge

All of you be of one mind, having compassion for one another; . . . be tenderhearted, be courteous. 1 Peter 3:8, NKJV.

THE TOWN IN WHICH I LIVE has grown to the point of having more cars than space for them on the roads. Traffic lights now dot once-quiet lanes. Four-way stop signs spring up like mushrooms along the sides of strangled intersections, and road rage infects rush hour as drivers become dismayed when they hear the local traffic reporter announce that once again a certain route is blocked by wrecked cars and emergency equipment.

One congested area in particular has fueled many heated debates now that a new gas station/convenience store clutters its busiest corner. Ultimately the debates target a nearby single-lane wooden bridge on an intersecting road.

"It's archaic! It should be removed at once!" some debaters decree, with statistics to back themselves up. "Leave it! It's a city tradition!" the opposing side challenges, sentiment their only evidence. This antique piece of roadwork has always been known as the Courtesy Bridge, and they are determined to keep it. Why, county-made signs at both ends of the bridge officially and proudly state it as such. It is so dubbed because it is still not uncommon for a pair of cars, approaching the bridge from opposite directions, to both wait for the other to cross. After a few seconds, one driver will flash her or his car lights, as if to say, "No, please, I insist. You go first." Then as the oncoming car passes the stationary one, each driver will wave, smile, and nod to the other.

Personally, I hope the bridge survives. While waiting for others to cross, I have chuckled at the antics of ducklings slipping into the creek below and have marveled at the wingspan of a great blue heron. Furthermore, the exchange of pleasantries with someone I don't know and with whom I may never cross paths again has become an oasis of friendliness in a growing desert of anonymity. But most important, it reminds me in a gentle way of my responsibility as a Christian to humbly put others first, to encourage them, and to rejoice in their success. It reminds me that courtesy is often a bridge over the rough waters of life, and that life is not just about getting somewhere as quickly as you can. It's about helping each other along the way.

LYNDELLE CHIOMENTI

Is God Still There?

But I say unto you, That it shall be more tolerable for the land of Sodom in the day of judgment, than for thee. Matt. 11:24.

IT HAD BEEN A BUSY day for me. As the mother of two small girls, I felt as if I'd been running a race, and I wasn't sure my arms and legs were keeping up with the rest of my body. After going from the bank, then to the commissary, then to get some shoes (again) for my sweet growing girl, I again put the girls in their car seats, jumped into the car, and started home. About 10 minutes later I realized that my purse wasn't in the car with me.

O dear God, I prayed. I pulled over and stopped at the side of the road. One of my girls wanted to pray and asked God to help. We all said a prayer asking God to show us where Mommy had put her purse.

We went back to all the places we'd been, and as we went I was getting more upset. What was I going to do if we didn't find it? My personal things, cards, money, pictures of my family, and my military identification card for the base were all in that purse. I know that God knew I needed those items. I didn't want to call my husband and tell him, so again I prayed and asked God what to do.

It was almost as if I could see God smile at me and bend down and whisper in my ear: "Go to the security office and ask them. I drove over there as fast as I could and walked up to the counter. The man at the desk smiled and said, "Mrs. Molé, are you looking for your purse?"

"Oh, yes, sir, I certainly am!" I cried in shock and relief.

A kind woman had found my purse and taken it to the office.

Praise the Lord! You are looking out for us mothers. You are my legs, arms, head, and thought! I do need You every day and thank You for going with me each step of the way. Remind me to help others as did the kind woman who found my purse. Help me to find ways of demonstrating a Christianity that only You would share. SUSEN MATTISON MOLÉ

Go Into the Shop

If you, then, though you are evil, know how to give good gifts to your children, how much more will your Father in heaven give good gifts to those who ask him! Matt. 7:11, NIV.

ON A COLD WINTER'S DAY I was on my way to visit a friend. I had to change buses in the town center of Tampere, Finland, because my bus, which ran on charcoal fumes in that war winter, had to stop for a half hour on the way to charge up. I missed my connections. I leaned against the wall of the town hall to get some protection from the cold driving wind. Suddenly I heard a voice say, "Go to Erdman's Fabric Store now." Startled, I looked around. There was not a soul in sight. Then I heard the voice saying again, "Go to Erdman's Fabric Store *right now.*"

My husband needed a new pair of work pants, and I had looked in vain everywhere. There just wasn't anything to be had, neither pants nor fabric. The war had made things scarce in the shops. That day before leaving home I had told my husband, "I talked to God about the pants. There is nothing I can do. I asked *Him* to look after the matter."

Well, I thought, *I might as well go to the store and wait there. At least it will be warm.* So I stepped into the shop and looked around. There were some customers at a counter. At that moment the owner of the shop came in with a bolt of thick durable cloth. He went to the salesclerk, put the fabric down on the counter, and told her, "Give that woman who is standing at the door as much material as she needs."

The people who had been standing in line objected. "But we were here before she came!"

"Never mind," said the owner. "Give her the material." I went to the counter and had the fabric measured out. As I went to the cash desk to pay, the shop owner asked me, "Have you got a baby's blanket yet?"

"No." I said. "I haven't received anything for my baby."

"Is it a boy or a girl?" he asked. When told it was a boy, he went off to fetch a blue baby's blanket. I was so stunned it didn't come to my mind to ask anything.

How did the shop owner know what I needed? He didn't know me. Who had told him that I had a baby? I will never know, but the Lord does. He will take care of our needs if we ask Him.

HILKKA ROUHE

My Flower Garden

As the earth bringeth forth her bud, and as the garden causeth the things that are sown in it to spring forth; so the Lord God will cause righteousness and praise to spring forth before all the nations. Isa. 61:11.

I LOVE FLOWERS AND HAVE many varieties growing in my yard. One year I counted more than 30 different kinds of blooming plants, from the first crocus in the spring (at times even forcing their way up through the snow) to the chrysanthemums in the fall. Since I don't have a green thumb, I prefer flowers I don't have to pamper, such as the lilacs out by the clotheslines, the yellow daffodils, the dainty blue hyacinth, and red and orange poppies that are scattered throughout the backyard. Some of my favorites are the old-fashioned pink roses that ramble along the edge of the driveway with the gladiolus and spiraea bushes.

I planted a packet of morning glory seeds my daughter sent me from her garden in South Carolina, and each year I save the seeds to perpetuate the blooms. I watch the progress of the blue and pink flowers as they climb the rows of green cord I've strung up on the old wagon wheel out by the mailbox.

When I see the tiny green spears emerge on the heels of the winter's slush, there is little promise of the beautiful flowers they will soon become. But in no time the fragrant white lilies are standing straight and tall beneath my kitchen window.

Each spring I look forward to the hanging basket filled with fresh geraniums by the front door. Many of the tulips and peonies have dwindled through the years from a lack of proper care, but along with the azaleas in front of the house they stand as a constant reminder of what used to be when this caregiver was more attentive.

I discovered through the years, mostly by trial and error, that both plants and people need certain elements in order to survive. Besides generous amounts of tender loving care, we all require the sunshine, pure water, and proper nutrients that our heavenly Father so lovingly provides for His earthly family.

CLAREEN COLCLESSER

March 27

Wrong Focus

He who began a good work in you will perfect it until the day of Christ Jesus. Phil. 1:6, NASB.

I NEED US TO PRAY FOR the bump on my head," said 7-year-old Josh, rubbing his forehead with a smudgy hand. "I fell, and my head hit really hard."

I was helping lead out in the prayer and praise part of children's meetings during our church's recent evangelistic series. I duly noted Josh's prayer request.

Five-year-old Davey was stating his prayer request when Josh's hand shot up again. "Pray a lot for my head because that bump just makes me feel awful."

I promised that we would. I moved on, but noticed that Davey kept looking at Josh. I was about to say "Children, let's kneel down for prayer" when Josh's hand went up. "Do you remember the bump on my head?" he asked.

I took a deep breath. "Yes, Josh, I still remember."

"Well, it's really, really big. You ought to feel it."

Thinly masking my impatience now, I abruptly—and unthinkingly—said, "Maybe later on this evening we can all feel the bump on your head." Josh solemnly nodded while an "I've-been-affirmed" smile flickered briefly across his face.

A guest storyteller arrived to deliver an animated version of Jonah and the whale. After the story, nine little hands shot up. Chris wanted to know, "What did it smell like inside the whale?" and Caitlan asked why Jonah didn't want Nineveh to be saved.

"And what did you want to ask about the story?" the storyteller asked Davey last.

As innocent as a cherub, Davey earnestly asked, "I was wondering . . . How long is it gonna be till we all get to feel the big bump on Josh's head?"

I burst out laughing. "Right after this activity."

Like Davey, I too misplace my focus as I become anxious about my faults and failures. This line of thinking makes me run the risk of losing the whole point of salvation's plan—that Christ died in order to finish the story He began in me. What a relief it is every time my patient, reassuring Teacher helps turn my attention back to The Story! CAROLYN RATHBUN SUTTON

The Sun Still Shines

Lift your eyes and look to the heavens: who created all these? He who brings out the starry host one by one, and calls them each by name. Isa. 40:26, NIV.

GRAY SKIES OVERHEAD MATCHED my gray thoughts that dull, miserable March morning, and the cool rain didn't improve my concerns for my family that day. I walked on around the park as usual with my little dog. But for her I would have stayed at home, warm and dry. With my head bent down against the driving rain, I saw only the equally gray path beneath my feet. Then suddenly from somewhere above me I heard the distinctive call of a red-winged blackbird. I stopped and looked up into the nearby tree. There he was in his elegant black-and-red plumage, singing his heart out.

Spring was coming—the blackbirds had returned. I saw something else. In the sky above the tree, right behind my blackbird so that I couldn't miss it, was a small circle of light. It was the sun trying to get through that heavy blanket of cloud. I still couldn't see any sun, but that small circle of lighter sky just where the sun would be reminded me that the sun was still up there even though I couldn't see it. I was feeling better already. When I got back home I found the first two daffodils of the season blooming in my garden.

I thanked God for His messages to me that day. He had used my dog, a blackbird, a small clearing in the cloudy sky, and two daffodils to tell me to look up. Although I could not see it at the moment, the sun was still shining and spring was still coming. I also realized that although I can't see Him, the Son is still up there and in control of my life, and a better time is coming, not just for me at one bad moment, but for always.

Lord, help me to keep looking up, to keep my eyes on You and remember You are the Creator of the vast universe. Your light never goes out. When my earthly world feels as though it is crumbling down on me, help me to remember always that You are there. Remind me to trust Your plan as I try to follow it each day.

RUTH LENNOX

March 29

Insomnia

When thou liest down, thou shalt not be afraid: yea, thou shalt lie down, and thy sleep shall be sweet. Prov. 3:24.

MY SLEEP HAD ALWAYS BEEN sweet and sound. I usually retired about 8:30 and was ready for the day by 4:00, rested and refreshed. But these days were different. I felt weary and sleep deprived. Disturbing thoughts kept my mind active far into the night. My husband had developed a serious health problem, and we were faced with important decisions—decisions I had to make alone. I had no doubt that God was guiding in our lives; He had given me abundant evidence. But I was tired, bone tired.

Deeply concerned one night, I presented the problem to my Father. Before I realized it, Bible texts began coming into my mind, one after another. Strangely, though, they seemed to come alphabetically. So I took up the challenge to see how far I could get through the alphabet. Before I had gotten far, I had drifted off to sleep. The next night it happened again. And the next, and the next. From then on I played my alphabet game nightly, always falling asleep before I could finish.

In a brand-new way I realized how caring and resourceful our Father is with the concerns of His children. Now I play my game while waiting for a doctor's appointment or just anywhere I have a moment of idle time. My list has grown to several pages now, and I'm still adding. Want to try it? It's a delightful way to remember Bible texts, and His promises are oh, so comforting! If you get stuck on a few letters, keep trying. You'll find them. The fun is in the searching. Here are a few that gave me a start:

"And I say unto you, Ask, and it shall be given you" (Luke 11:9).
"Behold, I have graven thee upon the palms of my hands" (Isa. 49:16).
"Commit thy way unto the Lord . . . and he shall bring it to pass" (Ps. 37:5).
"Draw near to God and he will draw near to you" (James 4:8, RSV).
"Even to your old age . . . I am he who will sustain you" (Isa. 46:4, NIV).
"Fear thou not; for I am with thee" (Isa. 41:10).

LORRAINE HUDGINS

A Little Red Car With Doors That Open

May the Lord grant all your requests. Ps. 20:5, NIV.

HOLDING OUT BABY HANDS, the 3-year-old looked at Auntie Sydney and said, "Bring me a little red car with doors that open."

Sydney's heart sank. Where would she get a little red car with doors that open? "What if I can't find it, my honey?" she asked, kneeling down and gathering the little girl in her arms.

"Oh, you will! My auntie can do anything!"

That was the little girl she had raised, the one who followed her everywhere, who loved to give big hugs and, yes, who thought she could do everything.

"Oh, she'll forget and love anything you bring her," whispered the grandmother at the door as Sydney waved goodbye to the tearful little face.

But the little girl didn't forget. Every time Sydney called, the little girl would end the goodbye with "Bring me a little red car, won't you?"

Sydney looked and looked for a little red car with doors that opened. Then on the last shopping trip, there in the middle of a display of toys was a little red car with doors that stood open. Quickly Sydney entered the store just in time to see a woman pick up the red car, along with two others, and go to the checkout counter.

"Please, Lord," Sydney prayed, "don't let the woman buy the red car."

Sydney gasped as the woman handed the car to the clerk. "I don't want this one."

"Thank You, Lord," whispered Sydney.

"What did you say?" the clerk asked.

"I'll not take the red car," she answered.

"It's the last one we have," the clerk commented. "I can't get any more."

Later a beaming little girl flew into Sydney's arms. "You have my car, don't you?" she chattered, as Sydney handed her the little red car with doors that opened. A little girl hugged an auntie who could do anything. And an auntie thanked a God who really *could* do anything.

EDNA MAYE GALLINGTON

March 31

Good All the Time

It shall come to pass that before they call, I will answer; and while they are still speaking, I will hear. Isa. 65:24, NKJV.

GROWING UP WITH A praying grandmother made me develop an attitude of constant prayer. She would awaken during the night to pray, and she invited her children and grandchildren to do the same. At church she would also encourage us to pray silently during audible prayer sessions. God had always answered prayers in our family in miraculous ways.

Our three children had always attended parochial schools. We had moved in faith from Maryland for them to attend Oakwood Academy in Huntsville, Alabama. Some of our friends thought we were out of our minds leaving well-paying jobs, a lovely suburban home, and family and friends to relocate 700 miles away. My husband stayed to get the house sold while the children and I worked on getting settled in Huntsville. He would make frequent weekend trips to see us. It was difficult at first. As a registered nurse I had to apply for my state license, which took time and money. God always provided just enough for tuition and food. I even applied for food stamps for a few months, unknown to my husband.

One Friday I received the second notice that the children would not be able to return to school the following Monday if their tuition was not paid. I took the letter to my room, closed the door, and laid it before the Lord. I told Him these were His children. He had seen us through previous tough times, and we were here in His school, following His instructions for them to be trained for His service. While still on my knees I heard a knock on the door. My uncle, who had bought a Volkswagen from my husband, came to bring him the payment. It was exactly the amount needed to pay the tuition. I thanked God for taking care of our needs one more time and shared this experience with the family that night at worship.

Since then we have experienced incredible answers to prayer in many situations. All three children have done very well in school and been blessed in their careers.

Sometimes we become discouraged and feel it is too difficult to do even what God directs us to do. Do not give up—go to your knees, and God will meet you there.

LYDIA D. ANDREWS

The Book

Can a woman forget her sucking child, that she should not have compassion on the son of her womb? yea, they may forget, yet will I not forget thee. Isa. 49:15.

DEB WAS GETTING MARRIED. The wedding was planned for July, and it was already early spring. With this short engagement, the approaching date would arrive in a blink of an eye. That's when the "book" entered my life and proved a truth I will not soon forget.

I had been asked to deliver a bridal book to Deb, a new believer. I slipped the book in my leather case for safekeeping. I ran into Deb several times, but not once did I remember the book.

One Saturday morning I vowed faithfully to deliver the package at a church meeting. I was determined to keep my word. I was going to make sure Deb received that book, no matter what.

That evening, while preparing to return for a youth meeting, it occurred to me I'd better take my leather bag. There was the book. It just seemed to cling to me like a piece of fine lint. I had spoken with Deb throughout the day. How could I have forgotten again? I was becoming very annoyed with myself. I finally prayed, *Lord, please help me remember to give Deb this book.*

After the youth program I went straight to the kitchen for refreshments. Deb served apple juice from a small table. The book never entered my thoughts. I set my leather case on the counter above a huge juice container that had been used for dinner earlier that day.

"Want some juice?" Deb asked.

"Sure would," I told her. "But I'd rather have the kind we had for dinner."

"Let me see . . . There might not be any left." Deb moved over to the huge metal container. "You tilt, and I'll press the spout."

When I reached for the container, my eyes fell on my leather bag. The book. Deb's book. I grabbed her shoulders, bursting with joy. "God helped me remember I have a package for you." I hugged her again and finally delivered the book. "Isn't God wonderful?" I beamed.

God is amazing. He created worlds by the word of His mouth, cradles oceans in the palm of His hand. Yet He's interested in the smallest details of our lives. That's a truth I will long remember. ETHEL FOOTMAN SMOTHERS

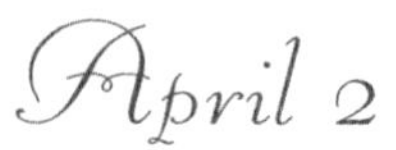

It's Going to Work Out OK Anyway!

We know that all things work together for good to them that love God, to them who are the called according to his purpose. Rom. 8:28.

THIS IS MY FAVORITE TEXT in the whole Bible! I am not sure when I adopted this text as the fundamental and foundational orientation of my life, but once I did, I did! This text says to me that my life is being orchestrated by God Himself. There is nothing, absolutely nothing, that happens in my life that He is unable to work out for my good. This text was illustrated for me when I was in junior high school.

My home economics teacher, Mrs. Owens, took a special interest in my sewing abilities. During the ninth grade I mastered bound buttonholes, matching plaids, adding collars, inserting pockets, and lining a two-piece suit. So for me to place the center fold of the dress front on the selvage while sewing during the summer was a very careless mistake.

At first I thought I would just have to trash the dress. Then I got the idea of adding black grosgrain ribbon down the center front to cover the selvages I could zigzag together. The ribbon bow at the center front turned the simple white dress into an elegant dressy dress.

But I couldn't wear it to church, because back in those days my mother wouldn't allow me to wear a sleeveless dress to church. So a matching white coat was added, with the stunning contrasting black trim around the neck and front edge. I felt so beautiful in this outfit that came together because of a careless mistake. It was a favorite for some time!

This is a good example of why Romans 8:28 is my favorite text. I am assured that God is able to take what appears to be a bad situation or circumstance and turn it into something far more beautiful than what I would have wished at the beginning of the mess.

This text is the foundation of my positive outlook on life and every situation. There is a blessing in everything! All I have to do is keep an open mind and a listening ear for the Holy Spirit's instructions about how to let Him turn things around 180 degrees. He can and He does!

I know everything is going to work out for my good again today. What a blessing! What an assurance! Thank You, Lord God. JUDITH W. HAWKINS

Let Thine Ear Hear

Faith cometh by hearing, and hearing by the word of God. Rom. 10:17.

OUR BABY-SITTER, PAT, told us that our daughter, Barbara, was saying all kinds of words by the time she was 1 year old. We could not believe it, because my husband and I never heard what Pat was describing. We heard cooing and other sounds, but nothing faintly familiar to a word.

A few months later those sounds took on a whole new meaning as we began to hear what Pat had been hearing. We could hear words such as "help," "thank you," and many others. While we were shocked, Pat was trying to figure out what had taken us so long to hear them.

We found it was very easy to get caught up in the other things of this life. In doing that, we may have missed hearing the important things. These kinds of distractions can be a hindrance in listening to God's instruction, too.

The other side to being distracted is being overly anxious to hear. In regard to Barbara, after we discovered what Pat had been hearing we began to analyze every utterance out of her mouth. It was quite funny when my husband and I would compare our notes. It appeared we were searching too hard.

Another example of straining to hear was the time my husband was on a business trip and I woke up in the middle of the night, thinking I heard something. A scary noise, of course. My hearing was in overdrive, and I think I was actually making up noises in my head. To my relief, sleep prevailed.

In Matthew 13:17 Jesus says, "Many prophets and righteous men have desired to see those things which ye see, and have not seen them; and to hear, and have not heard them." Also, Job 13:1 reads, "Mine eye hath seen all this, mine ear hath heard and understood it." The goal should be to keep so connected to God that we are neither so far from Him that we cannot hear Him, nor misconstrue His message in an effort to attain His glory. I found prayer and reading God's Word to be the key.

As time goes on, Barbara's vocabulary will grow. In the meantime we will continue to listen prayerfully for God's still small voice.

Mary Wagoner Angelin

Outward Appearances

People judge by the outward appearance, but the Lord looks at a person's thoughts and intentions. 1 Sam. 16:7, NLT.

ACCORDING TO MY VERY conservative orientation, this seemed like a strange assembly. Their dress was typical of the area, but I was uncomfortable with the clothing. We were in a remote Asian village to join in the orientation of a Christian group. I admitted that the gathering here in the shade of banyan and mango trees really did not demand formality in dress. However, my discomfort continued because of all the finery—wrist and ankle bracelets and bangles, fake stone rings, and dangling earrings. This did not, I thought, exemplify the simplicity Jesus had demonstrated.

Smiling groups of people continued to emerge from that small village and seat themselves on the lush grass. *Has the whole village become Christian?* I wondered. *And do they fully understand all this?* I had to admit, though, that they all looked happy, really happy.

Enthusiastic hymn singing was accompanied by harmonium and drum. There were sincere prayers. There was a reading of a biblical parable, then the explanation and relevant interpretation. The pastor invited those individuals seeking membership in the Christian fellowship to assemble on the grass right in front of him.

Twenty-five or 30 individuals emerged from the crowd. To my great amazement there was no jewelry, no gaudiness, no ornamentation—just neat, smiling people. These were the new members. And the others? They were their neighbors.

Although it was a solemn service with admonitions and instructions, happiness seemed to increase as the service progressed. It culminated with sheer joy in the Communion service. Throughout all this the visitors, too, had retained their happy faces. These new members had witnessed so enthusiastically that the entire village had responded. It was no longer their gaudy clothing and glittering jewelry I noticed. It was their happiness. They were sharing the new believers' joy in acknowledging Jesus as their Lord and Saviour.

Sitting there on the grass that day, I asked myself, "Do I allow people's outward appearance to form my opinion of them?" That, I decided, could be called judging. And "Do I radiate my relationship with Jesus joyfully?" That, I think, could be called witnessing.

LOIS E. JOHANNES

Help on Time

I will deliver you, and you will honor me. Ps. 50:15, NIV.

IT WAS LATE EVENING, about 9:30, and I wanted to go home after attending a computer course to which my office had sent me. It was my first time to go to that place, and I was not familiar with the way back home.

An uncomfortable feeling came over me as I drove down the road. There were no houses along the road, and a forest lined either side. I realized I hadn't seen any other cars. After driving for about a half hour, I found myself in a business area. *Thank You, Lord!* I sighed. At least now I could ask directions from someone. I left my car and walked to the nearest restaurant to ask directions from the cashier.

"I'm lost and I want to go to Virginia Beach Boulevard. Can you please show the way?" I asked.

"You *are* lost!" she said. "It'll take you at least an hour to get there. I don't know how to help you. Even if I give directions, I'm afraid you'll get more lost."

I was tired and frustrated. I stood there for about two minutes. *Please, dear Lord, help me!* I prayed. Those were the only words I could utter while my heart started to beat faster.

Then the girl shouted to a woman across the room. "Mom, this girl wanted to go to Virginia Beach Boulevard. Could you please help show the way?"

To my surprise her mom said, "I'm going to Virginia Beach Boulevard now because I would like to see the new car being advertised here in this newspaper." She pointed to a newspaper in her hand.

Praise the Lord!

Back on the road again, I thought about how instantly God had answered my prayer. *I asked for the help, Lord, and You sent it. I called, You answered. Thank You, Lord, for the assurance of Your guidance and help.*

LANNY LYDIA PONGILATAN

April 6

My Dog and Greener Pastures

Do not covet your neighbor's wife. Do not covet your neighbor's house or land, male or female servant, ox or donkey, or anything else your neighbor owns. Deut. 5:21, NLT.

WHEN WE GET HOME from work every evening, the first thing we do after we change our clothes is to take Abercrombie, our dog, for a walk. We got him from the animal control center when he was just a puppy. A German shepherd and a golden retriever mix, he had a lovable face we could not pass up, and we took him home and showered him with lots of love, affection, toys, food, and dog treats. Abercrombie has an annoying habit, though, that we cannot curb. He is a bona fide kleptomaniac. No matter what we do or what we give him, he always wants the toys that belong to the other dogs. He would steal them and bring them home if he could.

Every evening as we head toward the field behind the townhouses where he can run, play catch Frisbee, and meet up with the neighborhood's big dogs—Shane, Tam, Bo, Bear, Molly, Rudy, Skip, and Apollo—he makes a beeline for their toys instead of playing with his own. And at the end of the "social session" he is reluctant to return the toy that does not belong to him.

What is it about another dog's toy? Abercrombie does not lack toys; he even has similar toys. Nevertheless, all our efforts go to waste as he sits in the grass with a toy in his mouth, refusing to let it go, and giving us long doleful looks when we make him return it.

I wonder if dogs and humans aren't very much alike in many ways. Like our animal friends, we often think the grass is greener on the other side. We covet what our neighbors have and can't be happy with the abundance we receive. We don't see what the Lord has blessed and provided us with. Like Abercrombie, I have been guilty many a time of looking over the fence at the next pasture. Still, the Lord is patient with me whenever my human nature nudges me into one of those I-wish-I-had cycles.

Today, Lord, help me to recognize and give You glory for all You have given me. Help me remember that "Better is a little with the fear of the Lord, than great treasure with trouble" (Prov. 15:16, NKJV).

LYNNETTA SIAGIAN HAMSTRA

Does My Mirror Have Two Faces?

If any are hearers of the word and not doers, they are like those who look at themselves in a mirror; for they look at themselves and, on going away, immediately forget what they were like. James 1:23, 24, NRSV.

ONE OF MY TEACHERS in nursing school would say that it is good to look at ourselves in front of the bathroom mirror, but that it's better to do so before a full-body mirror, because the small mirror doesn't show enough to say whether one is overweight or not.

I must confess that I haven't always been satisfied with my image in the full-body mirror. Although at first I had no real incentive to do so, I began to exercise and tone my body. Now this daily routine has become one of my life's imperatives. Each day I stand before the full-body mirror. This is a moment of introspection that few make time for.

The truth of the matter is that we don't like to see ourselves as others see us. We like to think that we look better. So when we're out working or shopping or sightseeing, we are careful to straighten the hair, check the clothes, and make sure that nobody sees the wrinkles. All of us want others to see us at our best.

I wonder *How much time do we spend in front of God's mirror? Do we like the image it reflects?* I wouldn't like to speculate on numbers, but I'm sure many would not dare to look at this mirror for fear of what it might show. Would the mirror show idolatry, bad temper, envy, jealousy, disobedience?

"There's nothing to be afraid of," we might say. "This mirror can't show others what we're really like inside." So we keep these reflections hidden, like treasures, hoping that nobody will ever find out. But people are more perceptive than we give them credit for. More important, God sees and knows.

As we prepare for Jesus' second coming, getting ready means working on our reflections, our characters. We don't need to keep our treasures hidden; we can go directly to the Lord, because "he is just and may be trusted to forgive our sins and cleanse us from every kind of wrong" (1 John 1:9, NEB).

Ellen E. Mayr

April 8

Cling to the Cross

The message of the cross is foolishness to those who are perishing, but to us who are being saved it is the power of God. 1 Cor. 1:18, NIV.

WHEN I WAS A CHILD I clung to the cross, wearing a white robe, my arms stretched over the crossbars. It was a pageant in church at Eastertime, and I was to represent a person deeply grieved over Christ's death. As I knelt there and hung on to the cross, I decided to give my heart to the Lord. Although that image has been a part of me over the years, I am saddened to think of how many times I have lost sight of that experience.

This evening, when I can't sleep, this is my prayer. *Lord, help me cling to the cross when I am overcome with grief and sadness and engulfed with fear for myself and others. Help me cling to the cross when my loved ones suffer pain and hurt unbearably, and all I can do is pray and hang on to the crossbars.*

Help me cling to the cross when friends seem cold and unfeeling and lack sympathy for those around me. Help me cling to the cross when neighbors ignore or reject me and I feel alone. Help me stay at the cross when Satan's atrocities cause havoc over the world, when leaders fall down and things seem to come apart.

Help me find the cross when things are confusing and everything goes wrong, and when I'm crabby and can't get the housework done. Help me hang on for dear life when my health isn't good and I need healing and I worry too much.

And Lord, help me cling to the cross when the neighbors bring a casserole and the irises are blooming in the backyard and my husband remembers my birthday. Help me cling to the cross when there is someone I can help today and the budget works out for the month and our children call to say they love us. Help me cling to the cross when I feel better and there is hope and peace in my life and the sun is shining. Help me kneel at the cross and remember that You gave Your life, not to keep me from disappointments, but to give me victory over them.

Thank You, dear Jesus, for the cross. DARLENE YTREDAL BURGESON

The Saving Blood

Without the shedding of blood there is no forgiveness. Heb. 9:22, NIV.

AS A MEDICAL TECHNOLOGIST I get my hands into all sorts of body fluids and excrements. (Yes, I really do love my job.) One of those substances, of course, is blood. Each time I deal with a blood specimen I think of today's verse. Through my training I've learned that the life-giving fluid carries DNA molecules or genetic coding for our specificity and our individuality. It carries nutrients and oxygen that our body needs. It also disposes of wastes and harmful elements that we don't need. And sometimes the blood carries disease. Additionally, there are white blood cells that fight off infection and platelets that maintain blood vessel integrity. They are our first response to stop bleeding by forming a platelet plug, or scab.

Like the red cells, Jesus' blood gives us life—His blood has justified us. He gives us His blood so we can be free of the SIN virus. When a foreign substance invades our body, the white cells attack. Jesus came to attack sin in our flesh and to take the impurities and inflammation of sin from us. He knows and feels what we are going through, and He tells us that we can have a blood transfusion. He will give us His blood pure and free from all iniquities, and He died for us.

Just like the platelet plug, Jesus is our first response to the sin that wants to separate us from Him. He wants to maintain our vessel integrity and says if we let Him in, He will continue to do a good work in us. And He is faithful to complete it (Phil. 1:6). Not only does He start the healing and reconstruction process, He promises He is going to finish what He started in us.

The blood of Jesus takes us to the throne of God. Nothing but the blood of Jesus can wash away our sins. In the medical field you need type-specific blood for a blood transfusion. Jesus' blood is universal. It is for whosoever will. Unless we accept His life-saving blood there is no forgiveness, no life, no hope.

Lord, thank You for Your blood that cleanses me from sin. Please continue to be there to respond to sin's invasion in my life. I want to accept Your blood. Keep me close to the fountain filled with Your saving blood.

TRUDY SEVERIN

The Cleansing Breath of God

The wind blows (breathes) where it wills; and though you hear its sound, yet you neither know where it comes from nor where it is going. So it is with everyone who is born of the Spirit. John 3:8, Amplified.

SPRING IS MY FAVORITE time of year. I so enjoy watching the first flowers poking their pretty heads through the soil in search of the sun, hearing the birds singing praises to the Father, and watching the buds on trees burst forth in beautiful leaves. The bloom of colors in the spring is such a welcome sight after the dull of winter.

One day in early spring, early enough that not too much had yet started to bloom, I was driving home from work at the end of the day. On my travel route there are certain stoplights that are longer than others. When I am stopped at these longer lights, I have time to take a look at the world around me, which is especially nice after living in an office building all day. This day I was studying a huge tree at the side of the road while I waited for the light to change. The trunk was enormous and the branches large and sturdy. This particular tree was still covered with ugly dead brown leaves. There were some spring buds on it, but not as many as it could have had if those dead leaves weren't blocking the new growth.

While I was still watching, a very strong wind came out of nowhere and blew through the tree, engulfing my car in a dead leaf storm. The wind had done its work. As the stoplight turned green, I glanced out my back window and saw that the tree was now bare of dead leaves.

As I continued my drive I thought *If the wind had not blown the dead leaves off the tree branches, the tree would not have grown in the way it was created to grow.* I wondered what "dead leaves" were stunting my spiritual growth. I came up with a list and realized I needed the Holy Spirit to blow these dead leaves out of my life so that I could grow into the woman God had originally intended me to be.

Father, please send Your Holy Spirit to blow through me and remove those dead leaves. I want to remove everything that is not in conformity with Your will for my life. Amen.

SHARON DALTON WILLIAMS

Correct Pronunciation

The Lord direct your hearts into the love of God, and into the patient waiting for Christ. 2 Thess. 3:5.

I AM A SCHOOL NURSE. When I was still new to a particular school, a mother called to ask me to remind her second-grade son to come to the clinic to take an asthma treatment after lunch. This would help him avoid another asthma attack.

Because I had no orientation to the location of each class, the teachers, or the other staff, I didn't know the boy or where he was. I scanned the records and found the name of the student and the room where he would be. But I didn't even know which direction in the building I should go. I saw a staff member in a room close by and asked where Ms. Hill's room was. She directed me to go all the way to the end of the building and turn left to the last hallway. One room before the last on the left was her room.

When I got there, the teacher said that she was Ms. Gill and that Brendan was not in her class. However, a visitor in Ms. Gill's room directed me in the opposite direction, closer to the clinic. I finally found the room only to have the teacher, Mrs. Hill, say that she did not have any boy in the class named Brendan. So I began my search again, looking all over the place for any clue as to the boy's whereabouts.

After searching for a while I went back to Mrs. Hill. "I am still looking for Brendan Kearney," I told her.

The teacher looked surprised and embarrassed. "Oh, yes, he's here. I thought you said *Brandon.*"

"That is my native pronunciation," I apologized. "English is not my first language." I could have saved 20 minutes of precious time if I had pronounced *Hill* instead of *Gill,* and *Brendan* instead of *Brandon.*

Lord, I want You to direct my ways. Help me to listen carefully to Your words—I don't want to misunderstand anything.

Esperanza Aquino Mopera

Do You Remember?

Don't forget to show hospitality to strangers, for some who have done this have entertained angels without realizing it! Heb. 13:2, NLT.

THE YEAR WAS 1978, and I was working as a waitress in Fort McMurray, Alberta, Canada. Our beautiful little Andrea was 5. She attended Mother Goose Preschool, so I wasn't needed at home. I was working because I wanted to, not because I had to. I know very well that this is a blessing so many have never enjoyed, and I'm truly humbled at the thought. I was saving my paychecks to buy a nice bedroom suite, and my tips bought our groceries.

I knew in my heart when I awoke that this spring day was going to be special. I never kept a journal then, but I remember it was just before Easter, my grandma's birthday. Before going to work I decided that this day's tips would be spent on a gift for Grandma.

Not surprisingly, this was my best day ever for tips. A handsome man whom I hadn't seen before—and never saw again—came into the restaurant just before my shift ended. I can still remember where he sat, what he ordered, and what he looked like. As I passed his table after taking another customer's order, he slipped some money into my hand. The tip was more than his order. In those days I was very painfully shy, and it wasn't easy for me to make eye contact, especially with men. His smile was beautiful, saying nothing more than "I like you!"

I'm a victim of child molestation, and some details I have mentally blocked out. My mom told me that I had to go all alone before a grand jury to tell them what had happened to me. You don't have any idea how long and hard Jesus and I have had to fight together to get back my self-esteem, which was brutally taken away from me when I was 6 years old. I believe that Jesus inspires me to write for His glory. It's easier on me to do His will in this way—so that I won't have to look at people when I share unless He gives me the desire to do so.

With tips in hand, I ran like the wind through the mall to the jewelry store and purchased an ivory rose pin for my grandma and sent it to her with all my love.

Thank You for helping me remember the special days and blotting out the bad. You are so good.

Deborah Sanders

The Cross on the Hill

When I am lifted up [on the cross], I will draw everyone to me. John 12:32, TLB.

ALONE ON A CHILLY winter morning, I got out of a warm bed at 5:00 to pray. The room was dark as I groped my way to the window to draw the curtains apart in the guest room where I was spending the weekend. A never-to-be-forgotten sight kept me riveted on the spot.

Framed in my window was a mountain, and on top of it an illuminated cross in sharp contrast to a pitch-black sky. It seemed to be suspended in space, as I could not see what was supporting it. As the light shone from it, I found myself inspired to meditate on its significance.

There was something so compelling about that cross that urged me to remember another cross—a plain rugged wooden cross that stood on a hill nearly 2,000 years ago—the cross on which our Saviour was crucified. There was nothing beautiful about that cross, a symbol of ignominy and shame and on which the greatest indignity was inflicted on the One to be punished.

This cross, standing alone on the top of a mountain, reminded me of the loneliness of Jesus as He felt forsaken by His Father, His friends, and ungrateful humanity. I thought about my part in causing His suffering and loneliness and asked for forgiveness once again.

The illuminated cross was also beautiful as it shone out as a symbol of victory. As the light gleamed steadily in the darkness, I thought of Jesus, the Light of the world. The cross has dispelled the darkness of sin. It is our only hope of salvation, and when we are touched by the sacrifice of Jesus on the cross, our lives will never be the same again.

I didn't realize how long I had been standing there, but the sound of people awaking in the adjacent rooms jolted me back to reality. I turned to the clock and saw there would be no time for my usual morning worship; nevertheless, peace, strength, and His grace flooded my heart. I knew that there could be no better form of worship than to meditate on the cross and thank Jesus for His love.

When I turned back for a last glance at the cross, it was hardly visible, as the darkness was fast disappearing with the approach of daylight.

Never let Your cross fade from my mind, my dear Jesus.

FRANCES CHARLES

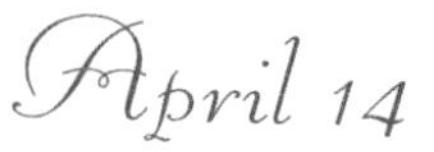

Pleasant Surprises

No eye has seen, no ear has heard, and no mind has imagined what God has prepared for those who love him. 1 Cor. 2:9, NLT.

IT WAS OUR FIRST TRIP out of the Philippines. We were new missionaries to Africa. Our girls were only toddlers, and the trip was long—18 flying hours and four stopovers. We were nervous.

Our knowledge about Africa was that of a famine-stricken people living in mud huts. We knew of prides of lions, tigers, and elephants. We packed plenty of food for the girls, but we thought that we adults could survive on whatever we could find where we were. We filled our boxes with plastic plates, glasses, and utensils. We also brought mosquito nets. We were committed to the mission and ready to sacrifice the comforts of home.

Saying goodbye to family and friends was not easy, especially when we felt it might be the last time to see each other. Tears were shed by the bucketful, embraces given, and words of comfort exchanged. "Let's be faithful and remain true to God and meet each other in heaven."

At last the plane landed. We felt nervous, scared, happy, and anxious. When we stepped out of the plane I noticed a worried look on my husband's face. I too was worried and wondered whether we were thinking the same thought: *Did we board the right plane? Is this Africa?*

As we entered the terminal building we were greeted and welcomed by the church president and treasurer. It was a relief to know we were in the right place. It was a great surprise for us. This was not the Africa we had expected. Here was a beautiful and fertile land of modern cities, tall buildings, huge supermarkets, beautiful landscaping, gorgeous flowers and trees, paved roads, plenty of cars, and well-dressed people.

As I recall these memories, I think of the great surprise awaiting God's people. You and I might have seen and visited many beautiful places, places that are so awesome that we cannot explain their beauty, but we are told that the surprises awaiting us in heaven haven't been seen, heard, or even dreamed of. We cannot imagine the beauty of it. I am looking forward to that grand surprise, aren't you?

JEMIMA D. ORILLOSA

Vanity of Vanities

We shall not all sleep, but we shall all be changed. 1 Cor. 15:51.

MY HUSBAND AND I ONCE attended a concert by Mildred, a renowned harpist, who was the friend of a friend of mine. I'd heard so much about her and was dying to meet the glamorous woman who had once taught Harpo Marx and many others to play the harp. However, the plain old woman who answered my knock on her dressing room door was vastly different from the picture that had been painted of her.

"Come in," she said. Ignoring my pleasantries, she demanded I help her get changed. "Help me into my corset," she insisted. "Now . . . that green gown over there, and my slippers. . . . They must be in the closet. Where's my makeup case and wig? Hurry now! I have to go on soon."

Annoyance mixed with amusement as I let myself be turned into an unpaid maid and scurried around at her bidding, even agreeing to be there during intermission to help her change. At last I was able to take my place beside my husband, and in amazement I watched the stage curtain open to reveal a glamorous woman, bathed in soft lights, seated beside an ornate harp. Slowly her delicate fingers caressed the strings, and sweet music filled the hall.

At intermission I raced backstage and helped Mildred change into a pink outfit, fetched her a drink of water, packed her other dress away, and listened to her constant grumbling about her maid who had failed to show up, the less-than-full hall, and many other things. Finally I was able to join my husband for the second part of the concert.

When it was over and the encores and whistles had died away, I returned to the dressing room and helped her change into street clothes. Once again she was a plain old woman who looked very, very tired. "Fetch me a cab," she demanded at last, adding that she was going to fire her maid immediately. Would I like to take her place and see something of the world? How thankful I was to be able to say I had a husband and children and wasn't looking for a job.

One day we'll all be changed, not just a temporary coverup of our tired old selves, but brand-new glorious bodies that will never grow old and never need fixing up. As the years take their toll on us, isn't this one of the greatest promises in the Bible?

EDNA MAY OLSEN

April 16

Serendipity

Behold, the eye of the Lord is on those who fear Him, on those who hope for His lovingkindness, to deliver their soul from death. Ps. 33:18, 19, NASB.

WE WERE ON OUR way to an evening church meeting. I was driving so my husband could rest after a busy day. The sun had set, but it was still quite light. As we entered the sharp curve not far from our home, we were horrified to see a huge tractor-trailer careen into the curve, out of control, and directly into our lane. With no time to think, I steered ahead and to the right. To our amazement, the truck was suddenly in its own lane, speeding past us while we continued on.

"How could that truck have gotten over so quickly?" my husband exclaimed.

We both agreed it had to have been the work of an angel of God. Had I had time to think, I would have known that there was no opening in the road there, as indeed we verify every time we drive past that area. There is the sharp curve with a narrow strip of pavement about three feet wide between the white line at the edge of the road and the railing that separates that road from the river. There was no opening, but in that moment of need God showed me a place to steer toward, away from the truck.

I keep a prayer journal, and in it I have a section I have labeled "Serendipities." Here I record unexpected happy events in our lives. I read these over sometimes, noting how God helps us find lost keys or glasses after a futile search brings us to call upon Him in prayer.

There are those times I've asked God for wisdom when facing various problems of life and, as James 1:5 tells us, He never has failed to help me. There are those times He provided unexpected help for our children when I've prayed for their needs. Now I've added this wonderful deliverance to the list. I believe it's important to keep track of all our extra blessings, so we'll never forget them.

We thank our Father God every day for His marvelous care in our lives. God is so good!

MARILYN KING

Your Father Knows

Remember, your Father knows exactly what you need even before you ask him! Matt. 6:8, TLB.

THE TEACHERS, THE STUDENTS, and their parents were all worried about the coming church school fete. They had been planning the event for weeks, but now it looked as if it might, quite literally, be a washout. The weather forecasts were grim, and there had been a clash of dates so that quite a few of the people who might otherwise have come along to support the event were committed to being elsewhere. It wasn't to have been merely a fun social occasion. The plan was to raise funds for much-needed new computers for the school; hence, the feeling of concern. In such circumstances there was only one thing to do—pray. Members of the local church congregations joined students and teachers in sending up petitions for a successful outcome.

The day before the function the rain bucketed down. The paint ran in streaks on the posters the children had prepared. The strings of colored flags they had helped to put up sagged damply. It continued to pour all night, and it was still raining when I looked gloomily out of the window the next morning.

Now, God is certainly into precision timing. As I finished my breakfast cereal the rain stopped and the sun came out. The day remained fine until midafternoon, when a further storm front swept through, bringing fresh torrents of rain—just after the fete had ended. Some thousands of dollars were raised for new computers. More important, perhaps, was the impact made on those parents who were not Christians and had not previously encountered a prayer-answering God.

I do believe that God answers prayer, but not always with such a clear "Yes." I confess to struggling sometimes with the "No" or "Not yet" answers. I find myself praying for what I want—and how and when I want it—rather than for what He thinks is best. A colleague recently e-mailed me a message with a timely reminder. It began "Good morning. I am God. Today I will be handling all of your problems. Please remember that I do not need your help." And it concluded, "Rest, my child. If you need to contact Me, I am only a prayer away."

JENNIFER M. BALDWIN

God Is My Strength

I can do all things through Christ who strengthens me. Phil. 4:13, NKJV.

SEVERAL YEARS AGO, as the single parent to two teenage daughters, I realized that in order to make ends meet I needed to have extra income. I mentioned this decision to a friend, who told me of an opening for a kitchen assistant in the nursing home where he worked. So I applied for the job. To this day I'm not sure how it happened, but by the end of the interview I had been hired as a nurse's aide. I had plenty of kitchen experience as a parent but knew nothing about being a nurse's aide. Nevertheless, I took three days of vacation from my full-time job and spent the time in training for the nurse's aide position.

After training I was assigned to the 3:00 p.m. to 11:00 p.m. weekend shift. It was not long before I concluded that the job was difficult and unpleasant. Most of the patients were helpless and needed total care. A few were combative, and it was a challenge to get them to do anything at all. The job needed not only intestinal fortitude but good physical strength. After about a month I felt that I had made a terrible mistake.

One afternoon I drove into the parking lot of the nursing home just before the start of my shift, and the thought of having to take care of the patients overwhelmed me. I couldn't get out of the car. At that low point the Holy Spirit brought to mind Paul's words to the Philippians: "I can do all things through Christ who strengthens me." As the meaning of those words seeped into my consciousness, the heaviness that had overwhelmed me evaporated. I walked into the nursing home with a new strength and confidence that enabled me to approach my job focused not on the difficulties or unpleasantness, but instead on the patients and their needs, seeing them not just as patients needing care, but as people. Most of them were placed in the nursing home and abandoned by their families. Others had no living relatives or friends, and there were the fortunate few who had relatives who still cared for them. I was able to see beyond the obvious and learned that these people at one time had led interesting and productive lives. They were happy to relate their experiences to anyone willing to listen. Indeed, I was able to do all things through Christ, who strengthened me.

Claudette L. M. Tang-Kwok

Moving House

Where your treasure is, there will your heart be also. Matt. 6:21, NEB.

ONE PERSON'S RUBBISH IS another person's treasure." This bit of folk wisdom made me think of the past few months of moving.

Someone suggested that I put all my accumulated keepsakes and other extra things in black plastic bags and dump them. Such an easy operation was too cruel for me. I had to take the long and hard way of going through every letter, card, book, and drawing by my children and grandchildren before deciding whether I should part with it or not. Was I being silly and sentimental? There were little gifts given by family and close friends, remembered with affection. My treasures—other people's rubbish.

I found it much easier to part with some things of value, especially when I knew they could be of use to others. A vanload of items went to the hospice, bedding to the homeless shelter, and blankets to the refugees. I tried to advertise useful clothing and some other items, but there was very little interest. An old drawn-thread tablecloth that had belonged to my grandmother and many black-and-white photographs of India and Guyana were saved. Over 24 years I had accumulated so much, and most of it had to go, as I was moving into a smaller place.

I am a natural hoarder, and it was an extremely hard process to learn to sort and cull. I am trying, with the Lord's help, to continue to identify the important things in my life and to get my priorities right. In this way I can prepare the greatest treasure of all, my heart. My heart and my character are the only treasure I can take with me when I leave this world. Besides, I have been promised a new home, more beautiful than anything imaginable, and it will last forever.

Thank You, dear Father, for helping me over this difficult period and answering my prayers. I am now beginning to appreciate the blessing of my new flat with all its advantages and not having so many things cluttering my life.

If we are faithful we can look forward to our final home, full of wonderful treasures, where we will never have to move again.

PHILIPPA MARSHALL

Just Look Up

I lift up my eyes to the hills—where does my help come from? My help comes from the Lord, the Maker of heaven and earth. Ps. 121:1, 2, NIV.

WHO WILL TAKE CARE of me today, Mommy?" Even though Abbie was only 27 months old, she knew that her nanny had told me to find a new nanny for her.

I soon learned what a mighty God we serve. He never fails. That was what Mom taught us. "Anytime you are in trouble, just look up. Tell Him your problem in prayer, trust Him, and wait; He knows what is good for us, and He will do just that at the right time," she always said. So that was what we determined to do.

I phoned my workplace and asked for permission for a day off, explaining everything to my boss. Then I put Abbie in her buggy, and we left for the town center to look for a new nanny. I met a sister from our church who asked where we were heading. I told her my problem, and she gave me the name and address of a person to contact. We went straight to that address, but the playschool teacher, Sonyia, told us that Abbie must be at least 3 years old to attend that school. I stood there in silence, lifting my eyes up to God, praying that He would intervene.

I told Sonyia that I could lose my job and that I was the breadwinner for my family, as my husband was a student. She was moved and advised me not to fill in the admission form showing Abbie's age. She promised to keep Abbie there for the day so that I could come later to see the headmistress for special consideration.

It took three days to see the headmistress; meanwhile, Abbie went to the playschool every day. When I met the headmistress she could not believe that Abbie was not 3 years old. She said, "Your daughter is bigger, smarter, and more mature than all the 3-year-olds. In fact, she goes around sharing toys, collecting them when it is time, and consoling those who cry for their mothers." She said Abbie knew many songs and Bible stories, too.

My heart was filled with joy, and I thanked God. He had done it again! I filled in the admission form and paid a minimal fee, less than for the former nanny. "I lift up my eyes to the hills—where does my help come from? My help comes from the Lord."

MABEL KWEI

Blessings in the Forecast

Encourage one another and build each other up, just as in fact you are doing. 1 Thess. 5:11, NIV.

CABIN FEVER HITS ME harder and harder each year. This winter it was complicated by my tediously slow recovery from two knee surgeries in the preceding 12 months. Snow kept me inside. The daily walks, vital to my sanity, were out of the question because of the reinjury possibility. Winter was cold and bleak and depressing.

I am a professional writer, but my writing, when it flowed, came out at such a sluggish rate that I despaired of ever meeting the demanding deadlines that loomed. To make matters worse, writing is an isolating profession. I didn't receive daily feedback and encouragement on my work the way I would have if I were out in the marketplace. While I don't necessarily expect a constant pat on the back for my labors, it does become overwhelming at times to throw your words into a vacuum and not find out what impact they have on your readers.

When my depression hit rock bottom and I couldn't write a single word, God started to send them. Messages from people who had read my books started filing into my e-mail box. Messages that said God was touching their lives through my writing. Messages that told me of their desperate struggles and how they'd overcome by the grace of God. Messages urging me never to stop writing. Maybe there were a half dozen in the span of a couple weeks, but to me, locked away in my isolated little world, it was an avalanche of blessings and affirmation.

These people took time out of their lives to share how God had used something I'd written to change their lives. As I read the messages I could almost feel God sitting next to me, patting my shoulder, saying, "See? You can trust Me. Do not be discouraged! Do not be dismayed! I am in charge, and I can see the bigger picture."

Satan specializes in despair and depression. He'd love us to believe we are fighting the good fight in vain. But God specializes in encouragement and hope. I thank Him again and again for prompting the people who write me. They will probably never know on this side of heaven how important their encouragement really was or how God used them. But I will never forget.

Céleste perrino Walker

On a Trek in the Hills

Where two or three are gathered together in My name, I am there in the midst of them. Matt. 18:20, NKJV.

WE HAD BEEN TREKKING for two days through the hills in northern Thailand, by the Burmese border. The views were superb, and the experience was unparalleled. We were 11 people from different walks of life who had come together on an adventure tour.

An avid traveler, I have visited six continents in the past three years, but I shun group tours because they do not afford me the freedom to choose my sights and company. However, because of the dangers in the area, solo trekking was highly discouraged. Sometimes different personalities mesh well. This was not the case with the 11 of us. The majority of the group were young students, out to experience life with no boundaries. Smoking cigarettes (and other more potent substances), imbibing alcohol, and engaging in shallow conversation were the preferred pastimes of most of the group. Those of us who didn't wish to share in these activities either kept quiet or found our own corner away from the action.

The group activities of trekking through the hills, rafting, elephant riding, spelunking, and visiting with the hill tribes were an adventurer's dream, but come evening time, there was a feeling of emptiness. It was at one of these moments that I decided to wander around the Lit-su village in the highlands. In the distance I heard someone playing music. I decided to go investigate. A young man was playing a guitar as several teenage girls sang. I inched closer but still kept my distance, not wanting to intrude on their lives. This was a village that saw many visitors who have subtly or not so subtly been changing the tribal customs; I wanted to minimize the effect of my presence. But the music was soothing, and soon I was close enough that the young people noticed me and waved to me. I joined them. The first thing I noticed was the sticker of a cross on the guitar. Using gestures, I asked them whether they were Christians. After some hand waving, we were smiling broadly at each other. We worshiped the same God. We shared songs—some new to them, some new to me, and some that we all knew. At that moment I no longer felt the emptiness. We were fellowshipping together in the only way we could communicate: through Christ in song. I was filled. *Thank You, Lord.*

CHRISTINE HWANG

So Many Rainbows

I have set my rainbow in the clouds. Gen. 9:13, NIV.

ONCE MORE I AM BACK with the little folk—the cradle roll children—in church, waving multicolored ribbons and singing enthusiastically, if not always quite in tune, that "God made the beautiful rainbow, that's why I love it so." For me it's a promise in the sky, the assurance of His hand in my affairs. We live in an area that has its fair share of rain. It makes our gardens productive, and the rainbows are a bonus. Sometimes I feel my life is punctuated by them.

For several months after we moved to Wales we house hunted without success. I began to doubt we'd ever find a home that really met our needs. One morning when I was feeling particularly negative, our daughter-in-law sent us a card that read "When God closes one door He always opens another." As if in confirmation, that very day there was a succession of rainbows—bursts of rain followed by dramatic heavenly displays. They really lifted my spirits, and a short time afterward we found our new home.

Another time, in despair concerning a particular problem, I wandered up our lane and sat beneath a familiar tree. Rain pattered gently on the leaves, eventually filtering through onto my head. It seemed to echo my mood. Then quite suddenly sunlight pierced the clouds and there, above my tree, was a great arch of color. I recounted the many promises God had fulfilled for me. I turned my problem over to Him and returned home with renewed confidence.

Still fresh in all our minds, though it happened some years ago, is a family holiday on Scotland's eastern coast. You can get glorious weather there on long white sandy beaches with magnificent seascapes—or you can get the other kind: somber skies and very wetting rain that persists for days. This was what greeted us, even though September was usually sunny. But you should have seen the rainbows! The great wide skies were full of them in the brief intervals between torrential downpours. "Look," one would say, "another rainbow!"

So what have these rainbow experiences taught me? Just this: However depressing things can get down here, God is always there, always encouraging the upward look, and always meeting my need. PEGGY MASON

April 24

Scattering God's Love

Whoever sows generously will also reap generously. 2 Cor. 9:6, NIV.

KAREN, THE THEME FOR the seminar is 'Scattering God's Love.' Do you think you could make a banner for us?"

"I suppose so," I said slowly, trying to imagine what I would put on it. "I'll think about it."

I thought about scattering God's love. I had grown up in a home in which my parents were always finding places to scatter God's love. Others had also scattered God's love in our lives. When we were studying at the seminary and had very little money, Bernie was sent to a small church in the Michigan countryside. That farming community scattered God's love by supplying us with home-grown goods that were welcome treats in our meager diet. Canned fruits and vegetables were ours—all we had to do was return the jars before the next canning season!

When we lost our first child, seminary families scattered God's love in bunches of hand-picked flowers, home-baked bread, and precious little gifts that I will always treasure.

Remembering what others have done for me, I try to find at least one person each week who could really use a dose of God's love, then I find a creative way to bring a small piece of happiness to their heart.

As I thought about these special moments I looked out the window at our lawn. It was covered with dandelions, their fluffy heads bobbing in the breeze, some white and some balding! The little parachutes somersaulted in the summer breezes, drifting over our neighbors' lawns.

That was it! The banner! A huge downy dandelion blossom on deep-blue silk. Floating away from the flower would be little parachutes of seeds, but each seed would appear as a tiny heart. Just as we can never tell where the seed will land, we can never guess all the effects of scattering God's love in a hurting world.

Think of someone today who needs a scattering of God's love. Pray for them and ask God to guide you as you choose to do something to brighten their day and help them to feel loved. Then go ahead and do it! Scatter your love far and wide. Let it land where it is needed, and pray that the love of God will take root in the hearts of others, too.

Karen Holford

Great Is Your Faithfulness

Your faithfulness continues through all generations; you established the earth, and it endures. Ps. 119:90, NIV.

IT WAS SPRINGTIME—such a beautiful time of the year—and we were happy and content living in our country home. Then without warning, tragedy struck. Our strong, active daddy was seriously injured in a logging accident. After three days in a local hospital he was transferred to a veterans' hospital 130 miles away. We couldn't make that long trip very often to visit him, and our two preschoolers and one second grader weren't allowed to go to his hospital room because of their ages. By the time the children were able to visit him in the lobby, three months had passed. He looked so different that the 2-year-old was afraid of him.

I knew we needed something to distract their active young minds from the trauma of the accident. Since the roadsides between our home and town were dotted with all kinds of wildflowers, we decided to make a collection. We pressed the flowers, and when they were dry each child made his or her own scrapbook.

As the months passed, Daddy progressed and returned home.

Thirty-five years have passed, and while preparing for a recent move I came across one of the old flower scrapbooks. Although the flowers were faded and brittle, I thought back to that long-ago experience. It's springtime again, and the same roadsides are dotted with flowers, made especially beautiful this year by heavy spring rains. Other tragedies came into our lives as the years passed, but through it all we have this reminder of what a great God we have and how He cares for us in all circumstances.

Lord, thank You for Your gentle reminders of the many blessings You have given me, and thank You for the tremendous courage You provide when troubles arise. May I be reminded each day of Your never-ending love and devotion, even when I have forgotten to remember You. Thank You, God, that Your faithfulness continues.

BETTY J. ADAMS

God Listens

Cast thy burden upon the Lord, and he shall sustain thee. Ps. 55:22.

IT WAS APRIL, SUMMER vacation time in India, where the school year runs from June through March. My two children and I were visiting at my parents' house. It was a happy time, free of responsibilities and worry, a bit of a breather before we had to move to the place of my husband's new appointment. He had already gone there to take up his duties.

On Friday morning I woke up my children, then went to my room to have my personal devotional time. Suddenly I heard my mother scream, "Joshna! Joshna! Come quickly!"

Leaving my Bible open on the chair, I rushed into the next room. There was my son stretched out on the floor, unconscious. I knelt down and cradled him in my arms. *Oh, God, please help me know what to do. Help him to be all right.* I felt numb with pain and shock. I kept repeating my prayer again and again, *Help him to be all right.* Meanwhile, someone had gone for the doctor, who came into the room where I held my son. After a brief examination he told me to admit him into the hospital at once for observation and tests.

The next day my husband arrived, but the doctors still had not decided what was wrong. I longed to make our son feel better, so I patted his shoulder and said, "Son, I love you so much!"

His eyes filled with tears. "And I love you, too." I could sense that he was worried too.

I got out my Bible and read a couple verses to him. One was Psalm 55:22: "Cast thy burden upon the Lord, and he shall sustain thee." Another was Psalm 103:3, where the Lord promises that He "healeth all thy diseases." Those verses made us feel better.

The next day our son felt better and wanted to go home. The doctors wanted more X-rays and other tests. They were clearly puzzled. We decided to trust in the Lord and take him home. The doctor agreed, provided we would bring him back if he had any more problems. Since then he has had perfect health.

I am so thankful to the Lord for His promises and for listening to my prayer. It is so comforting to be able to cast our burdens on Him.

Joshna Prakash

The *Strelitzia* Plant

I have chosen thee, and not cast thee away. Isa. 41:9.

IF EVER THERE WAS A plant I admired and wanted to have in my garden it was the *Strelitzia.* They are indigenous evergreen clump-forming plants with decorative oblong, spear-shaped leaves. The most colorful variety is the *Strelitzia reginae.* They have unusual colors of orange and blue or purple, blue, and cream flowers that look like birds, hence the common names for *Strelitzia* are crane flower or bird-of-paradise. Their growing position should be sunny, and they must be watered regularly in dry weather.

I always admired this plant in other gardens, but my husband would say, "We don't have the right type of soil in our garden, so stop desiring to have one."

"Some of our neighbors have *Strelitzia* growing beautifully in their gardens," I would respond. "So why can't we?" I wouldn't give up.

I asked several friends and relatives for a cutting, but each one had their various excuses to offer until one day I received a gift—*Strelitzia reginae.* I hid the potted plant where no one could see it or steal it. I watered it regularly. It started pushing out new leaves, and I was overjoyed at its progress.

My husband split the plant into three parts and planted it in the soil. Then one plant died, and later the second one died. I was very sad about my precious plants. Finally my husband said he threw the third piece away because it wasn't growing fast enough or blooming.

Plants teach us patience. One must have patience to wait for warmer weather for the plants to bloom and grow. The *Strelitzia* was my chosen plant. I loved its beauty; but now an impatient gardener, my husband, cast it away because it wasn't growing fast enough for his liking.

I'm so glad the Master Gardener doesn't cast me away when I have times of stagnation, when I am cold and do not bloom and grow as I should. *Thank You, Lord, for being patient with me and caring for me when I need Your nurturing most of all.*

PRISCILLA ADONIS

April 28

Surge Protector

If you want favor with both God and man, and a reputation for good judgment and common sense, then trust the Lord completely; don't ever trust yourself. In everything you do, put God first, and he will direct you and crown your efforts with success. Prov. 3:4-6, TLB.

WHEN I BOUGHT MY first computer for my office I was told I also needed a surge protector to protect the computer from uneven electrical surges, common in that area. They said that without the surge protector my new computer might be ruined. I could lose valuable reports held in its memory. So I promptly bought a surge protector. The surge protector proved to be a blessing and saved my new computer from many problems that it might have had otherwise.

One day I realized that I also needed a "surge protector" for my impetuous ways and unruly tongue. Because of making hasty decisions on the job or at home, I had made some dumb mistakes by trusting in my own judgment, by not giving myself time to meditate about it, or even to pray about it. My impetuous temper had led me to make wrong decisions that afterward caused destructive consequences. My regrets did not correct the situations—they were too late.

When I finally read the book *All I Really Need to Know I Learned in Kindergarten,* by Robert Fulghum, I realized that I hadn't yet learned all I really need to know. But sometimes it takes a lifetime to learn what we really need to know: simply to trust in God for every need, including what we need to know for every moment in our lives.

I realized that I had not been trusting God as I should in every moment of my life. I had been running on my own fluctuating power when God's sure power was available for the asking. He could be my surge protector.

I can become new every morning by turning to God with my problems and letting Him direct my paths in whatever the task is for that day. Things go a lot smoother when I do that. Can you join me in doing that each day, finding a happier pathway with God as our surge protector?

BESSIE SIEMENS LOBSIEN

Protection

See, I am sending an angel ahead of you to guard you along the way and to bring you to the place I have prepared. Ex. 23:20, NIV. Trust in the Lord with all your heart and lean not on your own understanding. Prov. 3:5, NIV.

MUCH PRAYER AND PLANNING had gone into our trip. This was a dream come true for my sister and me and a nostalgic memory-lane trip for my father. Having left Vietnam 57 years earlier, he was returning to where he had started his mission service. I was returning to where my life had begun—in Cambodia.

People in the various countries we would be visiting had been contacted via e-mail and fax prior to our departure, so at each airport we had either someone meeting us or a fax with the exact directions to give the cab driver. All went well until the second country, where no one met us at the airport. We waited in a strange country, not knowing the language or customs. Should we leave the airport, knowing that once we did there would be no way to be in contact? I had failed to take the address and phone number of the mission, and it wasn't listed in the directory.

A hopeless feeling engulfed me. I felt I had let my family down. I hadn't prepared thoroughly enough. To complicate matters, we were supposed to be getting tickets from our contact person to fly to Angkor Wat the next morning. My father had always wanted to visit Angkor Wat when he lived in Saigon, but never had had the chance. What a major disappointment! Feelings of desperation and anxiety overwhelmed me.

We finally hired a cab driver. We drove around the neglected city with its crumbling sidewalks and people everywhere. Suddenly we stopped in front of a hotel. Soon our driver returned and smilingly said he had gotten us a room.

We were comfortable and safe. I marveled at how trusting we had been of our driver. Because he knew a little English, we had trusted him with our very lives. He knew our contact hadn't shown at the airport. He could have driven us into the country or city and robbed or killed us, but the Lord is so good. Even when our best-laid plans go wrong, God is in control and uses the right people to help and befriend us. "What time I am afraid, I will trust in thee" (Ps. 56:3).

Louise Driver

April 30

Hear My Cry

The Lord hath heard my supplication; the Lord will receive my prayer. Ps. 6:9.

WHEN MY SON DON was 3 years old, he climbed up into the huge poplar tree that grew on the edge of our front yard. It was difficult to get up into the tree, and even harder to get back down. I didn't see him get up—or down. So I was surprised to see him standing before me, hands on hips, tear-stained face, and hear him say in an accusing voice, "Didn't you hear me cry?"

"I didn't hear any crying. Why did you cry?" I asked.

"Well, I climbed the big tree and couldn't get down, so I cried for you to come help me." Although annoyed, he admitted he wasn't hurt, so I asked why he was crying. "Because you didn't hear me and didn't come, so I got down by myself."

Years later my 3-year-old daughter, Lori Ann, confronted me, hands on hips, tear-stained face, and saying in an accusing voice, "Didn't you hear me cry?" She loved to climb up and down around the stalls in the barn. Her sweater had gotten caught on a nail. Since crying didn't bring help, she removed her sweater and hurried into the house to confront her delinquent mother.

My little ones knew that the instant I heard them cry I would hurry to their side to pick them up and comfort them. They relied on it.

I have also confronted my Saviour in the same manner. *God, don't You hear my cry? You seem to be ignoring my plea for help. Have You abandoned me?*

Many times I have rejoiced over answered prayers. Other times I have waited, trusting and patient, knowing that in due time the answer will come in some way. Perhaps He will expect me to use my own mind and resources and think through a situation or need.

It is a peaceful thing to know that the God who gave us so many great and precious promises really cares for us and will never forsake us. On occasion my children may have cried for me and I didn't hear them. But there has never been a time when my heavenly Father didn't hear my cries for help. Psalm 4:3 tells me that the Lord will hear when I call to Him.

VERA NELSON

Rainbow of Promise

I set My rainbow in the cloud, and it shall be for the sign. Gen. 9:13, NKJV.

IN SOME PLACES ON Planet Earth the month of May can be a great time to travel. The unpredictable storms of winter are mostly gone, flowers bloom in abundant splashes, the sun smiles more brightly. So it was then that Mom and I peacefully enjoyed the last leg of our journey from California to Michigan to visit much-loved, much-missed relatives.

We flew on a small commuter jet, anticipating the fun we would have for the next week. I could tell our airplane was about to descend to enter the flight pattern for landing. Years earlier Dad had taught me to fly our airplane, and landing had always been the most exciting part of private piloting for me.

But now I was about to experience more excitement than I had anticipated. The airplane suddenly was bobbing around like a cork on a stormy sea—not just one motion, but continuously. Turbulent clouds were all around us. I started praying to God for His wonderful protection, the same protection He had splendidly afforded me before on countless airplane trips.

Just then I gasped in amazement as I noticed an awesome sight out the right-hand window. There, on a nearby cloud, was a gigantic, perfectly round rainbow of the most brilliant hues. Filling the huge circle rainbow was the stunning shadow of our jetliner. The afternoon sunlight in a breathtaking shaft streamed across our jet's cabin in the direction of our rainbow.

"Look!" I pointed out the spectacular sight. Mom was awestruck too. "See," I continued, "it's like God's rainbow of promise to Noah back in the Bible!"

We both sighed as we felt a perfect calm come over us, as though God in His infinite mercy had allowed us that beautiful "mural" on a cloud to remind us that He had not forgotten us but would deliver us into the loving arms of our relatives.

Yes, May is a good time to travel, but whenever you choose to travel, don't forget to take along the wonderful God who wants to pilot your life. Who knows? You just might see a rainbow of promise too!

JUDY COULSTON

Unless We Become as Little Children

Whosoever therefore shall humble himself as this little child, the same is greatest in the kingdom of heaven. Matt. 18:4.

I MET HANNAH ONE DAY while I was taking my walk. Since I live on a busy highway, I choose a less-traveled side street a block from my house. She was playing with some neighborhood children as I walked by, so we just nodded and waved as old friends might do. Later she told me that she was 6 years old and her name was Hannah.

"What's your name?" she asked.

"You can call me Sissy," I told her.

As time went on we began to chat briefly as I would pause for a breather. Occasionally her mother would join us at the back of their house. One day Hannah came running and handed me a fuzzy yellow toy chicken. When I protested, her mother assured me that Hannah wanted me to have it, so I hugged her, took it home, and placed it on my hutch.

I continued walking throughout the summer and on into the autumn, when the leaves were starting to fall. It was on just such a day that Hannah approached me, carrying a large yellow leaf she'd saved for me. I took it and thanked her. She gave me my usual kiss, and I went on my way.

As the weather became more unpredictable, my walks were less frequent, with only an occasional venture outdoors. But I'd see Hannah standing in her doorway, and she'd call out to me, "Hi, Sissy."

I'd smile and answer back, "Hi, Hannah."

The love and friendship I've received from Hannah has been so neat. Children have such a special gift—they're truly uninhibited and very genuine. They haven't yet learned the art of wearing a facade. I'm so grateful to Hannah for giving of herself. What greater gift could a friend ask for?

I want to be childlike in my genuineness this day with You. I give myself to You because I want to be Your friend. CLAREEN COLCLESSER

Angels Unawares

He shall give His angels charge over you, to keep you in all your ways. Ps. 91:11, NKJV.

VENTURING ON HER OWN across the sea from her island state of Tasmania, Australia, to enroll in the University of Sydney had been like a step into the big bad world for our granddaughter, Kassie. Anticipation of her first term-end at home had been pent with excitement. Now it was time to return to the university, and the only available plane would land her in Sydney after dark. She would have to get a bus to the city, then a train to her suburb. Two weeks earlier a murder had occurred at that very station. To reach the unit she shared with two girls, Kass would have to walk through a dark alley and across a dark empty field. Nerolie, her mother, feared for her daughter. When saying farewell to her at the airport she told Kass, "As soon as I return home I'll begin praying for you, and I won't stop until the phone rings!"

It seemed a long, long time before the shrill ringing sent Nerolie scurrying for the phone. "You're safe," she breathed as she heard Kassie's voice.

"Mom, the weirdest thing happened," Kass replied. "When I got off the train a big cattle dog appeared and attached itself to me. I tried to shoo it away, but it wouldn't go. The more I shooed, the more determined it was to accompany me. I finally had to let it lope along, pressed tightly to my side. I sure was glad of it through that alley. It followed me right to the door. I got out my key and opened the door, then turned to shoo it away, but it was gone!"

"Well, angels come in all forms, you know," Nerolie told her in a strangely trembling voice. "Remember the promises we read before you left? 'The angel of the Lord encamps all around those who fear Him, and delivers them' [Ps. 34:7, NKJV]. Those promises were especially for you tonight, Kass."

What a comfort it is to be able to keep in such close contact with God that we can trust our loved ones with Him, even in the most dangerous circumstances.

L. WINSOME SPECK

I Intend to Fly!

He knows the way that I take; when he has tested me, I will come forth as gold. Job 23:10, NIV.

WHY DOES EVERYTHING always have to be so difficult?" Melissa's face looked like the proverbial thundercloud. She had just spent 30 minutes filling me in on all the "problems" of the past week. "I wish life were more easy!"

Having recently learned the art of making "smoothies," I suggested we create a delicious mango variation and retire to the patio. "Once upon a time," I began (those words usually worked like magic with Melissa), "some children found a cocoon and took it home with them. Several days later a small opening appeared, and the children watched, enthralled, as the butterfly struggled to force its way out of the cocoon through the little hole. Eventually, when it appeared as if it had gotten stuck, the children felt sorry for it and decided to help. Using a tiny pair of scissors, they snipped off part of the cocoon and voilà! The butterfly slipped out. But alas! Something was wrong. Its body was swollen and heavy; its golden wings shriveled and crippled. The children stared at the butterfly, expecting that at any moment it would spread its wings and fly away. That never happened. For the rest of its life the butterfly crawled around with a swollen body and shriveled wings."

"But why, why?" asked Melissa, peering over the top of her cool mango delicacy.

"What the children didn't understand," I replied, "was that the butterfly needed to struggle through that tiny opening in order to force fluid from its body into its wings."

Melissa was silent a long time. "Do you think that if I went through the whole week without any obstacles I might not learn to be as strong?"

"That's a definite possibility," I replied.

"But what if the obstacles are too big?" she persisted. And then we talked about the promise in 1 Corinthians 10:13 that says the obstacles would never be too big.

"OK," she announced with a big breath and a deep sigh as we went back into the house. "I'll struggle—because I intend to fly!"

ARLENE TAYLOR

Cobra Dance

Fret not thyself because of evildoers, neither be thou envious against the workers of iniquity. Ps. 37:1.

COME QUICKLY, DOROTHY," my husband said. "I want to show you something." There was a tinge of excitement in his voice, and I jumped up and followed him outside and over to the next-door neighbor's yard, where a small circle of people had gathered.

In the center of the circle a man sat cross-legged, facing a small cobra, coiled, head raised, and hood spread. It was a cream-and-rose color with black markings on its hood. The man was moving his hands, and the cobra was following his movements, swaying its hood from side to side.

It is doing its dance of death, I thought. What if the cobra bit the village man? I didn't want to be there to see him die, but stood transfixed for some time watching. Someone shone a flashlight directly on the cobra's hood, and the whole hood appeared translucent and glowed in the light.

Ron called again. "It's really beautiful from this side."

"Never mind the beauty," I said. "I'm staying here where it's safe."

Our neighbor had stepped out onto his porch and had seen the cobra just a couple feet away. He sent someone to the village for a man to catch the cobra. The cobra catcher had come and picked it up by the tail and moved it to the center of the sidewalk, where it now did its slow dance.

"It looks like a baby cobra," I said. It was pink and new looking.

"This one is at least 50 years old," the villager said. "Some live to be 100."

Not fair, I mused. Why are the lives of cobras so long and the lives of golden retrievers so short? There was my gentle, harmless golden retriever, Matt, whom we loved and who would do well to live to be 15. And this dangerous reptile that no one wanted might live to be 100 if the village man let him go. Similar thoughts have come to me when a good woman dies young, leaving behind small children. Why should she die, and the woman whose children had to be taken away from her because of her neglect live on to have still more children? Why does the village doctor die at 38 and the village scoundrel live to old age?

When I feel like arguing with God about His creation and the order of things, I read Psalm 37. I turned to it again that night and felt better.

DOROTHY EATON WATTS

May 6

No More Pretending

You will seek me and find me when you seek me with all your heart. Jer. 29:13, NIV.

LIVING IN A VERY lovely part of the city of Nottingham, England, surrounded by the beauty of blossoming avenues of trees and quietness, has enabled me to listen to what God has been trying to tell me for a while. He says, "I want to have a one-to-one relationship with you. I have been knocking, but it is up to you if you will open the door" (see Rev. 3:20). If and when we open it, He is there.

Until January 1999 it had been my privilege to work and care for the elderly in Nottingham. I led a very busy personal life and church life. Suddenly my life changed. I was diagnosed as having serious osteoporosis. All priorities had to be reassessed immediately, and I had to retire.

At this time of readjustment, during a quiet time while in much prayer trying to cope with the situation, I was given a text that has shown me new direction and the realization that many positive aspects can come out of a seeming crisis situation. Psalm 119:71 tells me, "It was good for me to be afflicted so that I may learn your decree" (NIV). Although I had loved my Lord deeply, my new situation helped me to realize that I had been too busy to appreciate my devotional quiet time in genuine peace with God. It almost feels as if I had been pretending at seeking and finding God.

My family lives in Belfast, Northern Ireland, and the telephone is a vital link. I had just received a call from my daughter, Fiona, when the phone rang again. It was my 3-year-old granddaughter, Cara, talking. "Hello, Nana," she said, sounding very surprised. Then I heard her call out, "Mommy, it really is Nana on the phone." After a precious few minutes Fiona came on the phone and explained that Cara had been playing on her pretend phone, and after Fiona had called me, Cara, by a fluke, must have pressed the redial button on the real phone. How surprised and overjoyed she was to talk to her real Nana.

I pray that by God's grace I will make my conversations with my God real and appreciate the time I now have to talk to Him. Not pretending, not by accident. *Thank You, Lord.* CELIA PARKER

Lost Suitcase

You are a people holy to the Lord your God. The Lord your God has chosen you out of all the peoples on the face of the earth to be his people, his treasured possession. Deut. 7:6, NIV.

IT HAD BEEN THREE DAYS since I had flown home from Michigan, and I still did not have my suitcase. I was not happy about the situation, so I was talking to God about it.

Father, You know how frustrated I feel. There is nothing I can do. I have tried everything to find that suitcase. It's not the money so much, but You know I don't have time to replace the items. And Father, there are some things that are unique and can't be replaced. Two of my favorite outfits are in that suitcase. And my blue purse and shoes. And my black purse and shoes. They were all hard to find.

The more I thought about it, the more depressed I felt about my losses. There was a skirt in the suitcase that was perfect for travel—it just did not wrinkle. Besides, I liked it. It was a favorite. My favorite travel pajamas were in there too—they were cool but modest, easy to wash, and dried quickly. I hated the thought of trying to find something else like them. In fact, I doubted that all those things could really be replaced. They were unique.

Suddenly a most astounding thought hit me. How must God feel when His children get lost? He has lots of daughters and sons. But I am sure He is distressed and feels really bad when anyone is lost, because each of His children is special, unique, loved. These persons cannot be replaced. A substitute really will not take the place of the one lost. My shepherd God once spent a night looking for a lost sheep even though He had 99 others.

I like to think about today's text and insert the word "daughter." "For you are a daughter holy to the Lord your God. The Lord your God has chosen you out of all the peoples on the face of the earth to be his daughter, his treasured possession."

I was blessed in that my suitcase showed up five days later, but I had had plenty of time to appreciate once again how special each of us is to God. His daughter. Unique. Special. Loved. He wants every one of us present and accounted for.

ARDIS DICK STENBAKKEN

May 8

Little Scientists

The wind blows where it wishes, and you hear the sound of it, but cannot tell where it comes from and where it goes. So is everyone who is born of the Spirit. John 3:8, NKJV.

I THINK CHILDREN ARE LITTLE scientists. If Hannah, 15 months old, wants to get down out of my arms (even if I am holding on tight), she shifts the top half of her weight to the bottom half, and her body propels itself like a flying artist to the floor. The force of gravity brings her freedom. However, when she wants to stay in my arms she clings to me, and the force of her body next to mine makes it impossible for me to extricate her.

If I want to know what things float or sink I just check her laboratory (the cat's water dish). Pennies sink, and rubber bands and dry cat food float. What is the litmus test for processing all incoming information? If it passes the mouth test, it is an OK object. She also has a built-in compass. While still in my arms and before she could even say her first word, she would point in the direction she wanted to go.

Her older sister Emily blazed the scientific trail before her. When just a toddler Emily discovered the theory of machines when she learned to pull a chair up to the sink to stand on the counter to reach and open the kitchen cabinet. However, getting a 7-year-old who's testing her independence off to school in the mornings is like living in the weather channel. If you want to calculate the velocity of a cyclone, just open her bedroom door. Selecting the day's clothes causes at least one volcanic eruption. Differences of opinion about what food items to put in the lunch box—well, I don't have to study the density and volume of planetary bodies in textbooks to recognize that I am face-to-face with an immovable mass!

But when it's time to say goodbye to baby Hannah, Emily says, "'Bye, Haney," and Hannah says, "'Bye, Emma," and the storm is calm.

This wind cometh from whence I know not, but with the gentle kiss of sisters, the tenderest of earthly ties, the solid ice melts to liquid and this warmth changes it to vapors of perfume that permeate the atmosphere the rest of the day.

ALEAH IQBAL

Blessed to Have Mothers

Children, obey your parents in the Lord: for this is right. Eph. 6:1.

AS MOTHER AND I listened to perplexing stories of brokenhearted moms on television one day recently, we witnessed the mothers literally crying because of the unacceptable behavior and problems of their teenage daughters. The audience showed great ambivalence as we marveled at what we heard.

"When does it stop?" I wondered. "How did this gap ever come into being?"

My mind started to race like a computer. I thought of how blessed I was to have my mother and to have her sitting by my side. She was frequently in and out of hospitals when we were children, but in spite of her poor health, her family was her greatest concern.

She played the piano for various churches, sold women's apparel door-to-door, stuffed envelopes, and did domestic work on weekends in addition to working eight hours daily in an ink plant to help make ends meet. Mother still found time to listen to our sob stories, wipe our tears, keep our doctor and dental appointments, attend PTA meetings and school programs, take us to amusement parks, and apply corrective measures when we got off on the wrong track. She took us to church every week.

Although I've made numerous mistakes and was quite rebellious at times, Mother always found room in her heart to forgive me. I thank God for allowing her to share the wisdom, knowledge, and understanding that He's given her. She encourages my sisters and me to this day, "Never look back, for you're going forward."

Sin has caused many mothers and their children to go their separate ways just as sin separates us from God. When God forgives us for our sins, He doesn't remember our sins; neither does He want us to look back on them.

Mothers are truly a special blessing to us from God. Mother's Day is a day set aside for us to honor our mothers once a year. Let's not wait until Mother's Day to express our heartfelt, unconditional love for our mothers, but let us recognize every day that God allows us to share with our mothers as Mother's Day.

CORA A. WALKER

Parent Tribute

Her children arise up, and call her blessed. Prov. 31:28.

WHEN OUR OLDER DAUGHTER graduated from high school she wrote and dedicated this tribute to me, reading it for the parent tribute ceremony.

"Words aren't sufficient in explaining my feelings for you. You've been by my side all the way and you never gave up, even when I was at my lowest. When I felt that things couldn't get any worse, a smile from you would change my world. In reflection of our years together, I can't honestly remember a time when you weren't willing to share of yourself and put other things aside so I would precede. You've helped me to make out of the shambles of my life a tribute to God. So now, as my final year in high school comes to a close, I hope I have become all you molded me to be, and maybe someday I'll have the wisdom and strength to be all that you are. I love you, Mother!—Stefani Allison."

Every time I read this I cry to think of the impact I made on my daughter's life. God entrusts in us, as mothers, the duty to guide and be models to our children by actions, words, and deeds. What a responsibility! There are so many mannerisms that my daughter has learned from me. It is awesome to turn back the clock—it is like looking in a mirror.

If you are not a mother, you still have an influence and a responsibility to the young women around you. Maybe there is a young woman in your church who is away from home, or a relative who needs a positive mentor. Through Christ, we are here to give our guidance to those less fortunate and to those who haven't found their path in life.

My heavenly Father, thank You for the guidance that You have given me. The responsibility is tremendous. But with Your help all things are possible, if it be Your will. I need this guidance because I want to see You and my children in the kingdom. Thank You for all Your blessings. In Jesus' name I pray this prayer.

DOTTIE ALLISON

Praise of a Childless Mother

Our sister, may you become the mother of many millions! Gen. 24:60, NLT.

WOULD YOU READ A poem in church for me?" a girlfriend asked a few days before Mother's Day. "I'm presiding elder for our church service. I've written a poem celebrating mothers, but"—angst leaked almost imperceptibly from her voice—"I can't read it in public. I don't want to cry." Mentally juggling my own schedule, I agreed.

Her poem was powerful. Beautifully crafted and majestically inclusive. Mothers of all ages, stages, and ethnicities were represented. The church members and I were all blessed. Dashing to another church five miles down the road, I had time to wonder why I had never felt deprived by my childless state. *Is it that I'm too selfish, too focused on other things, Lord?* I asked my heavenly Passenger. His answer came to me in beautiful phases.

Arriving at the next church, I discovered they were also honoring mothers. Before the minister spoke, young people distributed carnations to all the congregants who were mothers. The pianist, a college student who always seemed to need to be in my office, brought me a ruffly pink flower. "You're my campus mom," he informed me with a gentle kiss. I had been included in the special celebration. At the end of the service the choir director whispered, "Mentally, I dedicated the anthem to you, Mom." Again I felt part of the venerated group.

Picking up the mail that evening, I was delighted to find two Mother's Day cards from young women whom I had taught almost a decade earlier. One had scribbled a note: "You are indeed a mother in Israel." When my nieces called the next day for what my sister termed "Other Mother's Day," my cup was filled to overflowing.

Almost a year later, as I waited in the doctor's office with an injured student, I was touched by his answer to the secretary's quizzical look. "She wouldn't know my father's medical insurance number. She didn't birth me. She grew me. They do that at the university." Unwittingly he had explained why I had never felt deprived of my maternal status. God had created a niche in which I had the blessed opportunity to function as a mother almost daily.

GLENDA-MAE GREENE

Happy Mother's Day

Children are a heritage from the Lord, the fruit of the womb is a reward. Ps. 127:3, NKJV.

WHEN I FOUND OUT I was pregnant with my first child, I knew it would be an adventure but had no idea what a blessing childbirth would bring. I especially loved feeling the baby move inside me. The baby was active, but if I wanted to request a kick, I would knock on my stomach and get the requested response. I loved it!

As I was getting to know this baby I felt a temporary name was needed. My husband and I did not prefer a particular sex and did not want to know what we were expecting, so I called the baby "Wonder Muffin." A wonder it was, and definitely there was a muffin in the oven!

I reveled in the amazement of this process, and it seemed that more than in any other event in my life I saw God from a different perspective. What thought went into the making of human life. From the beginning to the end the specific growth and development stages are an orchestrated miracle. Although I stood in awe, the best was yet to come as I gave birth.

The actual birthing process stands alone as a main event. The labor aspect is as it is stated—a lot of work. I had prepared for an Olympic event and I was on the starting blocks. As I went through this part of the process I thought of the blessing to come and it carried me through. Eight hours later Wonder Muffin made her debut. Immediately after her entry into the world, I watched as the nurses cared for her. I could not believe she had been inside me. Again I was in awe of the creativity of God. She was so beautiful! She was not just any baby—she was specifically given to us by God. We named this precious gift of God Barbara Joy Valentine. She was joy throughout my pregnancy and continues to be the joy of our lives.

It felt strange having people refer to me as a mother, but in no time it became second nature to refer to Barbara as "my daughter." I remember my first Mother's Day and how surprised I was to receive a Mother's Day card from a friend.

As I am going through this process the second time, I am reminded of the blessing of God's creative powers. I hope all mothers have a blessed and happy Mother's Day while remembering the blessings with which God showers us.

MARY WAGONER ANGELIN

Two in One

She looketh well to the ways of her household, and eateth not the bread of idleness. Her children arise up, and call her blessed. Prov. 31:27, 28.

MY MOTHER HAD PASSED away. As my husband and I made the trip to Ohio for the final arrangements, I had very mixed emotions. Dear, as we children affectionately called her, had been in a nursing home nearly four years, confined to her bed most of that time, and in the final months fed by a tube. Sometimes when I visited she didn't seem to know I was even there, though I would talk and sing in her ear, hold her hand, clip her nails, and brush her hair. On that last visit before she died, there was no response at all. We prayed and sang while she lay there, semicomatose but breathing peacefully.

I miss my mother, and I know my two brothers and sister do also. For us she had been "two in one," our mother and our father. Our father abandoned us when I was 18 months old and never came back. After searching, I finally met him when I was 35 years old.

Dear never remarried and had literally given her life to us six children. But I am comforted and even brought to laughter as my sister and I rehearse the fun times we had growing up in Louisiana. Though our mother worked several jobs, she always made time to play games with us on the floor and make tents with blankets and pretend we were on a camping trip when the weather was too cold outside. She cooked delicious meals that were sometimes topped off with scrumptious blackberry dumplings from the berry bush out back.

Precious memories are countless. But if there is anything that I thank my mother for, it is that of living a God-fearing life before us and teaching us the importance of prayer and worship at home during the week and at church. Where money was lacking, our spirit was rich. Unlike my heavenly Father, Dear was far from perfect, but she gave us her life and made an impression on us that will never fade in this life or in eternity. When I think of her I think of Jesus, who lay down His own life for me, His child. A deep and lasting impression has been made in my heart to receive His gift of salvation, and that is mine as I accept it daily. I wait with great expectation to see my mother again, along with Him who is, even more, mother and Father to me.

Gloria J. Stella Felder

May 14

Healing Balm

He heals the brokenhearted, binding up their wounds. Ps. 147:3, NLT.

ONE DAY MANY YEARS ago, when my daughter was 2½ years old, we lived in an old farmhouse in southwestern Virginia. Eileen was playing with her four brothers in their upstairs bedroom. I was in the kitchen cooking when I heard a thud, followed by Eileen screaming and crying. Immediately the boys started calling for me to come quickly.

I ran up the stairs as fast as I could and entered the boys' bedroom to find Eileen with an L-shaped gash on her right cheek. My heart felt crushed as I thought of my precious, beautiful little girl being scarred for life! The cut covered most of her cheek. "What happened?" I asked the boys as I picked Eileen up.

"We were just jumping on the bed when her foot slipped off and she fell and hit her face on the bed frame and cut it," they explained, clearly concerned. Of course I scolded them for jumping on the bed.

I washed out Eileen's wound and put ice on it to stop the bleeding. Then I remembered a home remedy a friend who traveled around the country teaching the eight laws of health had taught me. I made a salve of equal parts of comfrey powder, honey, and vitamin E oil and put it on her cheek and covered it with a Band-Aid so she wouldn't pick at it. Every day until it was completely healed I washed off the old salve and put a new batch on. It caused the wound to heal from the inside out without ever forming a scab. She doesn't have any scar to remind her of her disobedience.

As we look around us we see many people who have been hurt, cut, and injured by sin. Many are crying out, not knowing what to do or which way to turn. I am reminded that God is ready to take us when we are broken and wounded and will heal us from the inside out, even though sometimes we do have to live with the scars of our actions.

Lord, today I want to be ready to apply the salve of Your love to the wounds I see around me. You will do the healing, and for this I thank You.

CELIA MEJIA CRUZ

A Lesson From My Violin

Check up on yourselves. Are you really Christians? Do you pass the test? Do you feel Christ's presence and power more and more within you? Or are you just pretending to be Christians when actually you aren't at all? 2 Cor. 13:5, TLB.

I PLAYED THE VIOLIN FOR six years—group lessons in grade school and junior high, private lessons (that we really couldn't comfortably afford), and participation in the school and county orchestras. Then I simply decided not to play anymore, because some neighborhood high school bullies (yes, they were girls) made fun of me. My hope of being a violinist dwindled with each passing day. I needed a firm musical foundation but was afraid of the risk—getting beaten up. Even recognition from my church friends and family for a job well done didn't inspire me. Playing the violin wasn't "cool."

I know I broke my mother's and father's hearts when I gave up the violin. They probably hoped I might be a great musician one day. And I broke my grandmother's heart too. She liked to hear me play and tapped out songs on her piano. She proudly volunteered me for every program at church.

Thinking about it honestly now, being afraid of the neighborhood bullies was an excuse. I really gave up the violin because I didn't practice faithfully. And not practicing caused me to fall to the back of the seating arrangement in the school and county orchestras, a position I didn't particularly like. The best and most accomplished violinist was always in the first seat of the violin section, and the worst (or almost worst) was at the end. I enjoyed playing the violin sometimes, but reading notes was slow and tedious for me because I didn't recognize them fast enough. So I practiced some at home and faked it in public—pretending to read the notes.

What about our "practice time" as a Christian? Are we strumming along to the beat of life, hoping that no one notices we're faking it? Are we relegated to the back because we haven't practiced what we preach? Do we memorize what a real Christian is, or should be, merely so we can keep up the pretense of being a true follower of Christ?

May God help each of us to be faithful today so we will truly be accomplished Christians.

Iris L. Stovall

My Wonderful Neighbor

Honour thy father and thy mother: that thy days may be long upon the land which the Lord thy God giveth thee. Ex. 20:12.

WE HAVE THE MOST wonderful next-door neighbor. She is more than 90 years old now, has a beautiful halo of white hair, still drives to town to make quilts at the Community Services center, goes to church and prayer meeting, and helps as many people as she can. Best of all, she is my mother.

When our house burned to the ground in 1991 we decided to use some of the insurance money to build a little apartment for her and my stepfather, who was 97 at the time. We moved them to Washington State from southern California in the fall of 1992, and the next spring my stepfather passed away. We were so thankful to have Mom already here with us, with no traumatic changes to be made in her life after losing her husband of nearly 25 years.

Whenever we are gone she looks after our shared kitty. If he can't get what he wants at our house, he goes to hers. If he doesn't like what is happening there, he comes back. Lucky cat to have two homes. Mom loves cats, but never had one for a pet until she started sharing ours.

When Mom goes to the Community Services center a couple times a week, she always asks if she can run some errands—go to the bank, the post office, or the grocery store. Talk about service!

Recently I've had to have a series of surgeries. I have been so fortunate to have my mother here to help make the beds and do the laundry. My husband is wonderful with the heavy cleaning, but he works and has not been here during the day to do the small everyday tasks that she has been so willing to do.

Not long ago we were teasing Mom that we moved her here to take care of her in her old age, but she has ended up taking care of us instead. Is it possible that we are seeing a little of what the Lord meant when He told us to honor our parents (make their days more enjoyable) and we would be rewarded with extra days ourselves? She surely has made our lives easier in many ways, and we are thankful that she is nearby so we can all look after each other. God has truly kept His word to us in this fifth commandment.

Anna May Radke Waters

Mickey Mouse's House

He who testifies to these things says, "Yes, I am coming soon." Amen. Come, Lord Jesus. Rev. 22:20, NIV.

LITTLE MISS FOUR AND I were busy coloring. She would choose the color for the dress, and we would both work to make the picture beautiful. It was a precious time together as our fingers were busy and we chatted about things important to 4-year-old girls.

After a minute of quiet concerted effort, she looked up into my face with obvious excitement and said, "I can hardly wait for Jesus to come. I can hardly wait to go to heaven!"

"Me too!" I exclaimed. "What do you want to do in heaven?"

"Play with the monkeys. We could swing from trees and jump, and if I fell it would be no problem. One of them would catch me. No one gets hurt in heaven."

We continued to color until her sweet little voice added, "But I really want to go to Mickey Mouse's house first. Before Jesus comes, I mean. That would be great! Do you think there will be time to visit Mickey Mouse's house first, Grandma?"

It was a classic. We all want Jesus to come. Sometimes we think we can hardly wait, but there is something we want to do first. I don't know what your "Mickey Mouse's house" wish is, but it can't compare to Jesus' house and being with Him.

It was a couple months later that Little Miss Four was visiting again, and we were making peanut brownies. She was saying for the third time "Can I do that?" and enjoying measuring and stirring. The little mouth was set determinedly to do a good job as she concentrated on the task when she suddenly shared with me, "I really want Jesus to come; don't you, Grandma?"

"Yes, darling, I do. I hope He comes soon."

"Me too," she said fervently. "But I hope there is time to go to camp meeting first!"

Dear God, whether it is something as fanciful as traveling from Australia to Disneyland or as spiritual as camp meeting, please help me not to let anything get in the way of my watching and waiting for Your coming.

URSULA M. HEDGES

Inches Away From Death

He shall give his angels charge over thee, to keep thee in all thy ways. Ps. 91:11.

WE WERE SERVING AS missionaries at Bethel College in South Africa. My daughters and I needed to go to East London, about an hour away from where we were living, to do some grocery shopping. I thought it would be nice to have an adult companion, so I invited Victoria Smondile, a good friend of ours, to come along. The road to East London zigzags through mountains and precipices. Not only that, people there say they don't drive, they fly.

It was noon when we finished with our shopping, so we stopped at a Chinese takeout and got something to eat before heading for home. I was so glad Victoria had come along to give me company, because the girls were soon fast asleep in the back seat. We were driving slowly and enjoying the beautiful scenery. Victoria was telling me of the many accidents that had happened on this road; her stories made me even more careful, making sure I didn't cut corners and looking out for blind curves.

On our last zigzag before reaching Butterworth, where we lived, a speeding taxi driver overtook another taxi on a blind curve. They didn't see me coming. I can still hear Victoria scream, "Lord!" I swerved the car just enough to avoid the head-on collision with enough space on the other side to avoid falling down into the canyon. He hit my side-view mirror, smashing it into pieces. We were inches from the edge of the cliff. With a trembling voice I said a thank-You prayer to the Lord. The girls woke up, and I heard Sunshine saying, "Mom, I'm scared."

I thank God for His angels that stopped my car just in the right angle to avoid the head-on collision and the precipice. As our text says, "He shall give his angels charge over thee, to keep thee in all thy ways."

Thank You, Father, for our guardian angels who keep us from danger. Thank You for guiding us. Please help us not to let go of Your hands so that we will not stumble on our way today.

JEMIMA D. ORILLOSA

The Wounded Monarch

Seeing the multitudes, He felt compassion for them, because they were distressed and downcast. Matt. 9:36, NASB.

THEY CALLED HER WILBUR. That name got the most votes in a kindergarten class election to name a delicate female Monarch butterfly. Wilbur came to us enclosed in a beautiful jade green chrysalis, decorated with a row of tiny golden dots called nails. Everyone watched with great interest at the changes and looked forward to seeing a butterfly come out of such a tiny package.

When the butterfly emerged from its chrysalis, there was a problem. One of its wings stayed curled and didn't unfold. It would never fly. I wondered what to say to the children. When the bell rang, boys and girls poured into the room, gathering about this fragile little creature. Something terrible had happened to their butterfly, and they looked at me with questioning eyes.

"Things often happen that we don't understand," I said, "unhappy things we'd like to change, but can't. Although Wilbur will never fly, we can keep her as a pet. We can feed her and hold her and make her feel special."

Their spirits lifted as they all accepted the challenge. The youngsters fed her diluted fruit syrup from a jar lid. They had fun seeing Wilbur use her proboscis to drink the sweet liquid. They fashioned paper butterflies, made up stories about her, and studied the life of Monarchs.

Qualities of love and compassion grew as the children took the responsibilities of caring for their fragile pet. The wounded wing of their brave little butterfly endeared her to them even more. They did all they could to make her feel special—because she was.

In the midst of a difficult problem I sometimes feel like that little butterfly, flapping my wounded wings and not getting anywhere. When I cry out to the Lord, He reaches down and touches me with love and compassion. My being far from perfect seems to endear me to Him even more. He makes me feel special.

Thank You, Lord, for sending little children to demonstrate loving care and compassion. Help me reach out to those who are hurting and show me ways to make them feel special—because they are. MARCIA MOLLENKOPF

Mental Illness

Be ye kind one to another. Eph. 4:32.

WE WERE SHOCKED WHEN we learned that our second daughter, at the age of 13, was seriously ill with an emotional illness. Her behavior became very inappropriate at times; she would get very depressed or very hyperactive and would do many strange things.

One day when she was in the "hyper" stage she took nearly everything out of the garage and scattered it on the back lawn. She said she was going to move into the garage. Many nights she would leave the house at 2:00 or 3:00 in the morning "for a walk." I feared for her life. She'd say she couldn't sleep and just "had to walk." Often the police found her and brought her home.

Now 43 years old, she lives in a large retirement home where there are many things going on to keep her bright mind active. She goes to a program five days a week and greatly appreciates the love and kindness. Friends take her to church, which she loves, and she handles her own finances, which is hard for her. But as we get older, we feel she needs to do this.

We now live in another part of the country, but she sounds happy and content when we talk with her on the phone. We have her come visit once or twice a year, and she enjoys the visit but realizes she needs to be somewhat on her own.

We have discovered that it is important not only to get the best professional help available for our daughter, but to pray—prayer partners help too. Diet, exercise, and water helped in our case, as did medication. We had to learn to stay objective and help her find avenues of service. Today she plays the piano for her friends, and she cuts felt for missions—which she does well—and it gives her joy. God does provide, and someday we will find answers to our questions.

Dear Lord, give us wisdom, strength, and comfort for the challenges we face. Help even those who enjoy mental and physical wellness to realize the simple pleasures You give us in life. Remind us of our everyday blessings and encourage us to give to those who can't appreciate those blessings. Amen.

FRIEDA TANNER

A Cry for Help

God is our refuge and strength, a tested help in times of trouble. Ps. 46:1, TLB.

IT WAS A TRADITIONAL saying at the school I attended that a month after the first jacaranda blooms appeared, the state examinations would begin. A month later the flowers would fall and carpet the landscape, transforming it into a sea of lavender-blue.

For some students the beauty of jacaranda time was lost and could be a very distressing time in their lives as they prepared for the exams—their goals in life depended on the examination results. It was also a time when the Education Department considered a pass in English and math mandatory to obtaining a certificate. A failure, particularly in English and despite straight A's in all other subjects, did not constitute a pass. The students who were weak in that subject had cause to feel uneasy about the exams.

One of the required reading books for English was one that most of us found very uninteresting. We were delighted when told that if a question was given on it, it would be a general one, so there was no need to know every story in detail.

It was a hot steamy day when we sat for the two English papers. The morning paper I managed quite well. As I opened the literature paper in the afternoon my heart rate shot up and the perspiration began to flow more freely. There were only four questions, one of which was to tell a particular episode from the uninteresting general book! To my dismay, I could not recall the story. If I omitted one question out of four, I was sure I could not gain enough marks on the other three to pass, and it seemed to me that all my plans in life were being dashed instantly.

As a newcomer to the Lord I was just beginning to experience His love and interest in my life. In my distress I cried out (silently) to Him to help me, as the future success of my ambitions in life depended on that one question. I began answering the other questions, and my heart rate began to slow down. Suddenly I recalled two lines of a jingle that described two characters in that particular story, and immediately I was able to recall in detail the whole narrative. A prayer of thanks ascended to my Lord, who heard and answered my prayer and turned my distress into joy.

In the years since, I have proved again and again that God is a tested help in times of trouble.

Joy Dustow

May 22

Life in Black Ashes

Weeping may endure for a night, but joy cometh in the morning. Ps. 30:5.

OPPOSITE MY WORKPLACE is a hill that was covered by grass, small bushes, flowers—a forest of vegetation that attracted our attention and made us appreciate the beauty while we walked nearby. On top of the hill was an old mill, now in ruins. During lunchtime we would often hear someone say, "Shall we go to the mill?" There we could walk a little, enjoy nature, view the beautiful scenery of Sintra, and breathe fresh air. Unfortunately, one day a fire left the entire hill in ashes. What sadness and desolation—all I could see was blackness and mourning. It seemed life was unable to exist there.

Several weeks went by, and the only thing I was able to do was to look at the hill from a distance, unable to get closer. I had enjoyed going there to meditate, to have an encounter with God, to rejoice because of the butterflies that stopped here and there on the beautiful small flowers. Now what kind of life did that hill have? Even the old mill looked dead.

One day, however, I decided to go up the hill again. Perhaps I was in need of meeting God, even if it was in the ashes. To my surprise, I found life in the middle of the black ashes! New life was coming, new grass of various species, born with new strength and energy and a green never seen before. Everything was smiling again! And even more, there were flowers! Elsewhere there might be beautiful flowers of different colors and shapes, but none like those by the old mill. They were small, simple, and of an extraordinary beauty.

Each day it seems my life has some destructive fire, leaving some smoldering ashes. I look to God for comfort. And there, in the midst of the black and the ashes, I find new life, life strong and triumphant.

What a wonderful lesson this has! Does not God perform miracles in our lives? Does He not take care of us, while the destructive fire leaves us completely exhausted, without hope and courage? Does not He renew His blessings? Believe me, He does! Let us trust and learn a lesson from nature. If He cares for each small seed, does He not care more for His beloved children?

EUNICE PINHEIRO PINA FERREIRA

The Other Side

Pay attention to your teacher and learn all you can. Prov. 23:11, TEV.

I NEVER LIKED SCHOOL. It was always either too boring or too hard. I read my way through the lower grades because the teachers went so slowly. Then, with subjects I didn't understand (such as math), the teachers rushed through while I frantically took notes. I was very happy when I could put the whole school experience behind me.

So I was probably the last person you'd expect to become a teacher. I agreed to teach a teen-adult class in writing because I needed the money. I was enthusiastic about my subject matter but not about the idea of teaching it.

Then came my first class, and I had to make a fast attitude adjustment. It was so strange. I would make a point and see everyone taking notes. After class was a revelation to me too. Instead of rushing out the door, students gathered around me, asking more questions. The walk out to the parking lot took a long time, because I had a cluster of students walking with me.

Now I understand my own teachers a little better. After five years of teaching the class I've had a wide variety of students—the youngest was 11, and the oldest was in her 80s. In spite of many successes, every now and then I run across a student I can't seem to reach. One student would only read from a booklet on gambling he had written before he ever took my class, even though he had talent and powerful observations to share on other topics. Even though I encouraged him to write more on those subjects, he stuck to the gambling booklet.

My experiences as a teacher make me think of the accounts of Jesus trying to teach His disciples. How frustrating it must have been for Him to be confronted with students who just didn't understand His message! No doubt He saw the potential for greatness in some of them.

Seeing a classroom from the other side of the desk makes me a more willing pupil. I want to be that student who walks the teacher out to the car, the one who asks questions, the one who wants to learn. I want the Lord to find me a willing pupil.

Lord, help me to learn from You in every way possible. Even when the lessons I should learn are difficult to face, give me courage. Help me to be the best student that I can be.

GINA LEE

May 24

Stand Up and Be Counted!

If serving the Lord seems undesirable to you, then choose for yourselves this day whom you will serve. . . . But as for me and my household, we will serve the Lord. Joshua 24:15, NIV.

WE RECENTLY VISITED Williamsburg, Virginia, which was the capital of Colonial Virginia and the largest colony of British settlers in the New World in the eighteenth century. We toured the restored capitol building, the site of colonial government activities.

We sat in the straight-backed seats along the sides of the dark, wood-paneled House of Burgesses chamber. The guide, who was dressed in the period breeches and three-cornered hat, recounted some of the major decisions made in that room. It was easy to imagine the sound of the buckled shoes shuffling on the wooden floor as the men, the loyal British subjects, arrived from around the colony to discuss the business of the day.

That chamber had heard the voices of important men in American history as they wrestled with their feelings of loyalty to Britain and still felt the growing urge to become independent. I could picture Thomas Jefferson and George Washington with their silver-curled wigs standing to speak. Then I could almost hear the echo of Patrick Henry's voice bouncing off the walls as with deep conviction and bold assertion he declared in 1775 the now-famous impassioned words "Give me liberty or give me death!" He had made a decision he was willing to give his life for. Mr. Henry, like Joshua of Bible times, knew that he had to act on his conviction.

Joshua, as the aging leader of Israel, summoned the Israelites together for his farewell fatherly counsel. "Be very strong; be careful to obey all that is written in the Book of the Law of Moses, without turning aside to the right or to the left" (Joshua 23:6, NIV). Then he went on to recount ways God had led them, mentioning important names in their heritage and stories of divine intervention. Joshua wanted to be sure the people had a foundation for their conviction. Then Joshua stated with firm decisiveness, "As for me and my household, we will serve the Lord" (verse 15).

The lukewarm, easy way to face life is to "go with the flow," "be part of the crowd," "not make any waves." But God is looking for women who will respond to the conviction of His Spirit, who will make a difference, who will stand up and be counted—especially for Him!

ROXY HOEHN

God's Miracle Prescription

Who forgives all your sins and heals all your diseases. Ps. 103:3, NIV.

THE GREAT PHYSICIAN HAS given us a prescription for good health called the Word. It is an antidote for doubt, discouragement, fear, selfishness, pride, and impurity.

COMMON USES: Vital to the treatment or prevention of spiritual illness or decline. It may be used as eye salve, balm for the soul, fuller's soap, or applied directly to the heart, depending on individual need. It is pleasant to take in any form.

BEFORE USING THIS MEDICINE: Consult your Great Physician. He is available 24 hours a day, using His easy access number, which you will find while on your knees. This is most important, as dosages are designed and regulated to meet individual requirements.

DIRECTIONS: The first dosage should be taken upon waking in the morning, followed by subsequent doses throughout the day in liberal amounts and as needed. It must be taken with generous measures of oil of the Spirit to be effective. Generic forms could be harmful.

PROPER USE OF THIS MEDICINE: Continue taking for the full course of treatment, even if you feel better in a few days. Do not miss any of the prescribed doses. You need not be fearful of overdose. Continued use will cause increased sensitivity to sin and worldliness. It must be continued for the rest of your life to maintain optimum health. You are strongly urged to join a support group weekly. The therapy of assembling together results in improved health for all patients in attendance. The Great Physician Himself promises to meet with you on a regular basis.

PRECAUTIONS: Certain habits and practices may seriously interfere with the effectiveness of this medication. Excessive television, imprudent use of time, and overwork will inhibit recovery. If you experience difficulty with swelling of the head, spiritual blindness, weakness of the will, seizures of temptation, attacks of failure, frequent falling into sin, sudden eruptions of anger, stiffness of the knees, or spiritual lethargy, call your Great Physician immediately. Delay may prove fatal.

This prescription should be stored in a prominent place in a well-lighted room. It may be placed safely within the reach of children and shared freely with others.

LORRAINE HUDGINS

May 26

Natural Phenomenon

The righteous will flourish like a palm tree, they will grow like a cedar of Lebanon; planted in the house of the Lord, they will flourish in the courts of our God. Ps. 92:12, NIV.

AS I TAKE TIME TO walk in the late afternoon each day, I have the privilege of walking among trees of various sizes and forms. Trees have fascinated me since I was a child. From my childhood point of view, trees were good for three things: climbing, producing fruit for me to eat, and providing shade. Later I discovered many things made from trees—furniture, objects, houses, charcoal, paper, medicines, and much more. My appreciation for trees grew with these discoveries.

As an adult I see trees in another way. A tiny tree sprouts from the ground and begins to rise upward from the dust and mud in the direction of its Creator. Its leaves are like hands in the prayer position, and it grows by following the light of the sun and absorbing nutrients from the soil watered by the rain. The air is the tree's partner in photosynthesis, producing oxygen to maintain life on earth. A tree gives of itself to humanity, animals, and birds.

The greatest enemy of the tree is human beings. They cruelly cut trees, place toxins in the air, and pollute the roots. This deforesting provokes disturbances such as erosion; droughts; death of animals, insects, and plants; ecological unbalance; and economic damage.

But the tree sprouts again and continues growing, not giving up on the very important task God has given it. It is renewed each spring, and in the midst of the breeze or the whirlwind, it graciously moves its flowers and leaves, beautifying the scenery and thanking the Creator.

God wants you and me to be like a tree planted in His temple and rooted in His truth, living witnesses of His power. He wants to make us a phenomenon of human nature. Between cuttings and prunings, without being recognized or receiving incentive, by the power of God we continue growing toward the heavens, following His light. In this manner we produce the fruit of the Spirit in welcoming, understanding, loving demonstrations, being useful to all, doing everything with joy, and finally raising our hands in gratitude. This is the task the Lord puts before us today. May He help us to fulfill it.

VASTI VIANA

It's Real

The Word became human and lived here on earth among us. He was full of unfailing love and faithfulness. And we have seen his glory, the glory of the only Son of the Father. John 1:14, NLT.

TEARS BEGAN TO FLOW that morning as I lay in my hotel bed in Tiberias beside the Lake of Galilee. This was my first trip to Israel and our second day of touring. I'd prayed before falling asleep that God would help me really absorb the meaning of this land where Jesus had walked. I awoke about 5:00 a.m., overwhelmed with emotion. All I could think of was that Jesus had actually been *here,* right *here!* He had lived and ministered, slept and ate, right here in Galilee. The Creator God of the vast galaxies walked *here.* It was just too much to take in. I cried softly, but eventually couldn't stifle my sobs. My husband awoke and rolled over to hold me. Time passed before I could speak.

It's hard to describe my feelings, but I realized in a deeper way than ever before that the King of the universe had really entered our world in flesh and blood. The human existence of Jesus is a historical fact, and this was the actual place where He had lived and walked.

But what a country He came to! Smaller than the state of Massachusetts; rocky and arid. A rugged beauty, yet nothing like the lush green of the Garden of Eden, or the picturesque countryside of Switzerland, or even the misty hills of the Smoky Mountains.

And what a people He came to! Burned out on ritual and religion, yet arrogant of their chosen status. Filled with hate toward the Romans, yet full of corruption within their own religious politics. Materialistic and fickle—one day ready to crown Jesus, the next to crucify Him.

My heart cried out. *It's not fair, Jesus. Coming from the rapturous color and beauty of heaven down to our little planet was condescension enough. But to come to a place that is brown and dry much of the year, ministering to people who didn't want You. . . . It's beyond my understanding.* I ached for Him and at the same time was in awe of His incredible love.

Now when I read the Bible I have vivid pictures in my mind of the hills, lakes, and valleys where so many of the stories took place. And I will long treasure that early morning by the Lake of Galilee when the reality of God sank deeper into my heart and His love overwhelmed me. HEIDE FORD

May 28

All You Need to Do Is Listen

Cast all your anxieties on him, for he cares about you. 1 Peter 5:7, RSV.

IT HAD BEEN A difficult time. I had arrived home early one evening to find an ambulance parked outside our home. A phone call to a nearby friend revealed that our next-door neighbor had collapsed at home and was fighting for his life. I later found out that Ian, who was only 47, had had a massive stroke and was not expected to live through the night. What could I do to help? Here was a man, our good friend for 15 years, fighting for his life, and I felt utterly helpless. It was a restless sleep that night.

The next morning we went through the normal family routine. There were children to get ready for school and my husband and myself ready for work. We had to carry on, as there was nothing we could do but wait.

That afternoon I got the phone call. My husband's quiet tone told me all I needed to know. Ian had never regained consciousness and had died peacefully. I felt totally numb.

I went to see Ian's wife, Sadie, that evening. She had always been there for me when I had been through difficult times. What was I going to say? With a prayer on my lips I sat and listened to her, her two daughters, and son-in-law recall their final moments with their loved one. I could do nothing but listen.

During the next few days I did a lot of that. I had many things at home that needed to be done (and probably still need to be done), but I knew they could wait—right now my place was to be there for those who needed companionship and a friend to share their burdens with.

While looking through the many expressions of sympathy Sadie received, I was reminded of today's Bible verse: "Cast all your anxieties on him, for he cares for you." I gained great comfort from these words in the weeks that lay ahead and hoped that they would also have meaning for those whose need was greater than mine. Jesus will always listen when we call on Him. We can do the same for those who need us.

JUDITH REDMAN

The Guiding Light

The Lord went before them by day in a pillar of cloud to lead the way, and by night in a pillar of fire to give them light, so as to go by day and night. Ex. 13:21, NKJV.

HAVING BOUGHT OUR monthly groceries in Nairobi, Kenya, we started the five-hour drive back to the university where we served as missionaries. We had been assured that the van we had been asked to drive back to the campus was in good condition, so my husband and I and a Kenyan friend set out on the long drive. We were still enjoying the sights along the way when we heard a noise at the back of the van. Right away we knew we were in trouble. Fortunately, our friend spoke the local language and managed to get some help. Later we had the same problem again, and again the van was quickly fixed. We left the station with some extra gas, certain that this time we would make it.

Unfortunately, we did not alert anyone at the campus that we had had trouble with the van. An hour later we experienced problems again. We put in some gas, because it appeared as if it were low. We were getting a little panicky because it was getting dark, and we had no flashlight, matches, or cell phone. By this time we were out in the real country. We drove a few miles farther, and the lights quit. There were no villages nearby or cars going either way, and we were getting really scared, not knowing what to do. We even imagined wild animals or robbers coming by. The good thing was that the car was still moving, even though the lights were dead. I really do not know how my husband kept the van in the middle of the road.

We began singing, "'Children, keep in the middle of the road, don't you look to the right, don't you look to the left, just keep in the middle of the road.'" Suddenly, from nowhere, the moon came up and shone brightly, making us as excited as little kids receiving a dreamed-of toy.

We drove slowly with moonlight as our guide, not realizing that the slower we were going the more gas we were using. Though the entire trip took us more than 10 hours, we experienced the mighty hand of God. We could have had an accident in the forest, or we could have run out of gas. But God was our driver as well as our guiding light that night. Isn't He awesome?

SIBUSISIWE NCUBE-NDHLOVU

My Other Child

For God so loved the world, that he gave his only begotten Son, that whosoever believeth in him should not perish. John 3:16.

THE RAIN WAS COMING down in torrents as our Chinese guide, Jane, deposited us at the "soft seat" ticket holder waiting room at the Shanghai railroad station. She handed us our tickets as we hugged each other warmly; we had become fond of each other after a 10-day tour visiting the grand sights of China. My sister, who was visiting me, and I were now returning to Hangzhou, where my husband and I worked at the Sir Run Run Shaw Hospital.

Now we were on our own with almost no knowledge of the language, but we could show our ticket. It was to be a one-and-a-half-hour ride with only one stop. We found our car but were disappointed, as "soft seat" was supposed to mean just that. This car had double-decker bunk seats and very thin cushions—definitely not soft. Evidently our guide had been given the wrong tickets.

When we came to the second stop, I indicated to the woman across from us, "Is this Hangzhou?" She motioned no. Another stop, and she still motioned no. We were getting into the second hour. And more stops. We were becoming more puzzled and somewhat fearful. Finally a young man sitting on the top bunk jumped down—he was a businessman from Taiwan and spoke good English. He looked at our tickets and informed us that we did not have "soft seat tickets" and that this was not the express train. It would take four hours. He would tell us when to get off. We relaxed and enjoyed a pleasant international conversation with him.

When we arrived in Hangzhou near midnight, the rain was still pouring. He insisted on carrying our big luggage up and down many stairs to the taxi stand. I kept trying to thank him and say goodbye, but he would not leave. He insisted on going with us, even in the taxi, to be sure we would be safe. I tried to pay him for the taxi at our apartment house. He smiled at me in the dim hallway light and said, "Just pretend I am one of your children."

I will never forget meeting "my other child" on that rainy night on a train in China. God has children everywhere, and it was a privilege getting to meet and work with some of my brothers and sisters in China.

Dessa Weisz Hardin

If Only We Could See Ourselves

You were taught . . . to be made new in the attitude of your minds; and to put on the new self, created to be like God in true righteousness and holiness. Eph. 4:22-24, NIV.

OH WAD SOME POWER the giftie gie us to see oursels as ithers see us!" When Robert Burns, the well-known Scottish poet, penned these lines, he expressed a wish that we could well echo and act upon.

I often wonder how I appear to other people. I don't mean my outward appearance—I can see that by looking in a mirror. No, I mean how does my character appear? What do other people think about me? What does my family think of me? Am I always friendly and cheerful? Is my conversation always optimistic and helpful? Do I come across as one of those lucky hail-fellow-well-met persons who love everyone and everyone loves them?

Or am I someone whose mood changes with the weather? Do my associates tell a newcomer, "Tread warily until you find out what kind of mood she's in; some days she'll kill you with kindness, and other days she acts as if she'd prefer just to kill you"? Do my friends say, "Oh, yes; she's a bit of a cactus on the outside, but she's absolutely lovely when you get to know her"?

What do people think of me? What do they think of you? It's a good idea sometimes to sit back and take a long look at ourselves. Our image is most important, particularly if we profess to be Christians.

The greatest miracle in the world is the change wrought in us when we truly turn our lives over to Jesus and let Him work in and through us.

Dear Lord, I have looked at myself today and I don't like what I see. I am ashamed of what others must think of me. Please take my life and make it over. Help me to become a true disciple. I ask it, please, in Jesus' name. Amen.

GOLDIE DOWN

He Showed His Love to Me

It is of the Lord's mercies that we are not consumed, because his compassions fail not. They are new every morning: great is thy faithfulness. Lam. 3:22, 23.

MY HUSBAND HAD LEFT early in the afternoon to attend a retirees' convocation. I picked up the local newspaper to read the news—but all of it was sad and tragic. "A Little Girl and Her Father Shot Outside Their Home," the headlines proclaimed. Only two streets from our home! I sat and thought a while about the uncertainty of life before I opened my devotional book to have worship. *Lord,* I prayed, *please keep me safe while I am alone.* Then gunshots were heard in the distance. In spite of that, I fell asleep, confident in God's loving care.

The next morning I was up early. Nature was coming alive again. The little birds who had started a nest outside my bedroom window were already busy, singing as they went about their work. I watched them through my lace curtain for a while before heading outside.

My pansy patch . . . How beautifully they were adorned in their various bright colors! One pansy seemed to face me and say, "A special welcome to you this early morning!"

I admired my rosebush. Never had so many blooms been on at the same time. It seemed to say to me, "God is love."

As I walked farther down the path, the sweet fragrance of the honeysuckle hedge wafted through the fresh morning air. I had to pause and pick a flower and lingered longer to enjoy that lovely fragrance. Then a white butterfly flitted by.

The arum lilies have no fragrance, but they reminded me that although they grow in mud, they come out straight and tall and spotlessly white. *I can have a good character despite my surroundings,* I thought.

My eye caught sight of my delicate fern that grew on the cord and reached to the roof of the house. It reminded me of hands stretched up in prayer to God in heaven. Yes, He had showed His love to me once more. And He had kept me safe.

There was no better way for me to start the day than to sing the lines from that lovely old hymn, "I come to the garden alone, while the dew is still on the roses." May you also experience His love today.

Priscilla Adonis

Blessed Assurance

In quietness and confidence shall be your strength. . . . The work of righteousness will be peace, and the effect of righteousness, quietness and assurance forever. Isa. 30:15-32:17, NKJV.

IT WAS HARD FOR me to accept the fact that I had the ugly disease called cancer. I didn't even like the sound of that word, so I couldn't say it for a long time. I just said "lymphoma" when I was asked about it. It was an easier word to accept, since it is a more easily treated type of cancer, according to the oncologist. He has been treating me since the surgery removed the tumor and my spleen, which is the body's defense organ for filtering infections. Suddenly I realized that I was very vulnerable now. That fact has kept me isolated from the public, from streets, and from crowds.

I finally had to admit to myself that what I had was a very real type of cancer and just as dangerous as any, given the odds. Now I am going bravely through the chemotherapy treatments with the usual side effects of hair loss, weakness, tiredness, and low-immunity dangers. By reading books and watching videos on the subject of cancer, I have learned the proper diet, attitude, and general health rules to follow for the duration of the disease. And most of all, God's presence and promises have answered my prayers for a healing attitude.

One of my favorite books is by Ellen G. White, *The Ministry of Healing.* Right now I especially like the chapter "Mind Cure." My copy is an old edition with pictures, songs, and verses, the pages decorated with flowers and scrolls. I've underlined and made notes in it through the years, maybe even tear-stained some pages. But it is ever new in its message to keep the spirit of gratitude and praise, even in our illnesses. One of my favorite passages says, "Often your mind may be clouded because of pain. Then do not try to think. You know that Jesus loves you. He understands your weakness. You may do His will by simply resting in His arms" (p. 251). And God is giving me His strength one day at a time.

Even if we don't have a dangerous disease, we need to keep an uplifting attitude toward life each day by trusting in God's promises, whatever our trials may be. Let's pray especially about that today.

Bessie Siemens Lobsien

June 3

Just One Touch

Before they call, I will answer; and while they are yet speaking, I will hear. Isa. 65:24.

THEY WERE TERRIFIED. I was mortified. I wanted to melt into the wall. I felt about 10 inches tall in the midst of a dozen officers in a maximum security institution. They had just responded to what they thought was a major disturbance. What had happened was that I had accidentally touched the panic button instead of the door buzzer and activated the emergency system. It took the officers only a short while to realize that the incident was a false alarm.

For the rest of the night I kept thinking of the many times in my life and in Scripture when God's response to just one touch of the prayer button was instantaneous. Like the time I lost a very small specimen on the operating field. This specimen was crucial to the prognosis of our patient, and I had to find it. The "amen" to my desperate prayer was still in my mouth when the surgeon asked me to send it off to the pathology lab—and there it was!

I also recall the time my husband and I were standby passengers on a connecting flight home. We had spent many hours waiting for a flight. We had missed two flights already, and should we miss this last one, we would be forced to spend another night on the road. *Father,* I began, *You know how tired we are. We must get home tonight. Please find us two seats on this flight, even if we—* My prayer was interrupted by the sound of our names over the public address system. We were to report immediately to Gate 62. My Abba had done it again!

Gabriel's response to Daniel's prayer came while Daniel's finger was reaching for the "button": "And whiles I was speaking, and praying, . . . yea, whiles I was speaking in prayer, even the man Gabriel, . . . being caused to fly swiftly, touched me about the time of the evening oblation" (Dan. 9:20, 21).

True, God does not always respond swiftly. But when in His wisdom He deems it necessary, and/or the situation is urgent, I can testify that before we call, He will answer, and while we are yet speaking, He will hear.

MARIA G. MCCLEAN

Thank You, Lord

O give thanks unto the Lord; for he is good: for his mercy endureth for ever. Ps. 136:1.

OPENING MY EYES AFTER a few minutes of lying awake in bed, I yawn and stretch. *Thank You, Lord, for allowing me to see another new day.*

Sitting on the side of the bed with my feet on the floor (which is a great accomplishment for me sometimes because of fatigue and chronic pain), I reach for my robe and slippers. I walk to the bathroom. *Thank You, Lord, for mobility.*

Starting with prayer, devotions follow. Having asked the Holy Spirit for guidance, I begin by reading the Morning Watch, my Bible lesson, a scripture, and sometimes I sing a song.

Then I call Irma, one of my prayer partners. I kneel at the foot of my bed for our intercessory prayer. What effort it takes to pull myself up! *Thank You, Lord, for the privilege of prayer and for helping me to my feet again.*

Now I make my bed, tidy my room, brush my teeth, and shower. *Thank You, Lord, for shelter, bed, toothbrush, toothpaste, towels, soap, and warm water to bathe.*

It's 6:15. I must be out of the house by 6:30. The phone calls usually start with my sister, Yvonne. I talk to her every morning. Sometimes my mom, son, niece, or sister, Jeanne, calls. Sometimes it's one of my nephews, my uncle, grandnieces, or grandnephew. They just want to say hello and see how I'm feeling. *Thank You, Lord, for my precious loving and caring family. Please let them feel my love for them, too.*

I race out of the house to meet my neighbor and coworker, Sharon, to ride to work together. Sharon has been very supportive in times of need. *Thank You, Lord, for friends like Sharon.* As soon as I walk into work I call my other prayer partner, Annie. We invite other coworkers to join us as we engage in a short intercessory prayer before starting the day's work.

I realize everyone's morning is unique, but we are all God's children. Jesus is a friend to everyone. He is the best friend you could ever have. I thank God for everything. It's a beautiful morning. God is worthy to be praised.

Cora A. Walker

I Have Chosen You

Ye have not chosen me, but I have chosen you. John 15:16.

I WAS RAISED IN A Hindu home in India. When our family broke up, my grandmother took the responsibility of bringing me up. She was well off financially and decided to put me in a good school. She tried several schools nearby, but for one reason or another my application was not accepted. At last she approached Lowry Memorial College, a Christian boarding school that also took in day scholars, and I was accepted.

One of my ambitions as a child was to be a great dancer of the Indian classical dance Bharathanatyam. One of my teachers encouraged my talent and always included one of my numbers in each cultural program. Because of my dancing, I became very popular. I felt accepted in this Christian school even though I was not a Christian and had no desire to become one.

Then my life took a new turn. My grandmother was robbed of her wealth when some of her own people exploited her. She could no longer take care of me, but God made a way for me to continue my education as a boarder in the Christian school. At first I felt deprived of my freedom. However, slowly I learned discipline and good work habits. I made friends with the Christian girls and learned to cooperate in all of the activities. I got involved in spiritual activities and learned to sing Christian songs and to pray to Jesus Christ.

The more I became involved in spiritual activities, the less desire I had for secular music and dance. My ambitions changed. I no longer wanted to be a classical dancer—I wanted to give my life to Jesus Christ and serve Him only. I joined the baptismal class and was surprised when none of my relatives objected to my becoming a Christian.

When I chose Jesus Christ, I was in reality merely affirming a choice He had made for me long before. Before I chose Him, before I was even born, Christ had already chosen me.

After my baptism I was a new person. My aims and goals in life changed. Instead of classical dancing, I took up teaching as a career. I married a pastor and am involved in working with women in my area. I love the work and rejoice that long ago God chose me for this purpose.

ESHWARI P. HALEMANE

Sandalwood Treatment

Is there no balm in Gilead; is there no physician there? why then is not the health of the daughter of my people recovered? Jer. 8:22.

AFTER THREE HOURS OF driving through semidesert country with the wind blowing in my face through the open car window, my skin felt dry and tight, almost as though it had been sunburned. It was late and I was tired, but I had to do something. Rummaging in my suitcase, I found where I usually kept a small bottle of body lotion. I picked out one labeled "Sandalwood."

"Mmm! Smells so good!" I said as I poured the creamy liquid into my hand and then onto my parched skin. "And it feels wonderful!" After my skin had absorbed it, I put on more.

The next morning my skin still felt tight and dry, as though it were chapped. I applied a liberal amount of the sandalwood cream, but almost immediately my face felt dry and prickly again, so I rubbed in some more. Midday I had a bath and rubbed some more sandalwood cream on my face and hands and arms. Still my skin felt tight, so I added more cream.

By bedtime I felt as though I had a bad sunburn—my skin felt as though it were on fire. Did I pick up the wrong bottle? No, it was the sandalwood lotion. By now I sensed something was definitely wrong. I held up the bottle to the light and read the small words at the bottom. "Bath foam." The sweet-smelling lotion was meant to remove dirt and sweat. Instead of soothing my skin, it had actually removed the natural oils and made it drier than when I started.

It took about three days and lots of real body lotion to feel normal again. In places where I had put the most bath foam, the skin peeled away as if it actually had been sunburned.

The words of an old song came to me: "There is a balm in Gilead to heal the sin-sick soul." *Ah, yes!* I thought with sudden insight. *And there is that which is not the real thing. How often have I looked to the world for the remedy for my pain? How often have I tried to heal my hurt with that which only made me hurt more?*

Lord, today when my heart is sore and I look for something to relieve the pain, help me to make sure I turn to You for the "balm in Gilead." I know that only Your peace, Your grace, will really make me feel better.

DOROTHY EATON WATTS

June 7

Prayer and Pork Chops

Listen to my prayer and my request, O Lord my God. Hear the cry and the prayer that your servant is making to you. 2 Chron. 6:19, NLT.

MY HUSBAND AND I were visiting my youngest brother in New Zealand for the first time in many years, and I was shocked to realize how thin he was and that he smoked far too much. The day after our arrival my sister-in-law told me that if he got sick from smoking she wouldn't stay home and care for him. She begged me to talk to him, as he wouldn't listen to her.

But I had no more luck than she had had. He merely laughed and said he'd quit if I'd stop eating phoney baloney, his name for the vegetarian food I ate. One day he said, "I'll tell you what, if you eat pork chops tomorrow, I'll stop smoking."

"Done!" I said quickly.

He looked astonished. "You mean you'd really eat pork if I'd quit smoking?"

"Absolutely!"

"OK. I'll bring back some pork chops tomorrow, and if you eat them, I'll stop smoking."

Now, I knew the danger of making rash promises—they'd gotten people like Jephthah into trouble before, so I spent some anxious moments before telling the Lord about it. The following day my brother came home from work as usual, still smoking, but, to my relief, he had no pork chops with him.

The week after we returned to the United States I received a short note from my sister-in-law. "Don't say a word," she cautioned, "but right after you left, your brother threw his cigarettes away, and he hasn't smoked since."

How I praised God for this! But would he stay smoke-free?

It is 15 years later, and my brother is still smoke-free. He can't even stand the smell of cigarettes and will walk up the stairs rather than ride an elevator in which someone has been smoking.

Father, You always want what is best for us. You especially want us to know You. Bless us today to share Your love. EDNA MAY OLSEN

God's Strength

I can do all things through Christ who strengthens me. Phil. 4:13, NKJV.

A SEVERE BREAKDOWN SOME years back left me very timid and prone to panic. Most of the things that came easily before were now out of my reach, both physically and emotionally. Riding in a car was traumatic. Flying was impossible. The joy of singing was erased, as my voice could now hit only a few low notes.

But God's promises are true. Somewhere along the line I began to say, "If God has something for me to do, He'll just have to provide the strength." And He did.

With the aid of a panic course and medication, flying became possible. Then it became easier. Voice lessons finally brought back my song. I was able to participate in some church activities and do a little writing. And I felt certain I'd conquered all when I braved an overseas trip to Europe, rode a cable car up the Alps, and later peered down from the Eiffel Tower.

But God had greater tasks in store. My husband wanted to leave our well-established home of safety and build a cottage on our 80 acres of woodland, way out in the "boonies." I was terrified. I prayed the house wouldn't sell. It did. In three weeks. "With God all things are possible" (Mark 10:27, NKJV). Sometimes they're too possible! We lived in a small tent trailer while a builder finished putting up the little house we'd designed. He didn't even need a building permit! We moved in without water and surrounded by clay. What a mess!

More firsts awaited: Learning to drive an old pickup with poor steering. Learning to use a telephone party line. Learning about wells and septic tanks and how to start a fire in a woodstove. Learning to stack and split wood.

I learned about plagues of flies in the fall and about smoke puffing back through the chimney and setting off fire alarms. I learned to organize and plan trips to town many miles away and to have extra gas on hand. I quickly found out about sharing the land with bears and skunks. Someone gave us an Alaskan malamute—my first dog, and a real challenge.

I learned that God's school is safe; He guides us and gives us strength for each task in life. Oh, the joy of doing "all things through Christ who strengthens me."

DAWNA BEAUSOLEIL

Wedding Guest List

The Spirit and the bride say, Come. . . . And let him that is athirst come. And whosoever will, let him take the water of life freely. Rev. 22:17.

MY WEDDING DAY WAS only four months away, and soon it would be time to send the wedding invitations. There was only one big problem that needed to be solved before dispatching the cards. We had planned to invite 400 guests to attend the church service. Afterward we planned to have a private wedding reception with only 100 guests—we could invite only very close family members and friends. The wedding list grew to 550. We would have to go through all the names and delete 150 of them. After several hours my fiancé and I had deleted the 150 names, but it was a painful exercise. How I wished that all my friends could be invited to my wedding, but it wasn't possible to invite everybody. I wondered how some of my friends would feel if they knew that their names had been deleted at the last moment.

Soon it would be time to send the invitations, and many of my friends would realize I hadn't invited them to the wedding. Since I was marrying a man from another country, that meant inviting about 200 guests from my country, Zambia, and another 200 from his country, Botswana. As I thought about the disappointment that friends would experience, another wonderful thought crossed my mind. We are all looking forward to attending a grand wedding feast. Unlike my wedding, to which I could invite only a limited number of people, Jesus Christ is inviting everyone to attend His wedding feast.

It would be impossible to accommodate all the people who wanted to attend our wedding, let alone the reception. How comforting to know that Jesus Christ has an open invitation for all the people who live on earth, and He has enough room to accommodate every one. "Let not your heart be troubled: ye believe in God, believe also in me. In my Father's house are many mansions: if it were not so, I would have told you. I go to prepare a place for you. And if I go and prepare a place for you, I will come again, and receive you unto myself; that where I am, there ye may be also" (John 14:1-3). PRISCILLA HANDIA BEN

O Puraqué

The wolf also shall dwell with the lamb, and the leopard shall lie down with the kid; and the calf and the young lion and the fatling together; and a little child shall lead them. Isa. 11:6, 7.

IT WAS ALL LIKE A beautiful dream! I married the man I loved, and I was going to live on a farm in the interior of the state of Amazonas, Brazil. This challenged my sporting spirit, and it was all that my 21-year-old mind could imagine was necessary for happiness. The landscape was truly enchanting: the immense Amazon River, hundreds of fish jumping in front of the boat, turtles laying their eggs on the riverbanks, flocks of parrots and exotic birds, monkeys leaping from limb to limb, and wild ducks. I was charged with enthusiasm!

But there was the other side: the heat was stifling; there was no electricity, no refrigerator or fan; the flies (called carpanãs) invaded the house by the thousands; we could not even talk because they would enter our mouths. But what really scared me were the enormous tarantula spiders that strolled along the ceilings and walls, not to mention the snakes that often visited our home.

Our baths were taken at the riverbank in a little wooden shed without a door. The opening faced the river, and water for the bath was dipped up from the river in a ladle-shaped gourd. One day, when I was three months pregnant, as I entered the house I felt like my legs went to sleep. Frightened, I noticed that the loss of feeling went up to my hips. When I left the house, the feeling returned to my legs, and I forgot the incident.

On the following day the same thing happened but with greater intensity. My whole body shook, and my legs became numb up to my hips. After the third day I decided to tell my husband. He smiled and said, "I think I know what it is." With some effort he pushed the bathhouse into the river, and we saw what had caused this strange sensation in my legs. An enormous electric fish had been releasing electrical charges. Later I learned that the charge of the puraqué, or electric fish, can reach up to 800 volts and can light up lightbulbs and ring doorbells.

How wonderful it is to have the promise from God that one day He will return us to paradise, where the animals will again be peaceful and "they shall not hurt nor destroy in all my holy mountain" (Isa. 11:9). My greatest desire is to be there one day soon. EUNICE MAFALDO MICHILES

The Hummingbird

The Lord is my light and my salvation; whom shall I fear? The Lord is the strength of my life; of whom shall I be afraid? Ps. 27:1, NKJV.

I HAVE ALWAYS ADMIRED hummingbirds. After we moved from Maryland to Tennessee my husband was in the process of arranging all the various items to be stored in our newly built garage. I went out to see how he was progressing. Suddenly I heard the whirring of wings. "What is that sound?" I asked.

"What sound?" My husband wears a hearing aid but still doesn't always hear the same things I hear.

I looked toward the ceiling of the garage and finally spotted it. It was a small hummingbird, vainly flying back and forth in the peak, looking for an opening. Since it was flying so high it wasn't able to see the light coming from the large open door. *Now what should I do?* I wondered. I knew it needed to find the light, but how could I get it to fly down where it could see the light? I finally called our veterinarian to ask what I could do.

"Get a feeder and hang it down where it can see it," he told me.

So off to the store I went to purchase a feeder. Then I mixed up the sugar and water and poured it into the feeder. I kept worrying that I might be too late and that the little bird would be so exhausted it would die from fright or lack of food before I could get the feeder ready. Finally it was ready. Now where to attach it? I decided to hitch it to the pull-down rope of the overhead door. When the hummingbird flew down to the food, it would be able to see the light and fly out to freedom.

And that is what happened. I went back to the house to finish working on other things, and when I went back, the bird was gone. I reattached the feeder to our carport and eventually got a second feeder. We have enjoyed watching the hummers as they come and go. They are feisty little birds and fight with each other for food, not wanting to share their feeder.

Are we sometimes like that little hummingbird, not knowing where to look for the light of the Lord? There are others who are ready to help us, if we let them, to lead us to the light of God. I pray that each one of us will follow God's light to heaven and eternity. LORAINE F. SWEETLAND

Why, Lord?

All things work together for good to them that love God. Rom. 8:28.

HAVE YOU EVER HAD an interruption in your day and wondered, *Why, Lord?*

I was 15 miles from home, picking strawberries in a U-pick garden. When my pails were full I carried them to the car. Alas! The doors were locked and the keys were in the ignition. It was evident I was absent-minded, but *Why, Lord?*

Fortunately, the owner of the berry patch had a portable phone. I called a friend who had keys to my house, and told her where my extra set of car keys was. An hour later I was on my way home. *What was the purpose of wasting a whole hour on a beautiful sunny day?* I thought. I wasn't angry, so I didn't need a lesson in patience! I just wondered, *Why?*

Have you ever had shopping-day blues? There have been times when I'm shopping for a special dress for a once-in-a-lifetime occasion. I'm elated to spot the very dress that's one of my favorite colors and a distinctive style that suits me, only to find it doesn't fit. Dieting is fruitless; altering the garment isn't possible. I rarely find something better to compensate for my disappointment. Money management isn't a problem I need to control, so again I wonder *Why?*

One time I was running late for an appointment. Three miles down the road I remembered I had forgotten to take my medication. It was imperative that I not miss a dosage, so nothing else would do but that I go back home. *Why, Lord?* I questioned. As I entered the house the phone was ringing. *Why, Lord?* I questioned again. *You know I don't have time to talk to anyone.* Being a curious person, I had to know who wanted me. It was an urgent call from my lawyer regarding an affidavit being issued to delinquent renters. I gave a sigh and thanked God for the inconvenience that had made it possible to get an important message.

I don't always discover the reasons for interruptions in my day, but I trust that God is in control and that whatever happens is for my own good. Does it really matter why? *Lord, help me accept each day's interruptions without questioning. Help me to remember that You always want what is for my good.*

EDITH FITCH

Reunions

Do not be afraid—I am with you! From the distant east and the farthest west I will bring your people home. I will tell the north to let them go and the south not to hold them back. Let my people return from distant lands, from every part of the world. Isa. 43:5, 6, TEV.

SOME DREAMS REALLY DO come true. For many years I had longed for a joyous family reunion. Some of my grandchildren had never seen each other, and it had been almost 10 years since my five children had all been together. However, the obstacles seemed almost insurmountable. One child lived in the Midwest. The rest resided on the edges of North America—north, south, east and west. Distance was one problem, and meshing professional schedules with high school and college vacations was another hurdle.

My eldest grandchild had two cousins on her mother's side die in a tragic accident. She began campaigning for a happy reunion of her father's family. How I blessed her for her insistence as my husband and I headed our RV toward the East Coast from our California home.

The miles ticked off the odometer, the days clicked off the calendar, and my excitement mounted. On Friday, June 11, 1999, my long-awaited dreams became a reality. My daughter's "new" 1840s farmhouse in New York's Hudson Valley began echoing with joyful greetings. By sundown the house was rocking with animated laughter, music, fellowship, and reminiscing. Twenty-two of us had finally gathered under one roof!

The days of togetherness rocketed past, but the precious memories will last as long as I live. Dreams of another reunion thrill me even more. Our Saviour has promised, "I'll come back to take you home with me, so you can be with me forever" (John 14:3, Clear Word). We have an enemy placing obstacles to keep us and our children from attending. We also have a powerful Saviour to remove all complications.

At this reunion the joy of togetherness will not be short-lived. Our fellowship and love will only grow deeper and stronger for millenniums to come. I can hardly wait for that gathering of all God's children from every era of this earth's history and from every corner of this globe. I want to be a part of that grand, spectacular family event, don't you?

Donna Lee Sharp

The Bride-to-be and the Mailman

Keep watch, because you do not know on what day your Lord will come. Matt. 24:42, NIV.

A YOUNG COUPLE FELL IN love and made plans to marry. The young man had a good job in the logging industry, but when the economy went into a recession, he lost his job. He began to hunt for another job. Each day he returned home, discouraged and jobless.

He wanted to get married so badly. Then he came up with an idea: he decided to go to work at a logging camp in Alaska where there was ample work at good pay. Emily protested. She couldn't bear to be apart from him for so long. She reasoned with him. She cried. All to no avail.

They parted with solemn promises to keep their love alive through letters every day. At the end of his day the young man was dead tired, but he couldn't disappoint Emily. By the light of a flickering lamp he wrote a love letter to her. She was equally diligent.

Every day Emily found herself eagerly waiting by the mailbox. As she collected her letters day after day, she visited with the mailman, telling him about her far-away love. The mailman began scheduling extra time to visit with her. To make a long story short, she married the mailman!

Letters from her love weren't enough. He was forgotten when someone else was available to interact with her on a daily basis. When I read this story I immediately thought of our devotional life. I believe it will fade away unless we stay intimately involved with God on a daily basis. We need to read His letters to us in the form of Scripture.

Another vital part is prayer. It is important to remember that the strength and peace derived from one day with God won't be enough for the next day any more than it was for Emily. Every day she went to meet the mailman with no thought of missing his visit.

Evaluate how Emily anticipated getting letters from her love—running to the door, waiting for the mailman to come. We too should have the same type of yearning to talk with God. The first thing each morning we should consecrate ourselves to God for that day. Our prayer should be *Lord, I give myself anew to You today and place my day's plans at Your feet for Your approval. Use me today in Your service.* NANCY L. VAN PELT

Delight Yourself in the Lord

Delight yourself in the Lord and he will give you the desires of your heart. Ps. 37:4, NIV.

WHEN I WAS JUST out of graduate school, single and looking for employment, I prayed for an answer to the promise in Psalm 37:4. I asked God to show me how to delight myself in His plan for my life, and I poured out the desires of my heart to Him. My desire was to get married and to have a family. As I was interviewing for jobs throughout the summer, I looked at the location of those jobs, hoping to find one in an area where there would be young Christian men I might meet. One by one the doors began to close on all of those jobs, until the only offer I had left was a mission position in Guatemala. The position was a volunteer one, but it would give me the much-needed experience my résumé was lacking. I remember asking God, *Are You sure this is the place You want me to go? Are You sure You know what You are doing, God? After all, I can't even speak Spanish. How are You going to answer my prayer for a Christian husband when I am in a foreign country where I can't even communicate? Please, Lord, provide me with something closer to home where I can at least speak the language!* But the answer remained unchanged, and so I went to Central America.

God truly does answer prayers. It was through my mission experience that I became acquainted with another single missionary, who has now been my wonderful husband for 12 years. And we can communicate in two languages! We are the parents of two children. God saw to the desires of my heart to have a family.

But there's more! Recently I was putting together a scrapbook of pictures and mementos from my time in Guatemala and came across the airline ticket stubs from my departure on that first mission trip. I noticed the date that I had traveled was September 29. My first child was born six years later—on September 29.

Be encouraged today that our God loves to answer our prayers. Delight yourself in Him and He will give you the desires of your heart.

You provided me with the desires of my heart. I will love and trust You always.

SANDRA SIMANTON

Keys and Tears

Thus saith the Lord, . . . I have seen thy tears. Isa. 38:5.

I WAS PLANNING TO JUST dash into the local supermarket on my way home from work to purchase items that were necessary for the evening meal. So with this in mind I drove into the car park, parked my car, got out, and locked it.

I noticed a number of people all around a vehicle parked in the next row. Walking closer, I quickly learned what was going on. A very distressed young mother had locked her car keys in the trunk of her car. That would be annoying enough in itself, but what was causing her anguish was the fact that her sleeping baby was in the locked car.

A young supermarket employee was trying to hook up the lock button inside the window with a straightened metal coat hanger. A second supermarket boy was telling him which way to turn the wire. Another person was writing down the model, color, and exact position of the car so he could go and phone for help. A fourth person was comforting the mother, and several more people were standing around, as people do, watching the little drama unfold.

I looked at my car. While her car was a different model, it was the same make. My car was assembled in Japan, hers in England. But I felt impressed to help, so with my car keys in my hand, I walked up, put my keys in the trunk lock, turned it, and the trunk opened. There were the elusive keys, sitting on top of a bag of groceries. Quickly the car doors were unlocked, while the baby still blissfully slept.

The mother was so relieved she flung her arms around me, her tears of anxiety turning to tears of relief.

Later that evening I thought how God had directed me to that exact spot so I could help—I usually went to a different part of the shopping complex car park. And I thought of how Jesus throws His loving arms around us when we unlock our hearts and let Him come in. No keys are needed.

LEONIE DONALD

The Human Condition

All have sinned, and come short of the glory of God. Rom. 3:23.

MY MOTHER WAS IN the living room folding laundry while I was ironing. My brother, David, who is six years younger than I, sat on the floor building block towers. Suddenly he looked up at us, saying, "Oh, I feel so good and bad and weak and strong and wise and foolish!"

Mama and I chuckled. "Wonder what prompted him to say all that?" she commented.

"I don't know," I answered.

"What makes you feel that way?" Mama asked David.

David grinned. "I'm not sure," he admitted.

But the more I think about what he said, the more I realize how profound his words were. Though only 6 years old, he had made quite a statement about the human condition.

All of us have been affected in some way by sin. Even the best of us are a curious mixture of good and not-so-good character and personality traits, strengths, and weaknesses. Most of us have to cope with health problems at least some of the time, while others of us find ourselves afflicted with some chronic illness. And even the wisest people occasionally do foolish things.

We can't overcome these tendencies, faults, and physical difficulties by ourselves, but we can tap into divine help. Philippians 4:13 promises, "I can do all things through Christ who strengthens me" (NKJV). With the aid of "him that is able to keep [us] from falling," we can become morally and spiritually better, stronger, and wiser, to the point where Christ will someday "present [us] faultless before the presence of his glory with exceeding joy" (Jude 24).

What a wonderful time that will be! I long for that day, don't you? A time when our spirits will be elevated to a height unknown. A time when all the positive things that we treasure in this world will be even better than our wildest imagination. A time when we can thank our Father face to face and truly appreciate the great gifts He has given. Bonnie Moyers

What Goes Around Comes Around

You will reap exactly what you plant. Gal. 6:7, TEV.

SOME YEARS AGO, WHEN I started my insurance agency, I occasionally would contact someone who already had insurance with the company I wrote with. It has never been my policy to take another agent's business for my own. Unfortunately, not every agent abides by this work ethic.

Years later a new agent proceeded to steal some of my policyholders. I found out about it when they called me to tell me that he had asked them to transfer their insurance to him. Because he was just starting out, they wanted to "help" him.

Several times since those days I've had some people request a transfer back to me because they could not get in touch with that agent and were unhappy with the service. I have always discouraged people from changing agents and tell them that I'm not in the business of taking another agent's livelihood away. But I am reminded of today's verse.

Just recently I had a contact from someone who wanted me to write some insurance for them. When I found out they already had some insurance with the same company, I told them they could also get the additional policy through that agent. They insisted that they did not want the same agent again. After completing the business, I found out that the agent was the same one who had stolen some of my policyholders years before. I reiterated that I did not encourage or ask people to change their policies to me when the same company already insured them. This policyholder, however, proceeded to be very urgent about wanting to make the change. His experience with the lack of service he was receiving made it necessary for him to seek a change.

You are the one who said it: "You will reap exactly what you plant." Help me remember the truth in my personal relations, in my business contacts, and in my relationship with You. Even when the rewards aren't evident, let me remember Your example and stick to Your "policy." PEGGY HARRIS

Be of Good Courage

Trust in the Lord with all thine heart; and lean not unto thine own understanding. Prov. 3:5.

WHILE I WAS STUDYING at the School of Practical Nursing in Illinois in 1960, my group was fortunate to be able to take some classes from the professor of psychology at a nearby college. One of our sessions involved a test in which we were asked to draw a picture of a person standing beside their house in the rain. From that drawing the teacher would attempt to give us an evaluation concerning our emotional makeup.

A few days later he called us, one by one, into his office to give us his findings. When my turn came, I entered the room eager to hear just what he had to say about my simple drawing. As I approached his desk I could see that he had before him my picture of a woman standing by her house in the rain. She was dressed in a raincoat, rain hat, and rain boots and held an umbrella. To top it all off, I'd placed a fence around the house.

That's all I remember about my drawing, but I do recall some of the teacher's remarks during our short session together. He proceeded to tell me something that wasn't entirely new to me—that his evaluation of my picture suggested to him that I was an insecure person.

I had known for many years that I was in need of some help in that area. After I got married and had my children I seemed to gain some ground. Since my husband was an emotionally strong individual, I was able to tap into his strength. Much of the decision-making in our home was a joint effort, but Harold took care of most of the business of our household, so I didn't have to worry about that.

After his death in 1994 that was all changed. Decision-making was thrust upon me, and the old pangs of insecurity came rushing in as never before. One of the biggest hurdles I had to face was my 100-year-old house, which seemed to be in a constant state of disrepair. I've lived alone now for six years, and my security rests in the Lord. Only as I'm learning to depend on my heavenly Father can I find strength for each new day.

Job 11:18 says, "Thou shalt be secure, because there is hope." *Thank You, Lord, for that hope. I rely on You and Your security.*

CLAREEN COLCLESSER

A Lesson From the Children

Oh, clap your hands, all you peoples! Shout to God with the voice of triumph! Ps. 47:1, NKJV.

NOT AGAIN! TO BE in charge of the children's story hour at camp meeting was not fun anymore. We had started with lots of enthusiasm, but with three camp meetings every year and so many unruly children who tried our patience, volunteers were difficult to find. Not even begging was giving positive results.

Then the Lord sent Barbara, an excellent teacher with many years of experience and lots of materials. Even more, she was willing to help. I remember our conversation. First I was afraid to ask, but she didn't have to be persuaded. Immediately she was offering ideas and I was answering with more ideas, and in a few minutes we had prepared the whole program.

The day came, and we had music, songs, and stories. The children were cooperating, and there were no discipline problems. At the end we had a slide presentation that showed a large variety of animals and children. We explained how Jesus loves all the animals, even though they are so different. The same is true of children. Some slides showed sick, sad, undernourished, and poor children. And then, as a solution to all the suffering, we showed pictures of the Second Coming and the New Jerusalem.

When the show was over I turned off the projector and walked to the front of the room, debating in my head if we should sing or just pray and dismiss the children. The children were quiet, and after a few seconds of complete silence they started applauding. They weren't applauding me or the show—they were applauding Jesus! The images of heaven, of children walking and talking and playing with the Lord, had made such an impression on their minds that it brought about their spontaneous applause.

I couldn't talk; it was so touching! An illustration of the saints arriving in the New Jerusalem came to my mind. A presenter had told us that as soon as they see Jesus the saved will become so full of love and admiration that they'll start clapping. Our children didn't wait till heaven; they were giving honor to the Master right there!

I can't wait until the day I will be able to put my hands together honoring my Saviour!

ALICIA MÁRQUEZ

Discretion

Prudence will watch over you; and understanding will guard you. It will save you from the way of evil, from those who speak perversely, who forsake the paths of uprightness to walk in the ways of darkness. Prov. 2:11-13, NRSV.

HAVE YOU EVER FOUND that during your most discouraging or low moments in life the evil one heckles you with temptations even more than when things are going well? Sometimes things become most overwhelming.

One such time in my life remains vivid in my memory. It happened during the most trying time in my entire life. You see, we had to put my dear mother in a nursing home more than 300 miles from where I lived. To place her in the nursing-care facility was something entirely against my will or wishes. Many times during her five-year stay there I made the trip to help the nursing staff care for her.

One day an orderly said to me, "I'd like your phone number."

Startled by his request, I looked at him, speechless for a moment, and then replied, "I choose not to give you my phone number."

The next morning during my devotional reading I discovered Proverbs 2:11-13 and claimed the promise of deliverance conveyed in these verses. I'm certain that that orderly did not have the best intentions in requesting my phone number.

Until I'd read these texts and claimed that promise as my very own, I felt uneasy about meeting that orderly again at the nursing home. He never asked for my phone number again and treated me with respect thereafter. Later I discovered he was married, and of course I was also happily married.

My daily Bible reading, prayers, and relationship with my heavenly Father sustained me during that exceedingly trying time in my life.

Thank You, Father, for giving me this precious promise—for granting me discretion and understanding, and for preserving me from evil throughout that most trying time. Amen.

NATHALIE LADNER-BISCHOFF

Finish the Good Work

He which hath begun a good work in you will perform it until the day of Jesus Christ. Phil. 1:6.

I AM NOT ASHAMED TO admit that I dislike gardening. As a child I was expected to work outside in the garden with my father and older sister. I disliked pulling weeds, hoeing, and carrying the sprayer on my back so my sister could spray the tomatoes. I soon learned that inside with my mother was a place of refuge. When my father suggested he needed my help outside, I begged for inside duties. My mother usually found some dishes or ironing she needed help with. She seemed to sense my dislike for the outside labor, even though we didn't talk much about it.

When I married Norman, I married a man with the same love for the outdoors that my father had. We decided early on in our marriage that I would keep the inside of the house clean, and he would be happy to keep the yard and garden.

Presently we have two living houseplants. They have had to be revived on more than one occasion with a healthy dose of Miracle-Gro. I like to see their pretty green foliage, but I do not love them or talk to them, and I forget to water them. My husband does not understand this but patiently reminds me to give them a drink by asking, "When did you last water your plants?"

While in the grocery store last spring I passed a display of lovely hyacinth plants. I purchased a white one with three blooms. The hyacinth bloomed its little heart out, and its sweet fragrance wafted through our kitchen/den area. Soon it was finished blooming, so I cut the top off and set it in the basement stairwell for my husband to throw away. I really never noticed what he did with the plant. I arrived home from work this past November to find the little hyacinth plant sitting on my kitchen counter, one little green shoot poking its head through the soil to once again bring me joy.

As I gazed at its small green bud I thought of how we worry about and pray for our loved ones. We do not see the results fast enough, but like the little hyacinth we cannot see what the sweet Holy Spirit is doing on the inside. We should have great comfort in knowing that "He which hath begun a good work . . . will perform it until the day of Jesus Christ!"

ROSE NEFF SIKORA

June 23

I Will Never Leave You

Fear thou not; for I am with thee: be not dismayed; for I am thy God. . . . I will uphold thee with the right hand of my righteousness. Isa. 41:10.

WHILE EXPECTING MY second child, I began to experience signs of a miscarriage. On my doctor's advice I stayed home from work for two weeks and rested. However, instead of getting better, I felt worse. I became lonely and despondent. My husband was away, and our 2-year-old daughter, Stacy-Renee, was staying with my parents.

In the third week of my illness I decided to put the Lord to the test. I prayed for intervention, because I knew that He cared for me. I felt impressed to take my Bible and open it. My eyes fell on a text that looked as though a magnifying glass were held over it: "Fear thou not; for I am with thee: be not dismayed; for I am thy God: I will strengthen thee; yea, I will help thee; yea, I will uphold thee with the right hand of my righteousness." This was the indication that I was not alone and that my God was with me in this life-threatening period. This text became my tower of strength.

That very night I had no rest and felt much discomfort. The next morning I was taken to the doctor, who sent me to the emergency room. The nurse prepared me for surgery. After she left, I whispered a prayer and repeated my "tower of strength" text. Soon I heard a knock on the door, and in walked a stranger. "Good morning!" she said cheerfully. "I understand that you are going to surgery shortly, and I'm here to encourage you and pray with you."

I told her that I had already prayed, but one cannot have too many prayers. "That's very good," she said and opened her Bible and proceeded to read. "Fear thou not; for I am with thee; . . . I will uphold thee with the right hand of my righteousness." I was amazed! I expected her to read on but she stopped, closed her Bible, and prayed. At the end of the prayer and before I could ask "Who are you?" she disappeared through the door.

God had sent His comforting angel to reassure me that He would be with me always. What an assurance! To this day I hold Isaiah 41:10 as my "tower of strength," and I thank the Lord daily for loving me so much.

PANSY COOPER

A Gift Given Three Times

Give, and it shall be given unto you; good measure, pressed down, . . . and running over. Luke 6:38.

A BUBBLE WITH LACY LEAVES—that was what the large pink carnation in the florist's window looked like. What was its destiny? Tracey walked into the shop. "I've looked and looked for a single pink carnation," she said. "It's for a friend in a convalescent hospital; I want it to be special." Then she added, "She will never walk again."

Loving hands picked up the carnation and wrapped it in a big corn-silk bow and added greenery, a stem of baby's breath, and a small water holder. It was beautiful.

At the convalescent hospital the woman in the bed smiled as she gently held the carnation. "I love carnations," she said softly.

"It has a water holder so you can keep it on your pillow and smell its spicy aroma," Tracey said.

That evening the telephone rang. Tracey answered. "I hope you don't mind. I gave the carnation away."

For a moment there was silence. Tracey did mind. That particular carnation had taken a long time to find.

"My nurse was so sad," the woman continued. "Her father has died, so I gave her the carnation. It made her happy. I hope you don't mind." Her voice was plaintive.

Suddenly Tracey didn't mind. "That's OK," she answered.

"But that isn't all. The nurse took it home and put it in the center of her dining room table and told her children it was for them. She said they loved it and said, 'It brightened our dinnertime.' I'm so happy I had something I could give her. I can't get out and buy flowers or shop. You brought it at just the right time."

"Yes, just the right time," said Tracey. "What I gave kept on giving and giving and giving. A flower given three times." And her heart was happy.

EDNA MAYE GALLINGTON

June 25

Stuffed Full

Seek ye first the kingdom of God, and his righteousness; and all these things shall be added unto you. Matt. 6:33.

THE NOISE AND VIBRATION of the small motor that works with the heating and air-conditioning system in our car got worse by the moment. We had no choice but to turn it off to avoid damage to it or to some other parts of the car. My husband disassembled it to see which parts needed to be replaced. He was so amazed at what he found that he called me out to the garage so that I could see. A small animal had stuffed the small basketlike area full of worthless junk.

I don't know where she managed to find most of the "stuff," but at this stage, although the original intent seemed to be to make a nest and raise a family, there was no room to accommodate a mother rodent of any size, not to mention having room to raise her offspring. The cost of repairs was about $300. What a silly animal! I kept thinking about the fact that the nest was so full of stuff that the whole intent of the project was defeated.

About a year later we sold our house. This meant that every closet, cupboard, and storage area had to be emptied, packed up, and moved. I found that in some ways I was very much like the silly rodent who had stuffed the chosen nest area with useless stuff. There were things I had planned to use or wear, things that I would fix or utilize in some way. I found things I thought I would use when we had a bigger house and a more adequate dining room so we could have larger groups for special occasions. Some things had been pushed to the very back of the storage area in order to store more things. We have made several trips to charities, and some things have been taken to the dump. I still have to go through many more boxes that are full of acquired stuff.

What about what we stuff into our lives? What do we cherish, save, and stuff? What do we throw away as of little value? Is there room for what is really important?

Lord, please fill our lives, our hearts, and our minds with all the joy, peace, and love we can hold. May we be stuffed full and brimming over with the fruits of Thy Spirit.

LILLIAN MUSGRAVE

God Can Do the Impossible!

The Sovereign Lord has given me an instructed tongue, to know the word that sustains the weary. He wakens me morning by morning, wakens my ear to listen like one being taught. Isa. 50:4, NIV.

AFTER THE BIRTH OF my fourth child (the oldest being only 4 years old) I faced the impossible. I knew that as a mother and a pastor's wife I needed to spend time in God's Word and in prayer. But where could I find the time? I never woke up in the morning naturally—it was always an emergency, with either a little boy tugging on my arm or a baby screaming. Since four little ones never took naps at the same time, there was seldom quiet time in my house. If, by chance, I found a few moments and sat down with my Bible, I always fell asleep! And by the time I had the last little child in bed for the night and finished the absolutely necessary housework (making infant formulas, ironing a white shirt for my husband to wear the next day, or folding a batch of diapers) I just fell into bed like a log.

But God so graciously kept wooing me, calling me to spend time with Him.

It's impossible, I told Him one night as I stood ironing a shirt for my husband. *I figure it'll be 10 years before I can have regular devotions again!* Then in desperation I burst out, *But Lord, I can't wait that long! Who's going to teach me how to be a mother? Who's going to teach me to be a pastor's wife? I need You now.*

Then I had a wonderful idea! *I'll make a bargain with You, Lord. If I use an alarm to wake up in the morning, the children will get up too, and my day will begin. But I'll put my Bible on the nightstand, and if You wake me up in the morning with a mind wide awake and ready to talk with You, I'll spend time with You. If You do that I'll know You can do the impossible.*

God did the impossible. He woke me up every morning, day after day, week after week, month after month, year after year. Yes, it's true I could have turned over and gone back to sleep. But I was so excited about what was happening in my life that I never even considered doing that.

It was several years down the line when I discovered Isaiah 50, verse 4, where God promises to do that very thing—not only for me, but for everyone who asks Him!

CARROL JOHNSON SHEWMAKE

June 27

Fake or Not Fake?

Do not be afraid of them; the Lord your God himself will fight for you. Deut. 3:22, NIV.

AFTER SPENDING MORE than five years in graduate school my husband and I know what it means to be broke. One day someone sent us $150 in cash. Happily I went to our bank to deposit the money. The woman behind the counter looked at my $50 bill with suspicion. She tested it with a marker. "Do you see this?" She showed me the mark. "It turned yellow. It is probably counterfeit money. I have to send it in. And to make sure that the $100 bill is not counterfeit also, I'll have to send it, too." She snatched the bill from the counter.

I felt like a criminal. Mumbling to the clerk that she had to do what was right, I left. Every Friday I went to the bank for news of our money. There was none. Not believing that the precious gift was counterfeit, I went to another bank to get more information. They suggested that I ask the bank clerk a couple specific questions. I did, and I could see that she was getting a little nervous. She had no answer for my probing questions. I had asked her for a receipt of the money in question. We had not gotten one.

Then my husband and I went to the chief of police. He first called our bank, then the Secret Service, where all counterfeit money needs to go. At first there were no results. Then the bank manager wrote us saying that the bills they took were indeed counterfeit. In the meantime we received two additional $100 bills. I checked the serial numbers on the three $100 bills and found they were all sequential (very difficult to counterfeit).

We went to the police chief immediately, and he called the branch where our bank had sent the money. The woman on the other end of the line was curt. She told him that it was counterfeit money because the mark on the $50 bill had turned black.

"But in the bank's letter it said it had turned brown. Now we have three colors—yellow, brown, and black!" Concerned, the chief called the Secret Service again and finally found out they had never received the bills!

After 10 long weeks we got reimbursed. We know what David felt like going up against Goliath. But we also know that when God is fighting on our side, we cannot lose!

KARIN LEPKE

Morning Dew

My doctrine shall drop as the rain, my speech shall distil as the dew, as the small rain upon the tender herb, and as the showers upon the grass. Deut. 32:2.

I WATCHED A YOUNG MOTHER and her preschool daughter sitting across from me in a crowded doctor's office. The young woman quietly explained why the little girl should sit in the chair with her. The child was reluctant to surrender her chair to a new arrival, but the mother did not exercise parental authority—she appealed to the child's compassion, apparently a well-established trait rather than a coerced one. Few words were spoken, and the child seemed comfortable with her ability to decide for herself. She quietly weighed her options and soon moved her books to her mother's chair, confidently smiling at the woman who stood across the room, silently inviting her to take the chair.

God's love is like that. He generously provides whatever is good and does not ask me to surrender anything unnecessarily. Almost daily my eyes stray from whatever task I am doing to check the mood of the sky. The expansive blue or gray, or sheets of falling rain, speaks to me about God. I watch the lightning and note the gentle force of raindrops against the windowpanes. I breathe the fresh scent of a newly washed earth and feel loved. Standing near the choppy edges of the Atlantic, I have felt the sting of moisture whipped up by the wind and felt awed by the power and the splendor of the ocean. This abundance of sky and ocean speaks to me of God. I am comforted when I feel overwhelmed by the largeness of something I cannot understand or perhaps see because I sense God's expansiveness.

When forces of difficulty launch themselves against my life, making my days unmanageable, I often remember that God manages the surging waves of the ocean. I then know that His power is adequate for my present crisis as well. God writes His power and generosity on the face of nature for my benefit, reminding me that He is nearby and is sufficient for any emergency I might experience. God's gentleness anchors my love. The dew explains my nurturing Father, who understands vulnerability. When I am most vulnerable He treats me not as He might treat a tree planted by the water, but gently, as a gardener who also understands herbs and grass.

STELLA THOMPSON

June 29

The Greatest Miracle of All

If there is no resurrection of the dead, then Christ has not been raised; if Christ has not been raised, then our preaching is in vain and your faith is in vain. We are even found to be misrepresenting God, because we testified of God that he raised Christ, whom he did not raise if it is true that the dead are not raised. . . . But in fact Christ has been raised from the dead, the first fruits of those who have fallen asleep. 1 Cor. 15:13-20, RSV.

NOTHING EVER PREPARES YOU for the real thing. Even the death of a much-loved pet is not the real thing. Three children ensured that a multitude of animals shared our home through the years. Fifteen rats, about the same number of rabbits, two miniature hamsters, one cat, and a hamster the cat was afraid of. They brought much joy, but of course they also meant that from time to time we needed to buy memorial rosebushes and hold solemn funeral services in the garden or the forest. Once one of the girls even telephoned a taxidermist before accepting that it was best to consign her beloved black rabbit to a plastic ice-cream container coffin. Saying goodbye was always hard.

For many years that was the nearest that sorrow had touched our family. Our daughters' cousin was cured of leukemia. Their uncle's brother-in-law survived a fall from the top of an empty grain silo. Maybe we had become too used to miracles.

Nilla was 9 when her grandfather first got sick. I knew she had written him in her prayer journal and was trusting Jesus fully to make him well. So the day he died I was worried for her. Would she blame Jesus? Later that day I tried to talk to her—giving away, unsolicited, all the old, tired, standard answers. I told her that it was OK to be sad and to cry, if she wanted to. She was sitting on the stairs, putting on her snow boots, and looked up at me indulgently.

"Of course, Mom. But Grandfather had a lot of pain. He knew that Jesus will give him a nice new healthy body at the Second Coming. And that's when we'll get to see him again."

And that, of course, will also be a miracle. Nilla had remembered that better than I.

No, nothing ever prepares you completely for the real thing—the place where theoretical doctrine meets real life. Or for the simple eloquence of a child's faith.

SUSAN BOLLING

Beautiful Women

How beautiful on the mountains are the feet of those who bring good news, who proclaim peace, who bring good tidings, who proclaim salvation, who say to Zion, "Your God reigns!" Isa. 52:7, NIV.

I WAS ASSISTING AN evangelist by singing songs, giving short talks, and telling stories. One day we invited a family and their neighbors in a small village to attend our meeting. The people all seemed interested in our talks and songs. Then the evangelist asked me to speak.

I talked about how God gave His only Son to save us. I told them about Jesus and His love and how He died to save us. I said that in spite of all God has done for us, we often forget Him or even forget to thank Him. I was happy that everyone seemed to be listening carefully. At the end of the meeting an old woman came to talk to me. She could hardly walk and was almost blind. She grabbed my hand, and with tears in her eyes she expressed her joy at finally hearing of God's love and grace.

"Before my husband died," she exclaimed, "he told me that someday I would see many new and wonderful things—real things. Here, tonight, his words are being fulfilled!"

Then she added how delighted she was to have the opportunity to meet me—a woman. It seems that it was the first time in her life she had heard a woman speaking publicly about the gospel message. To her, it was beautiful.

I thought of the words in Ephesians 3:8: "Although I am less than the least of all God's people, this grace was given me: to preach to the Gentiles the unsearchable riches of Christ." That was me, a woman preaching Christ.

Bible women, such as Miriam and Esther, made a difference in helping to deliver their people. They were beautiful women.

I have heard it said that "some people make the world more beautiful by just being in it." I think that describes women who are making the world more beautiful in Christ.

Lord, send me. I want to be a woman who is beautiful for You, telling the world of Your endless love and grace.

ANAUDI KANDULUNA

God Cares and Understands

Call upon me in the day of trouble, I will deliver you, and you will honor me. Ps. 50:15, NIV.

IT WAS THE FIRST NIGHT of our gospel meetings in a remote town in the Philippines. I was to present a talk about family life every other night and tell stories to the children. Just before the meeting began, I felt something happen to the crown of my left front tooth. I quickly went to the place where we were housed to examine the damage. Sure enough, part of the crown was chipped. *Lord,* I pleaded, *what am I supposed to do now? Please hold the crown together until these meetings are over. It is in Your hands because I have no where else to go.*

The place was so remote that no nurse or medical office was available. The nearest hospital was more than seven hours away on rugged, dusty roads. The only public transportation to the capital city left at 3:30 in the morning and returned late in the afternoon. I would just have to put all my faith and hope in the Lord.

I was a little nervous as I gave my talk. From previous experience, I knew the crown could split in two. But God cared. He saw to it that the tooth stayed together that night. In fact, it stayed together the entire time. How thankful I was! God understood my predicament. He cared for my uncertainty. He didn't leave me in a precarious situation.

I thought when this happened to me that certainly the enemy was working hard to discourage me. But the enemy didn't succeed. My God is stronger than the devil. The devil tried to stop me from doing my part in the sharing of the gospel, but God in His power overcame the scheme of that furious enemy.

In the end God's power was manifested, not only by holding my broken tooth intact but in the people who responded to the call to follow the Saviour's bidding. I am so glad I trusted Him, even though my faith was shaky when I first lifted my prayers to Him and asked Him to help me in my predicament.

You are an amazing God, showing concern for all of us, whether it is a broken crown or a person who does not yet know You. I thank You for hearing and answering my specific prayers. Bless each one who needs You in a special way this day.

Ofelia A. Pangan

Lost, but Not Forever

I have gone astray like a lost sheep; seek thy servant; for I do not forget thy commandments. Ps.119:176.

HE STOOD AT THE edge of the road, a small dog, filthy, bedraggled, and so very lost. His long hair, snarled and caked with filth, almost covered his eyes. Such sad eyes, filled with unutterable longing, pathetically searching the faces of those who passed by for a smile of recognition. Surely someone would scoop him up, dirt and all, and take him home. Someone would bring to an end the nightmare he had been living, hungry, cold, frightened, and so alone in a hostile world.

He had obviously once belonged to people who loved him and cared for his every need. They had gently brushed his long, silky hair until it shone, played with him, and kept his little stomach comfortably filled. But he had never really appreciated all these blessings. Instead he had longed for the "far-off fields," which, he was sure, were so much greener. He had chafed at the restrictions of his friendly yard with its sheltering wall, never for a moment stopping to think that it probably protected him from unseen and unimagined dangers. He had wanted only to be free, and now that he was free he would have given anything to be home again.

Sometimes we are not so different from that little dog. We see God's encircling love as restrictive to the full expression of our personalities. We long for freedom to "do our own thing" and, sooner or later, we end up like that little dog, spattered with the filth of sin, spiritually starving, and very, very lost. We walk the busy streets of life, a dull, hopeless look in our eyes, buffeted and bruised by our "free" living, an aching void in our hearts that only Jesus can fill.

Some of us do not know we are lost; we only know that happiness seems to evade our every effort to capture it. Others are fully aware of their condition but are confused and don't know how to return home. God is waiting patiently to piece together our shattered lives, to supply our every need, and to give us a glorious future. He longs to encircle each lost, sinful child of His in a love that knows no bounds and has no end.

May we all have a greater sensitivity toward the needs of those around us and the courage to reach out, in the love of Christ, to help Him bring His lost ones home.

REVEL PAPAIOANNOU

July 3

Tangled Paths

Thomas said to him, "Lord, we don't know where you are going, so how can we know the way?" Jesus answered, "I am the way." John 14:5, 6, NIV.

WE WERE EXPLORING the English North York Moors on lanes that meandered between high hedges and ancient fields, and crossed sparkling streams on small, humpbacked bridges. We drove past castles, ruined abbeys, and picturesque villages, up to a forest park.

Every time we go on vacation with our three children we try to find an orienteering course. The children love to follow the map and collect the letters from the hidden markers that show that you have genuinely followed the course. The orienteering course in Dalby Forest was beautiful. A lake nestled quietly in the valley; there were forest sculptures to discover, and acres of open moors to roam across. From the map we saw a good shortcut between two of the orienteering markers. The map described the area as "open forest—for running through."

But soon we noticed that the floor of the forest was becoming increasingly congested. There must have been a terrific storm since the map had been drawn! Trees had fallen down, lying in criss-cross patterns over our path. Soon we could no longer walk on the ground. We clambered over the horizontal trunks, sometimes six feet above the forest floor! We clung to the vertical branches for support, but they snapped off in our hands. At the base of the tree we would have to negotiate around the vertical roots, tangling up toward the sun. Sometimes we had to crawl on hands and knees under trunks, trying to avoid marshy spots and nettles.

One child began to cry. Every inch we covered demanded our full attention. I slipped, skinning my shins through my jeans. What should have been an easy five-minute walk became 40 minutes of struggle as we prayed that we would make it through and that the children would cope with the challenge.

Just when we all felt we had reached our limit, we broke through into a clearing and found the main pathway once more. Sometimes in life the way seems hard. Someday the path will be easy, but right now we feel lost, confused, struggling, and hurt. It is good to know we aren't alone. Jesus is there, every step of the way, helping us through to the other side.

Karen Holford

The Strawberry Patch

Come to me, all you who are weary and burdened, and I will give you rest. Matt. 11:28, NIV.

ONE HOT FOURTH of July I was out picking strawberries in the long patch beside our house. My thoughts were of all the families out picnicking and enjoying the holiday while I was on my hands and knees, picking and trying to make some sense out of a painful experience our family was going through. For days I had been trying to figure out "why," as so many of us do in a crisis. Today the longer I picked the berries and mulled over everything in my mind, the less sense it all made. We had tried to figure out a remedy for the problem—no answer came. We had prayed and asked God to help us understand and deal with the situation—still no answer. I was exhausted, physically and mentally, from sleepless nights and worry. Then while I knelt there, tears and perspiration falling in the dirt, I stopped and put my muddy hands over my face and said, "Here, take it!" Finally I did what I should have done in the first place—let God have it.

That was the beginning of the answer. The difficulty became His instead of mine. It dawned on me that in spite of the praying I had done, I was still hanging on to everything myself. How foolish! A peace began to come over me that the situation was in God's hands, and it would be all right. Satan tries very hard to get us to hang on to our troubles. As long as we are consumed by them, he has power over us. The last thing Satan wants is for us to tell God about them, to let Him take care of the situation.

Several days later I saw some dishes in the supermarket that had bright-red strawberries all over them. I knew that I would have to buy some so that each time I used them I would be reminded of that day in the strawberry patch.

That afternoon has been a blessing to me and helped me to learn to let go and let God. Won't you try it too? Just give it to Him and say, "Here, take it! I don't want this burden anymore. You promised rest, and I am ready to accept."

Darlene Ytredal Burgeson

A Miracle in the Sea

It shall come to pass, that before they call, I will answer; and while they are yet speaking, I will hear. Isa. 65:24.

OH, YES, I REMEMBER very distinctly what happened to me in the sea while I was at home on vacation. I almost lost my life on a life buoy.

It was a beautiful sunny day in July. My sister and I, along with her two grandchildren, went to the beach to bathe. Another woman and her three small children were there for the same reason, I thought. We immediately befriended them. We bathed and frolicked in the clear blue water. Occasionally I would ride a big foamy wave as it dashed to the shore; then for a few minutes I would float on my back. Everything was fine—it was fun in the sun.

Soon I went out to a life buoy. Bathing in the sea and gliding on a life buoy had been two favorite things I loved to do when I lived at home. I was gliding along very smoothly for a while; then a nightmare began. I began to slip from the life buoy that had drifted with me a long way from safe water. My sister and the others were far away. To make matters worse, I tried to stand on the sea floor, but couldn't. It was too deep. I was stunned!

I said a frantic prayer to God. I also had to do something to help myself. I tightened my grip on the life buoy because my life depended on it. Hoping to get my sister's attention, I looked toward her and yelled, "Catherine! Catherine! Catherine! Get someone to help me!" My sister looked at me but didn't respond. She really didn't know what was happening, because she was preoccupied with the baby in her lap. I lifted my head high and yelled with intensity over the noisy waves, "Catherine! Catherine! I can't stand up! Get someone to help!" Oh, it was frightening! The woman who had joined us saw my predicament, quickly said something to my sister, swam through the water like a fish, and brought me to the shore.

I felt that that woman was an angel in disguise. She didn't come to enjoy a sea bath with three children—she was sent on a mission. The Lord allowed my sister to hold the baby in her lap, because He was preparing the mother to rescue me.

CECELIA LEWIS

As in a Mirror

But we all, with open face beholding as in a glass the glory of the Lord, are changed into the same image from glory to glory. 2 Cor. 3:18.

MIRRORS SPELL DISASTER IN ancient stories and in life. Handsome young Narcissus fell in love with his own reflection in a pool of water. The ancient gods changed him into a flower so that he might worship his reflection forever.

Then there's the story of the mirror on the wall that turned a queen into a murderous virago when it informed her that she was no longer the fairest of them all. We can add to these the mirrors of Hamlet's mother and Oscar Wilde's Dorian Gray.

Usually we use our mirrors to admire a fine line of lip or eyebrow, or to mourn a single mole or shiny patch. We usually end up thinking ourselves prettier or uglier than we really are, lamenting with Robert Burns,

"Oh, wad some power the giftie gie us
To see oursels as ithers see us!"

It is the measure of God's love that He is able to replace the ugly reality of what we are with the incredible beauty that can be ours through Him. And it's all done with mirrors! Jesus steps into your and my personal histories with a cleaning cloth drenched in His own blood. With His righteousness He covers us and removes the dirt. Now we look in the mirror and see reflected a shining beauty that we never dreamed possible. "And we, who with unveiled faces all reflect the Lord's glory, are being transformed into his likeness with ever-increasing glory, which comes from the Lord, who is the Spirit" (2 Cor. 3:18, NIV).

See? Something is happening as we look. This mirror is alive. It has power. We are being changed into that same beautiful Christ picture. Bit by bit, glory upon glory, He is making us compassionate and gracious and patient and loving and faithful and forgiving!

The last earthly mirror falls away when, having seen "through a glass, darkly" (1 Cor. 13:12), we look upon the face of God in open communion throughout the ages of eternity.

IVY PETERSEN

July 7

What Is in Your Hand?

The Lord said to him, "What is that in your hand?" Ex. 4:2, NIV.

HIS HAIR WAS GRAY, his body slightly bent, his face leathery with wrinkles. Otherwise, he looked much the same as the other racers milling around. All were waiting for the loudspeaker to announce the winners in the various categories in the 10-kilometer race in Dayton, Ohio. I was waiting to find my son and daughter who were somewhere in this crowd of 100 or more people, each wearing race numbers on their T-shirts.

I wondered about the weathered old man. How did he dare to race with all these strong, muscular youth anyhow? His T-shirt was imprinted, "L.A. Marathon." Had he really run such a grueling 26-mile race some 2,000 miles away? I worked my way through the crowd to where he stood, drinking a glass of water, and asked him.

"I notice your shirt says 'L.A. Marathon.' Did you really run in such a race?"

"Oh, yes, ma'am. I have run in many. I fly all over the U.S. to run marathons."

This man was even more sensational than I had imagined. How could I quickly learn what made him tick, what motivated him? "How did you get started running marathons?"

"You want to know how to get started running?"

When I assured him I did, he said, "All right. Can you run 10 steps?"

"Sure!"

"OK. Get out there today and run 10 steps. Tomorrow run 11. The next day 12, and so on."

I was overwhelmed. How simple yet how profound was his training strategy! I began to follow his program and later ran in several races myself. His short lesson has been an inspiration to me ever since. It's not some great responsibility or achievement that God requires of me, only to use what I have and to continue to improve upon it.

Moses used his staff to strike the rock, and God poured out water for a million. A small boy used his lunch, and Jesus fed thousands. What is that in your hand?

RUTH WATSON

A Day to Remember

God is our refuge and strength, a very present help in trouble. Ps. 46:1.

JULY 8, 1999, DAWNED as a normal day for my family. But as the hours passed, things changed.

I turned the television on for the noon news and stood in shock as breaking news bulletins were being reported that Las Vegas, Nevada, had storms that had just left three inches of rain in two hours. Flash floods had caused two deaths, damaged cars, destroyed mobile homes, and damaged a casino and homes and businesses throughout the Las Vegas area. They reported that 163 people had been rescued from the raging waters by police and firefighters, and eight were saved by a helicopter. A near disaster!

As I listened, I thought about the two granddaughters and a former daughter-in-law living there, and I started to feel fear.

Then the news reports said that storms and a tornado had hit an area near Lewiston, Minnesota, which is only seven miles from the town where my grandson lives and where my son and his wife were on vacation at that time. The news was distressing, and I was frantic with worry.

Finally after many phone calls I learned that all my loved ones were safe and the damage to their properties was slight. As the reality of the experience sank in, I realized I could have lost my entire family in one day.

I spent much time in thankful prayer to God the rest of that day. I thought about how God must feel as disasters plague this sinful world of ours. Of course, He knows where and how we are, but He too is distressed when He loses His children. His Son died that we might have life and hope.

Thank You again, Father. Please keep us in the hollow of Your hand, according to Your will. Amen. ROSEMARY BAKER

The Stove-Top Miracle

Ask, and it shall be given you; seek, and ye shall find; knock, and it shall be opened unto you. Matt. 7:7.

THE BIBLE HAS MANY references to the invitation to come: "Come unto me, all ye that labour and are heavy laden" (Matt. 11:28). To the millennium woman, this call is like a magnet to a lost needle or an inexhaustible insurance policy. Too often we spurn the invitation, thinking, *God is too great, too important, too perfect to be concerned with the trivial inconsistences of careless, tired, forgetful, frustrated women, wives, or mothers.*

A few years ago, being a newlywed with a great need for affirmation as a capable wife and homemaker, I set about preparing an impressive dinner. Minutes before serving, when I took a last taste to ensure that all was as perfect as it could be, I discovered to my horror that the scotch bonnet chile I had put in the pot whole was now in pieces, and my entrée was a burning, spiked disaster. It wasn't an impossible situation, for there was always the option to begin again, but my ego and excitement wouldn't have allowed that.

I spoke to my God, my friend, showed Him my dilemma, and asked for a quick miracle. I trusted Him to honor His promise as stated in Psalm 91:15: "He shall call upon me, and I will answer him: . . . I will deliver him, and honour him." I needed deliverance, and quick! I recovered the pot and returned to the other finishing touches to complete the meal. Then dinner was served: I watched closely for my husband's facial expressions of discomfort, but the meal ended without a word said. With uncontrollable excitement, I shared my experience and thanked God for His intervention in what may seem trivial; He must have been smiling at me.

Matthew 19:26 says that "with men this is impossible; but with God all things are possible." God is not only able but eager to come to the rescue in all aspects of our lives. It takes a mighty, caring God to keep track of the hairs on our heads. First Peter 3:12 says, "For the eyes of the Lord are on the righteous and his ears are attentive to their prayer" (NIV).

Is there anything too hard for God? Is there anything too small with which to approach God's throne? Call on Him today. He is eager to surprise you.

PATRICE WILLIAMS-GORDON

Thanks for the Thorns

Give me understanding. Ps. 119:169, NIV.

I WOULDN'T BE CAUGHT dead in public with a run in my nylons!" Melissa was emphatic as she looked down at her growing legs, encased in sheer hose for the first time. Following the tilt of her head, I noticed the elderly woman standing a few paces ahead of us. Yes, there was most definitely a run partway up the back of her leg.

"Most people do about the best they can," I responded. "Undoubtedly, there's a reason."

"She acts like she doesn't even notice," Melissa observed. She remained adamant that nothing could induce her to wear "runned" nylons in public.

Experience, I thought to myself, *will be the only teacher.* And experience arrived mere weeks later. We'd stopped at the corner flower mart on the way to visit a dear friend. Getting out of the car, Melissa somehow tangled with the seat belt. During the extrication process the roses tumbled from her lap. A thorn on one particularly feisty stem grabbed Melissa's leg tenaciously. With record speed the tiny snag turned into a little run. Immediately there was consternation along with tears and protest. She couldn't possibly go into the convalescent hospital with a run! I tried to pull up the memory of how I'd felt when my first run had appeared, but it was a long time ago, and there'd been so many since.

We considered options from taking off her nylons (my shoes won't look right), to buying another pair ("you could lend me the money"), and everything in between. Fifteen minutes later she chose "You go in; I'll stay in the car."

"What would you like me to tell our friend?" I asked, my face as innocently straight as possible. "She'll want to know why you aren't with me." That did it. We made the visit together.

Melissa was very quiet (for her) as we drove home. Finally she said, "I bet something like this happened to that woman we saw standing in line." There was a pause. "Because of the thorn, I now understand her plight."

I think about Melissa's words—because of the thorns—and pray for wisdom. *Help me to understand the plight of others better.*

ARLENE TAYLOR

Before You Call

I will answer them before they even call to me. While they are still talking to me about their needs, I will go ahead and answer their prayers! Isa. 65:24, TLB.

THUNDER CRASHED, LIGHTNING illuminated the dark sky, and rain beat relentlessly against the windowpane. With each crash of the thunder, my heart quaked, and my fear escalated as the minutes ticked toward the hour when I would have to go out into the storm. It was the second year after we had moved to Maryland, U.S.A. One of the more difficult things I found in adapting to life in Maryland was the necessity of having to drive myself to work and my daughter to school and other social functions. I had been spoiled in countries like Singapore and Taiwan, where I didn't have to drive to work, since we were living on the school compound. Moreover, I had the misfortune of being endowed with a timid spirit; hence, the need to drive created in me exceptional stress. This stress was intensified when I had to drive at night or in a storm.

That particular evening my daughter had a banquet at school, and she had made arrangements for me to drive her to her classmate's house about two miles from our home. The road to the house ran down a steep incline and past a wooded area. The sun was still out when I had driven her to her classmate's house earlier in the evening. Since then darkness had descended and a storm had erupted. At 10:30 p.m. I would have to drive through the storm to pick up my daughter.

Ten minutes before the designated time, I turned in desperation to the Lord, requesting Him to still the storm so that my fear could be minimized. Just as I completed my prayer, the doorbell rang. I opened the door, and my daughter bounced in.

With a deep sigh of relief I welcomed her home. Yes, God had perceived my need even before I turned to Him and had answered my prayer in a way better than I had requested. He had impressed the mother of my daughter's classmate to drive her home. The happenings of that night were a fresh reminder that in all situations we have the assurance that God knows our every need, and before we present our request to Him, He will work to respond to our needs.

MARY H. T. WONG

Dear God

I will bless the Lord at all times; His praise shall continually be in my mouth. Ps. 34:1, NKJV.

DEAR GOD,

I had a wonderful day today, and I thank You and praise You for giving me this day. I have been able to remain at home throughout the day, and that is so good. The day's events were ordinary but so wonderful. It began with spending time talking to You before I got out of bed.

Beginning the morning with time spent skiing on the NordicTrack was invigorating. I gleaned insight into King David's life as I read the chapter about his anointing to become the next king of Israel. The Old Testament history book I am reading during my morning ski time reminds me of the wonders of Your goodness and divine guidance.

The telephone has brought messages of love and encouragement. My husband and I had the opportunity to talk with our daughters and hear of their joys and frustrations. Our daughter-in-law stopped in to chat. The grandchildren popped in for a few minutes. Our son stopped in after work and visited. What could be better for a mom and dad to experience all in one day!

The ordinary things were accomplished. Letters were written, reports sent in, bathrooms cleaned, and the bed was made. I made a noontime dinner for my working husband that we enjoyed together. I wrote my column for the paper. Calm, peace, and laughter reigned. Thank You, Lord, for this blessed day.

I treasure the memory of this day that has renewed my spirits and given me time to relax and enjoy our home. Thank You for blessing us with a happy home these many years. It has been even better than I would have believed possible. You have given us joy and delight, sadness and hard work, all of which blend together to help us remember You and that we live in a world plagued by sin. These gentle reminders help us to focus on the day soon to come, when You will come to take us home to heaven.

I praise You and thank You for this day in which you have again demonstrated your love and care for me and my family. I offer this prayer of thanks and praise in the blessed name of our Saviour, Jesus. Amen.

EVELYN GLASS

July 13

Touching His Garment

Commit thy way unto the Lord; trust also in him; and he shall bring it to pass. Ps. 37:5.

MY MOTHER HAD SUFFERED from arthritis for more than 12 years. Now she was bedridden and in constant pain. It was difficult for me to watch her sweet face lose that contagious smile. Though she was the subject of many prayers, years came and went with little change.

I thought of the unnamed woman in Scripture who had also suffered 12 long years without relief. As I read her story, I longed to join her as she trudged down that Capernaum road long ago. I envisioned the two of us among hurrying townspeople—one frail, the other robust—both seeking answers to our needs. We had a common bond: our Saviour, our only hope.

Young and old, rich and poor, sighted and blind, priest and profligate hurry past us. They too seek Jesus. With determined effort we struggle to keep up with the crowd. Then, far ahead, we catch sight of Him and our hearts kindle with hope. Our gaze is fixed firmly upon Him as inch by inch we draw closer. We must not give up. This is our chance, and we will plead our case.

Now, stretching forward, supporting one another, we reach toward the border of His robe. It billows toward us, and together we touch it. In that instant, radiance flashes across the face of this unnamed woman, and she turns to leave. She is healed. Healed! And her happiness is unmistakable. I watch her go, then turn back to meet the direct gaze of my Saviour.

As I sit beside my mother, peace suddenly flows like a flood into my trusting heart. My prayer too is answered in a way I had not expected, yet in a way that only my Saviour knew was best.

Sometimes He gives His beloved sleep—blessed, peaceful sleep. Mother is now cradled in His loving care, awaiting His voice. Soon it will awaken her, and that familiar smile will again wreathe her face as she looks into His noble smiling eyes.

I can hardly wait for the return of our precious Saviour-King. I know when He catches sight of us reaching out to touch His garment once again, it will fill His loving heart with empathy, and He will respond with eager arms open to receive us. And from that moment, through all eternity, His healing touch will remain. Please, God, may we all be there.

LORRAINE HUDGINS

Give Thanks

Give thanks in all circumstances. 1 Thess. 5:18, NIV.

TEMPERATURE: 90° FARENHEIT. Humidity: 90 percent. Energy level: 0. The morning was hot and muggy; thoughts of work were negative. *There might be a sea breeze up on the roof that would refresh me,* I thought. Languidly I trudged up the stairs to the flat roof of our apartment building. The atmosphere was sultry. Not a hint of air movement.

Looking down, I tried to analyze the cacophony arising from the street below. Drivers of huge trucks, mufflers nonexistent, were transporting wheat, cotton, and rice to the ships at the dock, continuously blasting their horns to clear a way for themselves. Desert camels, also with produce for the port, completely ignored the trucks. Their cameleers shouted at little donkeys, heavily loaded with vegetables for the market. No one had any intention of relinquishing his location in the street. A steady stream of women filed down the sidewalk on their way to market. I stood there contemplating the lives of those women until my meditation was distracted by activity on the roof of the embassy building across the street. A man was hoisting a flag into position—my country's flag! Noise, heat, and humidity became secondary concerns for me. I experienced a profound emotion of appreciation and respect for that flag and the country it represented.

That surge of gratitude returned my thoughts to the women on the sidewalk below. Most of those women had never been to school. They could neither read nor write. They had skills and interests, but those skills and interests had never been cultivated and enhanced. It's like that for women in some countries. The fact is, I am most fortunate. I am not better; I am not more intelligent. I have no more innate abilities and gifts than women in any other country. It is only that I have had more opportunities and advantages, having been born in a country that fosters education for all of its citizens—even women. God has provided the opportunity for me to develop every talent and faculty He has given me. And He wants that for women everywhere.

Time was passing, and there was work in my office. I turned from the street scene and descended the stairs, grateful for that interlude in an uncomfortable morning. It had renewed my awareness of God's amazing, unfathomable love, and increased my regard for my country.

Lois E. Johannes

Loving Hands of Grace

My little children, let us not love in word, neither in tongue; but in deed and in truth. 1 John 3:18.

I WAS TUTORING SOME students in their home one summer, helping them with reading and math. One of my students was a darling petite Korean girl named Grace.

At the end of our studies one day I went into the bathroom to wash my hands and Grace had followed me in. I washed my hands well and turned to discover there was no towel to dry them. Grace saw the situation and quickly took my hands in hers and proceeded to wipe them with the folds of her pretty full skirt.

I stood there as she lovingly and gently wiped my hands dry. I can't express how very special the moment was, making me think of a time long ago when Mary wiped Jesus' feet with her hair. How special He must have felt too. I really felt like I understood that story so much better by Grace's simple and loving actions. Grace's act was with love and sweetness that shone on her little 6-year-old face. She didn't even think about it—there was a need for her teacher, and she attended to it.

The innocence of a child . . . If we could but learn to do simple acts that bring joy and happiness into other people's lives. We think we have to do big things, to spend much money, when really there are many small, simple things we could do to make another person happy—a smile, a card, a word of encouragement. You never know when God can use you to create happiness for another.

Perhaps the person who needs a hug or a word of cheer can get that special feeling from you this very day, as I did from Grace.

Dear Lord, please make me Your instrument to make another person feel good about themselves and be uplifted. May we consistently show our love, not just in words, but in deed and in truth.

ANNE ELAINE NELSON

It's Worth It, Abbey!

I press toward the goal for the prize of the upward call of God in Christ Jesus. Phil. 3:14, NKJV.

THERE'S A LINE FROM an old gospel song that goes something like this: "All the trials of life will seem nothing, when I look in my dear Savior's face."

When we lived in Massachusetts, we would go blueberry picking every summer up on Mount Wachusett. We could drive partway up the mountain on a makeshift "road." Then we had to climb to the top of the mountain where the wild blueberries grew. People who had been coming there for years knew exactly where to go to find the best picking. Since we hadn't lived there very long, we had to do more exploring. At times it was slim picking.

One year we decided to head for a new spot we'd heard about. In order to reach it, however, we had to cross an almost impassable tangled mass of junipers and prickly bushes. Slowly, painfully, we made our way through the thick undergrowth, falling and half crawling or climbing, trying to get a footing through the maze. Finally we were there, and oh, what rejoicing! The large berries hung in clusters like concord grapes—so plentiful, low-hanging and easy to pick. We could tell that it wouldn't take long to fill our buckets.

Another man who had made it across the brambles was also enjoying the luscious fruit, but his wife was still struggling through the dense wilderness. He called to her loudly, "Come on, Abbey! It's worth it, Abbey!" Encouraged, she struggled on until she too reached us and realized that it was worth it.

Sometimes life's journey also seems very difficult. It is then that we need to remember to fasten our eyes on the goal and the joyful reward of our efforts—to be with Jesus. As we cling to Him we will receive the power and guidance of the Holy Spirit, enabling us to keep pressing on the upward way. When we see our Lord coming in the clouds of glory to take us home, we'll surely say, "Yes, it's worth it!" MAE E. WALLENKAMPF

So Close, Yet So Far

Then came she and worshipped him, saying, Lord, help me. Matt. 15:25.

I VISIT HUNTSVILLE, ALABAMA, frequently. My route takes me from the hotel to Oakwood College, the mall, and back. Once I stayed with a friend who lives a few miles from the college.

After dinner I went visiting. Carefully I wrote the directions, making sure I had all the turns for the 20-minute ride. I had a good visit. Before leaving, I phoned my hostess to tell her to expect me soon, and after about five minutes I left. Returning would be easy, just do the reverse, I thought. But somewhere along the way I made a wrong turn. Thirty, then 40 minutes passed, and I still had not reached my destination.

I kept seeing the same street signs. Some were familiar, but at night everything looked different. I should have stopped at the gas station for directions, but I was determined to find the way on my own. I told myself, *I went, so I can get back.* Time was passing. Fifty minutes passed. I still was not back at my friend's.

I knew the way to the college but could not even get there. In my frustration I thought of a story about a lost little boy who asked a police officer for help. He could not remember the address but knew there was a church with a cross on the top. He told the officer that if he would get him to the cross, he could get home. I prayed, *Lord, if You just get me to the college I can find my way to Juliaette's house.* At that moment I came to a street that led to the college. I thanked the Lord because then I knew where I was. I had crossed those same streets many times before, but now the signs looked familiar.

Finally I reached my destination. Juliaette had no idea what had happened. A 20-minute trip had turned into an hour. After telling her my predicament, she smiled. Her cellular phone had been there in the car—I had available help and did not use it.

Life is like that. There are times when we fail to follow the Christian road map. We fail to recognize the Holy Spirit as an available help for us. We miss many blessings because we do not plug into the lifeline through prayer and study. Seeing the cross will get us home. MARIE H. SEARD

Oh! To Be Like My Child

He said to them, "Why are you troubled, and why do doubts rise in your minds?" Luke 24:38, NIV.

BEING A WIFE AND mother is a wonder. Yet I love it so dearly. Being an international singing evangelist is a wonder as well. Being in the service for the Lord is rewarding, even when you can't see your way.

I travel often, and most of my trips keep me away from home at least two to six weeks at a time. As the calls come in I go to my Father in heaven and then to my husband. I also have to deal with our 14-year-old daughter. For 11 years of her life I have been working in the Lord's vineyard, having to leave her behind.

She used to ride to the airport with her dad and me, but not anymore. I once asked, "Why don't you come to the airport with us?"

"I just wish you didn't have to go," she responded.

I looked into her eyes and paused a moment to breathe. "Jessica, you know that I must go to do the work that God would have me to do. But don't worry, and above all don't doubt; God will take care of me."

Then a look of "What do you mean?" came across her sweet, coco-butter face, and she said the magic words, "I don't know how to doubt God, 'cause no one ever taught me how. When I talk to Him, I tell Him all about it, and I know that He has it all in control. So you see, Mom, I don't worry about you when you go. I just miss you, and I get lonely for you. But I know you're coming back home. I never doubt God, 'cause I really don't know how."

And at that moment my heart jumped a beat, and I began to praise Him for shielding her from doubting Him.

I said to myself, *Oh, to be like my child! God, help me today to trust and never doubt You. I love You, Father.*

KIMBERLY PALMER WASHINGTON

I'll Carry You, My Friend

Blessed are the merciful: for they shall obtain mercy. Matt. 5:7.

AS I HELD MY friend's letter in my hand I questioned whether I had read it correctly. I read it again: "I tested HIV positive" (human immunodeficiency virus). Unfortunately, I had read it correctly. I could not believe it. I have known this friend for many years, and it saddened me to know that he will have to cope with this illness for a long time to come.

Since the time I read the letter I have thought a lot about my friend and the perceptions regarding this illness. It is easy for us to judge, avoid, or even discount individuals who are sick. I am not talking only about people with AIDS (acquired immunodeficiency syndrome). Included in this group that I am describing are people abandoned in nursing homes, the spiritually sick, and people with disabilities. The mentally ill can also be included in this group.

I thank and admire Jesus for His compassion and consistency in this area. There are many places in the Bible that tell of Jesus' experiences with sick people. The truly amazing thing is how He treated each one with love and respect. For example, Luke 5:12 and 13 reads: "Behold a man full of leprosy: who seeing Jesus fell on his face, and besought him, saying, Lord, if thou wilt, thou canst make me clean. And he put forth his hand, and touched him, saying, I will: be thou clean. And immediately the leprosy departed from him." Another example is in Matthew 9:20 and 21: "And, behold, a woman, which was diseased with an issue of blood twelve years, came behind him, and touched the hem of his garment: for she said within herself, If I may but touch his garment, I shall be whole." What faith! She knew she would find acceptance and healing in Jesus by just one touch!

We all are sick in one way or the other and will be until Jesus puts His robe of righteousness on us. There is a lot to be learned by Jesus' example in our current age in which disease and sickness are so prevalent. I hope that prayerfully we can accept this challenge to love without judgment.

I want to carry my friend to You today for Your touch and for Your healing. Please touch us all.

MARY WAGONER ANGELIN

Vacationing in France

Thou wilt keep him in perfect peace, whose mind is stayed on thee: because he trusteth in thee. Isa. 26:3.

FOLLOWING AN EIGHT-HOUR flight to Europe, I boarded an ocean liner to sail the Mediterranean Sea. The itinerary covered France, Italy, and Spain. It was my first trip to Europe, a place I'd dreamed of visiting since my early childhood.

The ship anchored at sea, and we were taken to shore in a tender. We then boarded a bus to tour Nice, Monaco, and Monte Carlo. How exciting! When we got off the bus, our tour guide raced through the bus depot, making it clear that she would not wait for anyone who could not walk at her pace. I could not allow her out of my sight. My brain automatically canceled the remainder of tours with this particular tour guide. By the end of the day I was tired and disappointed. I waited for the tour group to return to the bus stop. This was the part that I enjoyed most on that entire tour. We were very happy to return to Nice. It had truly been a long day.

We noticed that the tender waiting to take us to the ship was almost twice as large as the one that had brought us to shore. On our way back to the ship the waters were so rough it seemed as if we weren't going to make it back safely. The tender was tossed from side to side by the waves. Those standing were unable to balance themselves, and those sitting down were being forced from their seats. We were wet from the water that splashed aboard. We finally reached the ship, but forces from the wind and the water would not allow the tender to become stabilized so we could get off. It was pushing us away from the ship.

I thought of Jesus and His disciples on the Sea of Galilee. I prayed, *Lord, please allow us to board that ship safely.* Within minutes we were on the ocean liner again. Jesus commanded the winds and the waves again for us! We later learned that our tender was the last one allowed to sail back to the ship that evening. God had prepared that tender just for us.

Father, You promised never to leave or forsake us. Thank You for going on vacation with us and for keeping Your promises. CORA A. WALKER

The Harvest and the Laborers

Then saith [Jesus] unto his disciples, the harvest truly is plenteous, but the labourers are few. Matt. 9:37.

THE FAMILIAR WORDS OF this passage came to life for my husband and me during the summer when we responded to a sign by a roadside vegetable and fruit stand. The sign read: "Canning Tomatoes—U Pick, $6.00 a Bushel." We decided to take a look, received directions from the farmer's wife to the specified field, and drove our car down the lane. What we beheld made us think we'd misunderstood her instructions. The connotation of "canning tomatoes" is that they are the small, less desirable fruit that's left over after the prime yield has been gathered. What we were looking at was a bountiful array of beautiful perfectly-shaped specimens worthy to set before a king. We eagerly filled our baskets, stopping frequently to comment to one another, "Look at the size of this one! Can you believe this?"

So pleasant was our experience that we went back for more containers, not willing that any of the matured crop should be left in the field to perish. We listened to the farmer's lament, wishing for more people interested in picking the premium crop. We thought of others who would appreciate the find as much as we, and we picked a few more . . . and a few more, all the while realizing we were only skimming the surface of what was available. Still scattered among the ripe fruit were green specimens needing the nurture of sun and rain to bring them to maturity.

As I contemplated our find, the words of 2 Peter 3:9 came to mind. Our long-suffering Saviour is "not willing that any should perish." He has children who are ripe and ready for harvest, as well as those who need the nurture of a more experienced follower to help with the maturing process.

I wonder if I am discerning of the people in my life who might be "ripe for harvest." Am I available to those who are still maturing? Am I willing to be one of the laborers in Jesus' harvest field?

Lord, help me to have the same urgency for others as You have, "not willing that any should perish."

FERYL E. HARRIS

On This Hill

I will lift my eyes unto the hills, from whence cometh my help. Ps. 121:1.

MY MIND WAS NOT at ease. I knew something had to be done. After tears and angry words I climbed Ham Hill, a beautiful and historic hill in Somerset. Many years ago John Wesley had preached here. I prayed all the way up for guidance.

It was a remarkably clear day. I could see for miles and in a complete panoramic circle. I found a huge flat rock to sit on. The sun was warm and comforting, the breeze was cold and refreshing. I wanted to record the beauty and my feelings. I had paper and pen and began to write. I realized afterward, as I read my notes, that a poem had formed. I had been given the words, and my burden became lighter. Painful decisions had to be made—I had to break a relationship that was going nowhere after many years. However, I felt a peace and strength fill me, and I knew it had to be ended.

I was in my early 50s, and my children were already adults and making their own lives. After much prayer and thought the way was cleared and I was free. I then asked the Lord to find me a companion who would also love Him. My prayers were answered, and the absolute joy of sharing our faith together was complete when we married a year later. To make it even more wonderful, my husband-to-be was praying at the same time, unknown to me, to meet someone with whom he could share his life.

It is often not possible to make certain decisions when we are too close to the problem. Jesus, our role model, often went aside to a quiet place, or "he went out onto a mountain to pray" (Luke 6:12), away from everyone, to speak to His Father. We need to do the same each day to keep close to our Father and to ask for guidance in everything, whether it is a crisis or a tiny query. He is always ready to help us.

I am sure that if we believe the Lord will answer our prayers, He will give us the strength to accept His will. Sometimes the answer is yes, sometimes it is no. Sometimes it is wait. I was blessed with yes!

PHILIPPA MARSHALL

Camp Meeting Fires

The sun shall not smite thee by day. Ps. 121:6.

CAMP MEETINGS ARE always such a special time for me. As a child I loved camp meetings at Ardmore, New Zealand. I can remember the excitement of staying with my grandparents and sleeping in a tent. We used wooden banana boxes for cupboards and straw and burlap for flooring, held down with nails pounded through bottle tops. There was the smell of canvas and the wonderful smell of the cooking from the camp kitchen. There were friends to see, including many cousins, from all over the country.

One night as I lay in my sleeping bag, drifting off to sleep, there were shouts, loud shouts, not too far away. My grandfather raced along the row of tents and helped put out a potentially dangerous fire caused by someone incorrectly lighting their little Primus cooker.

After I had grown and moved to Australia, I found the annual camp meetings here in southeast Queensland to be just as wonderful. Held at beautiful Watson Park, there are always friends to meet and greet. Guest speakers and guest singers from other states and overseas bring spiritual blessings. However, here in Australia there is always a very real danger of fires. Every year bush fires somewhere in the country cause heartache and loss. September 1994 was a bad month with no rain and extremely high temperatures. For the week while camp meeting was being held there were many fires burning in the state. At about 4:00 each afternoon the sun would disappear behind a huge hazy pinkish cloud of smoke in the western sky. Because there was very low humidity (8 percent), it was like being in a bonfire.

The camp meeting passed all too quickly and concluded with a wonderful concert on Saturday night. Sunday all the tents came down. And do you know what happened two days later? Bush fires raged out of control, and a lot of bush was burned across the main road, down the main road, and on neighboring land near Watson Park. What a tragedy there could have been if a few sparks had landed on those tinder-dry tents.

How thankful I felt to know God is in control. He who neither slumbers nor sleeps kept the bush fires well away until camp meeting was over. *Thank You, God.*

LEONIE DONALD

Saving Time

Come to me, all you who are weary and burdened, and I will give you rest. Matt. 11:28, NIV.

I SOMETIMES WONDER WHY we seem to have less time than women had in the past. They didn't have all those time-saving devices and still managed to get everything done. Of course, we still have 24 hours a day. Maybe I am packing too much activity into those hours.

When I put the dishes into the dishwasher I don't have to spend my time with my hands in soapsuds. But instead of relaxing and being grateful that the dishwasher is giving me a quarter of an hour's break, I will rush off to my next job. Although I have machines that do most of the work, I can fill my days with activities that make my head spin.

Have we lost the ability to do one thing at a time? To sit down and enjoy a moment of peace? Maybe that is the reason so many women are frustrated and at the end of their tether.

I know that I have a problem with this. There are many things I love to do. There are plenty of things I have to do. And to fit all of this into the time I have, I do several things at once. Usually I manage and everything works out. But sometimes I long to do just one thing and to savor every aspect of doing it in a peaceful way.

We had planned a concert in our church for Saturday afternoon. I was involved in all but two of the musical items, and I had to practice with everybody. Besides my family to take care of, I had invited friends to come over for the weekend. By Friday afternoon I was a nervous wreck. My heart started racing, and my hands trembled. All I could do was lie down on my bed.

I began to pray. *Dear God, I seem to have a mountain to push, and I don't have the power anymore. I know I've taken on too much. But please, Lord, if You want that concert to take place tomorrow, help me to calm down. I can't do it on my own.*

And God showed me that I don't have to do anything by myself. He'll help me. After a half hour I was able to get up with steady hands and peace in my heart. I will never forget that experience. I've also learned to cut down at least on the extras on such occasions.

Lord, I'm going to take You at Your word. Help me fix my priorities so I don't get overworked and too worn out to serve You. HANNELE OTTSCHOFSKI

Shampoo and Conditioner

Let us then pursue what makes for peace and for mutual upbuilding. Rom. 14:19, NRSV.

HAVE YOU EVER HEARD that song, "I'm gonna wash that man right out of my hair"? I was only trying to rinse the shampoo out of mine, but it was a tangled mess anyway. Then I reached for the conditioner. A little dab, and my hair behaved wonderfully. I could run my fingers through the remaining curls with no difficulty. I thought about my mother washing my much-longer hair when I was a child. When she tried to comb out the tangles I fussed and cried. Even lemon juice didn't help. I guess it was supposed to help rinse out the shampoo or give shine or something. It certainly didn't help the tangles. Luckily, back then my hair got washed only on Fridays, but how nice it would have been to have had conditioner.

I thought about washing my daughter, Rikki's, hair. At least by then there had been No More Tears shampoo, but there was not the conditioner that we have today. Sometimes we would meet up with a terrific tangle and there would be tears, in spite of the shampoo.

It is rather like life itself. We get ourselves into tangled situations. There is fussing and tears. Maybe in the past we have tried lemon juice, but it just added acid to the situation. How much better to use some No More Tears and a nice dollop of conditioner. Massage in gently and change tense frowns to relaxed smiles.

What is this conditioner? Grace. Grace lived through love. Grace that does not insist that things be done my way or no way at all. Not insisting on tearing out the tangles, but looking for a real solution that will smooth things out and get the frizzies under control.

It is so much easier to access and apply this conditioner of grace when I spend more time with God. He has an abundance of grace that He willingly dispenses and shares.

As I travel around the world I have discovered that conveniences such as good shampoos and conditioners are now readily available almost anywhere. They come in a wide variety of types, smells, brands, and prices. But they all work about the same. Likewise, grace is available to all. It may come in different packaging in different places or situations, but it is always a good idea to use it if a tangle gets in the way of smiles and happiness.

ARDIS DICK STENBAKKEN

Heavenly Sonshine

And I, if I am lifted up from the earth, will draw all peoples to Myself. John 12:32, NKJV.

IT'S SO EASY TO LOOK at other people and compare their actions with ours. Sometimes we think they are doing better or looking better than we are, and we feel discouraged or inferior. Other times we think we are performing better than they are, and we allow ourselves to feel just a little superior. Or we can dare to analyze their behavior and reason that if they are doing something, then it's acceptable for us to do it too.

Unexpectedly, I got a lesson in these matters. It was a beautiful sunshiny summer day, and my spirits were high as we drove to church and found a space for the car. I noticed that one of my outgoing friends had just arrived also. Getting out of the car, I went up the steps, while she chose the ramp. I waited for her on the landing, and when she was about halfway up, I decided to acknowledge her presence. I waved what I thought was a friendly greeting.

She didn't answer, but continued to chat with a woman who was walking beside her. *Perhaps she is so involved in conversation that she doesn't have time to speak to me,* I thought. But I was a little bit surprised by her lack of response.

When she was only a few feet away she smiled and made a statement that caused me to do some serious thinking. "Oh," she said, "have you been there all this time? I saw you drive up and get out of your car, but I couldn't see you here because the sun was in my eyes."

What if we could not see each other's faults or defects because the Son, God's Son, was shining in our spiritual eyes? What if we were willing to use our talents and work for Him, not because someone else was, or was not, using theirs, but because we were looking at the Son instead of our fellow human beings?

Dear Lord, please let Your Son shine in my eyes that I may always serve You to the best of my ability. I love You. Amen. MILDRED C. WILLIAMS

The Shopping Money

Bring all the tithes into the storehouse; if you do, I will open up the windows of heaven for you and pour out a blessing so great you won't have room enough to take it in. Mal. 3:10, TLB.

WHEN DAVID AND I met, he was not a member of any church and had not been raised in one. So as I told him about some of my beliefs he questioned me as to what tithing was. I explained God's system of tithing and how I always paid tithe on the income I made. Later we were married, and he consistently set aside tithe money from his income.

Soon we had two children, and of course expenses were growing as fast as our family. Often the devil tempted us to use the precious tithe money for other things, but my husband was very faithful in paying his tithes.

We started doing odd jobs on top of our regular work to have a bit of extra money for necessities such as baby diapers, tires for the cars, and such. Payday came, and the bills seemed to be more than the paycheck. David, as his custom was, set aside the tithe and offerings and counted out the money and bills. There was just enough to cover the bills except one item: there was no money for food. The temptation was great to dip into the tithe money, set so visibly on our dresser.

"No, we won't," we declared. "God said to test Him, and we shall do just that." The testing was difficult, but He was probably testing us also.

Thursday evening we got a phone call from a man whose lawn we had mowed on occasion. "Hi, this is Bud," he began. "Listen, my lawn mower is giving me trouble, and if you could get to my lawn by tomorrow, I would appreciate it."

Wow! What a blessing! He always paid $45 for us to mow his lawn, and that was what we generally spent on our weekly groceries. Does God keep His word or what? I know He does. CHARLOTTE ROBINSON

It's Rather Nice to See Behind the Curtains

Who knoweth whether thou art come to the kingdom for such a time as this? Esther 4:14.

ONE OF THE BIGGEST differences between being a lawyer and a judge is that I rarely ever know the "rest of the story." I almost never know how my orders impact the lives of litigants and their families, so I am always happy for any opportunity God gives me to peek behind the curtains and learn how He has worked through me.

My first assignment as a county judge was in traffic court. I didn't understand what a hardship my "tailor-made" sentence for an impaired driver created for the jail, although I was promptly made aware of the problems. However, about three years passed before I learned the rest of the story.

Since the litigant had gone through other rehab programs, his family was poised for another relapse. Instead, his wife reported that for the first time in more than 30 years he was truly sober. He is now a converted, alcohol-free husband and father. And none too soon, because his wife was later diagnosed with cancer. "For the first time in many years," she commented, "I am able to count on him; he is there for me now."

One day as I was eating in a buffet restaurant the server kept looking at me. Finally she identified me as the judge who had recently sentenced her for violating her probation stemming from cannabis charges. She told me how much she appreciated my continuing her on the drug counseling program rather than sentencing her to jail time. The program, she assured me, was what she needed—close supervision as she sought to overcome her addiction.

Because of the sentence, she was working and putting her family life back together. She was so pleased each morning that she awoke with her money on her dresser and able to remember where she had been the previous day and what she had done the night before.

Learning the "rest of the story" for these two defendants allowed me to know that my daily prayer, asking for wisdom to execute God's justice, is being heard and answered. I got a little peek behind the curtains of what God is doing through me!

JUDITH W. HAWKINS

July 29

Just Pray

I tell you the truth, unless you change and become like little children, you will never enter the kingdom of heaven. Matt. 18:3, NIV.

MY TWO BOYS, Gabriel and Joshua, were in the car with me one day while I was driving down a freeway when I realized I was lost. It was just beginning to get dark, and it wouldn't be long before Joshua was due for a diaper change and some food. Panic and fear gripped my heart, and I lost all sense of logic. *Am I going north or east? Do I have enough gas? H'mmm . . . How much money do I have in my wallet?*

Just then I spotted a restaurant and stopped to ask for directions. Unfortunately, the man didn't speak very good English, and I didn't understand his instructions. I began looking for a gas station. The man at the gas station gave me directions that were completely different from those of the first man. I climbed back into my car, still feeling panic and fear. Grabbing the steering wheel tighter, I began thinking out loud. "Should I just take this exit, or should I find a phone? Oh, dear, what shall I do?" The palms of my hands started to perspire, and I felt tears welling up in my eyes. I kept driving, but I didn't really know where I was going. After what seemed like eternity a soft voice said, "It's OK, Mommy; just pray." I glanced over at Gabriel and realized he had witnessed my panic and fear. Yet very calmly he reassured me, although I had almost forgotten for a moment that he was in the car with me.

I recalled all the times I told him to always pray when he was angry, frightened, or sad. How could I have forgotten to pray? Very quickly I asked the Lord to grant me the faith of a little child and to deliver us home safely.

I have never forgotten that experience and how the Lord used my son to remind me to trust Him. Gabriel is now 11 years old, and Joshua is almost 8. The experiences of motherhood with my two wonderful boys continue to strengthen my faith in God. No wonder the Bible tells us to be like little children.

VIOLA POEY HUGHES

Unconditional Love

Behold, what manner of love the Father hath bestowed upon us. 1 John 3:1.

IT WAS LOVE AT first sight. I had anticipated meeting him for several months, but when the moment finally arrived, an overwhelming feeling of love welled up inside me. It didn't matter that he was short and bald with sleepy eyes, or that he didn't even acknowledge me when I spoke to him. He stole my heart away with no effort whatsoever. And I loved him simply for who he was—my first grandchild.

Little Lorenzo has a tremendous influence on our family, although he's quite unaware of it. He doesn't even try to earn our love, but just being "ours" creates an unexplainable bond of emotion. Nevertheless, I'm eagerly awaiting the day that he will be able to respond to our love.

Sometimes I think of my relationship with God as being similar to this human experience. I have nothing to cause God, my heavenly Father, to love me—no physical beauty or outstanding personality traits. The fact that I'm His child seems to be sufficient reason for Him to shower His amazing and unconditional love on me. And it was enough to cause Jesus, my King, to leave everything heaven could offer to come down to this sinful planet to die an ignominious death, alone and rejected, just for me. Does He wait in vain for some grateful acknowledgment from me for this incomprehensible gift? Am I still a spiritual babe, unresponsive to His lavish display of love? I hope not.

One of the first questions I asked Lorenzo's daddy when he called with the news of the baby's birth was "Who does he look like?" I need to ask myself, *Whom do I look like?* Do I resemble my heavenly Father? Can others tell we're related? God longs to see His reflection in me—a continual outflowing of love toward Him and others. Does He see that? Do others?

Father, help me to resemble You more each day. Give me Your eyes that I may see others as You see them. Give me Your lips that I may speak words of encouragement to those who need them. May my hands resemble Yours in unselfish service to my brothers and sisters. And most important, give me a heart like Yours so that I can love unconditionally, the way that You love me. And then there will be no question as to whose child I am.

NANCY CACHERO VASQUEZ

July 31

Glimpses of Heaven

Wilt thou believe him, that he will bring home thy seed, and gather it into thy barn? Job 39:12.

AFTER SUPPER ON OUR last day of a four-day vacation at a lake, Emily, 7, was bored and said that the next-door neighbor had videos she could borrow. She came back with an old black-and-white Shirley Temple video. Movies bore me, so I sat on the porch. Before long there was a tap-dancing tune. The music pulled me back into the living room.

"I used to tap-dance," I called out to Emily. I couldn't really tap-dance; I could only scruff it up and pretend.

Pretty soon Emily joined me, saying, "This is how you do it!" One-and-a-half-year-old Hannah joined in, barefoot and spinning around with us. She was wearing a little dress, the skirt of which was twirling around in the air, exposing her diaper. For some reason, that little diaper under that twirling dress and Emily's laughter that seemed to float in the summer air stand out in my mind as one of the happiest times in my life. The movie was long since forgotten as we three danced around and laughed with the insects until dark.

I remember another camp. A youth pastor was giving a nature talk and weaving into the story things he'd observed in the juniors that day. He mentioned my oldest son, whom he noticed liked squirrels, and that the squirrels also seemed to like my son. My son's face lit up, and his smile literally glowed. Apparently, the visiting speaker didn't know this was my angry, rebellious son, and no one had ever said anything nice about him before. That shining, smiling face of my son so many years ago is also etched in my memory.

I wonder about the memories Adam and Eve carried of their first outdoor camp home—the beautiful carefree days in the garden of Eden, their personal companionship with God and the angels—memories to give them hope after generations of sin and toil came upon them, the hope that someday they would go home again.

Do you have memories that provide glimpses into that soon-coming eternal home?

ALEAH IQBAL

Wisdom's Years

They will still bear fruit in old age, they will stay fresh and green. Ps. 92:14, NIV.

HOW ARE YOU TODAY?" I asked a neighbor, who was pruning her roses as my husband and I circled the block one morning last year.

"Old age isn't easy, you know, my dear." The old woman stood up, slowly brushing clumps of earth from her knees. Startled at the unusual response and enchanted by the singsong voice that betrayed her Caribbean heritage, we paused to chat.

"Old age is like working for yourself." Leaning on her gate, she explained her metaphor. "And the work is hard. First I struggle to get out of bed, and then I spend 10 minutes on my eyes, and another 10 on my teeth, and yet another on my painy knees. The list goes on and on."

At the crest of my own 70-year experience, I could relate to her tale of woe. I wondered if my neighbor realized how closely she had echoed Solomon's words in his poetic ode to old age (Eccl. 12). Then one day I realized how reassuring Solomon's litany was to those of us who have passed middle age. "There is nothing more important for me than to . . . pass on to others what I have learned" (Eccl. 12:9, Clear Word). When I read the lines below, attributed to a Middle Eastern mystic, I caught another glimpse of the developmental theme of a way of living and praying:

"When I was young, I prayed, 'Lord, give me the energy to change the world.'

"When I approached the middle age, I prayed, 'Lord, give me the grace to change those who come into contact with me—just my family and friends—and I shall be satisfied.'

"When I grew old, I prayed, 'Lord, give me the grace to change myself.'"

How tragic it is that we rarely become wise before we grow old! *Dear God, please give us wisdom and Your grace to change ourselves first and then pass on our knowledge to those around us. May we still bring forth good fruit in our old age. Thank You for the assurance that our talents will stay fresh and green, even though our bodies don't.*

CAROL JOY GREENE

The Lost Son

They, supposing him to have been in the company, went a day's journey; and they sought him among their kinfolk and acquaintance. And when they found him not, they turned back to Jerusalem, seeking him. Luke 2:44, 45.

WHEN I WAS A small girl, we lived in Pune, India. Once every few years we traveled to Kerala to visit our grandparents and other relatives. Those were the days when coal engines pulled the railroad carriages. The journey was tedious. The compartments were crowded, and there were no facilities for sleeping.

On one such journey in the hot summer the steam engine chugged its way into the Madras station. As expected, the train for Trivandrum was already on the next platform and was ready to leave. My parents hurriedly dragged the luggage and us children to that train and managed to get in just as the train began to move. Then my mother screamed, "Where is Sunny? Where is Sunny?"

We all searched the compartment frantically, but he was not there. Immediately my parents threw the luggage through the windows, and we all jumped down from the slow-moving train. With tears streaming down their faces, they searched for Sunny among the crowds. They couldn't see him anywhere. They looked behind every mound of baggage and into every corner. They would not give up. Finally at the far end of the platform my father found Sunny, sitting with two porters. We spent the next 24 hours on the railway station platform, waiting for another train to Trivandrum. You can be sure that this time our parents made sure we were all there!

Two thousand years ago Jesus' parents missed Him on their return journey from Jerusalem. Mary must have felt much like my mother did in those anxious moments when Sunny was lost in the crowd. Mary and Joseph had thought He was with relatives and friends. When they couldn't find Him, they went looking for Him. We lost one day because of my brother, but they lost three days of their journey because of their neglect to keep in touch with their Son, Jesus.

How often we too have to experience sorrow and difficulties because we neglect to keep in touch with Jesus. We must keep in touch with the Son of God every moment of our journey. HELEN CHARLES

The Kiwifruit

The Lord seeth not as man seeth; for man looketh on the outward appearance, but the Lord looketh on the heart. 1 Sam. 16:7.

WHAT'S THIS?" AURELIA, my 5-year-old daughter, asked as she held up a strange-looking, hairy, brownish oval fruit she saw at the supermarket.

"Just put it down," I said. She loved fruit very much and begged me to buy one so she could taste the fruit. I didn't like the looks of it at all, so I refused.

A few years later when I visited Australia, my brother, his wife, and I were invited to a minister's home for lunch. I do not remember what the first course was, but I certainly remember the big crystal dish of fruit salad, decorated with whole strawberries, slices of green fruit with teeny black seeds, and dollops of fresh cream. I enjoyed the fruit salad so much that I inquired about those green slices. What was it? It was kiwi—the same fruit that my daughter had picked up at the supermarket and that I had despised in my ignorance and prejudice. I didn't know that under that awful-looking, hairy brown skin was the most delicious-tasting fruit. What I had missed all those years because of my refusal to become informed!

How often I have been prejudiced about some people, too, because I didn't know them. I looked only at the outside. I made no effort to speak to them or get to know them. Someone has said that "a stranger is only a friend you haven't met yet." There are many lonely and aching hearts around us, longing to have a friend, longing for a smile, a hug, or a word of cheer. "A word fitly spoken is like apples of gold in pictures of silver" (Prov. 25:11).

When Jesus' love comes into your heart, you won't notice the outer skin and blemishes of people; you will only experience the delicious fruit that a Christlike friendship gives.

Some may have a peaches 'n' cream complexion, and some may resemble the unpeeled kiwifruit, but with Jesus' love in our hearts each one of us is truly special!

PRISCILLA ADONIS

There's a Man in My Room

He orders his angels to protect you wherever you go. The Lord says, "I will receive those who love me. I will protect those who trust in my name." Ps. 91:11, 14, NLT.

A COUPLE YEARS AGO I conducted a stress management workshop for the wives of a group of salesmen in Wisconsin. The delightfully efficient person who gave me directions to the meeting place confirmed that it was about six hours from where I lived. I could not start traveling until midafternoon, so she promised to prepare the lodge receptionist for my 10:30 p.m. arrival. All I had to do was pick up the key when I got there.

Keeping an occasional eye on the map, I drove through the lush green lowlands to my destination. The summer breeze was a balmy reminder of God's love as I bypassed Chicago and Milwaukee. The highway was relatively unclogged.

Arriving at the lodge shortly after the stars came out in the darkening sky, I picked up the key to Room 9. Walking down the outdoor corridor, I marveled at the homey touch of the lodge. I could see inviting lamplight through the curtained window of my new room. I inserted the key into the lock. Suddenly cold shock waves rushed through my body. A man wrapped in bed covers emerged from the bed—my bed! My mouth fell open. Words lay unspoken in my too-dry throat. I could neither fight nor flee from the shadowed room. Moments dragged by on leaden feet. Then I heard a deep chuckle.

"Glenda-mae, what are you doing in my room?"

"Praise the Lord!" I exhaled, only then realizing that I had been holding my breath. It was my sister-in-law's uncle. He had come to meet with the salespeople the next day. The receptionist had inadvertently given him a key that opened all the lodge doors.

Settling into Room 7 that night, I barricaded the door and knelt by my bed to count my blessings. As I reached for my red-lined Bible, I paused at several promises before my favorite one appeared: "Do not fear, for I am with you" (Isa. 43:5, NRSV). Gratitude enveloped me.

As an added bonus, the Master Speaker had given me a powerful opening for my presentation the next day.

GLENDA-MAE GREENE

Set Free

So if the Son sets you free, you will indeed be free. John 8:36, NLT. Now make sure that you stay free and don't get tied up again in slavery. Gal. 5:1, NLT.

IT HAD BEEN ONLY a week since my three cats had been set free from the cages they had lived in for six months while it was determined that they were free of rabies. No contact with other animals. No human contact. Confined in cages in a room. It had been a long and especially hard wait for me. Each day as I placed food in the cages and cleaned out litter pans, I was reminded of my special kitty, Gretchen, who had died of rabies.

My husband and I had been remiss in obtaining the scheduled vaccines for all the cats, and in the meantime she had come in contact with something rabid, gotten very ill, and subsequently died. I missed her terribly. She had been especially affectionate, unlike my kitties in the cages, and I feared that this lengthy quarantine might have made them even less inclined to want human contact.

These cats were then required to spend six months in the cages. I had contacted the vet for the cats' required rabies shots, then the health department to advise them that the cats had been vaccinated, and finally the animal control facility so someone could check the cats and give permission for their release. At last the day came when their mandatory imprisonment was over. They were free again.

Once they were released from the cages they stood around, sometimes wandering back and forth, obviously disoriented. Our family tried not to make sudden moves to scare them, and began to pet them gently as soon as we could get close. Still, we could see their reluctance to be held or even stroked.

Sin must affect us the same way. We've all been exposed to the rabid enemy, Satan, and are susceptible to illness, disease, or even death. We too are confined to a life in the earthly realm, stuck in cages, as it were, while all heaven waits for the grand day when we will finally be released. And then our Lord and Saviour, who has already administered the antibodies to sin, will set us free. We will be free indeed. And in Him, and only in Him, our freedom will be eternal.

IRIS L. STOVALL

Trust God at All Times!

Trust in him at all times; ye people, pour out your heart before him: God is a refuge for us. Ps. 62:8.

MY TWO CHILDREN AND I had planned a visit to my homeland and to my mother in India. We arrived at the Maryland airport for our evening connecting flight in New York. To our dismay, our flight from Maryland was delayed, and we missed our flight out of New York. American Airlines arranged a hotel for us that night, assuring us that we would be on the next Singapore Airlines flight. In the morning, just to be safe, I called Singapore Airlines. I was very upset to hear that we could not be confirmed because it was not Singapore Airline's fault that we had missed our flight. We had to be on standby. Even worse, the woman told me that they were overbooked by 17 passengers, which made our chances almost impossible.

We didn't know what to do except to ask God to intervene and work a miracle. For worship I opened the Bible, and my eyes fell on Psalm 62:8: "Trust in him at all times." This verse lifted our spirits, and we all earnestly prayed that God would help us get on that flight. It was imperative that we make that flight, because we had no place to stay in New York, and my mother was planning to meet us at the airport in India, some distance from her home.

As suggested by Singapore Airlines, we were at their counter as soon as they opened. There were at least 12 other passengers in the same situation. This meant that our chances were even slimmer, as we needed three seats. We were also worried about our six suitcases that were checked through to India. We didn't know what to do, so we kept earnestly praying. We stood in line for two hours, and they kept calling names, but not ours. The final boarding call was made. We were still praying and standing in line. Other passengers were becoming irritated and were demanding to be on that flight. But we waited, claiming God's promise. Just when I thought there was no hope, they called our names. We rushed to the airplane, and they closed the door.

Miracle number two happened when we arrived in India two days later. We saw all six suitcases neatly lined up at the airport. One suitcase lock was missing, but nothing was stolen.

Our heavenly Father never fails. So trust in Him at all times!

STELLA THOMAS

Midnight Prayer-Praise Service

Let the peoples praise You, O God; let all the peoples praise You. Ps. 67:3, NKJV.

WE WERE CAMPING WITH 22,000 young people at a camporee in Oshkosh, Wisconsin. We were already in bed when our regional youth leader rounded up our group and said that it was very possible a tornado was coming our way and that we were to be ready to vacate the camp. We quickly had a season of prayer to implore God to spare the whole encampment. Soon the leader came back and said that all was clear. Everybody could go back to bed.

Ten minutes later all of us were told to dress and hurry to the hangars, where it was thought we would be safe. By the time we left our beds, it was already raining cats and dogs. The thunder and lightning became frightening. Water already covered the streets. When we reached the hangars about a mile away, we were wet and cold. We huddled together in groups, once again imploring God's intervention.

Soon the rains subsided. We tried to rest. Finally about 1:30 in the morning the leaders said we could go back to our tents. Again we lifted our hearts heavenward to thank Him who calmed the storm.

The following morning we learned that the tornado truly had passed over the encampment; however, that tornado had split into two—half went north while the other half went south, finally meeting together again. About 20 miles beyond our camp the tornado and hailstorm hit a town, destroying some property. God surely took care of the camp, averting a sure disaster. Oh, how we praised Him for His loving care! You can believe that the whole encampment had a thanksgiving prayer meeting.

Psalm 84:11 says that God doesn't withhold anything good from those who walk uprightly. Looking back to that experience, I recalled when Jesus commanded the raging storm to stop. I have often thought about the Israelites' crossing of the Red Sea. Oh, how wonderful God is! Yes, like the psalmist I will praise God again and again, for He has been so amazingly good to us.

Ofelia A. Pangan

The Voice(s) of God

Whatsoever ye ask in prayer, believing, ye shall receive. Matt. 21:22.

IT WAS A BEAUTIFUL sunny summer afternoon as my husband and I left the office of the neurosurgeon. My mood, however, did not match the weather. The doctor had just told me that he felt I should have surgery to repair the ruptured disc in my back. However, he gave me the option of doing some physical therapy and going to a pain control clinic to see what they might do. Rather than having the surgery, I opted for the physical therapy and pain control, but I wasn't sure I had made the right choice. As we drove along, my husband declared that he felt I should have opted for the surgery, but it was my choice to make.

I had already suffered nearly unbearable pain in my right leg for five months, and the anti-inflammatory drugs were no help. I had always been a walker, covering three to six miles nearly every day. Now I could barely stand to walk from my bedroom to the bathroom. I hated to go anywhere because I limped so badly. I was feeling really sorry for myself.

As my husband and I spoke of the options, I suddenly declared that I didn't know what to do, but I was just going to pray about it and ask God to help me make the right decision. I wasn't sure how God planned to do that, but I certainly was in for a surprise.

That very evening the doorbell rang, and there stood one of our former pastors, who had moved to another state. He noticed immediately that I was limping. I shared with him what had been happening, and he shared that he had gone through the same thing. He had had physical therapy and even acupuncture and still ended up having surgery. It was a great success, and he highly recommended that I go ahead and have it done.

Later, my oldest daughter, the wife of a physician, called, and when she heard of my dilemma, she said, "Mom, you have suffered so long; just go ahead and have the surgery and get it over with."

There were others who were encouraging me as well. I decided that God was using the voices of my friends and family to answer my prayers, and within a week I had the surgery. With time and lots of physical therapy, I am doing better. I am so thankful that God answered my prayers through the encouragement of others, and I am glad that I listened.

ANNA MAY RADKE WATERS

Love Wrapped in Plastic Wrap

Jesus called out to them, "Come, be my disciples, and I will show you how to fish for people!" Matt. 4:19, NLT.

THERE WAS A SMELL in our Toyota that was making me sick to my stomach. I repeatedly asked my husband to please find out what was making the offensive odor and to get rid of it. He would say OK, but then do nothing. On this particular day I was alone. That obnoxious smell overwhelmed me. It was coming from my hands, emitting from the steering wheel! I gave Ron a good blast. He was told that if he wanted to use our car for fishing, then he had better wash up before driving home. So Ron cleaned the car.

Just before we left on our next fishing adventure, he called me outside. The steering wheel was neatly wrapped in plastic wrap. With an ear-to-ear grin Ron said, "Does this please you, dear?" He had gotten the message, and his response was perfect! I laughed until I cried.

Fishing helps keep Ron and me balanced as we care for our 13-year-old mentally disabled son, Sonny. We have great memories, and we've made "friends for eternity" at Swan Lake, our favorite lake, only a 20-minute drive from home. I've given our little fishing boat a name, *Loveboat Number 55.* My favorite fishing lure is called a wedding band. My favorite fishing spot is across the lake by the big uprooted tree. I've caught some huge trout with my wedding band, worm, and some "special stuff" Ron put on my hook.

There have been several occasions Ron has accidentally put his fingers in his mouth after putting some "special stuff" on my worm. What a priceless look! It must taste worse than it smells.

Sonny always announces our arrival at the lake by running down to the water and calling out "Hi" to everyone he sees. Recently a kind stranger helped us. I will never forget what he said: "Fish are a dime a dozen, but people like you are rare—please let me launch your boat!"

Jesus sends His people to be witnesses for Him. He picks the time and place, but you must be willing to go. Jesus will say, "This is the way; follow Me!" *I want to keep fishing and inviting people to follow You until You come. And I pray that it may be soon.*

DEBORAH SANDERS

I Lost My Tummy Pack

I love you, Lord! You answered my prayers. You paid attention to me, and so I pray to you as long as I live. Ps. 116:1, 2, CEV.

WE HAD JUST ARRIVED in Paris and found a bed and breakfast hotel to stay in. As Americans abroad, we were also all thankful for the fact that there was a Pizza Hut next door. When we travel as a family, we have a hard time finding any restaurant that has food our girls will eat, so we usually look for an American restaurant, like McDonald's or Pizza Hut.

We were all starting to get hungry, so we headed next door for some pizza. After ordering four soft drinks and a medium pizza, we picked a booth by the window. I was hot, and my tummy pack was getting in my way. I took it off and placed it at my feet. All the papers we needed to get back home were in my tummy pack, so I wanted it close and safe. Sitting down to eat with some ice-cold sodas and steaming, bubbly pizza was relaxing, and soon we were full and content. We all got up and left, totally forgetting that my tummy pack was still nestled against the booth. In fact, I didn't realize it was missing until late that night. I hurried back to the Pizza Hut, but to my dismay, it was closed for the night.

The first thing in the morning I went back. To my annoyance, the restaurant was still closed. Somehow I was impressed to go around to the service door in back. A wonderful woman answered the door. I asked her if she had seen my tummy pack. She led me to the Pizza Hut safe, and there, safely locked away, was my tummy pack!

Again God had been with me. He had answered my prayer, even though I was the one who had made the mistake. He pays attention to all I do. Being a traveling woman has taught me this: Don't go anywhere without praying that God is right there with you.

Father, I need You again today. I don't know what crises I might meet, so I need You close. And I do love You. SUSEN MATTISON MOLÉ

I Remembered Martha

The Lord answered, "Martha, Martha! You are worried and upset about so many things, but only one thing is necessary. Mary has chosen what is best, and it will not be taken away from her." Luke 10:41, 42, CEV.

I'VE BEEN DESCRIBED AS a neat freak, a statement I acknowledge to be true most of the time. I cannot settle down to write, read, study, work on a research project, or prepare a Bible lesson in a cluttered room. Everything must be in order before I can focus on the task ahead.

Though it is commendable to keep a tidy house, my habit has become a preoccupation, which has its downside. I recall many occasions when I never did get around to a project because the tidying consumed the better part of the time allotted for that particular activity. For instance, I have noble intentions of being consistent in Bible research—there are so many areas begging to be explored. So on a scheduled night I assemble all the materials I intend to use, and prepare to dig into the Word. Then as I look around the room, I observe items out of place. A trip to the kitchen for a glass of water reveals a sink full of dishes and a kitchen floor that could benefit from a quick mopping. Before long, the sink is empty, the floor is spotless, and the misplaced items out of sight. Now I'm ready for the project! However, after five minutes' work, weariness overpowers me. The next thing I know, it's morning, books surround me, and I don't recall praying.

Martha must have shared my obsession with tidiness. She seemed absorbed in preparing this, putting away that, and fixing the other. It is painful to write that I feel the sting of that chiding more often than I care to confess. Occasionally home cares do tend to rival an intended private meeting with God.

I asked Him one more time to manage my life and bless me with a renewed focus. He has already provided an answer. One night I was checking the kitchen one last time before retiring to my study. Some dirty glasses sat in the sink. The kitchen floor was sticky in spots. The day's paper was scattered over the dining room table. I admit to being tempted to set everything straight; then I remembered Martha. That memory prompted me to leave everything as it was, turn off the light, and head upstairs to my waiting Bible.

MARIA G. MCCLEAN

Nearing Home

Forgetting what is behind and straining toward what is ahead, I press on toward the goal to win the prize for which God has called me heavenward in Christ Jesus. Phil. 3:13, 14, NIV.

MY OLDER SISTER AND I were holidaying in Tasmania, Australia's island state, with our younger sister and her husband, who live there. Tasmania has some lovely wilderness areas, and we decided to visit a well-known national park. We set out from the parking lot on a walk of several kilometers around attractive Dove Lake.

The first half of the walk was very pleasant. The path was fairly level, and the King Billy pines offered plenty of shade. We enjoyed views of the sunlit lake with majestic Cradle Mountain at its head, then the eerie beauty of the Ballroom Forest, its ancient trees festooned with moss. After a time, however, the track became more uneven underfoot and began to climb up a headland that projected into the lake. There was much less shade now, and the effects of other strenuous walks taken earlier in the week became apparent in weary, aching muscles. We grew thirsty, hot, tired, and hungry. It was hard to tell what progress we were making.

My younger sister, who had walked this part of the track before on returning from a grueling climb to the mountain summit, offered some words of encouragement. "Once we reach the highest point of the headland you'll be able to see the parking lot and know there's not much farther to go."

Sure enough, as we topped the rise we could see sunlight glinting on the windshields of the distant cars. That was where rest—and lunch—awaited us! As we descended the headland and pressed on with renewed energy, an old hymn came to mind: "Just over the mountains in the Promised Land, lies the holy city built by God's own hand; as our weary footsteps gain the mountain's crest, we can view our homeland of eternal rest. We are nearing home!"

I found myself humming the tune as we covered the last few hundred meters to our goal. And I was glad to think that we all have an Elder Brother who knows the path to our heavenly home and can provide all the encouragement we need along the way. JENNIFER M. BALDWIN

I Do Not Like Onion

Suffer little children, and forbid them not to come unto me: for of such is the kingdom of heaven. Matt. 19:14.

LYING IN THAT POOL of warm water, looking at the majestic palm trees, I thanked God for being the most adventurous of grandmothers. All my grandchildren were around me, running and jumping. My heart overflowed with joy each time one of them came to kiss Grandma.

Lunchtime arrived. Bernardo, my youngest grandson, his little nose covered with suntan lotion, jumped onto my lap. He began a session of questions: "Grandma, what's this?" "Why that?" One of the questions was "Grandma, can we ask for anything from Jesus?"

"Of course, dear," I answered.

He closed his little eyes, folded his hands, and reverently prayed for everyone before adding, "Dear Jesus, help Rosélia [the cook] to make good food without onion, because I do not like onion. In Jesus' name, amen."

I could almost see the angels smiling! Right there I learned a lesson: Take all our necessities to Him. God desires that we become like children in trust and simplicity. He understands when we face what we consider huge problems, such as unemployment, financial difficulties, marital misunderstandings, or differences with adolescent children.

I am certain that Jesus is also interested in our small problems, when, for example, I do not receive one single word of appreciation for my long day of work as a homemaker. He sees when I am restless about the bus that does not come or when I cannot find the car keys or the document that I need and am going to be late. Jesus knows when I am facing premenstrual tension and have to make an enormous effort to hold back my bad mood. He understands and helps if I am going through menopause with all those horrible symptoms of hot flashes.

How marvelous that He knows the individual difficulties of each of us and that we can take our problems, big or small, to Him with the simplicity of a child. In Isaiah He states, "You whom I have upheld since your birth. Even to your old age and gray hairs I am He . . . who will sustain you. . . . I will rescue you" (Isa. 46:3, 4, NIV).

EUNICE MAFALDO MICHILES

Healing Power

Jesus turned and saw her. "Take heart, daughter," he said, "your faith has healed you." Matt. 9:22, NIV.

HILKKA HAD SUFFERED excruciating back pain for five long years. Although still young, the doctors said she should be prepared to spend the rest of her life in a wheelchair. Her vertebrae had grown "spikes," and the bone mass was becoming softer. Soon the steel corset was not able to support her. Lying down was painful; getting up without aid or bending over was impossible.

It was time for the annual camp meeting. She was thinking of the Bible story of the woman who was healed when she touched the hem of Jesus' robe. How she wished she could touch Jesus.

"Will there be a meeting where you offer prayer for the sick?" Hilkka asked.

It was announced that there would be a special meeting Sunday morning for all sick persons who wanted to ask for intercessory prayer. Hilkka was sitting in the morning meeting, but she didn't hear a word of what was being said. She was praying. "Please, Lord, I don't know if I have enough faith for You to heal me, but please give me that faith."

A group of pastors joined and laid their hands on the sick people. One after the other, they prayed for the suffering. When Pastor Arasola prayed for her, Hilkka felt a power pass through her back, and she felt as if her backbone had been made straight again. The pastor later said, "I felt a healing power pass, and I so hope that it was you who was healed."

Later that day he decided to pray for Hilkka again, but he was stopped. He heard a voice tell him, "Don't ask, but thank!"

Hilkka told one of the pastors, "I was healed today!"

She went home, discarded the steel corset, got out the bucket, and washed the floor, bending her back—something she had not been able to do for years.

The doctors were amazed when they saw her again. One of them said, "I don't know how this can be possible, but your back has been healed."

Her back never again gave her any pain. Because God touched her back and healed her, she has never let anybody else tamper with it. I know, because I was that young woman.

HILKKA ROUHE

A Pattern of Good Works

In all things shewing thyself a pattern of good works: in doctrine showing uncorruptness, gravity, sincerity, sound speech, that cannot be condemned; that he that is of the contrary part may be ashamed, having no evil thing to say of you. Titus 2:7, 8.

WHILE ON A TOUR of Nashville, Tennessee, I visited the Hermitage, the home of General Andrew Jackson. Although he was a "volatile lawyer, military hero, statesman, and politician," his home attests to his hospitality and devotedness to his wife, Rachel. She became sick and died suddenly four days before Jackson's appointment as the seventh president of the United States. As I walked through the garden where his wife is buried, I was touched by the epitaph Jackson composed to mark her resting place.

"Here lie the remains of Mrs. Rachel Jackson, wife of President Jackson, who died the 22nd Dec. 1828, aged 61. Her face was fair, her person pleasing, her temper amiable, her heart kind; she delighted in relieving the wants of her fellow creatures, and cultivated that divine pleasure by the most liberal and unpretending methods; to the poor she was a benefactor; to the rich an example; to the wretched a comforter; to the prosperous an ornament; her piety went hand in hand with her benevolence, and she thanked her Creator for being permitted to do good. A being so gentle and virtuous, slander might wound but could not dishonor. Even death, when he tore her from the arms of her husband, could but transport her to the bosom of her God."

Truly, she was a wife Solomon described as more valuable than rubies (Prov. 31:10). I've never been married and haven't had the honor of being showered with the compliments of an adoring husband. However, I'm not depressed. Neither do I feel rejected. Each one of us can exemplify those selfless qualities in our interactions with family and friends, brothers and sisters in Christ. For me, my focus is on being met by Jesus, my heavenly Bridegroom, and hearing Him say, "Well done, good and faithful servant. . . . Enter into the joy of your lord" (Matt. 25:21, NKJV). EDITH FITCH

It Is Well With My Soul

You cast me into the deep, into the heart of the seas, and the flood surrounded me; all your waves and your billows passed over me. Jonah 2:3, NRSV.

I HAD GONE THROUGH SOME soul-wrenching experiences. I was betrayed by a loved one and then learned a shocking secret about another loved one. My soul was in turmoil. How could I survive this? I agonized and agonized, yet the hurt would not go away. "O Lord!" I cried out. "How could this happen? Why? Why, Lord?"

Peace would not come. Then one day I was going through my hymnal, playing hymns. I came upon "It Is Well With My Soul," by Horatio Spafford. I had always loved the hymn and was aware of the story behind the writing of it. Spafford saw his entire business obliterated by fire. He had planned a trip to England with his wife and daughters, but because of the disaster he had to stay at home. He let his wife and children go on, planning to join them later. But his plans were to take another turn. The ship was hit by another British vessel. He was informed that only his wife survived; his precious daughters were gone. Through all this turmoil his faith remained strong, and he wrote the words we know well about sea billows rolling.

As I recalled this touching story I began to think differently. I knew I could not change the things that had happened. I knew that I must forgive from the heart. It was not easy at first. I prayed and agonized with the Lord to give me His forgiving spirit and His understanding. I felt compassion for those who had caused the turmoil in the first place, and I prayed unceasingly for them. I prayed that whatever life's waves or Satan might toss at me, I would have the faith of Horatio Spafford and be able to say, "It is well with my soul."

Lord, please give me the strength I need to forgive those that hurt me just as I pray to be forgiven by You. Let me be reminded of Your example always so that no matter what I may face, I will remember Your grace and be able to share my praise with others. It is truly well with my soul. PAM CARUSO

Amazing Gracie

He does not punish us as we deserve or repay us according to our sins and wrongs. Ps. 103:10, TEV.

WHEN I LOOKED UP the word "grace" in the dictionary, I saw several definitions. The one I like best is "divine favor"; in other words, a gift. A gift isn't something you can earn. It's something pleasant that is bestowed upon you. It is beautifully represented in my cat Gracie.

I found Gracie in an animal shelter where I had gone to adopt a cat. I thought snow-white cats were gorgeous, and I really wanted one with long, silky hair that I could brush. I knew exactly what I wanted, but I visited two shelters without finding one. The third shelter didn't have a white cat, either. What it had was a scrawny black-and-white cat with short wiry hair that was falling out. That was Gracie, and she insisted loudly that I take her home with me. So I did.

Gracie taught me a lot about grace. As soon as I got her home, I discovered that she didn't like other animals. She was afraid of my dogs and disdainful of my other cat. Her coat improved with time, but not her attitude. She refused to mingle with the other animals. But here's where the grace part comes in. From the first time I saw her at the shelter, Gracie gave me her love.

She jumped on my shoulder when I passed her and kneaded enthusiastically. She greeted me vocally when I got home from work. It was too early in our relationship for me to have earned her trust, but she gave it to me anyway. When I cried, she rushed to my side to comfort me.

The love of an animal or a small child defies logic—it's not necessarily connected with the way we treat them. In that way, it's like the love of God. We do nothing to earn that love, but it's ours anyway. When one chooses to give you the gift of their love freely, the best thing you can do is to accept it gratefully. Like Gracie's immediate love for me, your love is amazing, a happy surprise. It is a gift of grace I was not even looking for. Grace—a divine favor, a gift I never earned.

Amazing, isn't it?

GINA LEE

My Prayer Rug

Do not be anxious about anything, but in everything, by prayer and petition, with thanksgiving, present your requests to God. Phil. 4:6, NIV.

WORKING IN PAKISTAN IN the 1970s on a one-year special service assignment, I was able to buy a few of their fine products. One item was a beautiful prayer rug. I had seen the Muslims use them, even in the fields where they worked. They would stop the moment they heard the call to prayer from the village loud speaker, roll out their prayer rugs, and kneel on them with their heads to the rug, always facing Mecca. These prayers took place five times a day in the home, in the business place, or in the fields. They began at 4:00 a. m. and ended at night.

My prayer rug was especially pretty with woven designs of a stately mosque in delightful colors and fringed all around the edges. I kept it packed up and took it home to the United States, where I hung it on a wall to enjoy its beauty.

When I later moved to a new place, I packed up my prayer rug to use in my new place. As I unpacked it, I took another look at my beautiful rug and remembered its real purpose. It was then that I decided that if this could be a reminder to pray more often I should—and would—use it that way.

My prayer rug gave my prayer life a new dimension of sincerity. As a praying Christian, I could face any direction and pray to my heavenly Father as Jesus had done. It reminded me to pray more often and to pray especially for those who are using similar rugs. They pray to God, but I can address God as Father and include the Lord Jesus and the Holy Spirit in my prayers. What a privilege to carry everything to God in prayer!

Even though we shouldn't need a rug to remind us to pray, I treasured my prayer rug because it gave me a special reminder to bring my prayers before my Lord in a consistent way every morning, evening, and sometimes in between.

Dear heavenly Father, thank You for giving me the privilege to bring before You my petitions today. Bless all those who do not yet know of Your wonderful grace.

BESSIE SIEMENS LOBSIEN

Reunited

Therefore keep watch, because you do not know on what day your Lord will come. Matt. 24:42, NIV.

THE LONGING TO SEE my sister, Ginger, was intense. I am accustomed to traveling in developing countries and adapting to different foods and customs, but I tolerate it better with a traveling companion. During this trip I had no companion and longed for someone to share the experience. Ginger and I were scheduled to meet in Miami and continue on to Jamaica for a Caribbean vacation. Our well-laid plans fell apart when her plane was delayed and I had to proceed to Jamaica alone. Our plans continued to unravel as my driver traversed two hours of winding, rough roads, and I realized that to hook up with Ginger the next day I would be forced to retrace this journey.

After the difficult drive the next day I waited patiently for Ginger, even though the humidity pressed upon me. I was encouraged because I'd no longer be alone. That thought reassured me. A half hour passed, but I didn't worry. I knew she had to clear both customs and immigration. After 45 minutes, however, I became slightly anxious and requested permission to look inside for her. Permission denied. I checked the monitor. Yes, her plane had arrived. Other passengers were coming out of the terminal. Where was Ginger? Anxiety produced concern when another half hour passed and still no Ginger. The humidity combined with new anxiety became oppressive.

Another hour passed, and I became distressed. After waiting nearly two hours, I again requested permission to enter the terminal to search for her. I was granted permission. She was not with immigration or customs. I finally located her in lost luggage. In spite of all the problems, we enjoyed one grand reunion.

I thought of my intense longing to see my sister. Did I have the same kind of longing to see my Saviour? Would I allow an inconvenience to interrupt time with Him? Would I endure winding, rough roads to see Him? Would I be willing to stand in oppressive humidity to get a glimpse of Him? Would I argue with security guards and press for permission to enter His presence? I have vowed to allow nothing to disturb my devotional time with Him each morning or the longing I have to unite with Him on resurrection morning!

NANCY L. VAN PELT

Vladamir

Be hospitable to one another without grumbling. 1 Peter 4:9, NKJV.

IT WAS HIS FIRST VISIT to Canada. He had come for my son's wedding. They had met and become friends when my son was teaching English in the Ukraine. (That's also where my son met his fiancée.) What impressed Vladamir most was Canada's fresh air. One day as we were walking, he commented again on the fresh air. Fortunately, it was August and not April, because there are a lot of chicken farms where we live. In spring, when the farmers clean out the huge barns, the air smells like dirty socks. But on that particular day the air was clean. I suggested that perhaps he could take some air back with him—in a Ziploc bag.

The days that followed were filled with completing plans for the wedding, which was only four weeks away. I also had the responsibility of preparing meals for three Ukranian houseguests. At one point it felt as if my son was expecting too much of me. Then I remembered him telling me of the kindness Vladamir and his mother had shown him when he visited their home. If this was going to be Vladamir's only visit to Canada, I would do all I could to make him feel welcome. For his birthday I made a banana cream pie, something he had never tasted before. He loved it!

I sent him an e-mail after he returned home, reminding him that he had forgotten the Ziploc bag with fresh air. Yes, he replied, he had forgotten the bag. However, he was sure that one day Bill Gates would find a way to accomplish sending air via e-mail. He was certain, though, that Mr. Gates would never be able to transfer the wonderful feeling of being part of our family, sharing warm and tender relationships, something incredible that he felt during his stay in our home. To this day, he said, he really missed that feeling.

Suddenly it all felt well worth the effort.

Lord, thank You for allowing me to show hospitality to a young Ukrainian man. Thank You for the strength I needed at the time. May I continue to be used by You in showing Your love to others. Amen. VERA WIEBE

Thoughts on a Cambodian Road

Finally, brothers, whatever is true, whatever is noble, whatever is right, whatever is pure, whatever is lovely, whatever is admirable—if anything is excellent or praiseworthy—think about such things. Phil. 4:8, NIV.

TODAY I THOUGHT THAT the road was smooth. I didn't always think that about this particular road. Only two weeks ago I thought just the opposite. The radical change in my view was the result of the adventure I had between the two recent trips traversing the same path.

It started with a seven-car convoy to Veal Veng, one of the last strongholds of the Khmer Rouge. The area had only recently reverted back to the Cambodian government. Land mines had been laid as recently as a few months before. This area was also home to a large tiger population.

After arriving in Veal Veng that night, it started to rain, something it was not supposed to do, as we were in the dry season. The rain made the roads almost impassable. The next morning three cars headed to a village 20 miles (30 kilometers) away. The other four would follow five hours later. Two minutes into our trip, one car was stuck. We hadn't even left the village. We reached our destination eight hours later, only to turn around to see the other four cars driving up behind us. They had caught up with us by our third stuck-in-the-mud episode. After that, the roads improved, and we managed to cover the next 30 kilometers in about an hour. Then our driver got a bit cocky and drove straight into a very large puddle. We were mired in a meter (three feet) of mud. Winches, chains, and military trucks were all used to try to free us. Somehow we managed to burn out our clutch and had to be towed by another car in the convoy for the next 10 hours.

Sin is like a road. When we are used to being in the middle of it for a while, we forget that sin is really ugly. We even see it as exciting. We continue along, despite the dangers. In fact, the knowledge of dangers lurking nearby adds to the excitement. Sometimes the discomfort is buffered by a cloak of normality, like good shock absorbers provide. After a while sin looks so inviting that we put all caution aside and dive right in.

I don't think that Cambodian roads are sins incarnated. They are only catalysts to a lesson worth remembering. CHRISTINE HWANG

Keep as Far From Evil as You Can

Keep thy heart with all diligence; for out of it are the issues of life. Prov. 4:23.

IT'S AN OLD STORY that I first heard as a sermon illustration nearly 70 years ago, but I'm retelling it for the younger generation.

A wealthy widow needed a new coachman to care for her horse and carriage and drive her wherever she wanted to go. She advertised in the local newspaper, and three men applied. She interviewed them separately and found they all had similar references and length of experience, which made for a difficult decision. So she decided on a simple test.

Calling the first man back, she asked him whether he had ever driven a coach around Rocky Mountain, a notoriously dangerous track near her town that had a precipitous drop on one side and a mountain wall on the other. "How close to the precipice could you safely drive on that road?" she asked.

"I've been over that road so many times I could do it with my eyes closed," he assured her. "I could run the carriage wheels within a hand-breadth of the drop and still get around safely."

When the second man was called back, the widow asked him the same questions.

"Yes, I know that mountain road," he said confidently. "I reckon I could drive a carriage within eight or 10 inches of the edge and still get around safely."

When the third man came in to answer the same questions, he replied, "Madam, I know that dangerous road well. I have driven over it many times, and I always keep the carriage wheels as far from the precipice edge as I possibly can."

Guess which man got the job? We are all traveling the danger-beset road to heaven. Our safety lies in keeping as far away from the precipice of sin as we can. We are all guilty of getting too close to the edge in some areas of our life. Let us determine to shun anything that might take us over the precipice.

Dear heavenly Father, please help me to see my "precipice edges" and to keep as far as possible from them. Give me power to resist evil and to keep my eyes fixed on Jesus. Thank You. Amen. GOLDIE DOWN

The Highway Angel

He shall give his angels charge over thee, to keep thee in all thy ways. Ps. 91:11.

FOR WEEKS MY HUSBAND and I had been looking forward to this day—visiting our grandson in prison 150 miles away. It was late summer, and the day was clear and beautiful, so we decided to take the scenic route instead of the interstate. About halfway into the trip, the old Chevrolet van started to sputter and lose speed. After pulling into a small country service station and looking under the hood, we found gas pouring out of the carburetor. It was Sunday, and no mechanic was available. Waiting until the next day was not a viable option.

Out of desperation my husband bought some bubble gum and asked me to chew on it. Feeling very silly, I chomped on the gum for a while. Then he stuck the chewed gum on holes in the carburetor, and we were back on our way. Somehow we made it to the prison.

The visit ended all too soon, and we were back in the old van and on our way home, this time taking the interstate. It wasn't long before the van started to sputter and then went dead. We coasted to the shoulder of the highway, where my husband tried to start the van. After repeated attempts, the battery wore down. The traffic was heavy and motorists were zipping by, leaving us feeling anxious, frustrated, and very much alone. It finally occurred to me that the only thing to do was to pray. *Dear Lord, we need Your help,* I pleaded. Motorists continued to drive by, and it seemed that no one was going to assist us.

Suddenly a young man pulled over and asked if he could help. He looked under the hood, stuck his hand in for a second, then said, "There, that should do it." He hooked up some jumper cables and had us start the car, and he was on his way.

I looked at my husband in amazement, and we too were on our way. Surprisingly, the van purred along and kept right up with the traffic. I was mulling over in my mind that there was no way the problem could have been solved with the touch of a hand when I looked out the window and saw the same young man stopped at the side of the road, helping another stranded motorist.

"Look! There's the highway angel again," I said excitedly. Instantly it became clear to me that my prayer for help had been answered in a special way.

Kathryn Hammond

Stormy Life, Calm Life

Thou rulest the raging of the sea. Ps. 89:9.

OUR SUMMER HOLIDAY WAS fast coming to an end, and it was time to travel back down the east coast to Auckland. We were away in our boat and had spent three wonderful weeks in the Bay of Islands, North New Zealand. The weather had been favorable, and our last night was spent at Kawau Island, a delightful place with several bays providing safe anchorage for boats. However, overnight the weather had changed dramatically, and we awoke to see the whitecaps of the angry waves outside the shelter of the bay. The wind was up to 20 to 30 knots. After breakfast we decided to head for home, hoping the seas would not be too tumultuous.

All went well until halfway across a stretch of open sea from Kawau Island to the next shelter at Tiritiri Maitangi Island. Suddenly the engine stopped, leaving us at the mercy of the conditions. One, two, three tries of the starter produced nothing. Our boat immediately drifted sideways with the wind, and I thought, *It will take only one big wave to capsize us.* The severe rocking of the boat caused drawers to fly open and objects to fall from bunks. The cabin was soon strewn with things that were normally stowed neatly away. I prayed, asking God to please fix the problem with the engine.

My husband climbed out the forward hatch and put the anchor out. It held! He lifted the engine cover and checked obvious things, such as the fuel lines, then tried the starter once more. The engine started! What joy to our ears! Soon we were on our way again, passing Tiritiri and, from there, to the shelter of large Rangitoto Island down a landlocked flat, calm stretch of water, and on to home water to safe anchorage. A few days later we read in the paper that contaminated fuel, innocently sold in the Bay of Islands, had caused problems with many boats over the holiday period.

The stormy experience of our boat trip is similar to life. Sin creeps in as did the dirt into the fuel in our boat. We can be in calm, peaceful conditions, but overnight life changes and becomes tough, rough, and stormy. With God in control, however, we have nothing to fear as He brings peace once more.

LEONIE DONALD

Dolphin Kisses

My soul thirsts for God, for the living God. When can I go and meet with God? Ps. 42:2, NIV.

I WAS BURSTING WITH EXCITEMENT—it was a dream come true! What a way to celebrate our fifteenth wedding anniversary. We would swim with dolphins, and not just swim near them but touch them and do tricks with them.

Arriving at Dolphins Plus in Key Largo, Florida, we were given instruction on dolphin behavior, anatomy, intelligence, and communication. Donning life vests, we slipped into the ocean water two at a time to take a turn with our wonderful new dolphin friends, Bob and Kimbit.

It was awesome being in the water with these graceful, nine-foot creatures of the sea. Sleek and muscular, Bob and Kimbit enjoyed being stroked as much as we enjoyed stroking them. They "stood up" to shake flippers with us, tossed water in a playful water fight, and had fun jumping through a hoop.

The most exciting part for me was being propelled through the water by dolphin power. My husband and I were instructed to link arms and settle back comfortably in the water. Bob and Kimbit put their noses on the sole of one of our feet and skimmed us across their pen. What exhilaration to speed through the water, holding Bob and Kimbit's dorsal fin.

Later, watching the trainers with their dolphins, I noticed what a bond they had. The dolphins were excited to see them and made happy sounds. The trainers could stroke their face and near their blowhole where we had not been allowed to. They could give them kisses and get kisses in return. That's the one thing I missed—I wanted dolphin kisses. As marvelous as my experience had been, I realized I had no deep relationship with these dolphins. I was just another client they did tricks for.

It made me wonder about my relationship with God. Is He just another client that I do religious tricks for, or do I have a deep relationship with Him? Do I get excited when I see Him? Do I let Him know with happy sounds? Do I get close and personal? Do I give Him kisses?

Some day I will skim across the sea of glass with my dolphin friends. But it'll be with greater joy and exhilaration that I finally get close and personal with my God, whom I long to see.

HEIDE FORD

Moving Again

Cast your cares on the Lord and he will sustain you; he will never let the righteous fall. Ps. 55:22, NIV.

THEY WERE GOING SLOWER than the rest of the traffic that Sunday afternoon, the shiny green sports car and the old, worn-out pickup, both with Florida license plates. They were north of Madison, Wisconsin, headed south, presumably home to Florida. The man driving the truck was in his 50s or 60s; the driver of the car was a girl in her 20s. Although the situation was not unusual at first glance, what caught my attention were the contents of both vehicles. The truck was loaded with household belongings. The car was loaded, too—with personal and breakable things.

I began to wonder about the situation. Were they father and daughter? Had the daughter tried school somewhere and, not liking it, was heading home? Had a job failed? Had a college degree finally been obtained? How many times had the father rescued his daughter before?

I then thought of the times my own parents have helped me move. Spending seven years in boarding school and college dorms meant many moves, in and out. Even the times they couldn't help, I always knew their thoughts were with me. When I graduated from college and moved to Chicago, they helped load the rented truck with my belongings. A few months later they drove to my wedding, their own truck loaded with wedding gifts from church and work families.

I thought of other people who have helped me move. While I was pregnant my husband and I moved into a new home across town. Four families of friends helped us move. I was allowed to drive the car and sit on the couch while they arranged things for us, even putting the bed frame together and putting sheets and blankets on for us. Clothes were put in the dresser, dishes in the kitchen cabinets, and other household items put away.

And now I think of Jesus. So many times He has rescued me from one situation or another. Each time, He helps me load my problem on His shoulders and patiently leads me back home. I am reminded of Psalm 55:22, which says, "Cast your cares on the Lord and he will sustain you." I doubt Jesus will carry boxes to the truck next time we move. But I am certain He will be there to carry any burdens I may have, now and in the future.

Marsha Claus

Religion Versus Spirituality

Do not consider his appearance or his height, for I have rejected him. The Lord does not look at the things man looks at. Man looks at the outward appearance, but the Lord looks at the heart. 1 Sam. 16:7, NIV.

DO YOU REMEMBER A time when you canned fruit for your family? You pick the freshest apples, pears, or peaches you can find, either on the tree or at the farmer's market. You want the best for your family—fruit fully ripened, full of flavor and aroma, the kind that won't need much sugar to process. Beautiful, perfectly shaped fruit gives you a sense of satisfaction and anticipation of how wonderful the flavors will be. You take it home, wash it, and begin cutting it up into chunks to be cooked.

But something's wrong. This lovely-to-look-at fruit is rotten at the core! You could never have detected that from the outside. It looked so perfectly shaped, firm to the touch, and colorful. You had no reason to doubt its sweet meat inside. Once it was cut open, though, nothing could be hidden any longer. What a joy when the beautiful fruit is sweet and tasty inside. How disappointing when the inside is pithy, dry, or rotten around the core.

Do we sometimes match this description of beautiful fruit? Are we saying we have the fruit of the Spirit—"love, joy, peace, patience, kindness, goodness, faithfulness, gentleness and self-control" (Gal. 5:22, 23, NIV)—only to have someone open us up and find pride, hatred, and envy inside? It can be revealing to have someone really get to know us on a deeper level and discover our inside rottenness. We try to do the right things, say the right things, and go to the right places so that by outward appearances we are like beautiful fruit. But inside we are wretched.

What will the Lord find inside you today? inside me?

Lord, I pray You will find only sweet, juicy meat inside each of us. May people we come in contact with not be disappointed by our words and actions but see and taste only You reflected in us. LOUISE DRIVER

Lost in the Fog

You will hear a voice say, "This is the way; turn around and walk here." Isa. 30:21, NLT.

RIGHT AFTER SUPPER I set off for a meeting at the library. On the way I stopped at city hall to pick up some notes from my desk drawer. To my surprise, during the few minutes that elapsed between entering city hall and leaving, a thick fog had rolled in from the ocean, obliterating everything in sight. As it wasn't far to the library, I set off confidently but soon realized that I was totally lost. Somehow I'd made a wrong turn and had no idea where I was. Praying for help and not daring to pull over, I opened the car door slightly so I could see the yellow line in the middle of the road. It soon occurred to me I was in the agricultural section of town, with nothing but flower and vegetable fields for miles, the road flanked by deep drainage ditches and no street lights whatsoever.

I knew the only One who could help me was God Himself. Suddenly the car went into a small dip in the road that I recognized as Dawson's Dip, near the gloomy federal prison. Home was behind me, but how could I get turned around in the fog? Again I asked for help, then tremblingly executed a complete U-turn and headed back to the faint lights of town.

Once safely home my husband said the library had called, canceling the meeting when the weather turned bad. But by then I was on my way, and he was unable to get in touch with me. He was on the verge of calling the police when I showed up, shaky but so relieved to be safe again. We realized that but for the fact I recognized Dawson's Dip, I might have been driving around all night. How thankful I was to our loving God for His help when I was totally lost. We can all have the assurance that the One who guides us in this life will surely guide us safely to our heavenly home.

Lord, thank You for steering me to the right destination without harming myself or anyone else on the way. I don't know where I may need to go today or what I may need to do. Please be my guide and lead me safely home.

EDNA MAY OLSEN

Let Go, Let God

Casting all your care upon him; for he careth for you. 1 Peter 5:7.

SHE WAS 87 YEARS OLD, frail and sickly, a woman who complained of anything and everything. She still felt that the world had to do what she wanted. She came from a wealthy family, but tragedy had come. War struck the island where she lived, and many of their properties were either destroyed or confiscated. Because her husband didn't "let go" of the thought of losing their properties, he got sick and died. Elizabeth was left with the children. She did manage to get back some of the properties and was well cared for. But money and wealth have their own limitations—they cannot make one young and strong.

I met Elizabeth while visiting one of the elderly care homes in Cyprus. At first I was not so sure if I would like to talk to her, but I prayed that if the Lord wanted me to befriend this woman, He would open up the way. After a few visits I greeted Elizabeth, and she invited me to her room. I didn't know how to open up the conversation, so I quickly whispered, "Lord, now what do You want me to say?" Words came freely from my lips, starting with a friendly "How are you?" and "Tell me more of yourself and family."

My visit with Elizabeth resulted in a bonding friendship. We enjoyed each other's company so much that I found myself turning to Elizabeth every time I got discouraged or just wanted somebody to talk to. We started talking about God and later developed a prayer chain with other friends. From this experience Elizabeth became a changed person. She was more understanding, cheerful, and loving, and never lost a single opportunity to tell others how good God is. She was often the first one to telephone me during the day and tell me that she had just prayed for me. Her friends noticed the change in Elizabeth and started asking her to pray for them. One thing I'll never forget about Elizabeth was her new motto: "Let go, let God." She told me, "Forget about yourself. Let God take control. Let God do everything; trust everything to Him."

Experience the joy of letting go, and enjoy the peace and joy that results.

Jemima D. Orillosa

Delighting in Distress

For Christ's sake, I [Paul] delight in weaknesses, in insults, in hardships, in persecutions, in difficulties. For when I am weak, then I am strong. 2 Cor. 12:10, NIV.

WHILE MY HUSBAND AND I were touring Michigan's Upper Peninsula late one summer, we noticed that autumn seemed to be arriving prematurely. Everywhere we looked, at least one maple burned red against the evergreens. At Tahquamenon Falls we learned from a forest ranger that these trees were changing early because they were in distress. How strange, we thought, that a tree in distress should be so beautiful.

In the Christian life this is also the case. Often during times of distress a child of God is more beautiful and stands out most noticeably against the backdrop of her or his environment. So it was with Mary, the mother of Jesus. We can only imagine the distress she must have felt when the angel disclosed that through the power of the Holy Spirit she would become the mother of the Messiah (Luke 1:26-35). Surely the marriage customs of the day intensified her distress. Being engaged to Joseph meant that the two were bound to one another as if they were already husband and wife. If during the engagement period anyone could prove that Mary had been unfaithful, Joseph had only two choices. He could bring his bride to public trial and judgment, or he could divorce her. Despite the social stigma and consequences Mary knew she would face when people realized she was pregnant, she replied to the angel, "Here am I, the servant of the Lord; let it be with me according to your word" (Luke 1:38, NRSV).

Just as trees change hues when the increased hours of autumn darkness break down the chlorophyll that keeps their leaves green, so we do not develop trust such as Mary exhibited during sunny times, when everything is running smoothly. We can only wonder about the difficulties, the times of darkness she must have previously endured, that enabled her to stand out so vividly against her environment. We do know that to have accepted God's will for her life, she must have used such situations to find her strength in Him.

Delighting in distress? Yes. For Christ's sake we then will be like the early-changing trees, signaling to passersby that to be His is far more glorious than anything else.

LYNDELLE CHIOMENTI

My Life-giver

I will lift up mine eyes unto the hills, from whence cometh my help. My help cometh from the Lord. Ps. 121:1, 2.

ONE NIGHT THE POWER went off as I sat down for dinner. At the same moment, Neena began to cry loudly. I felt my way to her cradle and picked her up. She felt very hot, so I carried her outside to the lawn where a slight breeze ruffled her hair. Within moments she was asleep again. I stayed on the lawn for quite a while holding her, enjoying the pleasant evening air. At last the electricity came back on, and I went back inside, put Neena in her cradle, and finished my meal.

It was midnight when I awoke with severe stomach pain and rushed to the toilet. Nearly 40 times I returned to the toilet with severe dysentery and vomiting. I became very faint and was unable to walk more than a few steps. I heard Neena cry for her food. I got milk for her but could not hold her, for I was too weak.

"I've got cholera," I suddenly realized. There was a cholera epidemic at the time, and I knew people died within a few hours of the onset of the disease. "I'm going to die if I don't get some help." But I was alone at home without a telephone. I had no strength to go out and call for help. I lay back on my bed and cried out to God. "Lord, help me, or I die!"

I looked around for medicine, but there was only a bottle of something for an upset stomach. I knew I needed more than that, but I took some of the medicine anyway since that was all I had. The dysentery and vomiting continued, and I got only weaker by the moment.

The words of Psalm 121 came to mind, and I used them as my prayer. I called the words as loudly as I could in my weakened condition. " 'I will lift up mine eyes unto the hills, from whence cometh my help. My help cometh from the Lord.' "

Again I took a little of the medicine and lay down on my cot, exhausted. When I opened my eyes it was morning. My dysentery and vomiting had miraculously stopped. I was alive! From that moment, I knew that God had saved my life for a special purpose, and I determined to use it for His cause.

KAJOL BAIRAGI

My Little Children

I tell you the truth, anything you did for even the least of my people here, you also did to me. Matt. 25:40, NCV.

I TEACH AT AN ELEMENTARY school and work with special education children. I love my job, and the children are extremely loving and kind, but they have many needs to be cared for each day. I thank God that He has given me the ability to help these children.

There are other children in my school, too, who have special needs. They come from all walks of life, from homes in which parents have left, died, or are abusive. They hurt for someone to love them.

God has given me the gift of motherly love. I try to use it each day to give a hug, a smile, or a kind word to each of God's children. There is one special boy whose mother left him and his older brother with their dad. He started acting up in class, being disruptive and disrespectful to his peers and teacher. His behavior in the aftercare program was terrible. I saw him crying in aftercare one day, so I talked with him to see if I could help him. When he said he needed a mother to hug him and hold him, I became that motherly person for him. I give him a hug anytime he comes to me at the school. I told him that if he felt he just couldn't go on with his day or if he needed to talk, I would be there for him. He is a very sweet child and still has some trouble coping, but he is better now.

Another little boy in our school, 5, is autistic and had just begun to talk when he saw his father shot and killed. He is a very sweet boy and is again beginning to talk a little since it was discovered he likes animals. I sometimes wear sweatshirts with horses on them, and he loves to talk about the horses.

I thank God each day that I can see the hurt of these children so I can show them a little of Christ Jesus' love for them. "Come to me, all of you who are tired and have heavy loads. I will give you rest" (Matt. 11:28, ICB).

Help me, O God, to be like You so I can give some of Your rest to the little ones around me. Help me to be sensitive to the needs of all others around me. Amen.

JEALANIE DAVIS

Where Are My Glasses?

When she hath found it, she calleth her friends and her neighbours together, saying, Rejoice with me; for I have found the piece which I had lost. Luke 15:9.

WE HAD ATTENDED THE ANNUAL Labor Day parade, and later in the evening I had taken a pair of slacks over to my sister Ruth's house to be hemmed. I noticed I wasn't seeing too well, so I reached up to adjust my glasses and realized they were not there.

When I arrived back home, I looked on the end tables in the den and on the dresser in our bedroom, where I usually laid the glasses, but they were not there. This was more than a casual misplacing of my much-needed glasses. I began a detailed room-by-room search. I even looked in the refrigerator. When my husband arrived home, he helped me look. But we couldn't locate the glasses. When we had our evening devotional time, my prayer included the plea "Dear Lord, please help me find my glasses."

Two days passed. I was due to work at the hospital, and I still had not found my glasses. I did, however, have an old pair I could use in an emergency. By the end of the day the right side of my nose, where I had had a skin graft, was aching from the weight of my heavy old glasses. The second day I again wore the old glasses and was miserable. The next day I called the optical shop at which I had gotten my special lightweight glasses and told them I would be in to order a new pair. I really didn't have the cash to buy new glasses without taking money out of savings, but I knew I had to have the lightweight glasses to prevent damage to my graft.

The next morning I prayed, "Dear Lord, You know where my glasses are; thank You if I find them, and thank You if I do not find them." I dreaded Monday, when I would part with the $298 it would cost to replace the lost glasses.

Later the light on the answering machine was blinking. I pushed the play button and heard, "Little sister, little sister, I found your glasses! Call me." Ruth had found my glasses on the floor of her living room, between an armchair and her daughter's keyboard. They had been virtually out of sight until the Lord drew her attention to the spot where He had safely kept them for me for the past six days.

ROSE NEFF SIKORA

The Watering Trough

If anyone is thirsty, let him come to me and drink. Whoever believes in me, as the Scripture has said, streams of living water will flow from within him. John 7:37, 38, NIV.

HURRICANE GEORGES STRUCK THE island of Puerto Rico with winds of 120 to 130 miles per hour. It left $2 billion of damage in its wake. For 10 hours the island was plundered with winds that left no corner untouched. The next dawn allowed our eyes to glimpse the destruction. It defied description. Gigantic avocado trees were uprooted, mango trees stripped of their foliage, and tin roofing material was scattered everywhere. Twisted utility poles, downed power lines, and mudslides across the road made all travel other than walking impossible.

The major road up the mountain from our home was blocked by a mudslide for six days before one lane for traffic was cleared. My family was without water for 45 days. During this difficult time God allowed me to see a miracle of His love. Our 400-gallon water tank supplied us for two days. Every two days my husband would travel the 1.5 miles to the fire station to refill our water jugs. We carried 150 gallons each trip. He would carry the jugs to the roof and deposit our precious water into the tank.

It was during one of our many trips that I noticed that midway down the mountain there was a stream of water coming through the rocks. It had not been there before the hurricane. Soon the mountain stream was flowing full and strong. People began to congregate there to fill their water bottles and wash themselves. By our next trip I noticed that an enterprising person had made a trough to deviate the water away from the mountain so that it was easier to obtain. It was not uncommon to see 20 to 30 people visiting, talking, and filling their water bottles. Early morning and late night the water trough carried its life for this community; old and young were comforted by its water.

Our water was finally restored 46 days after the hurricane. What a luxury to turn on the faucet and to see the water flowing. The community breathed a sigh of relief. It was a day of uninhibited celebration. What of the watering trough that had provided its precious gift for so long? The water continued to flow one more week; then, just as it had started, it stopped. It has not returned since. For 45 days it was the community well and place of refuge for our burdened lives. CYNTHIA ALEXANDER NKANA

One Impossible Day

With God nothing shall be impossible. Luke 1:37.

STARING AT THE CONFUSION of files that needed sorting, I wanted to scream. Instead, I settled for a weary sigh.

"What's wrong?" my husband asked. "You sound frustrated."

"Yes, I'm frustrated!" I shot back. "There's no way I can finish everything in time to make the plane tomorrow. I want to cry, but I don't have enough hormones to make the tears."

Ron got up and gave me a sympathetic hug. "I'm sorry your hormones are letting you down," he said. "Why don't you just go to bed?"

"I can't!" I said. "There is too much to do. It is impossible, but I have to try. Since we moved to this place, I have faced nothing but impossibilities, one right after the other."

Ron's hug gave me impetus to tackle the files. As I sorted them I began to tally the impossibilities in my life. They covered everything from work to family to health concerns. *It's all too much, Lord!* I thought. *I can't cope.* I thought of all the impossible situations I'd faced over the previous four months. Somehow God had seen me through each one. At that moment God seemed very present, and I heard Him whisper to my tired heart: "Dorothy, have you forgotten that I am the God of impossibilities?"

Suddenly my tears came. I had a good, soul-cleansing cry, realizing that God would somehow see me through my current impossibilities. It was such a release to cry and to sense the Lord lifting my burdens, soothing my stress.

"Glad your hormones are working now!" Ron called cheerfully. "Do you feel better?"

"Yep!" I responded. "I think I'm going to survive."

"That's good news," he said with a laugh.

It was amazing how much I accomplished in the next hour or so. I finally went to bed, then got up early the next morning and finished everything that still needed to be done. I was ready to leave on the plane and left with a sense of peace and a knowledge that God was able to see me through whatever impossible situation I might face in the days to come.

DOROTHY EATON WATTS

What's in a Name?

Adam called his wife's name Eve; because she was the mother of all living. Gen. 3:20.

IT WAS TIME TO GO TO school again. My granny walked me to the corner and kissed me goodbye, but I protested and wanted to go back home. Why would a 7-year-old girl not want to go to school? Because the children at school called me "Granny," "Fatty," and other names. I didn't like their teasing. I would come home in tears and tell my granny, "The children keep calling me names!"

Granny would say, "Tell them, 'Sticks and stones may break my bones, but names will never hurt me.' "

Because most of the children were older than I, I never dared say it to them. When I was 9, I had a very gentle, kind, and loving teacher. I loved her dearly and spent much time with her. She told me that she had experienced similar treatment. She really comforted me and gave me courage.

In naming their children, some parents consult books or name them after famous people. Some parents use ancestors' names; I am one who received such. Fortunately, as I grew older and started reading, I discovered my name in the Bible and was overjoyed at the thought.

Some names are humorous, some are strange, and some are even embarrassing. But no matter what your name is, the Lord says, "Fear not: for I have redeemed thee, I have called thee by thy name; thou art mine" (Isa. 43:1).

No matter what our names are here on earth, the Lord's promise is sure: "I will write on you the name of my God" (Rev. 3:12, NRSV).

Dear Jesus, please write my name in the book of life, and keep me from ever doing anything that would cause You to erase it from that record. And help me always to honor Your precious and holy name by what I do and say, by the way I live, and by the way I relate to others. Remind me that You died for others, as well as for me, and that You love them as much as You love me. Thank You for my special name, too.

PRISCILLA ADONIS

My Victory

Even a child is known by his doings, whether his work be pure, and whether it be right. Prov. 20:11.

GROWING UP IN A large family during the 1930s, there was never enough food to eat or clothes to wear, and just keeping shoes on the feet of so many children was a monumental task for my dad. Because we were poor we could not dress like some of the neighborhood children, so there were times we were picked on and taunted by the school bullies.

One such boy was Francis, who lived in another part of town, even though we all attended the same school. We had tolerated the taunting for some time, and I finally decided enough was enough and to take some action. One day on the sidewalk next to our house I met Francis face to face and lit into him like a mama bear defending her cubs. I had him down on all fours, beating him the only way I knew how—punching, jabbing, kicking, and slapping. But my victory was short-lived. Before I knew it, I saw blood coming from his nose (or was it his mouth—or both?). I got scared and let him get up. He was soon on his way home, and I was the victor. Or was I?

The teasing stopped, and he never bothered us again. I found out later that Francis was a sickly child. He had some physical problems besides the ones I inflicted upon him. The fact that he was a puny young boy was no doubt the reason he was unable to defend himself from my nasty jabs and punches.

I had to admit my actions that day were not my finest hour. I had been taught that 12-year-old ladies do not fight down on the ground like unruly boys, and I was sorry for the way I had behaved.

In the many years since that day I have never allowed my emotions to get the better of me in such an unladylike manner. I was soon to discover it's much more satisfying to patch up wounds than to make them.

Clareen Colclesser

September 7

Soggy Bread or Recycled Blessings?

Cast thy bread upon the waters: for thou shalt find it after many days. Eccl. 11:1.

TODAY'S TEXT WAS THE subject of a heated debate one evening in the college cafeteria more than two decades ago. I recall a question one of my friends asked: "But what will you find? Soggy, waterlogged bread?"

Our responses ran from amused chuckles to pensive deliberations. Unable to leave the question untouched, I said, "Of course not. That bread's waterproof. It has special preservatives!" I was grasping at straws; what I didn't know was how Spirit-filled my answer was.

My parents have developed a charming tradition for family birthdays. Tucked in our birthday cards are dollar bills representing each year of our lives. It does not matter that some of us are 3, others 43, and still others 73.

Just before my birthday my mother asked, "Would you prefer to have a year's subscription to one of our church's weekly magazines?" Recalling the pleasant hours I had spent in her study reading the cutting-edge articles, I promptly agreed.

Every weekend after that, I rifled through each issue, eagerly perusing the pages, then stacking them in piles. Although the piles began to take over our tiny study, I couldn't bear to throw them out. Saving a special few, I decided to give the rest to my friends—casting out the proverbial bread. They seemed delighted. One woman asked for all the ones I didn't want to keep. I learned later that after reading them herself, she took them with her whenever she and her husband went on road trips. She read them to him as he drove. Eventually she gave them to her daughter, who was attending law school several states away. Her daughter shared with others.

I found the bread when I saw the glow on my friend's face as she told me story after story of renewed or newfound faith. I learned then that the bread does, indeed, have special preservatives. What's more, the water on which it is cast develops in us, the casters, the pass-it-on philosophy of a generous mind-set.

Thank You, Redeemer God, for giving us that great mandate. Thank You for faith-filled eyes that help us recognize the gloriously enhanced bread when it comes back to us.

GLENDA-MAE GREENE

Fireflies

When I pray, you answer me, and encourage me by giving me the strength I need. Ps. 138:3, TLB.

I HAD JUST ARRIVED IN Quebec, Canada, the previous night after two long flights from South Africa. It had been 24 hours since I had left home, and my body clock was in total confusion, as Canada is seven hours behind South Africa.

I had come on a mercy mission. My cousin, whom I loved dearly, was dying of cancer. Other than her husband and two sons, she had no immediate relatives in this part of the world. When I saw her emaciated body and she clung desperately to me, I was totally devastated.

It was with a heavy heart that I awoke at 3:00 the next morning with a pall of gloom hanging over me. I was weary, depressed about her, homesick, and feeling discouraged. I looked out the window to find an impenetrable blackness that matched my mood. Wide awake, I knelt beside the uncurtained window to pray. *Dear Lord, please send me a small sign that You are listening to me—something that will lighten this burden on my shoulders. I need You so much.*

I opened my eyes and couldn't believe what I saw. In a small clump of bushes a few fireflies were darting in and out, making a significant difference as they lit up the darkness around them. Skeptics will say this was just coincidence, but for me it was God's answer to my prayer. I thanked Him for such a prompt answer and immediately felt a load lifted from my shoulders.

It is only in the darkness that we truly appreciate the light. How often, when the lights go off without warning, we fumble in the dark and appreciate even the feeble light of a candle. When we find ourselves in the dark tunnel of grief, loneliness, or suffering, how do we seek Jesus, the Light of the world, and appreciate Him? In the storms of life, when we walk through the dark valley or flounder in a sea of doubt and despair, it is the light emanating from Jesus that gives us hope and helps us find our way back to His safety.

The fact that the light is feeble or flickering at times, like the lights of the fireflies, is due to our own lack of faith, for the light of Jesus is always bright and radiant and compelling. *Light my life and my path, Father. I need You.*

FRANCES CHARLES

September 9

God Said No! Or Did He?

The mountains may depart and the hills disappear, but even then I will remain loyal to you. Isa. 54:10, NLT.

MY HUSBAND, OUR TWO GIRLS, and I arrived in Hong Kong for a short visit the Friday afternoon of Labor Day weekend. A taxi dropped us off at the mission hospital, where we were staying, and we collected our baggage. As we were counting the suitcases, the taxi rolled away. Almost at the same moment my husband realized that he had left his briefcase full of passports, tickets, and important papers in the taxi.

We tried calling the taxi company, but alas! There are hundreds of them! When we did get the right company, they couldn't help us. I prayed that the taxi driver would come back, bringing the briefcase with him, but time went by and no taxi. We went down to the Hong Kong police station and filled out the needed paperwork. No one gave us any hope of ever finding what we had lost. My husband called the American Embassy. They were nice, but everything was closed because of the American holiday. They told us we could replace our passports after the holiday.

We decided to continue with our vacation anyway. We saw Hong Kong and met some nice people—and some not-so-nice ones. One woman at the U.S. Embassy helped by showing us around, giving us suggestions and maps to help us find our way around the busy and crowded country. We enjoyed the sights and beauty, but the missing briefcase was always on my mind.

After the holiday we got to the embassy as soon as they opened. They were very kind and helpful. An hour and a half later we had new passports and visas. We were leaving that night, so our next stop was the airport to replace our airline tickets. We got them only at great cost, but we did get them, and finally we were on our way home.

Did God say no? Our mountains (personal things) disappeared. Our hills (personal feelings) seemed to end. But we know God was there. He didn't make that taxi driver bring our things back, but we were safe, and we had new passports, tickets, and credit cards.

When we go to heaven, I have some questions for God! God always takes our sadness and gives us peace. For that I can say, "Thank You, God!"

SUSEN MATTISON MOLÉ

Shut In

Whoever serves must do so with the strength God supplies, so that God may be glorified in all things through Jesus Christ. 1 Peter 4:11, NRSV.

I SPENT ONE NIGHT IN the mission guest room in Calcutta before my flight to Imphal the following noon. In the morning good memories of 25 years in teaching flooded my mind as I walked along the corridor. The sound of running steps broke my thoughts.

"Madam, did you see the principal?"

"No. He may be at home."

"The house is locked."

"Well, he may be somewhere in the school." The boys didn't think so but left hurriedly because school started at 8:15 and it was already 8:05.

I continued my stroll. Suddenly I heard someone call, "Hepzi, come to the window. Take the key. Open the door." Yes, it was the principal behind the locked door in his own house! Immediately I went to the window he pointed to, took the key, opened the door, and let him out.

He thanked me, saying, "A guest staying with me locked the house, thinking I had gone to the school. I called to the boys who came looking for me, but none of them heard me. I am so glad you came this way."

Why didn't the boys hear him? Maybe they didn't expect to see the principal locked in or couldn't see through the meshed window. It reminded me how Satan binds us in sin. He neither wants us to be free from sin nor wants anyone to free us. Yes, there are people who at one time or another, in one way or another, realize their "shut in" condition and cry for help. Do we stop to listen to the cries, however feeble they may be, and offer help?

Some bury themselves in hurt and long for healing. They need words of comfort, encouragement, and support that act like healing balm. Some shut themselves in because of guilt. They need relief from the guilt that boggles them.

Some call for help. Some don't. Dear Lord, tune my ears to hear the cries and sharpen my vision to see the "shut ins" and help them find healing and relief.

HEPZIBAH G. KORE

Your Cluttered Space

Thou, when thou prayest, enter into thy closet, and when thou hast shut thy door, pray to thy Father which is in secret; and thy Father which seeth in secret shall reward thee openly. Matt. 6:6.

WHY WOULD SOMEONE WANT to go into a closet to pray? If I am anywhere near normal, a closet brings to mind a small, confined space. A place where all the out-of-place items get tossed at the announcement of an unexpected guest. It is a place for empty hangers jutting out, half-dirty clothes waiting to be worn the last time, a hiding place for toys that cause conflict, and, yes, freshly laundered clothes. Sounds like a lot of clutter to me!

A closet is also a place in which you wouldn't fit comfortably with someone else. Why pray there? But that's just where Jesus waits for you. Not where things are neat and perfect, but at that place where things just lie, waiting to be fixed.

Here in your closet you'll find thoughts you have not dared share with anyone. Here are habits that only you know are still a part of your life and "half-dirty" attitudes that you have not yet gotten the courage to get clean. There are also empty hangers of decisions still to be made and confessions waiting to be spoken. Hidden "toys" that bring you pleasure at another's expense are there too. And, yes, there are usually a whole host of good intentions needing to be put into action.

What makes this particular closet even more ideal for prayer is that you can actually take its attitude with you anywhere you find yourself alone, where no one else is fitting comfortably with you—doing the dishes, taking a bath, weeding the garden, and even in those still hours of the morning when you can meet Jesus alone.

The truth is, closets are rarely neat and tidy, so Jesus is expecting your clutter. Meet Him there and enjoy the unique experience that awaits you in your cluttered space.

Here I am again, Lord, in the midst of the clutter of my life. Not only do You know all the chaos, You know the solutions. Take me. Clean me up. Organize me. Use me to Your glory. PATRICE WILLIAMS-GORDON

The Homecoming

I go to prepare a place for you. John 14:2.

SOME YEARS AGO AFTER a morning of shopping, my young daughters and I began walking to our car to go home. We didn't know it, but we were being followed. I opened the car door to let the girls in. Before they had a chance to move, a big Siberian husky dog jumped in and made herself comfortable on the back seat. We stared at her, and she stared back. It grew very quiet.

"You'll have to get out," I finally said, pointing to the open door. "You don't belong to us. Besides, we don't pick up hitchhikers."

I knew this dog understood me perfectly. However, she made no move to relinquish her newly found taxi. I pulled on her collar. She didn't budge. I pushed from behind. She didn't take the hint. After pulling and pushing from all directions, the dog reluctantly stepped out onto the sidewalk. We quickly got in the car and took off down the street.

We'd gone only a couple blocks when several automobile horns began honking. While trying to figure out a reason for all the noise, a woman stuck her head out of her car window. "Your dog is following you!" she shouted.

A glance in my rearview mirror revealed our four-legged friend in hot pursuit. "This can't really be happening," I muttered, and began easing my car into a parking place.

"OK," I said as I opened the door. "You win. Get in." I didn't have to ask twice.

Through the number on the dog tag hanging from her collar we obtained the owner's address and made a very special delivery. I watched with pleasure the joyous reunion of the husky and her master. She was so glad to be home!

The scene reminds me of a homecoming I'm looking forward to with my Master. The Lord has blessed His children here on earth. Yet my heart longs for a better home, a heavenly one that He is preparing for those who love Him. I'm excited! He's almost ready to come back and take us there. I can hardly wait for that day. How about you? MARCIA MOLLENKOPF

September 13

Floods of Life

You clothed the earth with floods of water, water that covered even the mountains. At the sound of your rebuke, the water fled. Ps. 104:6, 7, NLT.

MOMMY, THEY'S WATAH COMIN' outtah the sky!" she gasped in disbelief.

My 2-year-old had been born in the desert of southern California near Palm Springs and had never seen rain. On a visit to Grandma's in Atlanta we had gone to the zoo and spent happy hours watching and naming the animals, most of which she recognized from her picture books and our special-occasion treks to the San Diego Zoo. She wasn't used to enclosed buildings to house the animals, but accepted it as one of those variations in life between her home and Grandma's.

We were exploring the big cat house, an enormous edifice housing exotic felines of every description. While we, occupied and oblivious, were enthralled with the wildlife, storm clouds that had threatened all day suddenly fulfilled their thundering promise. Approaching the glass doors, we were greeted with more water than I had seen in one place since I had left Georgia. My daughter saw it with antediluvian eyes: the impossible.

Water—that back home we were so careful not to waste and that quenched our thirst and that we used to irrigate ever so sparingly and right at the roots of just a few plants—now poured from the sky in careless abandon, in frightening abundance. Wisdom dictates that water comes from faucets or five-gallon bottles, not from the sky. Water sprinkles, it doesn't pour; and it just can't fall from the sky. If it did, it might cover us up, wash us away.

I thought about those caught in the Flood when the last high places gave way and the furious forces of nature hurled themselves unopposed at any vestige of life—except the remnant, safe in the ark. I thought about my life when the impossible happened, flooding my soul with despair. Water out of the sky covering me up, washing me away.

"Mommy, hold me!" my little one pleaded. I scooped her into my arms. Safe. Protected.

Abba, hold me! Then I'll be safe—safe in the ark of Your arms.

HELENE HUBBARD

Housecleaning

Search me, O God, and know my heart: try me, and know my thoughts: and see if there be any wicked way in me, and lead me in the way everlasting. Ps. 139:23, 24.

MY HUSBAND HAD JUST taken over a new job as headmaster of a boarding school. As usual, I helped him set up his office. This first thing was to clean up the room, cluttered with books and paper stacked up in heaps on the shelves and on his desk. I went through the piles and sorted what seemed important. I also found many dead cockroaches behind the books in the shelves—*Lying there how long?* I wondered. I then swept, cleaned, and dusted the whole room, amazed at the amount of dirt I collected. After the cleaning, I arranged the books and furniture, making it fit for an office.

The next day I woke early to do my housework before going to my classes. To my surprise, I found my throat was sore and I was able to talk only in a whisper. I still went to class and did all my teaching by writing on the blackboard. My students asked me why I was not talking. I pointed to my throat, and they understood. It took days before my throat healed and my voice came back.

So often we allow our hearts to be cluttered up with junk. We fail to do the daily cleaning. Many times we don't get the broom into the nooks and corners of our hearts. Even dead sins lie there forgotten and unconfessed like dead cockroaches. The windows are closed, and no fresh air or sunshine gets in.

At least once a year we need to check up on our lives and do a deep cleaning. Many times no thorough cleaning is done, and old sins remain behind. Resolutions are made, then forgotten so easily. We fail to rely on God to help clean our hearts. Like David we need God to search our hearts and thoughts and to take full control of us. Let us not fear to ask God to do this, even if the cleaning hurts our ego, as the cleaning did my throat. With the cleansing, God also brings healing and sunshine into our life.

BIRDIE PODDAR

September 15

Time With My Father

Ye shall seek me, and find me, when ye shall search for me with all your heart. Jer. 29:13.

WITH TIGHT STOMACHS WE wandered in and out of the family waiting room on the surgical floor. Would Dad make it through his valve replacement and double bypass? After a short eternity the head surgeon, mask hanging from his ears and below his chin came into the room.

"The family of Mr. Roth?" he asked, looking around.

We quickly rose to our feet.

"The operation went well," he announced. "Even better than expected. Give us about one more hour, and you can go see him. Only two or three family members at a time, please, for only 10 minutes—and just once every hour."

How the hour dragged by! At last a nurse called through the intercom that our family could come in. We followed the nurse to the room where Dad lay, drained of color in his face, and unconscious. Plastic tubes snaked out from his arms, nostrils, lungs, and legs. Fighting tears, we held his icy hands and talked softly, though he exhibited no response. Suddenly our 10-minute visit time was over. The next 50 minutes seemed interminable.

During the second visit Dad's eyes were still closed, but he squeezed my hand in response to a whispered "I love you, Daddy." We had just started our visit, it seemed, when the nurse informed us that the hour's visit was over.

Deprived of my father's presence except for those fleeting 10-minute segments made me want to be with him even more. By the time our last short visit ended and the day's visiting hours were over, I left emotionally drained and with tears of frustration in my eyes.

As I was lying in bed that evening, a realization suddenly struck: I don't have any time limits on visits with my heavenly Father. He's left it up to me to set the visiting hours. Silently I confessed how often I have not taken advantage of this precious privilege of prayer. How often I've spurned spending time in His presence. Lying in the dark, I begged His forgiveness.

Then I asked my heavenly Father to cultivate the same kind of urgent desire to be in His presence as I had experienced while waiting to spend time with my earthly father.

CAROLYN RATHBUN SUTTON

Left on the Bus

I will answer them before they even call to me. While they are still talking to me about their needs, I will go ahead and answer their prayers! Isa. 65:24, NLT.

WHEN I WAS 12 years old my mother fell and broke her leg in five places. I had already started attending church, and one of the elderly sisters took it upon herself to come to our house every morning to get me and my three siblings ready for school and to spend the day cooking, cleaning, and caring for my mother.

One day after school Sister Balsa told me a story while she ironed our clothing. Several years earlier, when Sister Balsa was selling religious books and magazines, she left her satchel with the cash from her sales on the bus. She walked all the way home before she realized that she had forgotten the satchel. Once inside her house, she dropped to her knees and fervently prayed that the Lord would somehow return the satchel to her. While she was still praying, there was a knock at the door. When she opened the door, a young man was standing there.

"Is this your satchel?" he asked as he held it up for her to see.

"Yes, it is my satchel! I was just praying to God, asking Him to bring it to me! Thank you so very much!" she exclaimed.

He handed her the satchel, and she invited him in as she turned to put it down. When she turned around again and looked, he was gone. She looked up and down the street, but he had vanished. There was no one to be seen.

Sister Balsa assured me that it had to have been an angel sent by God in answer to her prayer. This story and others she told me gave my young heart a confidence and trust in the Lord that has never wavered. I thank God for promises that He is there to help us. I also want to thank God for people like Sister Balsa, who share their stories of faith with young people. I want to be someone like that, bringing hope and faith.

CELIA MEJIA CRUZ

A $1,000 Blessing

I will bless the Lord at all times: his praise shall continually be in my mouth. Ps. 34:1.

HONEY, SOMETHING IS definitely wrong with this car. It feels as though we are riding on bricks, and this shimmying when we brake is really worrying me," my husband commented.

Not in a position to buy a new car, we sought to get our 1993 Buick repaired. First we were told by a nearby mechanic that the brakes were bad. Not wanting to take a chance with faulty brakes, my husband authorized the repair, which cost nearly $300. As the problem persisted, the mechanic then told us we needed a front-end alignment, which was another $100. Still the car was riding very roughly, and we were then informed that we needed a new suspension system, which would cost more than $1,000. That definitely was not in our budget.

Finally my husband made an appointment with the Buick dealership to get their estimate. To our surprise, we were told that the suspension system was working perfectly. All we needed was a tire on the rear passenger side. No problem, my husband thought, instructing the mechanic to replace both front tires and put the old ones, which were still in good condition, on the back.

Shortly, the dealership called again. They did not carry that brand of tire. Since we really needed only one tire, we were advised to go back to the place from which we had purchased the four tires less than two years earlier. The cost for two tires, plus mounting, balancing, and rotation, would be less than $200—quite a difference from the price of a new suspension system!

In the meantime I decided to go back home and check our receipt box. Finding the receipt for the tires, I returned to the store and presented the receipt. We learned that the warranty had not expired—we would have to pay nothing for the job. In fact, we got a $45 refund.

Even though the other repairs were needed, we praised God on the spot for directing us back to the Buick dealership, where the real problem was pointed out, saving us more than $1,000. It is a reminder that just as Buick made our car and knows all about it, our "heavenly dealership," the Godhead, made us, knows us, and can fix us, no matter what the problem. May we surrender our lives daily for repair.

GLORIA J. STELLA FELDER

False Alarm

Depend on the Lord; trust him, and he will take care of you. Ps. 37:5, NCV.

IT WAS 6:50 A.M., and we were running late. At 7:10 my daughter was to connect with her ride to school, and I needed to get to work by 8:30. Quickly I keyed in the code of our alarm system and rushed out the door. My daughter, Alicia, was waiting in the car and motioning me to hurry. As I shifted the car from park to reverse to start our commute, Alicia hesitantly stated that she had left her lunch on the kitchen counter.

My first thought was one of immediate scolding, but then as promptly as this thought entered, it quickly faded. I told her I would go back into the house as soon as the alarm had completed its cycle. This would prevent it from sounding as I attempted to open the door. So we waited a moment, then I proceeded up the walkway. As I neared the porch I could hear a piercing sound that was becoming more deafening with each approaching step. Something had triggered the alarm. I entered, keyed in the code that would stop this earsplitting sound, and immediately called the alarm company to report the false alarm. The operator replied, "We will advise the police not to come and that all is OK."

I breathed a sigh of relief and informed Alicia that I would take her to school, and then hurry to work. "But Mom, you'll be late," she warned. Reluctantly I agreed, but continued with the new plan.

To my surprise, I arrived at work with five minutes to spare. At lunchtime a colleague, who occasionally rides with me, asked about my commute. As I began recounting the morning delays, she interrupted me with the story of a major traffic problem on our usual route that had caused her to arrive late. It was then evident that the morning mishaps of a forgotten lunch and false alarm that had forced a change in my travel routine had actually been a blessing in allowing me to arrive at work on time.

Thank You, Father. Thank You for being a God we can depend on, even in the smallest details of our lives, such as arriving at our appointments on time.

Yvonne Leonard Curry

Follow God's Orders

Whatsoever he saith unto you, do it. John 2:5.

MY ERRAND THAT DAY was to take a guest to the airport on the island of Phuket, Thailand. It was a hot, steamy, tropical day, and I was eager to get home and out of the hot car, which had no air-conditioning. I felt impressed to stop at the home of Thompen, one of our church members. He had been in the mission hospital for months, and I had visited him there many times. Because there was no hope for his recovery from tuberculosis, he had gone back home to die. *No,* I thought, *I'm too busy today. Another day I will visit him.* However, the impression was so strong that after I passed the house, I stopped, turned the car around, and drove back to the little dirt-floored shack.

His wife was at work, and I found him lying on his crude board bed, thatched walls and roof allowing in all manner of creatures and dust. He was overjoyed to see me. We talked about the glories of the home in heaven that Jesus is preparing for us and of his assurance of a mansion there. Somehow the dingy, dismal surroundings didn't matter. Thompen rejoiced in faith in the prospects of the bright future waiting him as a Christian. After a prayer I resumed my trip home.

A few days later we learned that Thompen had died. We returned for his funeral. The house was brightly decorated, and many church members and family members were there—but Thompen could not enjoy the beauty and the guests. At the service we talked about the glories of heaven—but Thompen could not hear and rejoice with us. I had been the last representative of the church to visit him. How thankful I was that I had listened to the distinct impression to visit him.

There are times when an opportunity comes to encourage someone. God may, or may not, give a distinct impression, but we can always be alert to the needs of others. Women are often especially gifted to sense when someone needs a helping hand or a word of comfort, sympathy, or cheer. We may share a visit, an invitation, a letter, or food to encourage another. I have learned that whenever God gives such an impression, such an opportunity, I had better do it. RUTH WATSON

Boxes of Promise

I am the Lord thy God which teacheth thee to profit, which leadeth thee by the way that thou shouldest go. Isa. 48:17. Call unto me, and I will answer thee, and shew thee great and mighty things, which thou knowest not. Jer. 33:3.

EVERY TIME WE PACK our home into boxes to move to a different place, I realize that so much of life is lived between moves. We move from one place to another, from one opinion to another, from one attitude to another, from one depth of relationship to another. Each move produces new packing boxes, change, uncertainty, new growth.

Sitting here among boxes, each containing mementos of change, I understand that my experience is not extraordinary. We all experience the ebb and flow of life. What is perhaps extraordinary is that as a believer I can claim a spiritual advantage, just as a visually impaired friend exercises the advantage of a dog and a cane to extend her physical visual range. The events upon my life's horizon from day to day often come as surprises. My visual range is limited—I do not always understand or appreciate the significance of each event, but the Scriptures promise providential leading and information for decision-making. I have a Friend who is willing to extend my visual range, to interpret my surroundings. He can sincerely ask in the face of each new challenge, "Is anything too hard for Me?" (Gen. 18:14), while untangling the complexities that certainly are too hard for me.

When I hear odd noises in my car or my house, when I must weigh competing opportunities or challenges on my calendar, when I contemplate the shadows and packing boxes of the future, I hear whispered promises, reminders that my questions have been answered in the past, that strength has always been given for the immediate task.

Perplexities are occasionally small ones, like the adventure of pressing ahead on an unfamiliar road to see where it leads. There are also larger ones, such as exams, evaluations, injury, and loss that demand our best courage. In either case, we are promised guidance and assistance proportionate to the difficulty. We have a Friend who can extend our visual range, who finds no difficulty too challenging.

STELLA THOMPSON

Baggage

Seek the Lord and his strength, seek his face continually. 1 Chron. 16:11.

WE HAD BEEN SITTING in the Adelaide International Airport waiting for our daughter's plane to arrive from Sydney. As we waited, I idly watched the passengers disembark from planes from other destinations. Most greeted their friends first, and then moved to the carousel to collect their baggage. The baggage caught my attention next. Some passengers had spic and span, very new, undamaged cases; others had well-worn travel ware. Some carried backpacks, and others carried huge bedrolls or cardboard boxes.

I considered the people carrying the baggage, all with the destination of Adelaide. Then in my mind's eye I saw again the worn green baggage that my friend, Leigh, had collected off the carousel two days before. That time was different because I knew the contents of the worn green baggage. It contained only two things: laundry detergent and presents, items that were going to bring joy and satisfaction to their recipients.

That set me thinking about the story of Gideon in Judges 7. God called Gideon to deliver Israel from the Midianites, then told him that he had too many people in his army. Those who were frightened and afraid were sent home. Israel's baggage at this time was their fear. All the travelers I saw at the Adelaide Airport had the same destination, Adelaide, but different baggage.

Spiritually, we are on a journey with one destination: heaven. But we carry different baggage. What is the spiritual baggage I carry? Fear of the future? Do I indulge in criticism or gossip or in a hard, unforgiving attitude? Do I harden my heart against the things that God wants me to do? Whatever it is, I need to take it off the carousel of life and give it to Jesus. He says, "Come to me with all your baggage."

Today I am determined to give all my baggage to Jesus and to let nothing interfere with my relationship with Him. When I have released my baggage into His hands, then I will experience the joy and satisfaction felt by the recipients of the contents of Leigh's old suitcase.

The Sydney plane is landing. My daughter has arrived! MAY SANDY

The Coming Storm

There will be a tabernacle for shade in the daytime from the heat, for a place of refuge, and for a shelter from storm and rain. Isa. 4:6, NKJV.

WE DROVE TOWARD HOME, winding across Minnesota on Interstate 94. The weekend with our daughter and son-in-law had been so pleasant. We reminisced on the happenings of the past days. As we drove on, we watched the sky grow darker with gathering storm clouds in an ominous-looking sky. It seemed as if we could feel the coming storm.

The birds followed their instinct as they sought protection from the storm. White egrets and ducks snuggled under the trees on the west edge of the ponds, a place of safety for them. A little farther along we saw the buffalo gathered around their barn as they too sought shelter. A few miles farther down the road we noticed the llamas had gathered into the barn as they felt the coming storm.

The rain came, driven by strong winds. The windshield wipers worked at their optimum speed, keeping the windshield clear so we could see to continue to drive. The air felt fresh with the cleansing of the rain. It was welcomed, and it was good to have noted the wildlife and domesticated animals all snug in their shelters. God's creatures have been given the gift of instinct to know when they need to seek cover from the storms that assail the earth. They also know where to go to find the safe shelter they need. Farmers and ranchers who raise animals and fowl provide places where their animals can go to be comfortable, warm, and protected.

When the storms of life assail me, I need to know where to go for comfort, shelter, and protection. I trust I am wise enough to seek shelter in the arms of the only One who can protect me. Friends may fail me and family may prove unreliable, but I can always go to the Lord. In the shelter He provides I will find the solace I need.

Lord, open Your arms to me and encircle me with Your love. Keep me safe and sheltered from the storms that beat around me. EVELYN GLASS

September 23

Playing in Concert

God is a God not of disorder but of peace. 1 Cor. 14:33, NIV.

I AM NOT MUSICAL. But for some reason people assume that all pastors' and chaplains' wives can play the piano. Not that I haven't tried. However, when we moved to our first pastorate, I told them, "I don't play or sing—I talk." It has kept everyone happier. This is to tell you that when I go to a concert or symphony I may see or hear things a little differently than some other folks.

Recently I was in Fort Worth, Texas, and was invited to a concert. For a variety of reasons, we were a few moments late getting to the Bass Performance Hall. The Fort Worth Symphony is very strict—no one is allowed to enter late. Not anyone. Not for any reason. The personnel were polite and sympathetic, but we were not allowed to enter until intermission.

We watched the first half of the concert on a monitor in the balcony lobby. We found a bench and pulled it around so we could sit down, but it was so noisy in the main lobby below that we could not always hear the music. Neither was the picture very clear. So I entertained myself by watching the bows of the violinists going up and down in unison and watching the hands of the cello players going back and forth in time with the conductor. I watched carefully to see if I could catch even one performer who was not in time with the others.

I got to wondering what would happen if even one bow would go up or down at another time—if only one musician decided he or she didn't want to play in concert (pun intended) with the rest. Obviously, that person would not last long, and no one would even have to wonder why.

Does this mean that the symphony does not want creativity? Individuality? Not at all. Music is based on creativity. It just means that there is a time and a place to be in time with others, and there are other times for creative endeavor and leadership.

There is a time and place for us to act individually, creatively, to improve things. There are other times when we need to be sure we are in step, in rhythm, in concert with the others. As it says in today's text: "God is a God not of disorder but of peace."

Lord, may I live in concert with Your will this day. May I be in tune with Your timing and in harmony with Your plan for me. ARDIS DICK STENBAKKEN

Big Plans

"For I know the plans I have for you," declares the Lord, "plans to prosper you and not to harm you, plans to give you hope and a future." Jer. 29:11, NIV.

I'M HAVING A MIDLIFE crisis," I mused out loud.

"At 35? A midlife crisis?" my older friends snickered. Their varying comments still echoed in my brain: "A mere babe." "Wait till those hot flashes hit you; then talk to me about crisis." "You're just beginning to live, kid!" Those my age, or a little younger, could be divided into two camps—they were either at the same point and were waiting for to me to say something profound, or they hadn't a clue about what I was feeling.

Now what? I asked the woman in the mirror with the blank face and a few sprinkles of gray. *Where to?* My poor husband offered support and encouragement but couldn't help me. I was always the one with the answers. I was the one with the goals decided, the steps written out. My plans were a veritable road map of what I wanted and hoped to attain. Friends called *me* for advice. Now I felt that nagging feeling that my life needed a change, that I was meant to do more. It seemed to me that I was merely treading water. My mantra through graduate school had been "I am destined to be the boss." But boss of what? That was the part I felt the Lord hadn't told me. "Hey, up there!" I yelled irreverently one day. "Boss of what?"

I must admit that the answer hasn't come quickly. There's been no flash of light or voice from above telling me which opportunity to pursue. No, it's been more like a slow dawning. It's been a journey of discovering myself and allowing God to teach me anew that His way isn't necessarily my way, and His timing may not be mine.

I've come to term this as the Moses syndrome. It took Moses 40 years to unlearn many qualities and to be prepared to be used by God. Journeying with Jesus is always interesting when you allow Him to lead. During one early-morning worship session I discovered Proverbs 16:3: "Commit to the Lord whatever you do, and your plans will succeed." I began to understand Jeremiah 29:11: "For I know the plans I have for you, . . . plans to prosper you and not to harm you, plans to give you hope and a future." *Help me to follow Your plan for me for today, Lord.*

Maxine Williams Allen

Brownie

Where can I go from your Spirit? Where can I flee from your presence? Ps. 139:7, NIV.

ONE OF MY COLLEAGUES gave my husband a little brown dog. She was so small and beautiful, with big brown eyes and fluffy brown hair. Her little white paws looked as if she were wearing tennis shoes. How we loved her! When we went shopping, Brownie would be on our minds. We bought many little things for her, as if she were a newborn baby. I even used two of my white Tupperware dishes for her food and water. We really took good care of her and trained her to do certain things.

Much to our disappointment and dismay, Brownie didn't want to stay home. She enjoyed wandering around the neighborhood. Most of all, she loved Lazzy, our neighbor's little boy. Usually she came home for meals and water but would then disappear again. Eventually she didn't come home for anything anymore. She followed everybody on the campus. She started eating out of garbage bins and even began sleeping out. I literally would have to go look for her, pick her up, and bring her home. But she would run away again.

One day, however, she disappeared for good. We think she might have followed someone off the campus, or someone might have stolen her. We had been touched by the loss of this little dog that we grew to love so much.

Many of us are like Brownie. We run away from the Lord, no matter what blessings He bestows upon us. He wants to give us His white robe of righteousness, but we love our sinful rags. We want to follow the pattern of this sinful world and ignore the promise of a mansion that is being prepared for us.

Let us return to the Lord right now before we are stolen forever by the devil and miss out on heaven. Our Master loves us, has paid a price for us, and wants us home with Him.

Heavenly Father, I've wandered too many times. I ask for Your forgiveness. I want to stay close to You today, because I do not want to get lost.

ZODWA KUNENE

Labels

As believers in our glorious Lord Jesus Christ, don't show favoritism. James 2:1, NIV.

IT WAS A NEW SCARF, a thoughtful gift from my daughter-in-law. I carefully chose a vest and blouse that would best enhance the scarf's soft yellow color. When I tried to tie the scarf, though, the ugly black label stuck out like a sore thumb. First I tried a graceful bow. As I looked in the mirror, the label seemed to be waving at me. Then I tried a plain square knot. The label was again too obvious. Labels, labels! What a bother they can be. Some scratch my neck so that I am forced to cut them out of the garment. Often, however, that leaves an uncomfortable remnant that continues to irritate my neck. Some labels fall out immediately, leaving me to wonder about the best way to clean the item.

In some countries, if one speaks with a foreign accent, he or she is immediately met with prejudice. Their accent is a label. In Russia, where my husband and I used to live and work, it was common to see brown-skinned men stopped by machine-gun-carrying policemen. Just the color of their skin and eyes or the shape of their face was reason enough for these men to be stopped. A Filipino man who worked in our office dared not leave the building without his passport and visa. He was frequently stopped because he didn't look like a Russian. Even the license plates on automobiles that belonged to foreigners were a different color than those on the cars owned by nationals. My own country, as well as many other countries, has a horrendous history of slavery and prejudice based merely on a person's genes. Labels, labels!

Much harm is done because of negative feelings caused by labels. The other side of the coin can be equally detrimental. Do we favor people because of their wealth, their dress, or their position? Do we give better treatment to an individual wearing a Rolex watch than we do to someone who has offensive body odor?

James tells us that favoritism is forbidden. Is there a label that is keeping you from a closer walk with God? Is there a label prompting you to sin? Pray about this so that those who see you can give you the labels of fairness, mercy, and kindness.

BARBARA HUFF

There's Always a Reason

[God's] ears are attentive to our prayers. 1 Peter 3:12, NIV.

THE BUSGIRL WAS PETITE and efficient. Melissa commented several times about the excellent service. Our water glasses were always topped off, the muffin basket was filled repeatedly. Momentarily distracted from her birthday breakfast, Melissa watched diners at the next table spread thick shiny globs of English orange marmalade on their French toast. "I'd like to try that," she announced, and promptly waved at the busy girl. "Please bring me some marmalade."

Five minutes later the marmalade had not arrived. "I want to try this stuff while my pancakes are still hot," Melissa said impatiently.

"There's always a reason for behavior," I offered, "even if we don't know what it is."

Melissa was out of her chair in a flash, repeating her request to the busy girl who was pouring water three tables away. She disappeared. No marmalade arrived. "This is patently ridiculous!" Melissa said (I coughed into my napkin at the use of the word "patently").

But within moments our waitress came to the table and asked, "What can I get for you? Janna thinks you want something."

"I do," Melissa replied. "Twice I've asked for orange marmalade." There was a slight hesitation and then a brief explanation. Janna had been beaten during childhood. Repeated blows to her head had resulted in deafness. She was learning to lip-read, but didn't know "marmalade."

The marmalade arrived. While Melissa sampled it, we talked about what her world would be like if she had a hearing impairment. When it was time to leave the tip, Melissa pulled a crumpled dollar bill from her pocket. It had long been earmarked for root beer candy on this special day. Now, however, she handed it to the waitress. "This is for Janna."

"Janna doesn't want anyone to feel sorry for her," the waitress said.

"Just tell her," Melissa replied, "this is for her excellent service on my birthday."

At bedtime Melissa expressed gratitude for her ability to hear and for God's ability to hear us. And she prayed for Janna. The birthday breakfast had given Melissa more than pancakes. ARLENE TAYLOR

Five O'Clock on Five-Cent Sunday

[She] and all [her] family were devout and God-fearing; [she] gave generously to those in need and prayed to God regularly. Acts 10:2, NIV.

SINCE THE ARRIVAL OF the computer in our home, family and friends have given up in exhaustion trying to reach us by telephone. We get e-mails stating exactly that. Talking with my mom on the phone is so rewarding for me, and I shall not be denied. Our long distance plan enables me to call her anytime for a Canadian dime per minute, and her long distance plan enables her to call me on Sundays for five U.S. cents a minute. I call her for quick visits during the week, and she phones me on Sundays at 5:00 so that we can talk as long as we want.

We share everything that's on our minds. We even pray together over the phone, making a three-way connection to heaven. By the time our conversation ends, we feel Jesus' loving arms surrounding our precious family. Sometimes we reminisce. Yesterday Mom told me something very special about my grandma, who passed away several years ago. Grandma had lived with Mom for a while after Grandpa died. Mom said that Grandma prayed before each meal, usually silently, because she was deaf. At times my mom actually thought Grandma had fallen asleep at the table, but she hadn't. Grandma's prayers were long because of the concerns she felt for her children.

I shared with Mom that I've started viewing important issues a little differently lately. I sincerely believe that Jesus does not leave His children in this war zone one second longer than necessary. Mom said that this was a good way to face the reality of death, should Jesus not come before we are laid to rest.

I look forward to another special get-together also. Jesus is waiting for us at church (a weekly family-day affair) prearranged like 5:00 on five-cent Sunday. The entire day is mine to talk with Him and to fellowship with other believers.

In advance, Jesus prepaid all the toll charges at Calvary, including even the quick little prayers. If you are connected to Jesus, He is your lifeline to eternity. Amen!

DEBORAH SANDERS

September 29

Prayer Deposit

It shall come to pass, that before they call, I will answer; and while they are still speaking, I will hear. Isa. 65:24.

IT WAS A TUESDAY, payday. I had written a number of personal checks that would clear the bank that very night, so getting my paycheck in the bank was of great importance. I left the office late, then there was unusually slow traffic. At six minutes before 5:00—and with 10 minutes' drive time remaining—I was clearly losing the race against time.

When I pulled into the parking lot of the credit union, the woman was standing at the doors. My clock said she had already locked the doors, but my prayer was that she hadn't. The former was the fact. As I approached, she lipped to me from the inside, "I'm sorry; we're closed."

As I wondered what to do, the woman let a couple on the inside come out. I stole the opportunity to beg her for mercy. Looking compassionately at me and fearfully at the tellers, she responded with her well-rehearsed line, "I'm sorry; we're closed!" and pulled the door shut. I prayed and stayed at the door. I thought, *She must hear hundreds of pleas every day. What makes mine special?* My plea may not have been special to her, but it was special to my Saviour. Seeing my dilemma and knowing my situation, He stepped in and spoke to her heart.

During one of the stolen moments, she mentioned the night drop. I asked where it was and when it would be posted. "Around the corner, near the drive-through," she said. "Posted tomorrow."

I quickly spoke again: "That's too late. I need this deposit to be posted to my account tonight." The fact that she even entertained conversation was my indication that the Holy Spirit was courting her heart on my behalf. Then the same Holy Spirit that was speaking to her heart spoke to my head: "Ask her if *she* would make your deposit for you."

She said yes. But in my haste I had not signed my paycheck nor completed the deposit slip. Neither she nor I had a pen. But when she cracked the door just enough to take my unsigned paycheck and my incomplete deposit slip, our eyes locked, and we both understood and agreed.

From my car phone I called the automated teller system and requested my account balance. She had made the deposit for me immediately.

Patricia R. Brown

A Glimpse of Eternity

I tell you, there is rejoicing in the presence of the angels of God over one sinner who repents. Luke 15:10, NIV.

SHE HAD HELPED ME stuff 42 welcome bags for my company's retreat after I had reprimanded her for calling me downstairs because she had a question. "You should come upstairs to talk to me. I'm busy packing for my trip," I scolded.

The tension spun us both, mother and woman-child, into an argument with me having the last word: "Because I'm the parent and you're the child." Then I went back to packing.

And it was after I had barked a command, telling her to shower and dress. She needed to be ready by exactly 3:15 so her father would have time to fight the Sunday afternoon football game traffic to take me to the airport.

And it was after her shower that she came and sat near me. "Are you busy, Mom?"

"Um-hum." I pulled out the cash and credit cards and arranged them in the travel wallet. Her hair was wet and clean. Nearly all of it was pulled into a ponytail. Two symmetrical strands refused to be corralled, and they cantered around her almost-12-year-old face.

"Can I ask you something?"

"Um-hum." Driver's license and business cards went into the wallet next. In my distracted state I hadn't a clue that at that moment one could hear a pin drop in heaven.

"Mommy, can I be baptized on my birthday? Because the thirtieth of October is on Sabbath. So I thought I'd like to be baptized then. Would that be OK?"

My mother-heart was laid open. "Why, sweetheart! Yes, of course. And if you did that, it would be as though you were giving Jesus a present on your birthday. It would be an answer to your dad's and my prayers."

She had such a look of contentment on her face. I pulled her close. The cheers in heaven were deafening. All the angels were high-fiving each other and throwing their halos up in the air.

And I got a glimpse of eternity.

SHEREE PARRIS NUDD

Jewels in the Word of God

But when you pray, go into your room, close the door and pray to your Father, who is unseen. Then your Father, who sees what is done in secret, will reward you. Matt. 6:6, NIV.

IT'S AMAZING HOW GOD teaches us through His Word, directing every desire of our hearts toward Him. Sometimes we discover a special gem for ourselves as we read Scripture, but often He uses people to lead us to the Scripture that will fill our need. It may be a book we are reading, a sermon we've heard, or a friend's comment. And sometimes that understanding may brighten up our whole lives, and we never forget it.

It happened that way for me the morning I discovered the five principles for prayer that Jesus gave in the one short verse that's our text for today, Matthew 6:6.

"When you pray," Jesus said. He wants us to set aside a special time for prayer.

"Go into your room," He adds. Have a place for prayer.

"Close the door," He goes on. Everyone should have a private time with God. Praying with family and friends is important, but nothing can take the place of time shared only by you and God.

"Pray to your Father, who is unseen," Jesus instructs us. We're not just praying into the air—or even just to a higher power. We are to pray to Someone we know, our Father.

And then the glorious climax of this little five-point jewel: "Your Father, who sees what is done in secret, will reward you." It's a guarantee. Jesus said it—God answers prayer.

The reason this insight means so much to me is that it's so simple I've never forgotten it! It's short and easy to share. Not only can I remember it, the people I tell will also remember it. I usually explain that Jesus spoke these words in the middle of one of His few recorded sermons, the one we call the Sermon on the Mount. That way, even if we forget exactly where the scripture is found, we can easily find it again.

Jesus always had something uplifting to add to any conversation. So should Christians. Storing our minds with gems of Scripture makes witnessing easier. And when others recognize our excitement about God's promises, they may respond and search His Word too. CARROL JOHNSON SHEWMAKE

The Weed Wacker

I can do all things through Christ who strengthens me. Phil. 4:13, NKJV.

SHE WAS NOT QUITE 5, and she had spent the night with me, her nana. Of course I adore her and enjoy spending time with my little Megan. We had stayed up late the night before, so she was still sleeping when I woke up in the morning. I carefully eased out of bed and quietly got dressed. Then I got a hoe and went out to start some weeding before the sun got too hot.

When Megan finally climbed out of bed, she started looking for me. Her auntie helped her dress, then led her to the back porch, showing her where I was. Meggie ran out and stood watching for a while. Then she asked, "What are you doing, Nana?"

"I'm digging up weeds." I knew what was coming next.

"I want to help you," she said, reaching for my big hoe.

I wished for a little one, just her size, but since I didn't have one, I let her take mine.

"Show me a weed," she requested. She lifted the heavy hoe as high as she could and whacked the ground with it, completely missing the unwanted plant. Before she could be disappointed with her efforts, I quickly pulled the weed by hand and thanked Megan for her help. She aimed at two or three other weeds that I also pulled, then wandered off to look for something else to do.

My efforts are very much like that in God's sight. How willingly He takes my feeble human efforts and perfects them. Jesus explained this principle when He was talking to the multitude who had come to listen to the Sermon on the Mount. He said, "If you then, being evil, know how to give good gifts to your children, how much more will your Father who is in heaven give good things to those who ask Him" (Matt. 7:11, NKJV).

Sometimes I want to help Him, and I really try to do my best, but my best falls short of what is needed. I realize I have not succeeded; then, to my amazement, everything turns out better than I had expected. I think those must be the times God gently takes over the task and does it for me while allowing me the gift of enjoying the results of my efforts.

MILDRED C. WILLIAMS

October 3

He Cares

Cast all your anxiety on him because he cares for you. 1 Peter 5:7, NIV.

AS I FINISHED MY DEVOTIONS early one morning, I looked through the sliding glass door to see our cat playing with a baby toad on the deck. Every time the toad tried to escape, the cat batted it with his paw. I tried to distract the cat, but the distance the toad had to travel to get away was too far. Finally, I grabbed a splinter of wood from the kindling box and went out, scooped the toad onto the stick, and put it on the lawn. At last it was free from its tormentor.

Back inside, I thought, *I wish someone would come to my rescue.* I was always the one helping other people and listening to their problems. Now I was feeling very much in need of someone who cared enough to come and save me from my feelings of loneliness.

There was no time to waste on those thoughts, though, because I had to finish getting ready to leave for work. In less than an hour I would be in my classroom, facing students, and my needs had to be put on hold. *A Christian teacher in a Christian school shouldn't feel the way I do,* I scolded myself.

It was the last day of our Week of Prayer, so after taking attendance I dismissed the students to go to their final meeting and started down the hall after them.

"I've been looking for you," a familiar voice called out from the other end of the hall.

It was my longtime best friend whom I hadn't seen in months. She just "happened" to pick that day to drop by the school to see me. I just "happened" to be able to spend half an hour talking with her while my students were occupied. And she just "happened" to give me the lift I needed that particular day by showing me someone did care enough to connect with me.

And Someone cared enough to arrange both our schedules so we could meet according to His plan. DONNA MEYER VOTH

For His Own Purposes

Now there are varieties of gifts, but the same Spirit; and there are varieties of services, but the same Lord; and there are varieties of working, but it is the same God who inspires all of them in every one. To each is given the manifestation of the Spirit of the common good. 1 Cor. 12:4, 7, RSV.

ONE OF MY MOST STUNNING experiences of knowing that God uses my black robe for His own purposes was the morning I substituted as the judge in a division outside my normal assignments. The Department of Children and Family Services brought my friend's two young granddaughters' case before the court. The department alleged that the girls' mother had abandoned them, so the girls were placed in emergency shelter care, awaiting a court order to place them in a foster home.

When I recognized the family's name, I asked the department if they had contacted the grandmother. They hadn't, because they didn't know where she lived. Only the weekend before I had eaten at her home and remembered being impressed to make note of her address. I gave the caseworker the grandmother's address, directing her to notify my friend about her granddaughters' dilemma, then continued the case to the next day.

When my friend appeared in court the next morning, she requested that the children be placed in her custody, which I did. In addition, I directed the department to provide her immediately with services that normally take weeks to receive. Today her granddaughters thrive in her care.

What were the chances of my being on the bench when these children were brought before the court? What were the chances that I knew where the grandmother lived? What were the chances that I would know both the services available and the necessity of ordering that the services be immediately provided? What if I had not been the substitute judge that day?

I am not always privileged to know the rest of the story, but I am confident of this: Because I begin each day with a prayer to be used by God for His own purposes, some day the curtains will be torn down, and in heaven I'll rejoice to finally know why I was sent to the bench for such a time as this.

JUDITH W. HAWKINS

As a Little Child

I tell you the truth, unless you change and become like little children, you will never enter the kingdom of heaven. Matt. 18:3, NIV.

AUTUMN HAD COME TO our little farm, and the walnuts were beginning to fall to the ground from the two trees we had planted many years before. I knew I must gather them soon or the squirrels would beat me to them. So one afternoon I took a bucket and began to pick up the nuts from the ground, one by one. Soon my neighbor saw me and came running out of her house.

"Oh, let me help you pick up the nuts! I really know how to do a good job at picking up nuts."

For just a moment I felt irritation because this woman, a grandmother and almost my age, was acting like a little child. Then God spoke to me. "If this was your 7-year-old granddaughter, you would be glad for her help and accept her actions. You know that Lou's mind isn't as good as it once was, so accept her as you would your own grandchild." Soon Lou was even climbing up into the trees to pick some of the nuts that were still clinging to the branches and throwing them down to me. And she was having such a good time that I couldn't have spoiled her fun if I had wanted to. By then I was enjoying her help.

Sometimes I have found myself judging older people by the way they act until I realize that we all seem to come full circle. We start out as babies, become children, and eventually reach adulthood. As the years pass and mothers become grandmothers and great-grandmothers, we gradually become more childlike. Our children now reverse the role and start telling us what to do. And many times that help is really needed.

Father, help me to have love for and patience with the children, both young and old. And help me to become humble and teachable as a little child so I may enter Your kingdom. Let me find ways to give simple pleasures to others. Help me to share my energies and give others opportunity for happiness, however small it may seem to me. Teach me to treat them as You would.

Betty J. Adams

Lessons From an African Violet

Yea, they may forget, yet will I not forget thee. Isa. 49:15.

MY NEIGHBOR, ARLENE, LOVED houseplants. So did I. We shared a common backyard fence, and over it we exchanged small plants, oven goodies, and occasional gifts. When she and her husband spent time away, I was delighted to care for their plants. She did the same for us. One spring my husband and I scheduled a two-week trip, and, as usual, our plants went next door. We were ready to drive away when I noticed a frail African violet sitting in the window. It hadn't thrived well, so I hastily deposited it under a shrub near the patio, sheltered from direct sun. I knew it wouldn't survive—African violets are temperamental—but I would consider it no loss.

Fall came, and we settled into a more stay-at-home pattern. There was catching up to do. Leaves had collected around bushes; shrubbery needed to be trimmed and roses cared for. I devoted the day to it. *Surprising how much can accumulate,* I thought, as I piled clippings and leaves together in a heap to haul away. Only one area remained, and I was weary, but I was determined to finish before supper. As I trimmed the last overgrown shrub, something purple and beautiful caught my eye. Tiny yellow centers seemed to sparkle out at me. To my surprise and joy, I reached down to reclaim the violet I had long since forgotten. I couldn't believe my eyes! Through the heat of summer, that dear little African violet had not only survived, it had grown large and beautiful. Now covered with delightful blossoms, its lovely deep-green leaves spread in perfect symmetry. God had taken special care of this little plant I had neglected, and I knew He had designed it to be a unique lesson just for me. Never again was my African violet forgotten. Sitting in beauty in my choicest spot, it became a cherished symbol of God's never-failing care.

I have had African violets since, and now they carry a very special meaning. At times when I have most needed His guidance, my loving Father seems to provide me with one, and each time it has flourished beyond my expectations and touched my heart.

God speaks in many voices, but the voice I love most is His gentle whisper through a purple, yellow-centered African violet. LORRAINE HUDGINS

Flying Kites

Here am I and the children whom the Lord has given me! We are for signs and wonders in Israel from the Lord of hosts, who dwells in Mount Zion. Isa. 8:18, NKJV.

WALKING ON THE BOARDWALK next to the beautiful beach of Long Beach, New York, on a sunny Sunday afternoon, I enjoyed watching a few families flying kites. I could see a daddy running, being very effective in his task. Other groups were led by mothers who had to work harder to obtain the same result.

My two boys are professional men now, but I remember trying to help them fly kites years ago. I really didn't enjoy it much. I got tired running, got angry when the kite didn't fly the moment I wanted it to, and once it was in the air, I got bored holding the cord.

Now I wish I had flown more kites. I wish I had spent more time with my children sharing adventures, rejoicing with their smiles seeing the tense cord, wiping their tears (and mine) when the kite fell to earth. I believe most memories my children have are happy, but they also may remember a mother too busy to play or listen or kiss their sore knees often enough.

If I had the opportunity again, I would fly more kites in the fall, put together more puzzles in the winter, camp out more in the summer, and ride more bikes in the spring. I would leave many things that I enjoy undone in order to spend more time doing the ones they like.

If I had the opportunity again, I would pray more with them, not only for them. I would not force them to eat broccoli. I would give them more opportunities to buy the clothes they like. I would negotiate more instead of ordering and imposing. I would listen more to their arguments.

If I could go back in time, I would have the house full of noisy children, organize more slumber parties, drive their friends back and forth. I would watch less TV and read more books. I would sing more hymns with them and would make sacrifices to pay for their music lessons.

I would give more compliments and bite my tongue to avoid negative comments. I would bite it even harder if tempted to scream or insult. I would tie my arms if I felt like hitting. And I would talk more of the love of Jesus every day—during worship in the morning, at night, all the time. And I would give them a good example so they could see Jesus in me. ALICIA MÁRQUEZ

The Tree Lesson

I am the vine; you are the branches. If a man remains in me and I in him, he will bear much fruit; apart from me you can do nothing. John 15:5, NIV.

I DECIDED TO STAY HOME today. My Bible study brought me to the conclusion that nature had something to teach me. I remembered the Bible saying something about going to the ant and being wise (Prov. 6:6), so outside I went. I had watched a particular tree from my basement apartment. From time to time, youngsters would pick the fruit off the tree. Now I sat on the steps and looked up at this tree, its leaves floating down in an autumn breeze. I didn't know what kind of tree it was—to me its leaves looked like leaves from other trees. I looked at its bark and its root pattern. It only impressed me how sturdy the tree looked for climbing. If I hadn't seen the fruit earlier that year I wouldn't have known this was an apple tree.

The spiritual lesson shocked me. Matthew 7:20 says: "Thus, by their fruit you will recognize them" (NIV). Do people know what kind of Christian I am? I started to panic. *Lord, where are my fruits? Haven't I done anything for You so that people will know I belong to You?* I looked at the strong root again and wondered how sturdy and rooted I was in the Word. I looked up at the branches at the top of the tree and wondered when was the last time I had reached for the Son. Here I was feeling sorry for myself, wondering where my fruits were, when all He asked was for me to remain in Him.

I was distracted from my pity party by a friend who came to see where I had gone. I explained what I was doing and what I had learned about myself. With compassion and understanding I was told that I helped out in church many times with little asking. I was a friend to the friendless. I share the Word of God with others and have a way of making people laugh, cheering them up. I felt better, but I remembered that fruit doesn't grow overnight. There is a certain maturation process, and I don't have to do much nor do I need to see my own fruits. It matters what Jesus sees, and Jesus says that if I remain in Him I will bear much fruit. It may take some time for me to see the fruit on my tree, but I am blossoming.

TRUDY SEVERIN

Canceled

Rejoice in the Lord always. I will say it again: Rejoice! Phil. 4:4, NIV.

I LOOKED OUT OF THE plane window over Salt Lake City. How I had wished to see the sights of that city, but I'd been told that with my kind of ticket I could not take a stopover there. It was so close, and yet I would not be able to get there!

I had only an hour to change planes, so I hurried to my connecting gate and made sure I was in the right place, then went off to the bookshop across the hall. A book caught my eye, and when I had paid for it, I looked over at the gate. My flight number was nowhere to be seen. The flight had been canceled! The airline personnel booked me on the next flight, which was scheduled to leave two hours later, and gave me a calling card and a meal voucher. I called my brother, who was going to pick me up at the airport, to inform him of my new arrival time and dashed down to the city information desk.

"How long would it take me to get to the city?" I asked the friendly woman. She gave me the necessary information, as well as a map of the city center, and recommended I go to Temple Square. The taxi driver even promised to come and pick me up at a given time so that I would be sure to get back to the airport on time for my flight. I was so excited! I was getting to see what I had hoped for! I was glad my flight had been canceled, and I thanked God for giving this bonus trip to downtown Salt Lake City.

Later on the plane I overheard a couple bitterly complaining to the cabin crew about how badly they had been treated by the airline that night. Of course, their situation was different from mine, but I suddenly realized how easy it is for us to get upset about little—or even bigger—things and make ourselves totally miserable. What was a treat for me was an annoyance for someone else. It all depends on attitude. I could have fretted about the delay and made myself miserable as well. I do not have to be a victim of the circumstances; I can decide to rejoice every day. There is always something to rejoice about, even if it's only something that isn't quite as bad as the rest of our lives! Let's try to see the good in all circumstances and take that as a divine bonus. It will make our day a happier one.

HANNELE OTTSCHOFSKI

Knitting in the Dark

Then Jesus spoke to them again, saying, "I am the light of the world. He who follows Me shall not walk in darkness, but have the light of life." John 8:12, NKJV.

BY THE TIME I WAS about 12 years old, I had lost my mother, a stepmother, and an 18-year-old brother. Each day for each meal I walked about three miles to eat with my girlfriend's family. I liked it much better than eating at a restaurant all alone. And my girlfriend's mother was a mothering person who had nine children of her own, yet was willing to mother me.

My girlfriend and I were very competitive. We both liked to knit, and each of us was sure she could knit faster and better than the other. That wasn't all. We liked to do it in the dark! Her house had a bathroom with no window. We would go into the dark bathroom and knit for a certain period of time (we usually had her mother time us), then measure to see who had knit the most during that time. And it had to be without any mistakes.

Knitting in the dark? Sounds like foolishness, you say? Well, I did learn to knit really well. But aren't we like that much of the time in our spiritual lives? We walk in the dark when we could have the light of Christ in our lives. We fumble around instead of getting to know Him, the source of our light. During a satellite evangelistic series, I offered to be one of the Bible counselors online through the Internet. I personally answered more than 70 questions for that event. It was very enlightening. So many people are searching for God's truth.

Last year I began to study my Bible in an entirely different way. Now, I had read my Bible through a number of times (I will admit that I tended to skip the "begats"). For the first time, I started keeping a notebook while reading the four Gospels. I'm only to the book of Luke, but I have found many spiritual lessons I never saw before. Taking time to write down what each verse means to me in my life has helped to lead me to His light.

Lord, sometimes we get tired of the same old way of studying even Your Word. Help us to try new ways of communicating with You. I know You will be there to bless us.

LORAINE F. SWEETLAND

Hide the Word

Your word have I hidden in my heart, that I might not sin against You. Ps. 119:11, NKJV.

I AM INVOLVED IN A chaplaincy program in a maximum security institution. In the beginning I used my acoustic guitar to accompany the singing as a refreshing prelude to the Bible lesson. One evening, however, the security staff on duty informed me that it was no longer safe to take the instrument to the restricted areas. The participants were disappointed. For the next few sessions, we sang a capella. The instrument was gone, but the music in our hearts remained.

I wonder what my reaction would have been if it were my Bible that had been prohibited. Would I have had enough of the Word stored in my heart to conduct the Bible studies with confidence?

Christians who lived during the days of the Reformation and throughout the Dark Ages cherished the Word, memorized its contents, risked everything to keep its memory alive, and faced death rather than turn their backs on the truths in its pages. In courts of law some were required on pain of death to quote texts in support of their beliefs—without a Bible in hand. These faithful ones faced their persecutors undaunted because they knew the Scriptures on which their faith was anchored.

Opportunities to witness present themselves in the grocery store, bus terminal, library, hospital corridor—when there is no Bible nearby with an extensive concordance. I don't know about you, but in those circumstances I'm not always as sure of Scripture references as I could be. To remedy that situation my family instituted a memory verse plan. Beginning on Sunday morning, we read a text at the conclusion of our worship. By Friday or Saturday we can repeat it from memory and are ready to learn a new text. At night we read a passage of Scripture before we pray, and do not "graduate" to another passage until we can all repeat the current one. Using this method, we have memorized several chunks of the Bible. With this Word hidden in our hearts, by God's grace we can "always be ready to give a defense to everyone who asks . . . a reason for the hope that is in [us], with meekness and fear" (1 Peter 3:15, NKJV). MARIA G. MCCLEAN

Our Ever Faithful God

Understand, therefore, that the Lord your God is indeed God. He is the faithful God who keeps his covenant for a thousand generations and constantly loves those who love him and obey his commands. Deut. 7:9, NLT.

WHAT A PRIVILEGE IT is to see the beautiful wonders of God's creation! My family and I have seen many beautiful places here in America, but one of the places I really wanted to visit was Yellowstone National Park. I wanted to see Old Faithful with my own eyes. I had read about it and been told that Old Faithful was truly faithful in spewing its water and mist up in the air at regular intervals.

Recently my husband and I traveled with another family to Yellowstone National Park. Early one morning we sat before the Old Faithful geyser to watch its performance. We decided to eat breakfast in front of Old Faithful so we would have plenty of time to watch it.

Sure enough, while we were eating, waiting, and watching for the geyser's activity, it marvelously shot water more than 100 feet into the air. Then we waited longer, because we wanted to see the interval of its performance, if it would be faithful the second time. And it was amazingly faithful.

What a lesson Old Faithful taught me that day! I should never doubt God's faithfulness to me. Even nature is faithful. I know I can trust Him in any circumstance. Sometimes when the enemy assails me with his darts of temptations, trials, and difficulties, when I don't see my way or perhaps there seems to be no way out, even then I should never doubt Him.

God truly cares. "Therefore know that the Lord your God, He is God, the faithful God who keeps covenant and mercy for a thousand generations with those who love Him and keep His commandments" (Deut. 7:9, NKJV).

Dear God, You who are faithful in all Your doings, please help me to trust You implicitly no matter what, as long as I live on this earth. I know You will guide me every step of the way.

OFELIA A. PANGAN

October 13

Not Guilty

We have an Advocate with the Father, Jesus Christ the righteous. 1 John 2:1, NKJV.

I WAS DRIVING NORTH ON Highway 27 in Leesburg, Florida, when a state police officer pulled in front of my car. It was impossible to avoid hitting him, although I was not going fast and applied my brakes quickly.

The officer immediately backed up his car and got out. "Is anyone hurt?" he inquired. Then he called Officer Cadiz, the investigating officer, to report the accident. After some time, Officer Cadiz started writing a citation.

"Why are you doing that?" I asked.

He insisted that I must sign the citation or he would arrest me.

"But I have done nothing wrong," I insisted. I did not intend to sign the ticket.

He declared me arrested and put the handcuffs on my wrists. He took me to his car and had me sit in the back seat.

A sheriff came on the scene and pleaded with me to sign the ticket. I finally did, under duress, but I wrote to the court to enter my plea of not guilty and to ask for a hearing.

The date was set. Our pastor, Rus Aldridge, is chaplain for the patrolmen in the area and offered to accompany me to court. On the day of the hearing Pastor Rus and my husband accompanied me into the courtroom. The police officer told the judge he had nothing to say. Since Officer Cadiz, who filed the false report, did not show, the judge said he had no alternative but to dismiss the case.

I am so thankful that on that great judgment day, although I will be appearing as guilty (unlike my case here), I am assured of having an Advocate who will say, "My blood, my blood!" to cover all my sins. And the great Judge of the universe will pronounce me "not guilty." RUBYE SUE

No Other Words

In the beginning was the Word, and the Word was with God, and the Word was God. He was in the beginning with God. All things came into being through him, and without him not one thing came into being. What has come into being in him was life, and the life was the light of all people. The light shines in the darkness, and the darkness did not overcome it. . . . And the Word became flesh and lived among us, and we have seen his glory. . . . From his fullness we have all received, grace upon grace. John 1:1-16, NRSV.

HOW DOES ONE PAINT with strong verbs and nouns the radiance of the aurora borealis as it weaves among the stars of a northern winter sky? Or how does one replicate in essay form the grim realities of any given tragedy? Indeed, there are numerous times in life when words are as inadequate as a dull knife or a flat tire.

And so it was for me one autumn evening. The phone rang. The words the caller relayed were concise, perfunctory. A friend of mine had died. Suddenly all words escaped me except those. They lingered, bold and haughty, as they echoed their refrain. There was nothing I could say to stop their dirge. "But she hasn't been married even a year yet! She's so full of life and hope!" I protested in the present tense to no one in particular, to everyone in general. But my grief held no special power. It was, after all, only words, and worthless ones at that, for at times of great emotion words only dance on the surface of the moment. What verb could possibly make this right? What adjective could possibly make anyone feel my spirit break or sense the stain of tears upon my eyes?

Leaves, forsaking their branches, tumbled to the ground. My heart sank with them. The geese that gathered in the field beyond flew from pond to pond, my house midway between their destinations. Together our cries rose gray against the low, lean slant of twilight.

Life went on. But there were no words, save the One I craved the most.

Word made flesh, from grace to grace, dance deep within my soul tonight.

LYNDELLE CHIOMENTI

Sermon in Shoes

Let your light so shine before men, that they may see your good works, and glorify your Father which is in heaven. Matt. 5:16.

THERE WERE 14 OF US who started our nursing assistant course. Only seven made it to clinicals and to the finals. It was not because the other half of the class were mentally incapable; it was because of the kind of teacher we had. She was a tyrant—she threatened us and didn't treat us as adults. The first two left during the first week. The others left in the third and fourth weeks. The class was always tense. If you are working and going to school, the last thing you want at the end of the day is tension. It was hard for the seven of us as well, but we managed to hang in there. I don't know how the others made it, but I just kept on forgiving my teacher every day. When I did that, every day was a new day for me, and I faced only that day's challenge.

Just before our clinical our teacher gave us orientation. She told us about the duties, and said that clinical is more difficult and that sometimes the instructor in the hospital is hard on students.

Then the big day came. Dressed in new white uniforms, we timidly pushed the elevator button to the fifth floor, where Miss Thomas was waiting. There was no talking, just a feeling of anxiety.

"Welcome to clinical," she greeted us. "I am Miss Thomas, your instructor." She spoke softly, looking each of us straight into our eyes. Her manner was friendly, and she coupled it with a smile. "Did you have any problem locating the place?" she continued. "Tell me if you have any problems or if there's anyone who has problems leaving their jobs earlier than usual to be able to come." Then she added, "Tell me if I can be of help."

We had a wonderful time with Miss Thomas. The class was not tense, and as a result, we were able to do our duties better. After the nursing director had invited the class to work for the institution, one of our classmates commented, "I think Miss Thomas is a Christian."

How do we portray God? Do we portray Him so that people will be fearful to approach Him? Does our life portray Christianity as tense, or does it portray a life of love and peace? Will someone comment, "No doubt she is a Christian"? Can the world see Jesus in us today?

JEMIMA D. ORILLOSA

Even Before I Knew Him

I have loved thee with an everlasting love: therefore with lovingkindness have I drawn thee. Jer. 31:3.

WHEN MY PARENTS DIVORCED and my mother remarried, I was 10 years old, and was I ever in for a culture shock! My parents had lived in the city, where we had every modern convenience known at that time. My stepfather was from southern Idaho, and the town we moved to had no electricity. Well, the country store had a generator.

Living in the city, I had no chores to do. I mainly read books and roller-skated. But now I had to milk seven cows every morning and evening in a cold corral where the cows would swish their icy tails around my neck. The outhouse door often stuck, and I had to yell for help to get out. Instead of walking to school, I rode 11 miles on a school bus. Instead of flipping on a light in a dark room, I lit the kerosene lamp to study by.

In the summer we lived on my step-grandad's homestead, and I rode a horse to herd cattle, drove a team to help put up hay, helped get in the winter wood, hunted, fished, brought in the water from the spring, raised lambs on a bottle, washed the cream separator, gathered eggs, and all the other things that needed doing on a farm. Our laundry was all done on a washboard, and baths were taken once a week in the same washtub as our laundry was done in. Quite a life for a girl!

Even though it was hard work for a young girl and my stepfather was not always kind, somehow I was able to enjoy it. I learned the value of work. During the winter months, when we lived in town, I had many young friends, and I enjoyed each one. When my stepdad decided to quit farming and move on, he told my mother I could no longer live with them. She would have to find a new home for me. I was heartbroken. I could not understand what was happening.

At age 13 I was taken to live with some elderly people until I could move into the dormitory of a Christian school. It was there, in that Christian school, that I learned of the love of Jesus and how much He cares for me, and all the pieces of the puzzle came together. Even before I knew Him, He was there, loving me, and in His time He drew me to Him.

Thank You for being a consistent and loving Father! Bless us each now this day.

Anna May Radke Waters

Priorities

Seek ye first the kingdom of God, and his righteousness; and all these things shall be added unto you. Matt. 6:33. My God shall supply all your need according to his riches in glory by Christ Jesus. Phil. 4:19.

WE HAD JUST COMPLETED signing all the papers required to close on our new home. As soon as that was accomplished, the closer at the title company handed me the house keys. Quickly I drove to the house and started moving some boxes and other small items that I could carry into the house through the garage door.

My neighbor, who had been friendly and had oriented me to the type of neighbors we have, noticed I picked up a casserole dish with some food in it. This Asian woman, who comes from the same province and speaks the same native tongue as I do, stopped me and said, "Wait; don't bring that in yet! You may bring that later. The first things you need to take inside a new house are rice, salt, water, matches, and images. Those were what we brought first when we moved in."

I was surprised and speechless. I had never heard of that superstition before. But I did not want to offend her since we were just getting acquainted. I returned the casserole to the car. Soon another helper took it back to the kitchen.

According to my new friend's superstition, the rice was for prosperity and good luck, water was for life, the matches were for light, and salt is a basic need. According to this thinking, if this superstition is not adhered to, it may decrease God's blessings or may even bring mishaps.

Jesus urges us to "seek ye first the kingdom of God, and his righteousness; and all these things shall be added unto you" (Matt. 6:33). This helps me prioritize what is most important in life.

Philippians 4:19 says, "But my God shall supply all your need according to His riches in glory by Christ Jesus." God's promise is sure. He needs to be a priority. God is the one who saves us from mishaps and adds all the blessings we need.

My prayer is for the Holy Spirit to help me remember to talk to God first each time I start my day.

ESPERANZA AQUINO MOPERA

The Gift of Listening

Oh that one would hear me! Job 31:35.

MY DEAR, SWEET, GENTLE Ceanne, a friend from church, can tell by the sound of my first word on the phone that I am having a bad day. She patiently listens as I unburden. Part of me wishes she didn't have to get these calls from me, yet I feel as if I'll die if I can't unravel what seems like an overwhelming sorrow.

"I like talking to you," she lovingly reassures me.

Later this afternoon, coming back from getting the mail, my elderly next-door neighbor stops me. Our usual amenities last only two or three minutes, so my hand stays on the open screen door. Surprisingly, her tone turns to anguish. I try to interrupt her untypical burst of grief with quick solutions and gems of wisdom, but each time this causes her to lose her train of thought, and she starts her story from the beginning again. So I let go of my hold on the screen door and just stand there and listen.

It amazes me that this incident she is relating, which I would consider trivial, is still bothering her 40 years after it happened. As the torturous confession comes to an end, her gratitude, like sunshine, breaks through the clouds in her eyes.

That's when I see God's plan for our emotional health. So simple. So profound. A new great truth comes to me that God has ordained that none of us have to cope with our own problems alone. God has arranged an interdependence for us. As I listen to another's burdens that are too hard to bear, He will give me someone to listen to the burdens that are too hard for me to bear. We too get in order to give.

Greater than this gift of human listeners is the One who hears before we cry, even when no sound is uttered. He is there. What a blessing for today!

ALEAH IQBAL

October 19

Lord, I Need Help

Jesus beheld them, and said unto them, With men this is impossible; but with God all things are possible. Matt. 19:26.

GROWING UP AS A teenager during the Depression era of the mid-1930s was very difficult. When I could not have even the barest necessities, much less the things I wanted, I rebelled in the only way I knew how. Two months before my sixteenth birthday I quit school.

Eventually I got married and raised a family, and when my children were in high school, I decided I wanted to return to school and become a nurse. With an educational background such as mine, I knew it would be difficult if not impossible for me to be accepted by any school of nursing. So at the age of 38 I opted for a practical nursing course that took only one year but still fulfilled my desire to care for the sick.

Since I did not graduate from high school, I would have to take the GED test in order to qualify. This was arranged for me by the registrar of a nearby college under the tutelage of my pastor. Without any previous study, I struggled for two days over the five subjects required. When I was notified that I had passed, I began making preparations to enroll in a school of practical nursing in Hinsdale, Illinois. I was both excited and nervous about meeting my new classmates and also the many challenges that I would be facing. I was soon to discover that going back to school would be one of the most difficult things I had ever done.

With my lack of proper education, how could I possibly compete with students half my age, most of whom were just out of high school? Nevertheless, I persevered, and with much prayer, encouragement from my teachers, and hard work, I was able to make it one day at a time. When the year was completed, I graduated with my class and went to work on the surgical floor of our local hospital.

This could have been an impossible venture, but as I found out that year, all things are possible with God. CLAREEN COLCLESSER

Wheat-free—Sin-free?

My dear children, I write this to you so that you will not sin. But if anybody does sin, we have one who speaks to the Father in our defense—Jesus Christ, the Righteous One. 1 John 2:1, NIV.

I CAN'T EAT WHEAT.

After years of being ill, I discovered that eating food containing wheat was causing most of my problems. At first it was really hard to find wheat-free foods and recipes. No pizza, no vegeburgers, no cookies, no cakes, and, worst of all, no more home-baked bread! Even ketchup, hot chocolate, vegetable stock cubes, and soy sauce could bring on a reaction of severe pain, lowered immunity, hormone disruption, chronic fatigue, and digestive problems.

I have to watch everything I eat. I even have to check margarine for stray crumbs. The tiniest crumb can make me ill for up to six weeks. I have had to become extremely scrupulous. Everywhere we go I have to take my own food and explain everything ahead of time to our hosts. I have to take my own bread into Communion.

But what about my spiritual life? Am I as scrupulous about that as I should be? If I can learn to live without wheat, why can't I exclude all sin from my life? If I can show such self-control in front of a tray of delicious-looking pastries, why do I find it hard to avoid such tasty morsels as a piece of gossip, a moment of selfishness, a hasty, sharp response?

It's probably because the result of my actions doesn't follow so swiftly, inevitably, and painfully as when I eat wheat. Yet the results of my sinful actions can have painful effects on others and have much longer-lasting results. When I do eat wheat, I have medication that numbs some of the pain. Then I cleanse my system again, eating fruit and drinking lots of water.

I'm learning, with Jesus, how to apply what I've learned to my spiritual life. It's not so easy! Instead of ingredient lists, I need to read the Bible to check the consequences of my actions. I need to pray, to ask the Holy Spirit to strengthen my self-control and be my guide in everything. I need to realize that some of my actions can have painful, and eternal, consequences.

But best of all, when I do "eat" some sin, I have Jesus there, to cleanse me once more and take away the pain!

KAREN HOLFORD

Our Shepherd

The Lord is my shepherd; I shall not want. He maketh me to lie down in green pastures: he leadeth me. Ps. 23:1, 2.

I SLEPT RESTLESSLY BECAUSE the traffic sounds of the busy streets below wafted up through the thin walls, even to the fifth floor. There was always the zooming of the fast motorists, then the clip-clop of horses' hooves, and the bleating of sheep. During the day I would jump up and run to the window and pull aside the curtains when I heard the horses or sheep. Horse-drawn carts on their way to market carried produce or sometimes the whole peasant family. Or a shepherd would lead his herd of sheep to the market, coming right through the city streets, competing with the cars and other traffic.

My husband and I were visiting our daughter, who was doing a year of teaching at the University in Sibiu, Romania. She was well into her second semester and no longer paid attention to the street sounds. I was fascinated, watching the powerful shepherd leading his sheep, followed by a young man or two and some strange breed of dog. Donkeys hauling the cooking utensils and all of their other living necessities mixed among the sheep. I would muse through the twenty-third psalm as I watched this parade. Truly, the shepherd was the leader, and the sheep knew it.

Do we remember that we have a Shepherd—a Shepherd who is able and willing to lead us by day and night? Do we remember the Shepherd knows well the paths that He is leading us on, or do we take off on little jaunts to this side or that to taste of activities or little sins? We may think the grass is greener on the other path and forget our Shepherd knows the best green grassy path for each of us. He will not fail us but be with us through trials, difficulties, sorrows, and joys to lead us to His heavenly home. Can we trust our heavenly Shepherd as much as the sheep in Romania who faithfully follow their earthly shepherd?

The Lord is my shepherd; I shall not want today or any other day because He is leading in my life—all I have to do is to follow. DESSA WEISZ HARDIN

A Life-saving Peace

And the peace of God, which passeth all understanding, shall keep your hearts and minds through Christ Jesus. Phil. 4:7.

IT WAS STILL DARK when they came to take us away. I can still remember that feeling—it was something I had never experienced before. I had always hated being in the hospital. Having nurses poking and prodding my body was not my idea of a peaceful time. But that morning was different.

My father had been on the dialysis machine for two years already. He was not doing well. Several infections had nearly taken his life. His kidneys were completely nonfunctioning. It was clear that without a transplant he would not live much longer.

My sisters and I had made the decision that one of us would begin the testing process to see if we matched and could become my father's donor. We had agreed that I would be tested first. If I failed any of the tests one of my sisters would then proceed. I had spent many hours praying about all the medical testing I would go through. I specifically asked God to give me a sense of peace about it all. I wanted so much to have a part in saving my father's life, but I hated hospitals and needles.

A week before the surgery my husband and I flew from Maine to California, where the surgery would be done, for more tests. Our family gathered together early that morning for one last circle of prayer. I remember suddenly realizing that I had not felt one twinge of anxiety through this entire process. In the preoperation room, they had us side by side, surrounded by our family. When the nurse came to give us some medicine to help us relax, I said that I didn't need any. Never had I experienced a deeper level of peace than on that day. I had given it all to God—the outcome was in His hands.

Today, more than five years later, my dad is doing great, and we are praising God for His awesome healing power and for allowing us to go through this experience. It not only brought our family closer together, I believe it brought each of us closer to God. Now I know what it means to have that peace that passeth all understanding. And I know that it can come only through a total surrender to my Jesus!

KELLY VEILLEUX

Walking in the Light

I am the light of the world. Whoever follows me will never walk in darkness but will have the light of life. John 8:12, NRSV.

WHEN MY HUSBAND AND I take our morning walk in the winter, it's not just the cold I mind, it's also the dark. So still and forbidding. Each streetlight, yard light, and porch light is welcome. I keep my eyes on the ground so that I don't trip and fall over a shadow or crack.

About the middle of March, however, it is light by 6:00, and how wonderful it is to be met by the singing of the birds. Even the raucous crows are more bearable in the light. As we walk we can watch the clouds turn from gray to pink to scarlet and fuchsia. There are a few brave crocuses who show their faces and reflect the rising sun. We watch for rabbits and deer and are sometimes rewarded.

We lived in Alaska for three years. Sometimes my husband tells people it was three years and six winters because the dark winters seemed so long. Many people there suffer from SAD—seasonal affective disorder. Then in the summer when they never see the sun go down, people become hyper. They have to remind themselves to look at their watches to know when it's time to go to bed. One has so much energy it seems you never get tired.

I have to believe that God intended for us to walk and live in the light. While walking in the winter, I keep telling myself that God really didn't intend for me to get up and out that early, but modern life dictates differently. Artificial light governs my hours.

I know that God intends for us to walk in the light spiritually. He Himself is the Light of the world. I consider one of the saddest lines in all of Scripture to be that found in the story of Judas after the Last Supper. John 13:30 says, "So, after receiving the piece of bread, he immediately went out. And it was night" (NRSV). Judas had chosen to leave the Light, and his life was filled only with darkness after that one grim night.

I look forward to walking in a place that "has no need of sun or moon to shine on it, for the glory of God is its light, and its lamp is the Lamb. The nations will walk by its light" (Rev. 21:23, 24, NRSV). That is where God intends for every one of us to be—and soon!

ARDIS DICK STENBAKKEN

Nurturing Relationships

How great is the love the Father has lavished on us, that we should be called children of God! 1 John 3:1, NIV.

RECENTLY MY FRIEND KATHY passed away. Kathy was one of the women in the church who was well-loved. She was an extremely creative person, and one would find her behind the scenes in many church events, such as baby showers, women's ministries secret pal programs, or church camp outs. During the time of her illness, a special bonding occurred among some of the women at the church as we reached out to her and to each other.

My thoughts of Kathy are easily triggered when I see a Beanie Baby, when I play Pictionary, or when I'm talking to a girlfriend. Since that cold, rainy day in December when Kathy was laid to rest my friends and I have talked about how important it is to nurture our friendships and spend time together. So my friend Anita started a monthly tea party group. We enjoy a devotional and fellowship over tea, scones, muffins, and other goodies. I've been having the women over on Saturday evenings to enjoy cooking, eating, and watching movies together while our husbands play basketball or go bowling. Last week we all went out for dinner, and then went bowling. We had a blast! Kathy's husband joined us for this. We joked, laughed, and reminisced about Kathy's bowling skills. Kathy was very athletic, and both she and her husband played in a bowling league. I know the moments we spend together will be cherished forever, as are our memories of Kathy.

This special nurturing of our relationships reminds me of the type of relationship the Lord wants with us. It's not enough for us to go to church once a week, just as it wasn't enough anymore for my friends and me to see each other once a week—we want to spend time together. In order for our relationship in Christ to grow we must seek the Scriptures and His will daily. The type of strength and faith that Kathy's husband demonstrated during Kathy's illness and her passing is the type of strength and faith I want. The only way we can have that type of strength, faith, and assurance is through a growing relationship with the Master. VIOLA POEY HUGHES

Daughter of Encouragement

I long to see you so that I may impart to you some spiritual gift to make you strong—that is, that you and I may be mutually encouraged by each other's faith. Rom. 1:11, 12, NIV.

SKIPPING CHURCH WAS NEVER an option. My father thought church attendance was important and being of Welsh ancestry, though somewhat diluted, he gave me the traditional Welsh choice: church or chapel. So in the absence of a third alternative (which I had been hoping for), I decided to try another church. I was put in the care of a neighbor who belonged to an influential church.

I was 7 at the time and going through a romantic religious phase, so I wasn't totally unhappy with the arrangement. Dreaming of stained glass windows and gleaming, golden altar crosses, I was to be sadly disappointed. The neighbor's church was a simple prefabricated construction, hastily erected in the aftermath of World War II. Even the name of the church was a disaster. St. Mary's, St. Peter's, or St. Paul's are most elegant. But St. Barnabas? Who was he? When Paul claimed to be least of all the saints (Ephesians 3:8), he obviously hadn't heard of Barnabas. I certainly hadn't!

But of course Paul had most certainly heard of Barnabas, who had accompanied him on his first missionary journey. They might have continued working together if they hadn't quarreled over John Mark. Paul, fearless, determined, and dynamic, had no time for a quitter. Barnabas was all for giving the young man a second chance. Barnabas' name means "son of encouragement," and he saw only John Mark's potential and judged encouragement to be his greatest need. Eventually Paul seems to have decided that Barnabas was right (Col. 4:10). Perhaps by then he had understood that encouragement always produces far better results than censure and criticism.

There have been times when I have felt like John Mark. How thankful I have been then for the "sons and daughters of encouragement" who have given me hope and renewed enthusiasm and taught me the importance of dealing kindly with others.

I'm glad that someone in my childhood town appreciated Barnabas' gift—encouragement—which they must have done to name their church after him. Most of all, I would be glad to be a "daughter of encouragement" and to lavish it generously upon those around me.

Susan Bolling

The Protection of God

The Lord will protect him and keep him alive; he shall be called blessed in the land; and You will not deliver him to the will of his enemies. Ps. 41:2, Amplified.

LIVING WITH THREE CATS is always an adventure. Each cat knows exactly which buttons to push to be irritating, and sometimes they gang up on me. In spite of this, I love those little furry bodies and would do anything to keep them safe.

We live in a quiet neighborhood, and we have a fenced-in backyard. This arrangement is perfect for our cats, who love to go outside and play. In fact, if they are kept indoors too long, they get jittery, and each in its own way lets me know it's time to let them outside.

I usually feel very safe in letting our cats outdoors. However, during a recent Halloween season, I heard that some people were stealing cats and using them as live Halloween decorations. I made the decision not to let the cats outside until after Halloween. After one day of being indoors, they began to pace around the house and meow loudly. They would stand in front of the door and pointedly stare at it, hoping I would open it.

I tried to explain to them that they were being kept inside for their own protection. I tried to explain the horrors that could befall them if they went outside and were kidnapped. They didn't understand what I was saying or why they were being held captive. They only knew they wanted to go outside and weren't being allowed to.

I sometimes react toward God in the same way my cats were reacting toward me. There are times when I really want God to give me something or to let me do something, and He in His wisdom says, "No." I don't understand His perspective any more than my cats understood mine. So I spend days whining to the Father.

It would have been so much easier if my cats had just trusted me and spent a quiet week indoors rather than whining and crying. Sometimes God explains why He says no; sometimes He asks me to trust Him. I know, deep inside, that God always has my best interest at heart. How much easier my life is when I trust my Father and rest in His arms, knowing He is protecting me and working everything out for my good.

SHARON DALTON WILLIAMS

October 27

Ready or Not?

But of that day and hour knoweth no man, no, not the angels in heaven, but my Father only. Watch therefore: for ye know not what hour your Lord doth come. Matt. 24:36, 42.

EXCITEMENT AND ANTICIPATION pervaded my mind. My sister and husband planned to visit for a week! We seldom see one another, so in order to spend maximum time with my sister I made a "to do" list. baked and cooked ahead and froze the food. The house cleaning I left to last. The night before my guests' arrival, my husband needed help installing a new gas tank in our VW Bug. I held the light and handed him tools and screws. At 10:00 we'd completed the task.

"I'm going to bed," I told my husband. "I'll vacuum the house in the morning."

After I'd entered the house, I heard voices in the garage. Peering out the window, I saw car lights beaming toward our garage. My sister had come!

"You've come a day early!" I exclaimed, tightly hugging her.

"Yes, our sightseeing tour went faster than we expected, and we didn't want to take a motel."

"That's fine, but I'm not ready for you, sis. I didn't get the window wells in your bedroom vacuumed after our recent dust storm. I'm so glad to see you, though, and for your safe trip! Let me help you bring your luggage inside."

After a short visit we all retired for the night. For a long time before I succumbed to dreamland I thought about how unready I felt for my special guests' arrival. I asked myself, *Am I going to be this unready for my friend Jesus when He comes? Is He going to arrive to find my soul's window wells filled with cares, unrepented sins, or whatever needs to be made right? What if He comes earlier than I anticipate?*

Dear Lord, I prayed, *though I've been caught unready for my guests tonight, please forgive me where I've failed in many ways during the past. Please help me avoid being caught up with the cares of this life so that I'll be unready to meet You when You come in the clouds. Help me be watchful at all times, because I do not know the day or the hour of Your soon coming! Amen.*

NATHALIE LADNER-BISCHOFF

The Longest 500 Meters

I press on toward the goal to win the prize for which God has called me heavenward in Christ Jesus. Phil. 3:14, NIV.

ON A CLOUDY SATURDAY afternoon in autumn two friends, Priscilla and Daisy, and I wanted to go walking in the mountains. We found a nice place to start quite high up in the mountains. We discovered a signpost pointing to a lake and decided to follow that path. Then we saw another sign announcing that there were only 500 meters left.

At least this was what we thought. Full of expectation, I started to run. *It must be right there after the bend,* I thought. After about 200 meters I waited for my friends. Then we continued on together. To our great disappointment, there was no lake after that turn—nor after the next one, nor the next. Daisy was tired. I was thirsty, but I had left my water bottle in the car. While Daisy sat, Priscilla and I went on a ways with great optimism. Maybe the lake was around the next corner. But the path simply went on, higher and higher. Disappointed, we returned and sat next to Daisy. When some farmers coming down from the mountains passed us, we asked them how long it would take to reach the lake.

"A half hour by foot," they said.

Daisy was tired; we had no water; my shoes weren't as comfortable as I wished them to be. However, our desire to see that lake won over the alternative of simply returning to the car. We encouraged each other, shared Daisy's last three candies, and after a couple more turns we arrived at the lake. What a joy that we finally made it!

As we admired the beauty of God's creation, I thought how we will one day have overcome all the struggles and have been faithful to the end. Then we will stand together as God's big family, not in front of a lake, but by the sea of glass and give praise to the Lord.

Dear Lord, please help me to be faithful today and to follow the way that You show me. Help me to overcome struggles and difficulties and to go on, because there will be an immeasurable reward waiting at the end—the encounter with You.

HEIKE EULITZ

Canning Jars

But we have this treasure in jars of clay to show that this all-surpassing power is from God and not from us. We are hard pressed on every side, but not crushed; perplexed, but not in despair; persecuted, but not abandoned; struck down, but not destroyed. 2 Cor. 4:7-9, NIV.

HARVEST AND CANNING season go together—reaping the harvest of our labors and coadventures of gardening with God. Fruits and vegetables have been chosen with care. It is time to assemble the canning kettle, knives, cutting board, tongs, jars, and lids. The sugar and fresh fruit pectin to keep the fruit's color looking its best are also set out. We inspect the lids and jars carefully, looking for any defects, cracks, or uncleanliness. Then the jars and lids are scalded with boiling water and placed in the oven to keep hot while the fruit is cooking.

All is ready to begin the process. Fruit is washed, cut, and cored. When it is cooked just right, we carefully ladle the fruit into the hot jars, savoring the aroma. Lids and seals get placed on tightly and set into the large cooking kettle for the canning process of sealing the jars. Our spirits are high with anticipation about how wonderful the fruit will taste throughout the fall and winter months. How attractive the jars will look neatly lined up on the pantry shelves!

But wait a minute; something is dreadfully wrong! What is happening to one of the jars? It looks as though the fruit is seeping out of the jar into the boiling water. The fruit is being ruined! What could have happened? The jar looked fine, but it had either a hairline crack that couldn't be seen by the naked eye or a weak spot that couldn't handle the heat and pressure of the water, subsequently cracking and spilling its contents.

The Lord tells us He will refine us, His jars of clay, in fire to perfect us as His disciples. We will all need to go through that refining process in our lives, but God isn't asking us to do this alone. "When you pass through the waters, I will be with you. . . . When you walk through the fire, you will not be burned" (Isa. 43:2, NIV). What great promises He gives us! He is our provider; He fills us with His goodness; He is our protector against the pressures of life and our sustainer through the fire and trials that come our way. What a mighty God we serve!

LOUISE DRIVER

An Unexpected Answer to Prayer

When they were filled, he said unto his disciples, Gather up the fragments that remain, that nothing be lost. John 6:12.

EACH OF THE FOUR Gospels tells how Christ and the disciples gathered up the leftover bread and fish after feeding the 5,000. Yet another such instance, the feeding of the 4,000, tells of seven baskets of fragments being taken up. What these texts say to me is that our resources are valuable and nothing should be wasted.

One spring my husband and I had "fragments" of another sort to dispose of. He asked me, "Honey, are you going to the dump tomorrow?"

"Yes. Why?"

"Because we need to throw away these leftover onion sets and seed potatoes now that our garden is planted."

"Are you sure that nobody wants these?" I asked. "It seems a shame to waste something perfectly good."

"Everyone around here has plenty," he assured me.

The next day I took everything to the branch landfill, but I couldn't bring myself to throw the potatoes and onion sets into the dumpster. I set the boxes on the wide railing next to it and took a black marker and wrote on the front of the boxes: "Today's Giveaway." I started toward my car when a little old woman rather timidly approached me. "Can anyone who wants to take those boxes?" she wanted to know.

When I assured her she could have them all, she smiled. "Oh, thank you, thank you! My prayers have been answered." She explained, "I'm on a fixed income, and these will be just right for starting my vegetable garden. You can't know how glad I am to get them!"

"I'm pleased you can use them," I told her. "I hope your garden will do well."

As we went our separate ways, I was thinking about how one person's "trash" may well be another one's treasure, and how God was able to use me and my wish to recycle to help answer a prayer and bring joy to the heart of one of His needy children. BONNIE MOYERS

October 31

The Secret Visitor

The Lord does not see as mortals see; they look at the outward appearance, but the Lord looks on the heart. 1 Sam. 16:7, NRSV.

ON MY WAY TO WORK one morning I noticed that my left indicator light was not functioning properly. The light on the dashboard wouldn't blink when I tried to use it; it simply glowed. Pulling into the nearest service station, I asked the manager if he had the time to fix it immediately. I thought that all he needed to do was put in a new bulb or perhaps a fuse.

"No problem," he said, smiling. "It'll only take a minute."

He returned 10 minutes later with a ball of fuzz about 12 inches in diameter. "We'll have to make an appointment for tomorrow. This is your problem." Seeing my perplexity, he continued. "I think you have a mouse using the insulation under your hood to make a nest. She's starting to chew on the wiring as well. The lights on the outside don't work either."

Goose bumps dotted my skin. The thought of what would happen if I had been driving down the highway and suddenly felt a furry rodent climb up my leg boggled my mind. Accurately diagnosing the cause of my consternation, he said soothingly, "Don't worry; it's under the hood. It can't creep inside. We'll take care of your car first thing tomorrow."

Going back to my Jeep, gleaming in freshly waxed black-and-gold splendor, I wondered about the startling turn of events. "No one would ever know what's under this hood." I couldn't wait to regale my friends with the latest development. "There are mice all around," a colleague said, reminding me that we lived in a rural setting.

A sermon I heard recently helped me to decode the message embedded in my dilemma. "It's what's inside that counts," the minister told us. It didn't matter that on the outside my car looked the picture of perfection. It's what happens when we are put to the test. As was the case with my indicator lights, the real test is in how we respond when we are called to labor.

Please, Master Designer, help me expunge whatever hidden sins dwell in my heart. Help me to grow in Your grace so that what people see on the outside, You also see on the inside. GLENDA-MAE GREENE

False Mercy

I will not . . . offer a burnt offering which costs me nothing. 1 Chron. 21:24, NASB.

A FEW WEEKS BEFORE Thanksgiving my first-grade teacher asked that members of our class bring toys for Christmas care packages to be sent to Native American children. My classmates gasped the next morning when I walked into the schoolhouse carrying Rosie, a beautiful, nearly child-size doll.

I smilingly accepted their effusive compliments about how "sweet and generous" I was. But down deep inside I was wracked with guilt. I knew my apparent merciful compassion came neither with cheerfulness nor was it genuine. In fact, it was absolutely false.

The previous Christmas I'd dropped very specific hints to my parents concerning which doll I wanted as my primary gift. It was a small, golden-haired gem neatly packaged in a little blue box. I had repeatedly pointed it out to them as it sat high on a toy section top shelf in the local five-and-dime.

However, on Christmas Eve my generous, loving parents had instead chosen to give me a large, life-size doll with brunet hair. Disappointed and rather resentful, I named the new doll Rosie, after a bossy classmate whom I didn't much like. When I laid Rosie atop the other contributions on the teacher's desk that crisp November morning, my classmates watched in awe. They treated me with new respect, as if I had placed the prize sacrificial lamb on an altar. But both God and I knew differently.

Once when King David wanted to offer great sacrifices to God, he declined using freely proffered oxen, firewood, and wheat for the grain offering. His rationale was this: "I will not . . . offer a burnt offering which costs me nothing."

Giving Rosie to the needy children of New Mexico cost me nothing in terms of emotional loss, or even material loss. I had other dolls at home. My brands of mercy and compassion were cheerless (Rom. 12:8), if not actually based on a mean spirit.

God's compassion and mercy (James 5:11), on the other hand, are genuine. How do I know? Because when He gave up His Son to die for needy people, that Gift cost Him everything. CAROLYN RATHBUN SUTTON

The Healed Car

Then you will call upon Me and go and pray to Me, and I will listen to you. Jer. 29:12, NKJV.

MY HUSBAND HAD PICKED me up after work on Friday afternoon. We decided to drive the short distance from the high school where I parked the school bus into town to see the house our friends had purchased. Not only was it a lovely house, but the yard was attractive, with a monkey tree in the front. After checking my watch, I suggested that we go home so as to get there before sundown.

As we began our nine-mile (14-kilometer) drive home into the country, my husband announced, "There's something wrong with the car. Do you hear that noise?"

There was no question. The clutch was giving problems again. Would we even make it? As we crawled up to a busy intersection, I breathed a quick prayer, asking the Lord to get us home safely. Soon after, my husband noticed the clutch seemed to be working again. We had no problems going up the steep hill. It was a relief to get parked in our own driveway. We would have to make adjustments in our plans for the following day.

It wasn't until Monday morning that my husband decided he had to somehow drive the car to our mechanic, about 12 miles (20 kilometers) away. I followed along behind in case he ran into trouble. He arrived at the mechanic's without any difficulty, but the mechanic could find no problem.

At supper that evening my husband indicated that nothing could be found wrong with the car. I told him of the quick prayer I had offered Friday afternoon. Could it really be that our car had been healed?

Lord, I find it hard to believe that You would be bothered with something so insignificant as our car when it wasn't working. But You have promised to be there no matter what we are going through. Help me never to forget that. Amen.

VERA WIEBE

Gift of Life

I have come that they may have life, and have it to the full. John 10:10, NIV.

IT WAS EARLY IN November, and already my mailbox was crammed with pre-Christmas advertising, donation pleas, and big winner claims. Impatiently I piled them onto my desk, quickly sorting out personal mail from the ever-present bills. Much of the rest went into the wastebasket, unopened.

I was down to the last piece. *Probably a travel advertisement,* I thought. But something impelled me to open it. I stared at a round-trip ticket to Chattanooga in my hand, and my mind went back to the phone conversation I had had earlier with my son.

"Mom," he had inquired, "how would you like to visit your new great-grandchild as a Christmas gift from your five children?" A gift from all my children? Of course I would! What mother wouldn't!

A few days later our dear little great-granddaughter made her entrance into the world, but nothing about her birth was normal. She seemed destined to die, and those first critical days of her life sent us to our knees often. But for the care of a skilled physician and the great love of our heavenly Father, she would not have survived. I could hardly wait for my trip there on January 6 to see this little girl and her grateful parents.

My first glimpse of her moved me to tears. The sacrifice each of my children had made to bring me on that long flight was a thousand times more appreciated. Now this child, who is part of me, lay in my arms, perfect in every way, totally dependent on love for her very survival. And love she gets! She is surrounded by it, breathing its atmosphere and thriving on it day by day.

Again and again the thought overwhelms me—if I could experience such joy over a cross-country trip to see my great-granddaughter, how much more joy will our heavenly Father feel when He makes that long trip through the universe to be with us, His children! We too were destined to die but for the nurturing care and sacrifice of our Great Physician. We are a part of Him, created in His image, and dependent on His love for our survival. One day soon He will restore us to His perfect likeness, and throughout eternity we will thrive in the atmosphere of heaven. Thank God for His gift of life—and love!

LORRAINE HUDGINS

November 4

Extravagant Love, Intimate Friendship

The amazing grace of the Master, Jesus Christ, the extravagant love of God, the intimate friendship of the Holy Spirit, be with all of you. 2 Cor. 13:14, Message.

AS I CAME INTO the house I sighed, "Home at last!" The disaster of the car quitting in the midst of snow and sleet and having to hike to the nearest store to call Ben was not what I had planned for that dreadful Friday. Now Ben and Laura had left for Seattle, Washington, for a new job opportunity for Laura. When I opened the door to the empty house, filled with all the boxes, clothes, and barrels that wouldn't fit in Laura's car, the harshness of loneliness faced me. I sat down in the living room with tears streaming down my face. I was praising God for being alive, yet I was frustrated because I had to trust Him more than usual—which is sometimes painful for me.

As I was talking and crying to the Lord out loud about the dreadful day, the phone rang. Wiping away my tears quickly, I answered the phone quietly. The voice on the other end was a very dear friend whom I'd not heard from in four long years. Through divorce and her choice of separating herself from anything Christian, our friendship had been severed. Only the week before, her name had been laid on my mind by the Holy Spirit. I had poured out my heart in her behalf that the Lord would shake her up, letting her know what His love was like. Now as I listened to her cries for help, the first words out of my mouth were "Oh, how I've missed you! How I've missed hearing from you! I've been thinking about you. . . . God put your name on my heart, and I've been lifting you up in prayer."

"You have?" She sounded surprised. "I thought you'd forgotten about me." Her voice trailed off.

"Oh, my dear, I love you so much," I assured her. "I don't care what you've done. I've felt your pain—I've hurt for you. I'll always love you, no matter what."

There was dead silence for what seemed a long time, then the sound of a tearful, broken voice. "I've never had anyone love me like that," she sobbed.

Reader friend, whoever you are and whatever you may have done, Jesus loves you even more than that too. Accept that love right now with me.

MARY MAXSON

Widow's Mite

He saw also a certain poor widow putting in two mites. He said, . . . "She out of her poverty has put in all . . . that she had." Luke 21:2-4, NKJV.

A FRIEND OF MINE WAS once traveling from college to his hometown. I asked for a ride to a town near there to apply for an apartment. As an afterthought I invited a 5-year-old neighbor boy, Wesley, to go along. It was summer, and he never seemed to get to go anywhere. When my friend dropped us off, he said he would pick us up in an hour. Finishing the apartment application, Wesley and I walked around town on the cobblestone walks and to a waterfront view. It started to rain. We didn't have enough money to seek shelter in an indoor restaurant, so we settled for an ice-cream cone from a street vendor. I said, "We must be crazy to be eating ice-cream cones in the rain!" He laughed too.

After I moved away, things got so bad in Wesley's home that his mother lost custody of him, and he was placed in foster care. No one, including his mother, knew where he was. At that time I had a car that was running again, and I went to visit friends living in the town where I had tried to apply for an apartment three years before. No one was home, so I stopped at a nearby mall. I was walking by an escalator when I saw a boy standing on the top step. It was Wesley! He was holding on to a woman's hand; I presumed she was his foster mother. His eyes met mine, and excitedly we waved and smiled, calling each other's name for the length of the descent. But the foster mother wouldn't stop or talk. She just kept walking. Wesley, looking back at me and talking to her, said, "I told you I had been in this town before! That's the lady who bought me the ice cream!"

I was so glad I had given a little boy a special memory. So many times we don't give, because we think what we have is too little or is not good enough. If you have nothing, give what you have—a smile, a hug, a laugh, your time, yourself. Someone needs your widow's mite. ALEAH IQBAL

X Marks the Time

When he had received the drink, Jesus said, "It is finished." With that, he bowed his head and gave up his spirit. John 19:30, NIV.

THE PEOPLE HAD GONE crazy. Some were honking their horns and driving around wildly. Others were yelling. Church bells were ringing. It seemed like a great party. People were terribly excited about something. The Greyhound bus on which I was traveling had stopped briefly for rest at this small village.

"Whatever is the matter?" we asked.

"The war is over! Japan surrendered!"

World War II was finished. That day was a time marker in history.

Many years later I carried with me a bunch of spring flowers and hurried into the nursing home where my mother had spent several painful months. As soon as I reached her bedside, I knew something dreadful was happening. I called the nurse, but nothing could be done. I held her hand as she stopped breathing. Her life of unselfish love and service was finished. That day was a time marker for our family.

Many are the events that are time markers for us: sometimes sad, such as a serious accident or financial disaster; sometimes happy, such as a graduation or new job. These events are markers that ever afterward divide our lives into "before the house burned" or "after Perry was born."

Long ago a war more dreadful than World War II broke out in heaven. "Michael and his angels fought against the dragon, and the dragon and his angels fought back. But he was not strong enough, and they lost their place in heaven. The great dragon was hurled down—that ancient serpent called the devil, or Satan, who leads the whole world astray" (Rev. 12:7-9, NIV).

That is what Jesus meant when He said, "It is finished." The victory was won over the controversy for good or evil in this world. Jesus had paid the price; He had become the sin offering for us. Our salvation was assured.

That day was a time marker for eternity.

RUTH WATSON

My Coworker the Angel

The poor is hated even of his own neighbor: but the rich hath many friends. Prov. 14:20.

THE GROWTH OF OUR company has led to many new positions being created at my workplace. The new positions have brought many new employees into our fold. My office is near human resources, so I see many of these folks as they go through orientation. After a while they are just another new face. I never would have realized that one of these would be an angel to me.

As I got to know Sue Hallet, I found her to be one of the biggest blessings at my work. No matter what was happening, she would bring encouragement through prayer and references to God's promises. She always seemed to say the right thing.

One such instance was when my 2-year-old nephew, Joshua, was found to have a very large tumor in his leg. This was a very trying time for the family because of the threat of cancer. I knew I could always talk to Sue about this, and she never seemed bored as I would talk of the events from beginning to end. I would find her at my office door as our workday began to make her daily inquiry about his physical status. She also was praying for the family and Joshua and making sure it was mentioned at her church's prayer group. When we found out that the tumor was benign, you would have thought by her response that he was *her* grandchild.

It is a blessing beyond compare to have a Christian friend in a secular workplace. It is so easy to get caught up with cares of this world—the gossip, the negativity, and the judging of others. Sue makes it seem simple to hang on to God and get through the workday with joy on her lips. I thank God for people like Sue. I understand better Paul's comments in Philippians 1:3-10, where he thanks God for his friends in Christ.

Sue's actions remind me that we have the opportunity every day of our lives to be an angel for God. When I am the recipient of the gift of friendship, it helps to remind me that I can share that gift and know that there will be an overabundance of blessings to come. I pray that God uses me as an angel for someone who needs a kind word, encouragement, or prayer.

Mary Wagoner Angelin

The Broad Screen

Come to me, all you who are weary and burdened, and I will give you rest. Matt. 11:28, NIV.

I CAN'T RESIST IT. I have to say something on God's behalf. I am overwhelmed by the way most people blame God for everything that goes wrong. They scoff at the idea of a devil being in existence and causing all the trouble. "No," they say, "it's God's fault. Why doesn't He fix everything up?"

Insurance companies refer to floods and hurricanes and earthquakes as "acts of God." The bleeding hearts whine and wring their hands: "How can God stand by and see innocent children suffer in these cruel wars, famines, and epidemics? Why doesn't He do something?"

Others say piously, "God is no respecter of persons; bad or good, misfortunes happen to all." Even sincere Christians who are suffering sickness or sadness say earnestly, "God is allowing this pain or sorrow to draw me closer to Him/develop my character/be an example/witness to others."

There might be some truth in what they say. In one specific instance God allowed Satan to afflict Job as an example for all time. But it is wrong to assume that all the misfortunes that happen in the world are allowed by God. Most are homemade.

For 6,000 years this sad world has been searching for a universally satisfactory answer as to why God permits sin and suffering. We can only cling to the truth that God is love.

The whole world and everyone in it is involved in the battle between good and evil. It is inevitable, as in any war, that each inhabitant of the warring nations will be affected. God's own Son was a special target when He was on earth.

God knows what is going on down here. He grieves over what went wrong with His original plan for the whole world's happiness, and at the propitious moment He will end the warfare. Until then, no matter how heavy our burdens, our verse says He will bear them for us.

Dear Father in heaven, sometimes my grief/trouble/poverty/loneliness/pain seems too heavy. I cannot bear it alone. Please help me to lay it all on Your Son's strong shoulders. Increase my faith and love today and every today. I ask this blessing in Jesus' name. Amen. GOLDIE DOWN

His Characteristics, His Likeness

As for me, I will see Your face in righteousness; I shall be satisfied when I awake in Your likeness. Ps. 17:15, NKJV.

THE LITTLE FINGERS ON both my hands are crooked. The left one is slightly misshapen, the right one considerably more. On many occasions people have noticed and asked if the fingers have ever been broken. No. I inherited my crooked pinky fingers from my father. A friend, Gail, had even joked that when I had my first baby I'd better check for crooked fingers while I was still in the hospital. That way, I'd know the child was mine.

I gave birth to my first child, Greg, in 1972. A while after the delivery he was brought to me, snuggled up in a soft, blue blanket. I held him close. My child. Oh, how I would love him! What plans I'd have for his life—and only the best! As I looked at him, I was amazed at how much this little bundle of joy looked like his father and so little like me.

Before long, Greg was screaming his head off. While I nursed him, I admired his curly hair, the color of his skin, his eyes, and the big smile he had as he drifted off to sleep. Soon after, he was back in the nursery again, sleeping soundly, until time for the next feeding, which came all too quickly. In pain, and overwhelmed with the responsibilities of being a new mom, I did little else except nurse him and give him back to the hospital staff.

The next day I was wrapping Greg in the blanket when suddenly he yawned and stretched. I touched one tiny hand and gently began feeling each finger—the thumb, index, middle, ring, and then the little one, which I discovered was crooked. I immediately grabbed for the other little finger. It was crooked too. He had gotten both my crooked fingers. I was ecstatic!

Since then I've had two more children—my second son also had crooked fingers; my daughter did not. But each in unique ways has one or more of my characteristics.

Passing my characteristics to my children has made me think of my relationship with my heavenly Father. He gave me life. He holds me close. I am His child. He loves me so, more than I could ever know. What plans He has for my life—and only the best! Which of His characteristics do I have?

IRIS L. STOVALL

November 10

My Estate

Lay not up for yourselves treasures upon earth, where moth and rust doth corrupt, and where thieves break through and steal: but lay up for yourselves treasures in heaven. Matt. 6:19, 20.

WHILE DRIVING AROUND TOWN doing some errands, I spotted a yellow sign tacked to a telephone pole. Should I, or shouldn't I? In a split second of indecision I passed it, then made a U-turn at the next corner. Something about estate sales pulls at me like a magnet. Perhaps it's a dream that one day I'll come across a real treasure—a rare old book or a valuable antique at a bargain price.

Following the yellow signs through the neighborhood, I finally came to the house. There were lots of people and lots of noise. I wandered through the kitchen. Silverware, pans, and a potpourri of other items spread over the counters and dishes stacked high on the tables. People were opening cupboards, looking under the sink, pulling out the drawers. In the living room people were waiting to purchase the "treasures" they had found. A salesperson was taking private bids on the furniture. Upstairs in the bedrooms I looked at items laid out on the beds, at clothes hanging in the closet, and even took a peek into the bathroom.

How sad, I thought. *This was once someone's private domain—their refuge from the rest of the world. And now strangers' eyes are peering into the most private places of their house, picking through the treasures they had probably spent a lifetime accumulating. How would the owners feel if they could witness this scene?*

I began to think, *Isn't that the way it is with earthly possessions? In the end, we leave them all behind.* I left, sobered and empty-handed.

Lord, help me to put earthly things into perspective. Help me to live this life as a temporary state, hanging on lightly to the treasures here. Help me to spend more time preparing for my heavenly estate by perfecting my character, for I know that is the only thing that I will be able to take with me from this world to the next. NANCY CACHERO VASQUEZ

The Lost He Will Rescue

All that the Father gives me will come to me, and whoever comes to me I will never drive away. John 6:37, NIV.

THE EERIE ATMOSPHERE OF the hospital room was pleasantly transformed by the soft playing of Christian music as our eldest daughter, Carol, lay seriously ill. In fact, she was dying. The nursing staff remarked that she was a very different kind of patient, always uncomplaining, never demanding anything of them. This type of behavior was quite unusual and rarely seen in a patient suffering such intense pain. They said they sensed a different kind of spirit in her room, that we, as a family, were different.

When asked about her relationship with her Lord and Saviour, Carol intimated that she felt it was much too late for her to turn to Him, as she had strayed from Him for so long. We assured her that it's never too late to go to Jesus; He is the one who never leaves or forsakes us but loves us with an everlasting love. We prayed the Lord's Prayer together and, with much effort, she raised her arms and clasped both hands together, resting them upon her breast.

When the pain was almost more than she could bear, she would cry out and ask God to help her. My family and I pleaded with God either to heal her or to let her fall asleep. It seemed that He wasn't listening. I tried to understand why He was hesitating, what He was waiting for.

Carol's last hours were very quiet, with barely a word spoken. Then with almost the last breath she could muster, she clearly and distinctly cried out to God, confessing her sins and pleading for His forgiveness. Oh, what a truly blissful moment, during which I came to the full understanding of the Saviour's delay in answering our prayers.

Our heavenly Father is the most kind, patient, loving, and caring Father any of us could ever hope to have. He waits and listens for the cry of the repentant sinner. With His outstretched arms He welcomes the lost ones home and covers them from head to toe with His righteousness.

Thank You, wonderful Father and Redeemer, for waiting for my child, who was once lost and now is found, and for the hope I have of seeing her again in Your heavenly kingdom. And also, Father, please remember that I love You!

VIRGINIA F. CASEY

Water, Clean and Pure

Whosoever drinketh of the water that I shall give him shall never thirst. John 4:14.

AS I WASHED MY sticky fingers under the tap after breakfast this morning, I thought what a marvelous commodity we have—water, running water, that we take for granted. Turn on the tap, and out gushes an unlimited supply of either hot or cold water.

Water. We shower first thing in the morning, wash our dishes, wash our clothes—all with clean, clear water. We drink glasses of water to quench our thirst. It really is a luxury to have water simply by turning the tap.

Many people in the world do not have "on tap" water. Afutara, a vocational training school in the Solomon Islands, was one such place. There young men and women study to give themselves and, indirectly, their families a better future. Our church "adopted" Afutara, and for several years we raised money to rebuild dormitories and other buildings. But the most appreciated gift we were able to give the school was the convenience of water "on tap." There was no shortage of water. The Afutara River was not far away, and there was a spring up the hill at the back of the school, but the water was not directly connected in any way.

The main food supply for students and teachers alike comes from the large garden that was previously watered with great difficulty and a great deal of time from the river at the bottom of the hill, some 300 meters away. The students plugged up holes in an old 40-gallon drum with sticks, filled it with water, and laboriously rolled it uphill to their garden.

With our fund-raising efforts, an electric pump was installed, and irrigation pipes and taps were put all through the garden. The students' work, as far as watering the vegetables was concerned, was practically eliminated.

The following year a holding tank was provided so fresh, clean water was supplied to the dormitories. A second tank by a teacher's house brought the availability of water for showers. It was such a thrill to be able to give to others the convenience of water, easily accessible.

Just as easily accessible to each of us is Jesus, the living water. The connection is free. What better gift? LEONIE DONALD

Of Pots 'n' Things

My command is this: Love each other as I have loved you. John 15:12, NIV.

THE TIME HAS COME," the housewife said, "to speak of many things: Of pots and pans and pizza break, of cabbages and kings."

Though the original Alice in Kitchenland, through many years I've come, willy-nilly, to acquire some kitchen craft. For instance, when I bought a nonstick Teflon-coated pan, I knew instinctively that you do not scour this item. Imagine my dismay when my weekly help ignored my stern warnings, and scratches appeared on the surface.

"But I told you: You don't scrape a pan like this. You soak it; then you wipe it clean!"

Neither do you win over an adversary by scouring. Don't allow the damage to equal the dirt. A gentle soak in warm, loving detergent will often clean up a sticky situation admirably and smooth a path to the future.

I also have a couple cast-iron pots. When necessary, they take a scouring and come up bright and smiling. People like these are a boon to work with. When they make mistakes, they can be quickly corrected without leaving hurt feelings, and one can get on with the job.

I am not a pizza addict. I like the toppings but find the bases a trial to dicey dentures. However, I've learned to accept the many split personalities around me in their totality, enjoying the pleasant and chewing bravely on the rest, while appreciating and affirming the whole.

I don't like cabbage much. With the kids grown, I don't often cook it anymore. For important projects it's better to pick teams with which one can interact well, leaving out the cabbage, mostly. On a wider level, a diversity of temperaments is necessary and welcome.

Even with the help of walrus and carpenter, we cannot sweep up all the sand on the beach. But in our own living space (including, *gulp*, the kitchen) we can soak and clean and tolerate and share and empower in the bright light of John 15:12.

IVY PETERSEN

Being Like Salt

You are the salt of the earth. But if the salt loses its saltiness, how can it be made salty again? Matt. 5:13, NIV.

JESUS WANTS US TO BE the salt of God to those around us. In order to do this we should be scattered, seasoning temperaments, giving flavor to life, and preserving virtue. We were not created to remain only in the company of other grains of salt inside the saltshaker. What is the saltshaker to us if not the place where we feel safe and comfortable?

Am I comfortable within the saltshaker? Or do I have a charity project? You remember that virtues that are not put into action become debilitated.

There is a variety of cooking salt. I ask myself, *What type and amount of salt have I been?*

Do I use too much salt? Instead of seasoning, things become too salty. When an individual is fanatical or exaggerated, even in good things, they become bitter and difficult to swallow. Do I not use enough salt? Too little makes life tasteless and uninteresting. Am I like enriched salt? It nourishes, in addition to giving flavor and grace, and I can even share this with others.

Am I coarse salt? Am I careful about being kind to others? It is no use to want to change others. What is worthwhile is the desire to change myself for the better. My change reflects positively on the people who are around me, and my world becomes more pleasant.

A poor woman wanted to have a large amount of money to provide food for several families in which the breadwinner had lost his job and the families were going hungry. In her simplicity the only thing that she knew how to make was paper flowers that were worth only a few cents.

After praying, she had a new idea: make many paper flowers, arrange them in a basket, and visit several people, exchanging a flower for a package of nonperishable food. Her project was so effective that she soon called her friends to help her. Soon many families had their basic needs met. This lady had decided to be salt outside of the saltshaker and was a blessing to many.

You and I also can be the salt that Jesus wants us to be today. May He motivate and help us toward this today. VASTI VIANA

Apple Pie

She considers a field and buys it; out of her earnings she plants a vineyard. She sets about her work vigorously; her arms are strong for her tasks. Prov. 31:16, 17, NIV.

USUALLY THE FRAGRANCE of an apple pie baking in the oven gives me a sense of satisfaction and contentment. It was not so that particular day in my apartment in Moscow, Russia. In fact, I felt guilt for the extravagance of it all. A pastor's wife had given my husband a small bag of little green summer apples, and I had decided that a pie was in order. However, I wasn't sure that I would be able to enjoy eating it when I recalled the story surrounding the apples.

The pastor and his wife have four delightful little boys. She and the boys are often home alone as her husband frequently travels. Her brother, who lives in a less deprived country, gave her a car so that she could be more independent. Almost immediately the frugal little homemaker realized that the car could elicit more expense than pleasure and convenience. They didn't need a second car. They needed a larger garden. They needed fruit trees.

In her country of skewed values, the money from selling the car enabled her to buy a dacha. On this two-acre garden spot, besides a little cabin, there were many apple trees. She was undaunted by the fact that the dacha was beyond the bus lines, and she had no easy way to get there. With great pride she showed my husband her lush garden and her gravid apple trees. With great joy she picked a bagful for us. Her generosity compelled her to share her blessing.

"Last winter," she told my husband, "we would cut an apple in fourths so the boys could each have a taste. Now they can eat all they want. I praise God for His blessings."

Apple pie will never taste the same to me. It will probably taste a little bittersweet. Sweet because of the wonderful delicacy that it is and that I have taken for granted all my life. Sweet because of a mother's innovative way of providing for her sons. Bitter because it will remind me of the harsh reality of poverty. It will remind me of the four little boys who had to share an apple because there weren't enough for each to have his own.

BARBARA HUFF

Attitude of Gratitude

They must thank the Lord for his constant love, for the wonderful things he did for them. Ps. 107:31, TEV.

EVERY YEAR I MAKE a pilgrimage south to the California coast. One of the first things I do is head for the beach. A friend drove me there and sat on the rocks while I stood in the ocean for an hour. It was a sunny November day, but the water was like ice, and I was the only one brave enough to go in.

"You know, that felt so good!" I exclaimed when we got back in the car. "I wish I could go stand in the ocean every day. It's so relaxing to just listen to the waves. I felt like my problems were washing away."

The woman looked at me in surprise. "You'd probably be happy living under the pier with a shopping cart!" she told me. "Standing in the water isn't going to make your problems go away." As we drove around town she told me how sick and tired she was of being poor. "This isn't the car I wanted," she said, "and I didn't get the kind of couch I wanted, either."

I pointed out that her car cost as much as my mobile home, and her couch cost five times as much as any of my furniture. But she wasn't happy, because they weren't her first choices.

Taking stock of my living situation, she didn't think I should be happy, but, in fact, I was. The week before, my cat had been in the hospital. However, after throwing up two feet of typewriter correction ribbon, he was on the mend. I was poor, but I had a job I enjoyed, a roof over my head, cats for company, and piles of books waiting to be read. I had less material wealth, but I actually enjoyed it more than my friend enjoyed hers.

Of course, if someone were to hand me $1 million, I would cheerfully accept it. But having so little in the way of material things has helped me to cultivate an attitude of gratitude for my many blessings. God is good to me. And yes, I could be happy just living on the beach! GINA LEE

Sometimes He Even Supplies Our Wants

My God shall supply all your need. Phil. 4:19.

IT WAS THE WEEK before Thanksgiving, and some very dear friends were coming from out of state for the weekend. I was busy preparing casseroles and making sure everything was in order for their stay when I noticed the dishwasher was making a terrible noise. When my husband came home, he said the bearings were obviously going out in the motor, and it was done for.

I couldn't believe it! It was Tuesday already, and I wondered how I was going to get everything done. Oh, I know, for years we all washed dishes by hand, and many people still do, but now I was used to having a dishwasher. I told my husband I thought we should get a new dishwasher.

He agreed, and the next day I found a top-of-the-line washer at a price that sounded really good. My husband picked up the dishwasher, and by Thursday morning the installer had it in and running. However, when I loaded the dishes and turned it on, nothing happened. The only selection I could get to work was the "cancel and drain." I called immediately and was told several things to try. Nothing worked. No repairman could come until the following Tuesday, so I prayed the Lord would give me strength to get through this problem.

Then the phone rang, and the repairman called to say he would be there on Friday. When he arrived, he announced the entire selection panel was dead. Nothing worked. He would have to order a new part. When he left, I prayed that somehow God would help me be able to use that dishwasher, even on one cycle. I pressed each control in turn. When I pressed the "light wash," it came on, and the dishes were washed cleaner than my old dishwasher had ever done. Nothing else is working yet, and the repairman can't figure out how even the one setting works when the entire panel is dead and will be until the new part is installed.

But I know why it is working. It is a little message from God that He is still in the business of working miracles, and that He really does care about all the little details of our lives. After all, this may have seemed more like a want than a need, but He took care of it.

Anna May Radke Waters

Designer Clothes

Buy your clothes from me, clothes designed in Heaven. Rev. 3:18, Message.

AS I DRESSED FOR church I thought of my early-morning meditations on Revelation 3:18. I put on my favorite pale-blue dress and chose white accessories. "You're looking very nice today, dear," Ron said. I smiled, but thought, *I wonder if the Lord can say the same about me when He looks at my character. I wonder what kind of dress He has designed for me to wear today?*

I had written in my prayer journal: "Please clothe me with heavenly designer-brand clothing today, Lord. Give me Your holiness to cover my nakedness, that I might be the woman that You want me to be."

During the service I noticed friends visiting from out of town. Then I noticed that they were with another family—10 in all. As I came near to greet them, I overheard someone else inviting them for lunch. *Good!* I thought. *I couldn't possibly feed so many!*

As I talked to Ruthie, Ron joined us. "Have you invited them for lunch?" he asked.

I gulped. "No, I don't have anything prepared."

"Give them soup and sandwiches," he suggested.

Ruthie said, "I'll help you. We'd love to spend the time with you. Don't worry about it."

Oh, but I was worrying. I knew the fridge was almost empty. There weren't even the usual cans and packaged foods to fall back on. There were only six slices of bread.

Once in the kitchen, Ruthie said, "Let's make noodles. That's easy."

"I have no noodles," I replied. "I do have rice and lentils. That's about it."

"Then we'll make kichadee" (rice and lentils cooked together with spices), she said. "And we can make potato curry." But I had no potatoes.

I was so embarrassed. Eventually, we had a simple meal and laughed about the whole thing. They had turned down the other invitation, thinking they would get a better meal at our house!

After they had gone, I thought, *So it was the robe of hospitality that You had designed for me today, Lord. Thank You for supplying it, even when I didn't feel like wearing it.*

DOROTHY EATON WATTS

Enough Food?

So they ate and were filled. Mark 8:8, NKJV.

I WAS STILL A YOUNG woman when I befriended a new girl who visited our church. I asked Mother if I could bring this girl home to lunch one Sabbath. A date and place were arranged where we would meet her.

Our family consisted of five children, plus our parents. We grew up in a very humble home. Dad didn't earn much at the cereal factory where he worked. Mom cared for us at home, but there was always something to eat, even for someone just visiting our home. My parents were well known for their hospitality.

Mom cooked the usual food for the Sabbath Alida was to visit. When Dad and I went up to the road to escort her to our home, we were met by her whole family—a beautiful, recently widowed mother, five pretty sisters, and one little brother! My thoughts started racing. Would the food be enough to feed everyone?

After scurrying around to get extra plates and looking for every seat we could find, we finally settled down, and Dad prayed for a blessing on the food. As Mom dished plate after plate, I was sure someone would go without. Praise the Lord, the food was enough for all—and some left over! How the Lord blessed that little food is a miracle that I will never forget.

In this experience I am reminded of the mother who thoughtfully put in a little lunch pack five barley loaves and two small fish for her curious little son, who wanted to hear more of Jesus. The little lad so unselfishly shared his lunch, asking no questions, but handing it over. And Jesus blessed it, feeding more than 5,000 people. Everyone was filled and happy.

Will you be prepared to share the bread of life with someone today, prepared to feed someone who is hungry and thirsty?

I don't understand how You multiplied the food when You fed the 5,000 or when You fed my family and friends. But I know I can trust You to meet our needs. Now help me to meet the needs of people around me too.

PRISCILLA ADONIS

Deep Cleaning

Have mercy upon me, O God, according to thy lovingkindness: according unto the multitude of thy tender mercies blot out my transgressions. Wash me thoroughly from mine iniquity, and cleanse me from my sin. Ps. 51:1, 2.

THE KIDS ARE COMING home! I'm cleaning my house. Oh, not your normal, everyday cleaning. This is deep cleaning—you know, moving furniture to vacuum under it instead of around it. The kind of cleaning that when you are done, you feel so good because everything is the way you want it to be all the time. The way it should be all the time. And this time I make myself a promise to keep it this way. If I had kept it this way all the time, however, I wouldn't have to be scurrying around now.

Isn't that the way we do? We do just enough to get by most of the time. At least we think we are getting by. Perhaps we are thinking we'll do a better job the next time. Jesus is coming! Do we need to do some deep cleaning? Do we need to move any sin out, polish some things, and maybe wash the windows of the mind? Or do we think everything is in place as it is supposed to be, and that we've done enough to get by.

Of course, there is a difference between the kids coming and Jesus coming. The kids don't really know what shape the house was in before they arrived. (They may have a good idea!) Jesus always knows what shape our spiritual house is in. We might let our earthly house get messed up, but our spiritual house should always be ready.

Do you know what? We can have help with our spiritual housecleaning if we only ask Jesus to help us keep it clean. He wants us to ask Him. He wants to help. He is happy to do it. And the thought crosses my mind that if we can ask Him to help with our spiritual housecleaning, then we can also ask Him to help with our earthly house cleaning. He wants to help us do that, too!

Have mercy on me, O God. I need Your cleansing; I trust Your lovingkindness to direct my spiritual housecleaning. Help me today, too, to keep my house clean.

DONNA SHERRILL

Don't Be Afraid

Make sure that your character is free from the love of money, being content with what you have; for He Himself has said, "I will never desert you, nor will I ever forsake you." Heb. 13:5, NASB.

I'M NOT A PROPHET," the preacher intoned, "but I believe this country will face a financial collapse sometime in the near future." Hearing these words, I felt a thrill of fear, a feeling I felt whenever I heard a negative prediction regarding the financial status quo.

Driving home from the service, I tried to analyze why it was that I, a Christian, should quake before any threat to our livelihood. Hadn't the Lord always been there for us and cared for us? Hadn't He proved again and again the promise in Malachi 3:10 that He would pour us out a blessing, and we would not be in need?

I thought back over the events of my life, an exercise that evokes strong feelings of gratitude for His care. I'd been born at the start of the Great Depression into a family rich in love but ill-equipped to face financial reverses. Nevertheless, we never lacked for anything all during my years of childhood. In my teen years my widowed mother had always been able to keep a comfortable home for us. When her health failed, God enabled me, still a teenager, to have just the right job to keep us stable.

All through our long and happy marriage God helped my husband and me to raise our family securely and blessed us in our respective careers. There were times when we, in our financial naïveté, rushed ahead of Him and made poor investments, yet He saw us through. Thanks to God, we could enjoy a modest but comfortable retirement. We had always followed His counsel regarding tithes and offerings, and He in turn never failed us.

Was I depending more on monthly income than I was on God, who provided it? In my Bible study I came across Hebrews 13:5, and I repented of my fears. I rest in His assurance that He will never fail us or forsake us. I can confidently affirm, as in verse six, "The Lord is my Helper, I will not be afraid" (NASB).

Thank You, dearest Lord. MARILYN KING

November 22

Reconciled

In this one body to reconcile both of them to God through the cross, by which he put to death their hostility. He came and preached peace to you who were far away and peace to those who were near. Eph. 2:16, 17, NIV.

A WOMEN'S MINISTRY GROUP decided to have a secret prayer partner project to draw the women closer to each other and to God. Each woman wrote her name on a slip of paper and dropped it into a basket. Then each drew a name. She was to pray daily for her name for a month.

In this group were two women who hadn't spoken to each other in months. They were from the same church, were part of the same women's ministry group, and loved the same man. To one he was a son, to the other he was a husband. The two women who loved this man hated each other. They had had an argument, some misunderstanding, and it had led to anger.

Now these two God-fearing, churchgoing, committed Christian sisters sat in the same group and kept their distance and their eyes averted. The basket circled the room, each woman drawing a name. The mother-in-law was appalled when she saw her daughter-in-law's name printed on the paper she drew. No less shocked was the daughter-in-law when she drew her mother-in-law's name. Each went home, questioning this comedy of errors while wondering if she had the capacity to pray for the one who had wronged her.

Nevertheless, each began praying for the other daily. The more each prayed for the other, the more hostility faded away. One month later both attended another women's ministry meeting to reveal for whom she had been praying. When the mother-in-law revealed she had been praying for her daughter-in-law, shock registered on the daughter-in-law's face. The daughter-in-law rushed across the room to embrace her mother-in-law. The joy of this public reconciliation was a blessing and a lesson to all. Tears were shed; hearts healed.

When I heard this story, I thought how creative our God is in getting our attention. I can picture the tongue-in-cheek smile that played on His face when He thought up this trick.

Anyone you need to forgive? Call on God's creative powers to do what you feel you can't do for yourself. He'll make it possible.

NANCY L. VAN PELT

Call Now!

Call upon me in the day of trouble. Ps. 50:15, NIV.

HELMI WAS A WOMAN whose husband was not a believer. He didn't want her to go to church, so Helmi had a hard time trying to please her husband and keep her own faith. People in church didn't know of her problems. One morning she was so discouraged and fed up with the situation that she decided to give up. She said to God, *I won't be going to church anymore—it's just too difficult. If You want me to change my mind, have somebody from the church phone me within the next half hour for no special reason!*

The same morning I was doing my housework when I felt the urge to call Helmi. There was no special reason; I just had the feeling that I should give her a phone call. I was a bit flustered. What would she think if I called her without reason? What should I say? But the feeling that I should call her was urgent. After a little while I picked up the phone. "Hello, Helmi; this is Hilkka. I don't know why I'm doing this, but I had the feeling that I should call you. Is everything all right?"

"Are you calling for some special reason? Do you want me to play the piano next week?"

"No, I'll play this time. I just had the feeling that I had to call you."

"Are you sure there is no reason for your call?"

I wondered why she was asking that. Then Helmi told me about her deal with God. Now she couldn't leave the church. She was sure God wanted her there.

Years later I met Helmi again. "I have often thought of that phone call long ago. Do you remember it?" I asked.

"Oh, I have never forgotten it! How could I? God showed me that He cared for me and that He wanted me to keep my faith. Your phone call changed my life for good!"

We don't always know the reason we are impressed to do certain things or the reason some people come to mind and won't leave our thoughts. Maybe God is asking us to call or to write to somebody who is in need of special comfort. God asks us to be His hands to pick up the phone and His mouth to speak for Him. God hears every prayer. Some He leaves to us to answer.

HILKKA ROUHE

Signpost Error

It is not good to have zeal without knowledge, nor to be hasty and miss the way. Prov. 19:2, NIV.

I DISLIKE DRIVING ALONE IN unfamiliar territory. I had just driven with my husband to the city airport two and a half hours from our daughter's home. We had found our way there quite easily—the way was well marked. Now John had left on the plane, and I was driving back to our daughter's. Finally I saw it—a signpost that clearly stated "Lethbridge," an arrow indicating straight ahead.

I've done it, I gleefully told myself. *I've found my way around this city, and from now on all I have to do is follow the signposts. I will soon be on a road I know.* Following the advice of the sign, I did not turn onto the main road but continued straight on over it.

A little voice seemed to say to me, "You should have turned there."

But the sign said straight on, I argued. So ignoring my better judgment, I kept on going. Soon I found myself out of the city and realized I was still heading east. The Rocky Mountains were visible about 50 miles ahead of me. I had to admit I had missed the turnoff to the south. I pulled over to the side and tried to find where I was on the map, but couldn't.

There was nothing to do but to turn around at the next opportunity and head back the way I had come. When I reached the main road again, there was a clear sign to turn right onto this road and head south to Lethbridge. This I did and was soon on familiar ground.

What had happened? Did the sign get twisted? Did it mean straight on at the approach to the main road, and I missed the on-ramp sign at the far side of the road because I was so busy congratulating myself? I fear it was the latter.

In life, as in driving a car, "it is not good to have zeal without knowledge," and it's possible to lose our way by being too hasty in our decisions. I pray that I will remember the lessons I learned that day: to listen to my conscience, and not to lose the way because I think I've got it right and don't need to be careful anymore.

RUTH LENNOX

I'm Too Little

Well done, good and faithful servant; you were faithful over a few things, I will make you ruler over many things. Enter into the joy of your lord. Matt. 25:21, NKJV.

MOMMY," PLEADED 2½-year-old Helen, "I want to dry the plates for you."

"No, darling. You are too little. I'm afraid you would let the plates slip through your fingers onto the floor. When you are bigger you can help me."

"Oh, I wanted to help you now" was the somewhat disappointed rejoinder.

About a half hour later her mother called, "Helen, come here!"

The child quickly came running.

"Helen, help Mommy by closing the door. The wind blowing through makes it too cool in here."

"No," pouted Helen. "If I'm too little to dry the plates, I'm too little to shut the door."

Mother was rather amused, but she didn't let my little sister know it. She explained that as one gets bigger, he or she is able to do bigger jobs and take more responsibility. Before she can learn to do big things she must learn to do little ones well.

This truth about receiving responsibility gradually is also in the Bible. The parable about the talents (Matt. 25:14-30) states that the man going to a far country gave differing amounts of money to his servants to invest, "each according to his own ability" (verse 15, NKJV). Did the one-talent man envy those who had been given more? The Bible doesn't say. We do know, however, that this man had his own version of "I'm too little." "You're a hard man to work for," he whined. "I was afraid that I couldn't please you, so I didn't do anything with the money."

Do we have modern counterparts of Helen and the one-talent man today? If we don't get the job or church or political office we covet, do we refuse to work or serve at all? Do we fail to see that even small jobs, done well, can bring a sense of accomplishment and may, as in the case of the two faithful servants, lead to greater things?

May our prayer be *Lord, help us get rid of our I'm-too-little mentality and make us realize we can be just right for whatever work You may want us to do.*

Bonnie Moyers

November 26

Storms Never Linger Forever

Be strong and of good courage, do not fear nor be afraid of them; for the Lord your God, He is the One who goes with you. He will not leave you nor forsake you. Deut. 31:6, NKJV.

FOR TWO YEARS MY husband and I had tried everything possible to get a scholarship sponsor, but to no avail. The little savings that we had while working in our home country had gone quickly. The few dollars we earned from odd jobs were nothing compared to the huge expenses we incurred, and life had become miserable. We sold all we had so we could meet all the expenses. In fact, we were left with nothing, and the help we had sought everywhere never materialized.

Praying became even harder, though we never ceased, and the few friends that we had distanced themselves from us. Some even gave us the impression that we weren't praying enough. Others thought we were praying for the impossible. We tried to keep our everyday smiles with a spark of hope in our hearts because God never changes. That same God who accompanied us from our homeland was still the God who was going to show us His mighty power.

We sat down one evening for our worship when we somehow reflected how our old folks had prayed for rain when there was no rain, but the dams never dried up. How the congregations prayed for people with demons, and they became free. How God had even supplied our own people with food during the heavy years of tribal wars. In all these incidences we realized that God wanted to show us that He is still that same God. All we had to do was to stand still and see the results of our fervent prayers.

Yes, it took us months and months to actually taste all these blessings, but it was worth the waiting. Each day has become something to look forward to because of the blessings that we receive every day. Our mighty Father rebuked the storm when it was time. Today we are a living testimony because of what the Lord is doing in our lives.

Friends, it all boils down to one simple thing: there is nothing the Lord will not accomplish for us if we faithfully ask Him, believing that He will and that He is able. The storms linger for a while and then pass. Praise God for that.

SIBUSISIWE NCUBE-NDHLOVU

Rejoice With Me

When she hath found it, she calleth her friends, and her neighbors together, saying, Rejoice with me; for I have found the piece which I had lost. Luke 15:9.

I SAT IN THE PEW of our small church. My grandmother heart was fairly bursting with pride as I heard my oldest grandson, Tyler, play his first trumpet solo. He had started lessons only three months earlier and was showing real motivation to improve his talent. His mother frequently had to remind him, "Put that trumpet down and go do your chores." As he played I glanced down and noticed that his church pants were again too short. I made a mental note to replace them soon.

Several weeks later my daughter, Julie, and I planned a day out doing one of the activities mothers and daughters do best—shopping. We were doing some early Christmas shopping. She had brought along her active 2-year-old son, Grant, safely secured in his stroller. We had shopped in several stores in the mall, looking for bargains. In my favorite store I found a rack of nice slacks on sale and hastened to buy a nice khaki pair for Tyler. Soon it was noon, and we were getting hungry. We decided not to take the time to go outside the mall for lunch, and ate our food leisurely. Then Julie made a trip to the bathroom, after which we gathered up our things to go.

That's when I noticed I had only two bags. We carefully checked the area around our table, but could not find the other bag. We opened the remaining bags to check the contents and, to my dismay, the bag containing the slacks was the missing one. I said a quick, silent prayer for help, and we quickly began to retrace our steps, hoping against hope to find the package. We checked at the mall information desk and were told we would have to fill out a form that described the lost item and list our phone number. We decided to look in one more store before completing the form. No bag.

We sadly returned to the booth to complete the form. Julie had just taken the pen in her hand when the booth employee said, "Here comes the mall guard now, and he has a bag in his hand from the store at which you purchased the slacks."

As we turned to head for the car, I told my daughter, "Jesus helped us find these."

"I know, Mama," she said.

ROSE NEFF SIKORA

Stretch Your Tent Curtains Wide

Enlarge the place of your tent, stretch your tent curtains wide, do not hold back. Isa. 54:2, NIV.

IT WAS A COLD PUBLIC holiday morning when I quietly slipped out of bed. I didn't want to disturb my husband, who usually sleeps so peacefully—like a baby. I took my Bible and went to the church that was in the same yard as our house. I treasured those quiet moments in that little church, for I was consumed by self-pity, discouragement, and much anxiety. I desperately wanted a child. I cried to God to perform one of His miracles, to enable me to conceive and bear a child. I really longed to carry a child within me and experience the miracle that God had given so many others.

After praying, I opened my Bible and read some promises from the Psalms. Then I turned to Isaiah 54. Oh, what a blessing these life-changing verses were! My heart leaped with joy and amazement. I read and reread the first two verses again and again. I could not believe that my Lord had answered me so quickly. My friend, the Holy Spirit impressed and explained these verses to me right there and then. "'Sing, O barren woman, you who never bore a child; burst into song, shout for joy, you who were never in labor; because more are the children of the desolate woman than of her who has a husband," says the Lord.

"'Enlarge the place of your tent, stretch your tent curtains wide, do not hold back'" (Isa. 54:1, 2, NIV). The Lord was telling me I should "enlarge the place of [my] tent" and I should "not hold back." From that moment I decided to ask the Lord to help me take each and every child on this planet as my own.

He really answered this plea. Since that cold morning my life has been blessed by the warmth of many children who have entered my "tents." The Lord answered my prayers and gave me peace. He even gave me strength and the resources to take care of and love any child who needs my love and care. What a blessing—blessings from above.

Thank You, Father of all children. Zodwa Kunene

Right Place, Right Time

Watch therefore, for you know neither the day nor the hour in which the Son of Man is coming. Matt. 25:13, NKJV.

TO GATE F, PLEASE!" the young flight attendant directed me after looking at my ticket. I was at the Changi Airport in Singapore, on my way from my country, Indonesia, to the United States. My itinerary showed I had a two-hour stopover in Singapore. Following the flight attendant's instruction, I walked to gate F. It was 3:30 in the afternoon, and my flight to Los Angeles would be at 5:30. I bought a newspaper to read. But time went so slow, and I felt bored. Finally, I decided to call my cousin and my friend, who lived in Singapore.

Coming back to gate F, I found that the passengers had started checking in. I was standing in a long line. When it was my turn, the attendant said, "Excuse me, ma'am, your ticket shows that you're going to Los Angeles; this plane is going to Japan."

"What!" I exclaimed. I was astonished. I could not believe what I heard.

After checking his list, he said, "You have to go to gate R, ma'am."

I looked at my watch: 5:25. I had five minutes to get there. Tears ran down my face as I ran as fast as I could. I realized that I didn't have enough time. *Lord, help me; I don't want to miss my flight,* I prayed as I ran. It seemed to take forever to reach gate R—Changi Airport is huge.

When I arrived at gate R, they had almost closed the gate—I was the last passenger to enter. What a lesson for me! I could not believe I made that mistake, waiting at the wrong place. I was there, I thought, at the right time and at the exact place. But I was wrong.

Could it be that as we wait for the Lord's return we may be waiting at the wrong place? While sitting on the plane, I pondered this and thanked God that I did not miss my flight.

I want to be ready when You come, Lord. I don't want to be found in the wrong place. Please send Your Spirit today to guide me into all the truth, to the place I should be when You return. Please help me, God, I pray.

LANNY LYDIA PONGILATAN

God's Stretched Out Arm

Ah Lord God! behold, thou hast made the heaven and the earth by thy great power and stretched out arm, and there is nothing too hard for thee. Jer. 32:17.

AS EURASIANS, MY SISTER and I were born into a family that was very English in its heritage. According to the British raj in twentieth-century India, children of English executives were packed off to boarding school at the tender age of 5. Situated in the Himalayas of northern India, these schools afforded a salubrious climate away from the sizzling heat of the big cities and gave certificates from Cambridge and other universities in England.

Barbara was a few years older than I and had a beautiful soprano voice, natural good looks, and a keen sense of humor, which made her very popular. So of course I was that "kid sister" who always seemed to get in the way. When we grew older, we finally came to a ladies' agreement. We became close friends for life, and although we lived oceans apart, we visited when we could and corresponded frequently.

It was when Barbara became a widow that my family and I increased our visits to her in London, England, from our residences in North America. Imagine my shock upon returning from a five-day trip to northern California to find a distressing message on my telephone recorder: "Come to London immediately—Barbara in hospital—not expected to live."

I took the next plane. Upon arrival at the hospital I was told that because of cancer, she had only three days to live. I was with her constantly for nine days. When she died, I was devastated. Sorrowing at her bedside with my head buried in her blanket, I cried, "O Lord, she's gone till the resurrection morning. Please help me now to know what to do. I feel so terribly alone!"

Suddenly I felt the weight and warmth of an arm around my shoulders. I glanced around. There was nobody there, but that divine "stretched out arm" and comforting presence stayed with me till all British death duties and other legal matters were duly met. A local Christian group and neighbors and friends of Barbara, few of whom were known to me, rallied to my aid.

Oh, how good is our God! Always rely on His "great power and stretched out arm" to help.

JILL WARDEN PARCHMENT

Poor Solomon

Yet when I surveyed all that my hands had done and what I had toiled to achieve, everything was meaningless, a chasing after the wind; nothing was gained under the sun. Eccl. 2:11, NIV.

POOR SOLOMON! HE WAS the wisest man who ever lived, so wealthy he could not even count all his riches; he was powerful, inventive—and miserable. He had tried everything. And everything was meaningless. Meaningless.

I just finished reading the book of Ecclesiastes again and found it a bit depressing. What was wrong with Solomon? Worldly wisdom would say that there is happiness in wine, women, and song. As a woman I find that less than exemplary, and the truth was that even with 700 wives and 300 concubines Solomon was miserable. His life was miserable. Why? What didn't he have? Relationships. Not with people nor with God. With 1,000 women there was no time for relationships. No time to enjoy understanding and sharing private jokes. No time to know any of his wives as friends before they were lovers, and then tossed aside.

There was no time for God, either. No relationship. Instead, he tried the wine. He tried the pleasures. He says he tried labor, luxury, lust, leisure, and learning. He tried the gods of his wives, Ashtoreth and Molech. "So Solomon did evil in the eyes of the Lord; he did not follow the Lord completely, as David his father had done" (1 Kings 11:6, NIV).

All was vanity—meaninglessness. What is so sad is that Solomon had every chance in the world for happiness. He could have helped his people—they needed it. He could have shared his wisdom to make life better. He could have told the nations around who admired him about his wonderful God. But he didn't.

I am so glad Solomon finally did find what had meaning. What's even better, you and I can gain from it today. It is just so sad that he was too old to profit from it. "The end of the matter; all has been heard. Fear God, and keep his commandments; for that is the whole duty of everyone" (Eccl. 12:13, NRSV). God was and is the answer. Today, I have a chance to build that relationship. I can have a joy, a wisdom, a meaning to life that Solomon missed. He said there was nothing new under the sun. What is meaningful is the Son.

ARDIS DICK STENBAKKEN

Wrong Time, Right Place

Thus says the Lord, your Redeemer, the Holy One of Israel: "I am the Lord your God, . . . who leads you by the way you should go." Isa. 48:17, NKJV.

I DO NOT BELIEVE IN coincidences in the lives of God's children. The King of the universe happens to be my Father, and before I start each day, I ask Him to direct my every thought, word, move. Because I take His promises seriously, I know that He is only too willing to manage my life. So I cling to these texts:

"With all your heart you must trust the Lord and not your own judgement. Always let him lead you, and he will clear the road for you to follow" (Prov. 3:5, 6, CEV). "Whether you turn to the right or to the left, you will hear a voice saying, 'This is the road! Now follow it' " (Isa. 30:21, CEV).

When I ended up in an area of the maximum security center after finishing a program one evening, I knew God had directed my steps. I was not scheduled for a second program that evening, but I was looking for an individual who had requested a Bible. He had been relocated, so I stopped to ask the officer in charge of the unit of his whereabouts. The officer was busy on the phone, but he recognized me and, without waiting to hear my request, announced that I was there to give a Bible study. By this time I realized that God had added an item to my agenda. Instead of offering an explanation to the officer, I waited to see what my mission would be.

One person responded to the announcement. During the session this individual revealed that he was at the end of his rope and had just pleaded with God to send someone to encourage him with a message from the Bible. For a few seconds no one spoke. The awesome presence of the Holy Spirit was palpable. Unquestionably God was in charge, so we listened as He ministered to our hearts.

Lead me again through this day, Father; I am ready to follow wherever You choose to lead.

Maria G. McClean

Morning Prayer

My voice shalt thou hear in the morning, O Lord; in the morning will I direct my prayer unto thee, and will look up. Ps. 5:3.

GOOD MORNING, GOD. IT'S morning already! The children are still asleep. I have so much to do today—getting children off to school, work, errands, meetings—but I want to begin my day quietly and with You, my friend. As the sun begins to rise over the plains, painting its brilliant streaks of pink across the sky, I seek You prayerfully on my knees. I ask You to give me courage and strength for what this day brings. Please, Lord, place Your hands under me today and lift me up so that I may be able to face my struggles with a smile and a song. I pray that You will empty me this morning of sin and selfishness so that my heart will be truly open for the pouring out of Your divine Spirit in my life.

The rays of morning sun reflect beautifully off the snow-covered trees, reminding me of Your goodness and faithfulness. Today, Lord, I place my life in Your hands. I want to be Your dedicated servant, a tool for Your use, completely consecrated to Your purpose. Fill me with Your love, O Lord, so that my words and my deeds today reflect the incomprehensible love You have for me. Make me sensitive to those who are hurting and in need. Give me the words to say to those who ache inside for understanding, compassion, and encouragement. Make me a messenger of Your love to them.

I know that without You, Lord, there is nothing I can do. But with You, my God, all things are made possible. Help me to rely on You for all my needs today. Remind me, Lord, of how much I need You all throughout this day for Your strength and Your guidance in my life. Nudge me, please, when I stray from my focus on You and what You would have me do today.

Tomorrow, Lord, is an uncertainty. I leave my tomorrows in Your hands. But for today, just for today, take my life and my plans. Let them be a witness of Your love. May my today glorify You to all with whom I come in contact.

I hear the children's feet on the stairs, so another busy day begins. *Thank You, Lord, for this quiet time. Thank You for being the friend who listens, cares, and never leaves me. Amen.*

SANDRA SIMANTON

December 4

No Pilot

This God is our God for ever and ever; he will be our guide even to the end. Ps. 48:14, NIV.

ONE DECEMBER MY HUSBAND and I flew from sunny Florida to spend a wintry Christmas with our daughter in Michigan. Our son and his family would drive from Iowa to join us. I was looking forward to a white Christmas, the first one I'd experienced in many years. I knew that the warmth of family fellowship would be more than enough to counteract the frigid temperature. We boarded the shuttle that was to take us to a small aircraft for the final leg of our journey.

Then we just sat. The unusual delay in boarding the plane concerned us. "Why won't they let us off the bus?" my husband wondered.

"You will have to go back to the terminal building. There is no pilot for this flight," a voice over the intercom instructed us.

Stunned, we returned to the gate. Later, we learned that there had indeed been a pilot, but he had already logged in his quota of hours for the day. Soon we boarded another plane, only to hear the pilot announce that there was a red light flashing on deck. "I don't know what that means," he said. We couldn't take off until the situation was checked out.

"Now how long will we be delayed?" I muttered to my husband. We waited for about three hours until the maintenance crew rectified the problem and gave the OK.

Thinking about our experience as the snowflakes frosted my mittens on my noonday walk the next day, I realized again that I had much for which to praise God. I was thankful that our safety had not been jeopardized. More than that, I was glad that our heavenly Pilot does not have a specified number of hours for His workday. Jesus never slumbers nor sleeps and is always prepared to guide us to heaven. There may be delays as we stop to make repairs that we may have necessitated, but He waits. He is always there to lead us to our final glorious destination.

Thank You, ever-present Pilot. We accept Your offer to be with us even to the end.

Carol Joy Greene

No Visa Required

The meek shall inherit the earth; and shall delight themselves in the abundance of peace. Ps. 37:11.

RECENTLY MY HUSBAND AND I made a very foolish mistake, and we had to pay dearly for it. We had made plans to visit our son in Thailand. We looked forward to seeing him and visiting Thailand for the first time. We told our travel agent our plan and our need for visas. The travel agent assured us that we need not worry as we could get visas at the airport itself in Thailand. We were surprised but delighted.

The joyful day arrived when we boarded the plane, knowing that within four hours we would see our son. Sure enough, at the airport we were guided to the counter for our visas. We filled out the forms, writing down our plan to stay in Thailand for three months. We gladly paid the fee, which we thought was very reasonable indeed. Our papers were stamped, our visas were granted, and our stay assured. We were so excited that we didn't even see the need to check our papers. We rushed to get our luggage, and then to the exit, straining our eyes to see our son. There he was, wearing a broad smile, waving his hand to get our attention. Oh, what joy!

After 17 days my husband suddenly remembered our passports. To his dismay, he discovered we had been given only transit visas. That meant only two weeks—not three months! Our son rushed us to the embassy. We talked to the officials, but they could not change their rule. We had to pay a fine for the three days of overstaying, and they extended the visa four more days to complete the third week they usually give.

When we got back home, our agent was surprised to see us so soon. When he learned his mistake by giving us assurance for three-month visas, he was very apologetic. He was wrongly informed, so he gave mistaken information.

There is another "travel agent" who has known all along that he is wrong, but is misleading people. His promises are tempting, but at the end we get only transit visas. On the other hand, God has promised us an eternal inheritance. He has paid the full fee to give us a free ticket to enter His kingdom—no visa required. Make sure, dear reader, yours is not a transit visa.

BIRDIE PODDAR

Take a Closer Look

Man looketh on the outward appearance, but the Lord looketh on the heart. 1 Sam. 16:7.

IT WAS A PINK CERAMIC frog planter—a very ugly pink ceramic frog planter, holding a sprawling, straggly plant. Why would my mother want something like that? While she was visiting one of my sisters across country, I was keeping her plants. I dutifully watered the frog plant, along with the others, but was still puzzled why anyone would keep it. The frog sat on its haunches, staring balefully ahead, unaware of my dislike.

One day, to my amazement, I discovered gorgeous pink blossoms on the ends of each branch of the straggly plant, transforming it into a graceful thing of beauty! The Christmas cactus had changed the frog into a handsome prince. The biggest change, however, was in my attitude toward it. Eventually, the plant and the planter went back to Mother, who still has it and says she's going to will it to me.

Just as I judged the frog by first impressions, I must admit that I have sometimes been too quick to form an opinion of another person without taking time to discover her inward beauty. Perhaps we should view new people we meet as potential friends and follow Solomon's counsel that "a man that hath friends must shew himself friendly" (Prov. 18:24). A real friendship takes time—time spent getting acquainted; sharing common interests, joys and sorrows, likes and dislikes; being able to confide in each other; and trusting each other. Such friends are priceless.

There is a Friend who meets all the qualifications of friendship and goes far beyond. One who "sticketh closer than a brother" (Prov. 18:24). Isaiah had prophesied that He would have "no beauty that we should desire him" (Isa. 53:2). Just as we must spend time with someone to develop earthly friendships, we must also spend time with Jesus if we would be friends. We can confide in Him, and He will never betray our trust. He cares about everything that concerns us and wants to share our burdens, joys, and sorrows.

I don't have a pink ceramic frog, but I do have Christmas cactuses—two of them. One is large, with graceful curving fronds; the other rather straggly, but valued. You see, the little piece it started from was given to me by a friend.

MARY JANE GRAVES

Found It

What woman having ten pieces of silver, if she lose one piece, doth not light a candle, and sweep the house, and seek diligently till she find it? And when she hath found it, she calleth her friends and her neighbors together, saying, Rejoice with me; for I have found the piece which I had lost. Luke 15:8, 9.

MY DAY HAD NOT started out very well. It seemed that there had been quite a succession of days like that. We had experienced some rather unusual and what seemed to be really unnecessary problems with our business, as well as our personal lives. There was just too much going on.

I had put my contact lenses in rather late in the day and was trying to get a couple more things gathered together to run some needed errands. I began to notice that I was not seeing that well. A check of the eyes showed that there was no lens in the right eye. Immediately I sent up an *Oh, no! Please, God, You know what this means. Please help me find that lens.*

Quickly I rushed back to the sink, hoping that I hadn't let the water out. The sink was dry. I crawled around on the floor, pleading in prayer with everything I had in me. No luck. The counter, my clothing—I checked everything. As a last-ditch effort, I rummaged around and found a wrench so that I could remove the sink trap. I was doing fairly well until one of the washers split in half. When I removed the trap, there was no lens. *Great! Not only did I lose a lens; now I have broken the bathroom sink.*

I was able to get around with the one lens pretty well, but it was uncomfortable. I went to do what errands I could. Then my husband called to tell me the clutch had gone out on the truck. I told him about the lens. This was too much. Our only option was to pray again.

After praying with my husband and exchanging comforting words with him, I went into the bathroom. I lifted the stopper. There was my lens, balanced on a metal lever that raises and lowers the stopper. I was greatly humbled and gave heartfelt thanks.

I have thought often of the woman who cleaned her house to look for something she lost. God does not ever consider us lost, yet He searches "diligently" and finds ways to bring us closer to Him. Even if it means keeping a contact lens from going down the drain. MARY E. DUNKIN

December 8

Riches Untold

Charge them that are rich in this world, that they be not highminded, nor trust in uncertain riches, but in the living God, who giveth us richly all things to enjoy. 1 Tim. 6:17.

AS I WAS ENTERING a local store a man stopped me; he wanted to admire my baby. As he walked away he smiled and said, "You are rich."

I have thought about what he had said many times since then. Yes, I am extremely rich.

When people think of wealth, they usually think of a high-paying job, a mansion, a new vehicle, and a large savings account. Although I wouldn't rate as a millionaire, these secular standards could apply to my life, sort of.

High-paying job—I work and am very thankful. So many people don't even have a job to go to. As a social worker I don't make a mint, but the people I have encountered and the lessons I have learned at my work are priceless.

Mansion—I have a home to live in. It has a roof to keep out the nasty weather and doors to keep most of the dust out. Even our baby has her own room. Our home may not be four stories high and on 50 acres, but it serves its purpose well, and we are blessed.

New vehicle—We have two vehicles, and that is a miracle in itself. They may not be new, but they do the job. An added blessing is that our mechanic is trustworthy.

Large savings account—Well, if accounts wore shirts, ours would be in an extra-small size. That's OK, because God keeps our finances flowing to cover the necessities. We do have CDs, but they only keep us rich in music.

All these riches, in and of themselves, are something to be grateful for, but my real wealth comes in knowing that God loves me. No matter what happens in life, I know He will be there—always. His attitude never changes, and His abilities are unlimited. There is no monetary amount that could replace that relationship. It helps me to remember that we are all rich, and we can revel in the thought that we have an inheritance that cannot be taken from us.

MARY WAGONER ANGELIN

Come to the Light

I am the light of the world. John 8:12.

EVERY TREE IN THE FOREST is different, but each one reaches for the light."

Those words on the upper inside corner of a Christmas card have given me much food for thought. So it is with humans: Each one different, but we are all meant to reach for the Light. How can we each reach for the Light? It's as simple as recognizing our great need and asking Christ into our hearts, saying, as did the tax collector in Christ's parable, "God, have mercy on me, a sinner" (Luke 18:13, NIV).

Then there seems to be another step. Not only did Christ say "I am the light of the world"; He tells us that we also are to be the light of the world (Matt. 5:14). In 1 Corinthians 12 Paul talks about different kinds of "spiritual gifts" (NIV). I feel these were given so that we can also be the light of the world.

What I believe to be my spiritual gifts, such as writing, listening, and sharing my faith, no doubt fit somehow into some of the categories Paul mentions.

There's a nearby store where customers can buy beautiful greeting cards, two for $1.00. One day I picked out 11 cards and paid for them. When I got home and sorted them, I found I'd accidentally put two cards with one envelope.

The next day I returned to the store and explained the situation. "I want to get an envelope for this card and pay for it," I told the clerk.

She smiled, but when I handed her the cash, she said, "It was good of you to come back."

"What would Jesus do?" I asked.

"He would have come back to pay for it."

As the song says: "This little light of mine, I'm going to let it shine."

Father, as You draw us to the Light, please show us the "spiritual gifts" You have given us so that we too may become "the light of the world." Thank You, Lord of love.

PATSY MURDOCH MEEKER

Prepared?

And while they went to buy, the bridegroom came, and those who were ready went in with him to the wedding; and the door was shut. Matt. 25:10, NKJV.

MY HUSBAND AND I had prepared for a 10-day vacation with our son and his wife in Texas. I had visited them several times, but my husband hadn't seen them recently. We were doubly excited about seeing our granddaughter.

With a friend's help, we arrived at Fresno Yosemite International Airport. Forty-five minutes before flight time our luggage was checked in. The ground host asked for my identification card, and I showed my driver's license. However, my husband had forgotten his. "Is it all right if I present my grocery membership card or health insurance card? I'm a clergyman, and I'm sorry I forgot my driver's license," he explained. I showed a picture of us from my wallet.

After the worker had consulted her boss, she said only government-issued cards were honored. Then she said, "There's plenty of time before the plane takes off. Why don't you go back home?"

But our friend had already left. My husband called another friend to help us in our dilemma. I prayed hard that the traffic wouldn't detain him or that perhaps the departure time could be held back.

After a while the American Airlines workers at the checking station left. The woman trying to help us suggested that I proceed to the boarding area. Before I could reach the boarding station, I heard an announcement over the intercom: "Calling for Mr. and Mrs. Pangan. Last call for Mr. and Mrs. Pangan." I was getting panicky—my husband was nowhere in sight. The worker was giving instructions to pull our luggage, and suggesting that we take the next flight, when my husband dashed in.

In the parable of the 10 virgins, all prepared, but only five made it to the wedding. The Bible spoke of two people in the field, but only one was taken; two women were grinding, and only one was taken. What a sobering thought! Every day you and I are reminded to be ready for Christ's coming. It's going to be an individual enterprise. Yes, very personal. No loved one can help. Others can encourage us, but it's going to be our personal relationship with Jesus that will be our security or identification card.

OFELIA A. PANGAN

My God Sees

The Lord hears his people when they call to him for help. He rescues them from all their troubles. Ps. 34:17, NLT.

HAVE A GOOD TIME! I'll meet you in about an hour down by Red Rock Road," I said to our older daughter, home for a few days during the year-end holidays. My husband, a railroad buff, had been wanting to ride his bicycle down the old railroad bed for many months, and now he had someone to ride with him. Our 14-year-old grandson was more than happy to join them on the ride too. Since I haven't ridden a bicycle since I was a teenager, my part is always to drive the pickup vehicle.

We had driven about a mile off the main road to the site of an old foundry for the start of their ride. I had gone only a short distance out to the road when I sensed there was a problem. The ride seemed rougher than it should be, even on a gravel road. I stopped and checked the tires, and sure enough, the left rear tire was flat. Now what to do? Although I had a jack and had helped my husband change many tires, I knew it was too much for me by myself. The spare tire was fastened under the truck in a way that would be difficult for me to get loose.

Slowly I drove out toward the road and stopped. Since the main road was narrow and steep at this point, there was no place to park there. I could see a few houses scattered about, but not a sign of a garage or store. The foundry was deserted, so I could expect no cars to be coming from that direction. *Please, God, send someone to help change my tire,* I prayed. I could imagine my family arriving at the pickup point and I would not be there.

After about 15 minutes a battered truck pulled up behind me. "That doesn't look nice," said the young man who got out and looked at my now-shredded tire. He spread a large towel on the dusty road and began to loosen my spare tire. In no time he had my tire changed, and I was ready to go.

When I offered to pay him, he said, "Oh, no. This is my Merry Christmas to you." He was my angel, and I told him so.

Thank You, God, for sending me help when I needed it so desperately.

Betty J. Adams

December 12

Perspective

Humble yourselves in the sight of the Lord, and he shall lift you up. James 4:10.

IT HAD BEEN ONE OF those hectic, exhausting days of Christmas preparations. Even though it was a little after midnight, I dutifully continued to hang ornaments so that chore would be completed before the busy work week began. Checking the water level in the Christmas tree stand, I fumbled the water can and spilled the majority of the water on the floor, causing quite a mess.

With the mess cleaned up, I surveyed my handiwork. Glancing up at the tree, I noticed that it appeared to be leaning. I put my hands through the branches and pushed here and there on the trunk to straighten it. It didn't budge. I proceeded to get down on the floor and twist and turn the screws on the tree stand. That didn't seem to correct the problem either. Giving up, I decided I was too tired to fuss with the tree anymore and would just let it lean.

Then it happened. The tree fell, scattering ornaments everywhere, dangling the garland, and spilling water all over the floor. Again. In anguish I cried out loud, "Lord, why did this happen? You know my time is so limited. And look at this mess!" I was starting a real pity party and was just about to burst into a flood of tears when, for some strange reason, two stories popped into my head that I had read the afternoon before. I recalled a story of a mother who lost a son to suicide, then lost another son and his wife to a senseless murder, and her struggle to overcome her debilitating grief. Then a tragic story of a young African university student also came to mind. He had experienced anger from an irrational mob that torched the building that held him and his friends captive. The story told of his miraculous escape from almost certain death, his long recovery from physical and emotional wounds, and his forgiving spirit to those who almost took his life and who had killed his friends.

Humbly I looked around and thought, *So what is a fallen Christmas tree? Certainly not anything to cry about.* After a struggle to get the tree upright, I leaned it against a wall, tossed the fallen ornaments on a chair, and went to bed. I had a good night's sleep, awaking in the morning, refreshed and ready for the challenges of the new week—including redecorating a Christmas tree.

BONNIE C. HUNT

A Christmas Memory

If you . . . know how to give good gifts to your children, how much more will your Father in heaven give good gifts. Matt. 7:11, NIV.

I LIVE SOME DISTANCE FROM my three children; Christmas was approaching, so I was feeling some of the loneliness that can come at this season of the year. Two of my children get no extra time off work during the holidays, making it impossible for them to make a long trip with their families. My teacher daughter always comes for Christmas, and I was so looking forward to her visit. She had even told me to think of something that I would really like to do.

Then the call came that the visit would be a short one—Christmas Eve and Christmas. What happened to something I would really like to do? What can you do on Christmas Eve? I must admit that I was feeling sorry for myself.

Now, I love books. I even love the book *I Love Books,* written by the father of a friend of mine. But what does that have to do with my Christmas memory? A friend of mine had sent me a check for Christmas and suggested that I buy a book. Before my friend moved, I had gone to a Barnes and Noble bookstore and really enjoyed it.

Now it was the one day in which to do something with my daughter. I thought of Barnes and Noble, and off we went. The drive is about 30 miles, and we decided to take a country road rather than the highway. That in itself was especially enjoyable with my daughter at my side. We arrived at the store and had no trouble finding a parking space. Inside, Christmas music was playing. It was so cozy. We took our time and really enjoyed browsing among all the books.

After paying for our purchases, we went into the store café and had a hot chocolate. I was soaking up the atmosphere and the pleasure of my daughter's company when I happened to glance out the window and saw that snowflakes were falling—the first this winter. Wow! I suddenly realized how much I had to be thankful for. That short visit had given me a warm Christmas memory that will stay with me for a long time.

How good God is! He doesn't leave us drifting alone but has promised, "Lo, I am with you always" (Matt. 28:20, RSV). *Thank You, Lord, for daughters and for Your presence.*

ANN VANARSDELL HAYWARD

December 14

That's Me

It is no longer I who live, but Christ lives in me; and the life which I now live in the flesh I live by faith in the Son of God. Gal. 2:20, NASB.

JUST BEFORE THE FRENZY of the Christmas holidays began, some friends and their toddler son stopped by to visit. As we settled in the living room to catch up on the benchmarks of our professional journeys, I noticed that little Zachary was beginning to show signs of intense boredom. Taking him by the hand, I led him through the house, nonverbally granting him right of passage to any room he chose, and then rejoined my friends.

Minutes went by before a beaming little boy came back to the front room and tugged at my hand. "Gina," he begged, calling me by a name he had apparently decided should be mine, "Come see!" He pulled me down the hall. His parents, unaware that most rooms in my house are virtually childproof, followed quickly. Trepidation hastened their steps.

Climbing up on a couch in the study, Zachary pointed to three charcoal sketches by a renowned Jamaican artist hanging on the wall. Singling out the drawing of an adorable little urchin in overalls, he returned to us. His bright eyes and broad grin mirrored the expression of the boy in the picture. "That's me," he informed us. "That's Zachary!" Relieved parents looked on in doting affirmation. He did indeed look like the child in the portrait.

I put that precious incident in a spiritual frame a couple days later. I realized that in two words— "That's me"— Zachary had captured the essence of being a Christian. As soon as we announce to the world that we are Christians, God measures us with His Yardstick—His Son, Jesus Christ. And so will the world.

When people look at me, I want them to be able to say, "Isn't she just like Jesus!" Christ came to earth and endured excruciating agony to show us how to overcome the fruits of our foreparents' fall from grace. We have His God-breathed example to follow.

Thank You for that reminder, Master Model. I want to be just like You. With Your help I know I can.

GLENDA-MAE GREENE

My Own Christmas Miracle

Before they call, I will answer; and while they are yet speaking, I will hear. Isa. 65:24.

WE WERE REMODELING OUR house over the holiday season. One Saturday evening my husband hitched up the trailer and went to the lumberyard to pick up supplies so we could be ready to work on the house early Sunday morning. The purchases were made—bales of insulation, a glass door, and other various supplies—and securely tied on the trailer, and we headed home.

About halfway home we stopped a second time to check on the load. With horror my husband informed me that everything was gone except the wood. We quickly asked God to help us find the lost items. The bales of insulation could easily cause someone to have a terrible accident. They were large, and the back roads were dark and curvy. About 200 feet from where we stopped, on the opposite side of the road, we found our door. Not a scratch on the glass. What a miracle! But the nine bales of insulation seemed to have vanished.

Lord, we prayed, *we are so thankful no one was hurt, but we need that insulation—we have dedicated this house to you. Please, help us.* Right after our prayer a policeman with a car in tow pulled up in front of us. He had two bales of insulation in the trunk. We excitedly jumped out of the van and ran toward the two cars, yelling, "You found our insulation!"

The story unfolded in a way I'll cherish for a long time. An elderly man had witnessed the insulation falling off the trailer and quickly stopped and proceeded to stuff as much in his car and trunk as possible. A young man also witnessed the event and questioned the elderly man about what he was doing. The old man said he knew us, but the younger man, questioning that, threw the rest of the insulation in his truck and headed for the police station. The policeman on duty immediately took off. All the insulation was recovered, and the elderly gentleman was happy we didn't press charges.

We felt doubly blessed that no one had been hurt, that all had been recovered, and that new friendships with the policeman and the young man were made. The realization again occurred to us that God is always there, giving us those whispers of love and touches of grace through His guidance and through others, even before we ask! VICTORIA L. WICKWIRE

December 16

Those Christmas Letters

I will tell of the kindnesses of the Lord, the deeds for which he is to be praised, according to all the Lord has done for us. Isa. 63:7, NIV.

IT WAS ALREADY MID-December, and I had not yet written our annual letter to friends and relatives. I was tired and a little depressed. How could I write anything in that mood? Should I write at all? Who cared to hear what had been happening in our family, anyway? But then, if I don't get down to writing at least once in a year, we'd lose contact altogether. All our friends live quite a distance away, and we don't have the chance to see them very often.

So I sat down at the computer and pressed a few keys. *No, that won't do. Forget it.* No letter this year. I started scanning some photos and decided to just print out some pictures of our family and let the people figure out for themselves how things were going.

The photo collage turned out really nice. That gave me a boost. But something was missing. The next day I sat down to write again. Even if others might not be interested, it would do me good to take a moment to look back at what had happened during our last year. I started thinking with gratitude about the things that God had allowed us to experience during the year. There were so many things to be grateful for. In fact, I was sometimes almost scared about all the good things happening to us when I thought about all the tragedies around us in the world. This attitude of gratefulness got me out of the dumps, and the words started flowing.

Sometimes we feel so worthless. But that's not true—it's just a feeling. There's always something that is worth doing, and it will finally work out right. There is somebody who cares about us. If we can't think of a person this would apply to, there is always Jesus to live for, because He died for us. Our worth is not measured in what we do, but in what God does for us.

It's not always easy to snap out of the negative mode, but there are some things we can do that will help. Singing or listening to uplifting music will make it easier for us to think positive thoughts. Gratitude will make creativity flow. Creating something beautiful will make us happier. Before we realize it, we are happy again. God loves us. What more do we need?

HANNELE OTTSCHOFSKI

Help Me Understand

God demonstrates His own love for us in this: While we were still sinners, Christ died for us. Rom. 5:8, NIV.

THE STORY IS TOLD of a 21-year-old woman in a land recently torn by war who was in desperate need. It was Christmas Eve, and she was almost ready to deliver her baby, fathered by a foreign soldier. No one wanted her or the baby. She started to the home of a missionary, but the baby was almost ready to come. She stopped at a home along the way to plead for help.

"Where is your soldier now? Let him help you," the couple answered.

She stopped at another home and again was refused assistance. She finally reached a bridge close to the mission where surely she would find help. But there was not enough time—the baby was coming now. She crawled underneath the bridge and delivered her boy.

It was a bitter winter night. She took off her jacket and wrapped him in it. The baby was still so cold. She took off her blouse, and then her skirt, to cover him. She gave him everything she was wearing and cradled him close to her, giving the last measure of her body warmth until she herself lay frozen under the bridge.

The next morning the missionary started over the bridge to distribute Christmas gifts. He heard—could it be?—a baby's cry. He climbed down underneath the bridge and found the boy for whom the mother had sacrificed everything.

The missionary adopted the child. When the boy had his tenth Christmas birthday, the missionary thought it was time to tell him the story. So the man told the boy how his mother had given everything she had so that he might live. The next morning the child was gone. The frantic father began looking for him. He found his clothes on the bank by the river. Climbing down, he found the boy, kneeling, naked, and praying: "God, help me understand how cold Mama was the night she died for me."

We can never understand how cold Jesus was the day He died for us; how He felt misunderstood, betrayed, beaten, spit upon, ridiculed, rejected, separated from His loving Father, executed—for us. "Greater love has no one than this" (John 15:13, NIV).

RUTH WATSON

Surprise Packages!

Every good and perfect gift is from above, coming down from the Father. James 1:17, NIV.

IT SEEMED AS IF we were right there in Bethlehem. We knocked on the inn door and met the innkeeper and his wife, who took us to see the stable. We peeped inside and saw Mary and Joseph and their tiny baby snuggled in the manger. A donkey munched hay in the corner, and chickens scrabbled around our feet. We visited the shepherds, who told us about the exciting night that had just past; we helped them to count their sheep to be sure that none had gone missing during the night. Then we found a tent of silk and satin, where three Wise Men sat before chests full of treasures and spices and charts of the sky. Their camels lowered their necks and eyed us suspiciously.

But we weren't really in Bethlehem; we were visiting the annual live Nativity at the London Zoo. We were next shown into Santa's grotto, a wonderland of ice and twinkling lights and interactive storytellers. We saw a video about reindeer and finally saw Father Christmas himself. As usual, he asked the children what they wanted. Seven-year-old Joel was rather bemused. As long as he could remember, he knew that Mom and Dad were behind the surprises, but he duly told the nice old man what he really wanted and was given a small wrapped gift.

Later Joel remarked, "It was really funny. We told Father Christmas what we wanted; then he gave us something we didn't want!" Joel didn't mean that the gift he had wasn't wanted; just that it wasn't what he'd asked for.

Do we sometimes feel that we tell God what we want, then He gives us something else? Several times in my life I have asked for an answer to prayer, and the answer has been quite different from what I had expected. At the time I may have been surprised, even deeply disappointed, but I can honestly say that none of these "surprise gifts" has ever been returned to the store as unwanted. Each time God knew what I really wanted, even better than I did myself! Some of the more unusual gifts, even the tragic gifts, were all transformed into something beautiful from God, things that I now treasure deeply.

So whenever I unwrap an unusual present from God, I can't wait to see how He will turn it into something beautiful, something for me to treasure forever. And He always does.

Karen Holford

A Christmas Never to Forget

All things, whatsoever ye shall ask in prayer, believing, ye shall receive. Matt. 21:22.

CHRISTMAS WAS NOT TOO far away. My parents had warned us there was no extra money for presents. For months, without telling a soul, I had been praying for a Raggedy Ann doll. I was 7 years old, and the news of no presents for Christmas did not deter my longing for a Raggedy Ann doll. I continued to pray for one anyway.

My dad was a hunter. Often, he would be gone until after we children were in bed for the night. I knew the sound of his footsteps by memory: he would open the door, then walk in the house through the living room and down the hall to his bedroom. It was a comforting sound.

Now it was Christmas Eve. As usual, Dad had been out hunting with friends. I listened for the familiar sound of his footsteps. Sure enough, after we were in bed for the night, the door opened. But instead of the familiar footsteps, I heard a commotion and scuffle of several footsteps. Startled, I wondered what that was all about. Then all was quiet, and I drifted off to sleep.

Since Christmas was not to be anything special that year, my brothers and sisters lingered in bed for an extra snooze. But I awakened early and tiptoed down the stairs to occupy my time until everyone else was up. To my utter amazement, there on the dining room table was a large tub full of toys. Sitting on the very top was a lovely Raggedy Ann doll. I made such a commotion squealing with delight that I woke up the whole family, and they came running. My dad's hunting friends had found out about the bleak Christmas in store for us and gathered these toys to brighten our day.

This incident had a profound effect on my relationship with God. I developed a trust that has never wavered. No matter what circumstances I have had to face (and I have had to face many tragic ones), I know, deep down in my soul, that God is there watching over me and will answer my prayers in His own special way. God answers prayers—all we need to do is develop a complete trust in the special ways He answers them.

Dear God, I want to thank You again for that special answer to prayer that has provided me with much comfort through the years. MELINDA GLADDING

December 20

The Present Counter

Then they opened their treasures and presented him with gifts of gold and of incense and of myrrh. Matt. 2:11, NIV.

I ROLLED MY EYES. MOM was at it again. My mother-in-law had a fixation with counting Christmas presents. Not only did she make sure that everyone in the family got the same number of presents but that the same amount of money was spent for all of them. My first Christmas in the family, she had given me a pair of pantyhose to make up the three-dollar difference between my presents and some of the other girls in the family. I felt this was ludicrous.

Now she was kneeling under the tree, counting the presents again into neat piles, trying to figure out whether everyone had the same amount. "How many presents are you bringing—one for each person, or two?" she asked.

"I don't know," I said. "I haven't even wrapped them yet."

"Well, I just need to know for the count," she said.

I rolled my eyes heavenward again. I couldn't believe this woman. The next year things were different. I had been in bed from complications of pregnancy, and my little sister had come to help out. She was going to be part of the Dillon Christmas. I knew she missed Mom and Dad, and I felt really badly that we weren't able to buy her a whole pile of presents. I was afraid she would feel really left out, going over to the Dillon Christmas, where everyone else got so many. Bruce and I had been able to buy her only two gifts.

Christmas Eve, as people started opening their gifts after dinner, I suddenly realized that Bonnie was opening gift after gift. Mamma-Jo had counted all her gifts as usual, and then gone shopping and made sure that there were the same number of presents for my little sister as there were for Bruce's sisters.

All of a sudden my eyes filled with tears as a great wave of affection swept over me. Instead of feeling angry and contemptuous at her present counting, now I realized that her present counting had been an act of love. I was so grateful to her for making Bonnie feel an important part of the family that Christmas. I never minded her present counting again.

SALLY DILLON

My Favorite Cookies

He made us, and we are his. Ps. 100:3, NLT.

WHEN MY DAUGHTER, BETH, and I get together for our annual visit, one of our favorite things to do is bake. We love to bake special cookies from carefully selected ingredients, the best we can find: gourmet vanilla, real butter, exotic spices. Each one different. Even if we use the same mold or cutter more than once, every cookie is decorated or flavored or iced in its own special way. Each Christmas cookie sparkles with ornaments unlike any other on the tray. Every Valentine heart is laced and ruffled like no other. We wouldn't think of giving any one of our dear ones an *imitation* cookie, an ordinary cookie like any other cookies. Our cookies are an art form.

You might have heard the story often told about how the various colors of people came to be. God baked the first batch too light and scorched the second batch. The last batch came out right—a nice golden brown. But I don't like that explanation. My God is a better baker than that. He pays closer attention to His carefully crafted cookies than to take them out half done or to let them burn. God does not make mistakes!

My friends are made exactly the way He designed them, each with a unique flavor, shape, and consistency. On purpose. He made the delicious, tangy, lemon-crisp cookie that is my friend Martha. He inhaled deeply as He sprinkled in the fragrant cinnamon and pressed in the plump raisins for my dear Vera. Kim is a subtle vanilla, with a little nutmeg for body. And Erica is a ginger cookie, sweetened with molasses. Some of my friends are thin and crunchy; some are chewy and soft. Some are aged to perfection, like Christmas lebkuchen, while others are still warm from the oven. All are works of art, made from the finest ingredients, created to be admired and enjoyed by Someone special.

We are His, for He made us. Let us rejoice and be glad for each and every one.

HELENE HUBBARD

A Simple Snow White Blessing

Lord, all my desire is before thee; and my groaning is not hid from thee. Ps. 38:9.

IT WAS MONDAY EVENING, and even though the weekend had just ended, I was not refreshed mentally, emotionally, and certainly not physically. I had done all the errands and chores I never seemed to have time or energy for during the week when I got home from the office. So there I was, as exhausted on Monday as I had been on Friday. What a way to begin a new workweek! It was very cold outside. The wind blew softly, but all was "clear on the eastern front."

As I finally finished my evening regimen and climbed into bed, I sighed out loud, "Oh, for a day just to relax and do nothing; to regroup and be refreshed." Then I groaned, "But it's only Monday."

All too soon I felt my husband's faithful nudge, signaling that it was time to roll out of bed and get on with another day. With great effort and reluctance I peeled away the covers and felt my way to the bathroom, hoping to hang on to one last moment of sleep. Peering out the window, I saw a sight that was unexpected and beautifully white. A thick blanket of snow had fallen quietly during the night, and continued falling.

I said to my husband, "Honey, there's a lot of snow out there," but because of my usual joking, he didn't believe me. Soon he realized I wasn't teasing this time. Clad with warm clothing, coat, hat, and gloves, he went out to begin shoveling. It seemed useless, for the snow just kept falling. Soon he was back inside. Eventually we received almost eight inches of new snow.

By now we had tuned to the Weather Channel. A winter snowstorm watch was in effect for our area. "If you don't have to be out today, stay inside. Roads are bad, some impassable, and a number of accidents have occurred, but with no serious injuries. Snowfall is expected to continue until 10:00 p.m.," the newsman reported. Immediately I made a phone call to one of the officers at my job and, after exchanging a few words about the weather and road conditions, was again advised to stay where I was. What a welcome blessing!

Thank You, God, for honoring my heart's desire for a day at home to relax and be refreshed. May I welcome Your soon return more than I did the day of my "Simple Snow White Blessing," when I will spend eternity at home with You.

GLORIA J. STELLA FELDER

Christmas Enough

This very day in David's town your Savior was born—Christ the Lord! Luke 2:11, TEV.

THERE HAVE BEEN MANY Christmas trees in my life, but the one I remember best wasn't a proper tree at all, merely a branch.

It was a bleak Christmas at college. I had a full scholarship for my tuition, but I had to pay my own room and board out of my meager earnings as a typist. My roommate, Cathy, wasn't much better off, and one evening in December she began speaking wistfully of past Christmases back home. She looked around our utilitarian dorm room, with just our beds, desks, and a shared dresser, and said in despair, "We can't even afford a Christmas tree!"

"I'll get you a tree," I told her.

I grabbed a pair of scissors from my desk and went out to the courtyard where I snipped off the end of a tree branch. I took the branch inside and stuck it in a flowerpot with some dirt, also gleaned from the yard.

When I brought it back in, Cathy asked, "What is that?"

"I don't even know what type of tree it is," I admitted. "It certainly is not fir or pine."

But we had a tree. We didn't have any store-bought decorations, so we made paper chains and strung them around our tree. We topped it off with a star made of the gum wrapper tinfoil.

When I think of our little tree, I remember another couple who spent Christmas without a tree or stocking or decorations. They had nothing to cheer them up or make their environment more comfortable. It was the very first Christmas, and Mary and Joseph celebrated it without any of the traditions that we hold so dear. But these people had a new Baby of love, the Christ Child, who would grow up to offer salvation to the human race.

When lack of money keeps us from buying the presents we wish we could, when circumstances keep us away from our loved ones on this special day, we need to remember that first Christmas with none of its modern trappings. Christmas is still Christmas, even if we spend it alone in a dorm room. It is the time we remember Jesus Christ and the birth of hope. It is enough.

GINA LEE

Todd and the Christmas Stocking

Let the little children come to Me, and do not forbid them; for of such is the kingdom of heaven. Matt. 19:14, NKJV.

I HAD BEEN A CHRISTIAN for only one year when I found myself alone, raising three children, David, 9, Todd, 6, and Adam, 14 months. We were too poor to have Christmas, although we found a real tree out in the woods by the highway. This we decorated with mementos we had collected over the years, using crib mobile figures as tree ornaments. We also had a record player and were able to listen to Christmas music. I was grateful to have this much, but I had to tell the children there would be no presents. The children insisted that we pray for presents, and although I obliged their innocent desires, I secretly did not have the faith that a way could be found to answer their prayer.

On Christmas Eve a telephone call came from Treasure City, a department store behind our apartment complex. They told us that Todd had won the giant stocking filled with toys. That was the first I'd heard that he had entered his name in the drawing. All of us ran, not walked, to the store, including neighborhood children, who kept falling onto the ground in hysterics, saying, "You lucky! You lucky!"

The stocking reached almost from the ceiling of the store to the floor. The variety of toys and gifts seemed to meet the need of everyone Todd knew. There was jewelry and perfume for me; books and trains for his older brother, David; a squeeze toy and rattle for baby brother; marbles and a cap gun for his two best friends next door; and he gave their little sister a doll.

If that wasn't enough, it was Gabriel's birthday during the week of Christmas. Gabriel was Todd's best friend from church. Todd was so happy that he could surprise him that Sabbath at the Hartford church with a birthday present. And there were still games and trucks to spare.

It was a miracle that my faith needed that day, too, to see how God does answer a child's prayer.

ALEAH IQBAL

No Room in the Inn

She gave birth to her firstborn, a son. She wrapped him in cloths and placed him in a manger, because there was no room for them in the inn. Luke 2:7, NIV.

THEY TOO HAD COME from a long distance. Travel-worn and hungry, they had no beauty to assure their welcome, those little gray-brown birds that swarmed around the inn. The inn offered comfort, a lodging place, and a sheltered home on which to build their nests. But the little birds would only be a nuisance—dirty feathers floating in the coastal breezes, their nests muddying the walls, their chirping disturbing guests. Little did it matter that they had flown for so long, braving wind and storm. Now there was no place for them at the inn.

Legend tells that the angry innkeeper chased the birds away and tore down the mud nests they were trying to build at the inn in San Juan Capistrano. At the nearby mission one of the priests observed what was happening and said to the birds, "Come, swallows. Come to the mission. We will give you shelter. There is room enough for all."

The birds did come and built their unique little nests under the eves of the old mission. Year after year they have returned to the mission in San Juan Capistrano from their winter home in South America. In their wake the swallows have brought blessing to the old mission. No one remembers the inn, but each spring on March 19, thousands of visitors gather at the mission of San Juan Capistrano to welcome home the swallows with a day of festivities. Through the years the swallows have been celebrated in both song and literature.

At Christmas we remember the blessing another innkeeper missed who turned away travelers, road-weary and unassuming, and the stable that gave them shelter. And we pause to ask, "Have we made room in the shelter of our hearts for the Christ Child?"

Lord, on this Christmas Day, let us open our doors to Your love and guidance. Help us to carry You in our hearts each day of the year.

EDNA MAYE GALLINGTON

Faith in Prayer

If ye have faith as a grain of mustard seed, ye shall say unto this mountain, Remove hence to yonder place; and it shall remove; and nothing shall be impossible unto you. Matt. 17:20.

MY FRIEND TRACEY TOLD me that weather conditions had grounded many flights. Stranded passengers were tired and annoyed with the inconvenience. The Saskatoon terminal was one of the crowded airports with passengers anxiously awaiting their flights. Tracey and her nephew were among the lineups to Kelowna, British Columbia.

"Kelowna has been covered with fog for three days. No planes are coming or going," Tracey was told when she reached the check-in counter.

"But we have to get there. My nephew is a teacher and has preparations to do."

"I'm sorry, ma'am. We can offer you two choices: You can fly to Calgary and take the bus to Kelowna, or you can fly to Victoria, where we'll pay your lodging in a hotel for one night. Then you can decide how to get to Kelowna from there. Which option do you want?" the clerk asked.

Tracey thought for a moment and replied, "I think we'll take the third option."

"Third option? What's that?" the clerk questioned.

"We'll pray about it," Tracey said calmly.

The clerk and those standing nearby gave strange looks. Amid stares Tracey declared, "We have to get there. God knows that. If God wants us there, He can lift that cloud." Tracey and her nephew left the airport and had a season of prayer. When they returned 45 minutes later, they were greeted with smiles.

"We have good news for you," the clerk said.

"I know what you're going to tell me," Tracey said. "Praise the Lord!"

Tension changed to amazement when people heard about the woman who prayed for the fog to be lifted in Kelowna. The same clerk received boarding passes at the departure gate. As Tracey passed through, the woman said, "Thank you for praying." Tears glazed her eyes. EDITH FITCH

It Pays to Read the Instructions!

Search the scriptures; for in them ye think ye have eternal life: and they are they which testify of me. John 5:39.

WHEN I RECEIVED THE beautiful bird clock for a Christmas gift, I was eager to hear it work. Each hour a different bird picture indicated the birdsong to be sung. Without carefully reading all the instructions, I pulled the clock out of its box and put in the required batteries. Then I hung the clock on a wall in the dining room. Soon the birds began to sing, a different one at each hour. I even decided to memorize the bird-calls so I could know what time it was without looking at the clock.

After about two days, however, I noticed that the birds singing on the hour were not the ones pictured on those hours. The oriole sang when it was time for the titmouse to sing, the robin sang when it was time for the little wren. And all the way around the clock the wrong bird sang. It was all mixed up!

Thinking the clock was defective, I even considered returning it to the store. Then, as I took it down and turned it over, I saw the instructions glued to the back and finally stopped to read all the instructions. There were three steps to follow which, in my haste, I had not read previously. Those three steps told me what to do. Number 1, take out the batteries. Number 2, rewind it to 12:00. Number 3, reset the clock's time, reinstall the batteries, and rehang it evenly. This time I hung it flat against the wall, as I should have the first time. It has worked perfectly ever since.

When I run into trouble in my spiritual life, I need to reread the instructions given in God's Word—to search them. In the prayer of Jesus it says, "Sanctify them through thy truth: thy word is truth" (John 17:17).

We need to read, study, and pray for guidance. Then we will know how to live each day. As in the promise of Psalm 32:8, God will instruct and teach us in the way that we should go.

BESSIE SIEMENS LOBSIEN

Every Shade of Red

A happy heart is a good medicine . . . , but a broken spirit dries the bones. Prov. 17:22, Amplified.

I saw an outfit on the sale rack that caught my eye. The price was right, so I bought it. The pants were really ugly, but the top was attractive. I wore the top several times, twice to church, out for an evening with my husband, to the doctor's office, to Sonny's school, and all around town while shopping.

The other morning I decided to wear the complete outfit. As I was checking out the bargains in another store, I noticed that there were more outfits like mine. I turned every shade of red and exited the store before the sales clerk noticed that I was wearing those ugly pants. I had just discovered that what I was wearing were pajama bottoms.

Now it makes sense why the clerk said, "I bought a pair like this too, and they are just perfect to wear at home while snuggling up with a good book." The comment had flown right over my head until it landed in every shade of red. I wonder how many giggles I got from others who identified my outfit as nighttime attire. How thankful I was that it was still chilly outside. I said, *Lord, You are really testing my sense of humor! Last week a sales clerk offered to give me a 10 percent discount because she thought I was over 50. I won't be the big 5-0 for another 30 months, and I thought I looked younger than my age, not older. And now this!*

Then He let me remember that when I was around 6 or 7, I kept having a reoccurring bad dream. In the dream I forgot to take off my pajamas. I wore them to school, causing myself great embarrassment. Forty years later it actually happened, and together my Jesus and I laughed.

This was just too funny to keep to myself, so I told a few friends and my husband. Yesterday I went shopping again. I was happy to find that there were three pairs of pajamas left on the sale rack. I bought them for my mom and my two sisters for next Christmas. This special gift is to remind them to thank the Lord for my sense of humor and for taking such good care of me. At Sonny's school they have "pajama day," and the kids and staff do wear their pajamas to school. I will be ready.

My heart is cheerful, Lord. I thank You for the good medicine.

Deborah Sanders

Still Small Voice Ministry

I heard the voice of the Lord, saying: "Whom shall I send, and who will go for Us?" Isa. 6:8, NKJV.

AS THE CHRISTMAS SEASON approached, I went shopping for the daily devotional books I always give my family. Before I left the book display I added a couple extras to my stack, even though I didn't know what I was going to do with them. A few days later my husband mentioned he would like to give his friend something for Christmas. When I suggested a devotional book, my husband was pleased. The second book was one of the women's devotional books. When I still had it a few days after Christmas, I remembered a sick friend. I felt sure she would enjoy a gift that she could read all year.

I realized a still small voice had directed me to those who would appreciate and enjoy the two books. Elijah's experience came to mind. I pictured him standing in the mouth of the cave while God displayed His power in the wind, earthquake, and fire, then contrasted His might by a still small voice (1 Kings 19:11, 12). So I have named my giving of devotional books "The Still Small Voice Ministry."

Small voice ministries can take other forms, too. It might be the impression to send a short note to someone who is sick or discouraged. Or mailing a card to a friend who is still grieving over the loss of a loved one. After the funeral they long to know somebody is thinking about them and praying for them. Their name or face coming to mind may be your commission to let them know you care.

This ministry can be even as simple and inexpensive as a handshake at church or a friendly smile in the supermarket for a mother who is struggling with a difficult child. Chances are she has already received her quota of frowns.

If He has not already done so, may God show you your still small voice ministry. Big deeds are needed in this life, but often it is the little loving things that give happiness to others and, in turn, a special kind of joy to you.

MILDRED C. WILLIAMS

Breakdown at Exit 5

Hear my cry, O God; listen to my prayer! In despair and far from home I call to you! Take me to a safe refuge, for you are my protector. Ps. 61:1-3, TEV.

I WAS READY TO HEAD back home to Maryland after spending the Christmas holidays in New York with my mother. My children, ages 14, 6, and 5, were with me. I decided to visit my aunt Dolly, who lived just off exit 5 on the New Jersey Turnpike, the road we would be traveling. I called to let her know we were on our way.

After we settled in the car, I said a quick prayer. "Lord, we've had a good trip, and now we want to get home safely. I don't want the car to break down, Lord, but if it must, please, let it be near exit 5. Thank You. Amen." I lifted my head and saw my older son, Greg, giving me a strange look. I'm sure he was wondering why I had prayed such a prayer. I was wondering the same thing, but I knew that at least if we broke down at exit 5, my aunt wouldn't be far away, and we'd be safe.

The day was extremely blustery and cold with the wind chill at -10° F. Even with the heat in the car pumping out at full force, pockets of frigid air whirled around us. After driving about an hour and a half, we began approaching exit 5. *Almost there,* I thought. I signaled and began changing lanes. Suddenly I saw thick, black clouds of smoke coming from the rear of the car. Within seconds I couldn't even see the road or any cars around me.

Oh, God, I thought, *help!* I continued driving, praying there were no cars immediately behind me as I completed the lane change. Almost instantly the car came to a halt. I tried to start the engine, but nothing happened. There we were, stuck at exit 5—frightened, hungry, and very cold. We tried flagging someone down. No one stopped. In desperation my older son ventured onto the roof of the car, waved wildly, and yelled at the passing cars. Still no one stopped. Finally, two hours later, a state trooper appeared, a tow truck was called, and the car was towed to a nearby service station. Within an hour we were at Aunt Dolly's, where we stayed for two days. Inconvenienced? Yes, but I praised God anyway. We could have broken down anywhere in the 225-mile stretch from my mom's house to mine, but it happened at exit 5.

IRIS L. STOVALL

A Narrow Escape

The angel of the Lord encamps all around those who fear Him, and delivers them. Ps. 34:7, NKJV.

IT WAS THE CHRISTMAS holiday season. My husband, our children, our son-in-law, a niece, and I all planned to spend New Year's weekend in Maryland with my mother and other family members. We were hoping to get to there in time for the annual New Year's service in our home church at sunset December 31. This is part of our holiday tradition.

After praying, we started out around 1:30 in the morning in a rental car packed to capacity with belated Christmas gifts, food, and clothing. As we headed north, the highway was clear, but snow covered the grass on both sides. Toward morning, about five hours into the trip, my niece was driving in the right-hand lane. Suddenly I heard a bang. I looked up and saw that the car was spinning out of control. Two other bangs followed, and the car came to a stop, parallel to and up against a guardrail. The car had made a complete U-turn—we were now heading south in the left lane, facing oncoming traffic.

We were in the middle of nowhere, had no cellular phone, and my niece was shaking with fear. The rest of us were in shock, trying to figure out what to do next. My husband and son got out to survey the damage in the predawn light. It was minimal. After a while a truck came along, and the two occupants offered to call the police. We thanked them and continued to pray, stuck there in freezing temperatures. After what seemed a long time, the police arrived. For quite a while they couldn't get the car started because they couldn't find the safety restart fuel button; they finally found it only after unloading the trunk. Then they stopped the oncoming traffic, enabling us to get back on course.

We were thankful that no one was hurt, but most of all we were thankful to God that no other vehicle was traveling behind us or beside us when our car spun around on that icy bridge. God had sent His angels to protect us by keeping the road clear of traffic right at that time. As we continued on our journey, quite conscious of the Lord's protection, my husband reminded us of our text for today. We did make it to Maryland in time for the sunset service, which had special meaning to us that year.

LYDIA D. ANDREWS

BIOGRAPHICAL SKETCHES

Betty J. Adams is a retired teacher, mother of three adult children, and grandmother of five. She is active in women's ministries and community service, and contributes to her church newsletter. She enjoys traveling, quilting, writing, and her grandchildren. **Apr. 25, Oct. 5, Dec. 11.**

Priscilla Adonis is a retiree/housewife. Her hobbies include writing, floral arranging, and crocheting. She writes from Cape Town, South Africa, and is the mother of two married daughters. **Jan. 26, Apr. 27, June 1, Aug. 3, Sept. 5, Nov. 19.**

Maxine Williams Allen resides in Orlando, Florida, with her husband and two small sons. An entrepreneur with her own computer and business consulting company, she loves to travel, meet people, experience different cultures, and teach a series on management and leadership strategies she created. Other hobbies are writing and reading. **Sept. 24.**

Dottie Allison, a teacher for 35 years, has taught at all levels, from kindergarten to college. She has been recognized as Teacher of the Year and as an outstanding teacher by the American Biographical Institute and the International Biographical Center. She is a pianist and writer and is women's ministries leader at her church. **May 10.**

Lydia D. Andrews is a registered nurse with 25 years' experience and a certified nurse-midwife. She has been in nursing education for 10 years and serves with her husband at the University of Eastern Africa as the midwifery lecturer and chair of the degree nursing program. She enjoys cooking, nature study, motivating and helping young people, attending prayer groups, and encouraging others. **Mar. 31, Dec. 31.**

Mary Wagoner Angelin lived in Kingman, Arizona, until moving to East Ridge, Tennessee, in 2000. She is a social worker at an inpatient psychiatric facility. She and her husband, Randy, have two daughters: 3-year-old Barbara, and Rachel, who is brand-new! Mary's hobbies are exercising, writing, vegan cooking, volunteering, and being a mom. **Feb. 16, Apr. 3, May 12, July 19, Nov. 7, Dec. 8.**

Kajol Bairagi was a teacher for 18 years and has served as conference director of women's ministries, children's ministries, health ministries, and communication. She enjoys her three teenage daughters, Neena, Idly, and Evi. Her hobbies are reading, singing, cooking, speaking, and visiting the sick and aged in her community. She lives in Jallundur, Punjab, India. **Aug. 31.**

Rosemary Baker, a freelance writer living in Iowa, is author of a children's religious book, *What Am I?* and has had articles in *Shining Star, Kids' Stuff,* and other magazines. She is a member of the Iowa Poetry Association, is active in church, and does volunteer work. Her hobbies include arts, crafts, music, poetry, and painting. **July 8.**

Jennifer M. Baldwin writes from Australia, where she is the clinical risk management coordinator at Sydney Adventist Hospital. She enjoys church involvement, travel, writing, and has contributed to a number of church publications. **Apr. 17, Aug. 12.**

Dawna Beausoleil, a former teacher, is living in northern Ontario. She loves to sing and write, does jigsaw puzzles during the long winters, and enjoys the outdoors during the glorious summers. **Mar. 7, June 8.**

Priscilla Handia Ben is women's ministries director of the Eastern Africa Division of Seventh-day Adventists. Priscilla previously worked as a home economics teacher, a full-time literature evangelist, and assistant publishing department director. She is married, with one stepdaughter, and enjoys cake decorating, homemaking, and reading. **June 9.**

Annie B. Best is a retired public school teacher. She and her husband of more than 50 years have two grown children. She enjoys being with her three grandchildren, reading, and listening to music. She has worked as leader in the cradle roll and kindergarten departments of her church, an activity she enjoys and finds rewarding. **Mar. 18.**

Susan Bolling, a pastor's wife, is a layout artist for the Swedish Seventh-day Adventist publishing service. She and her husband, president of the Swedish Union Conference, have three daughters, born in 1978, 1981, and 1989. Susan holds a B.A. in theology from Newbold College and an M.A. in religion from Andrews University. She enjoys reading, writing, swimming, and skiing. **June 29, Oct. 25.**

Irena Bolotnikova is associate director of the Ellen G. White Research Center at Zaoksky Theological Seminary in Russia. Her interests include gardening, playing in a Russian folk instrument orchestra, reading, studying languages, and traveling with her husband to the numerous extension schools where they both teach. **Feb. 18.**

Elizabeth Boyd, a physical therapist, is founder/owner of Traveling Medical Professionals, Inc., a traveling physical and occupational therapy registry. She lives on her farm in Harpswell, Maine, enjoys horses, entertaining, and music. She coaches young people in Bible study and prayer activities on the weekends. **Mar. 5.**

Patricia R. Brown from central Florida, works as senior director in organization development for the public education system. A graduate of Oakwood College, she is working on her master's in project management. She's a Sabbath school teacher, assistant treasurer, and director of finance in her church and enjoys yard work, walking, bike riding, and playing her violin. **Sept. 29.**

Darlene Ytredal Burgeson is a retired sales manager. Her hobbies include sending notes and seasonal cards to shut-ins, writing, photography, and raising prize irises. **Apr. 8, July 4.**

Pam Caruso has 10 grown children and 10 grandchildren. Her interests include classical music, fitness, and grandchildren. She is women's ministries leader at her local church. **Aug. 16.**

Virginia Casey is retired and resides with her husband in the town of Conception Bay South, Newfoundland. A born-again Christian who was baptized into the

Seventh-day Adventist faith January 1, 1994, she enjoys to the fullest her new life in Christ. A volunteer worker with Discover Bible School since 1996, she just loves people. **Nov. 11.**

Frances Charles is a retired school principal. She is women's ministries coordinator for the Kwazulu Natal-Free State Conference in South Africa. She is a bereavement counselor and a caregiver at a hospice. She has had a book, *My Tears, My Rainbow,* published. Her hobbies include writing and making pretty things. **Apr. 13, Sept. 8.**

Helen Charles writes from the Central India Union of Seventh-day Adventists in Pune, Maharastra, India. **Aug. 2.**

Lyndelle Chiomenti, editor of the *Easy Reading Adult Bible Study Guide* and associate editor of the *Adult Standard* and *Adult Teachers Bible Study Guides,* lives with her husband, Peter, in Frederick, Maryland. She and her dog, Elke, are members of PAL, a Washington, D.C., based organization that provides pet-assisted therapy and activities for nursing homes and hospitals. **Jan. 11, Mar. 23, Aug. 30, Oct. 14.**

Marsha Claus taught elementary school for two years. After her son was born five years ago, she chose to be a stay-at-home mom. Her husband is the manager of the Wisconsin Adventist Book Center. They enjoy traveling around the state on the bookmobile. Her hobbies include traveling, writing, and crafts. **Aug. 26.**

Clareen Colclesser, a retired L.P.N. and widow since 1994, has two children, six grandchildren, and five great-grandchildren. She enjoys her family, homemaking, and quiet times with a good book. Clareen stays active in her church. Hobbies include writing letters and short stories and her collection of interior decorating magazines. **Mar. 26, May 2, June 19, Sept. 6, Oct. 19.**

Pansy Cooper, a retired auditor, lives with her husband in Runaway Bay, St. Ann, Jamaica, West Indies. She is currently elder, treasurer, community services member, and Sabbath school teacher at her church. She is the mother of one daughter, Stacy-Renee, and enjoys sewing, gardening, and reading Christian literature. Her greatest joy, though, is witnessing for Christ. **June 23.**

Judy Coulston has a Ph.D. in nutrition and a private practice in Fresno, California. She has done a speaking tour of Australia and hosted and coproduced a highly rated weekly television program. Her latest venture is teaching pathophysiology. She also teaches adult Bible classes, is active in women's and prayer ministries, and is ever longing for Christ's second coming. **Feb. 9, May 1.**

Celia Mejia Cruz, now living in Georgia, was the women's ministries director for the Potomac Conference at the time of this writing. She is the proud mother of five young adult children and the grandmother of three. Celia collects Siamese cat figurines and decorative plates. **Feb. 23, May 14, Sept. 16.**

Yvonne Leonard Curry is a scientist who works as a director for minority programs in science. As a single mom of two teenagers, she enjoys running, crocheting, reading, and writing. **Feb. 26, Sept. 18.**

Jealanie Davis works in the Special Education Department of the Chatsworth, Georgia, Elementary School. She is involved with Pathfinders, women's ministries, and the Georgia Parent-to-Parent support group for families with children with disabilities. She is the mother of three boys and is a member of the Chatsworth Seventh-day Adventist Church. **Sept. 1.**

Fauna Rankin Dean lives in rural Kansas with her husband, three children, four dogs, three cats, and two horses. She enjoys her church family and spends her spare time on her hobbies: writing, photography, handicrafts, and a church music ministry. **Feb. 17.**

Winifred Devaraj enjoys her work for women in the southern part of India. She works with women from the states of Kerala, Tamil Nadu, and Karnataka. She loves to have her twin grandsons visit her. **Jan. 28.**

Sally Dillon lives in New Market, Virginia, with her husband and one son (and his 14 parakeets, two parrots, six finches, five cockatiels, and a 48-inch iguana) and really misses her other son, who is now in college. **Dec. 20.**

Leonie Donald has lived in Australia since 1987, when she, her husband, and son moved there from New Zealand. Her adult son now lives in Belgium. Her interests include reading, gardening, and walking. **Feb. 15, June 16, July 23, Aug. 24, Nov. 12.**

Goldie Down lives in Australia. She and her pastor-husband, David, who served as missionaries in India for 20 years, have six children, one of whom is an adopted Indian daughter. Goldie has had 23 books and hundreds of stories and articles published. Since retiring, she and her husband publish an archaeological magazine and are still active in church work, preaching, and teaching. **May 31, Aug. 22, Nov. 8.**

Louise Driver lives in Beltsville, Maryland, where she pastors with her husband, Don. They have three grown sons and four grandchildren. At church she is involved with music, youth, women's ministries, and Bible studies. She loves to sing, ski, read, do crafts, garden, and travel to historical places. She works at the General Conference in women's ministries. **Apr. 29, Aug. 27, Oct. 29.**

Mary E. Dunkin was born in a "hospital" on Route 66 in Albuquerque, New Mexico. She holds a B.A. degree in home economics and an Associate in Business Administration degree. She has held various offices in her home church. At present she helps run a business with her husband, Al. Mary's passions are God's will, being Doc and Nellie's daughter, Pathfinders, and her four Muttlets. **Dec. 7.**

Joy Dustow is a retired teacher who enjoys taking an active part in the social and spiritual activities in the retirement village where she resides with her husband. **May 21.**

Heike Eulitz comes originally from Germany. She left her home country when she was 19 and became a secretary in the Euro-Africa Division in Switzerland. She is active in the prayer ministry of her local church. Her hobbies include all kinds of crafts, baking, nature, and swimming activities. **Oct. 28.**

Gloria J. Stella Felder works in the communication department of the

Northeastern Conference of Seventh-day Adventists. Her husband pastors in Brooklyn, New York. They have a merged family of four grown children and four grandchildren. Gloria enjoys singing, listening to music, writing, public speaking, practicing the guitar, and working on her second book. **May 13, Sept. 17, Dec. 22.**

Eunice Pinheiro Pina Ferreira lives in Lisbon, Portugal, and is a graphic designer at the Portuguese Publishing House. She grew up in a Seventh-day Adventist home and has two sisters. She has been interpreting the role of Marie Durand (prisoner at the Tower of Constance in France) in special programs for women's ministries. She likes photography, reading, and writing. **May 22.**

Edith Fitch retired after 41 years of teaching, the last 28 in the church school at Canadian University College in Alberta, Canada. She enjoys writing and has devoted many hours of research to church and school histories. She volunteers in the college's archives. Her hobbies include needlecraft and traveling. **Mar. 10, June 12, Aug. 15, Dec. 26.**

Heide Ford is the associate editor of *Women of Spirit,* a Christian women's magazine. A registered nurse, she holds a master's degree in counseling. Heide and her pastor-husband, Zell, live in Maryland. She enjoys reading, hiking, and whale watching. **May 27, Aug. 25.**

Linda Franklin is a florist and runs a greenhouse in northern British Columbia. She grows and plants the flowers for the city of Chetwynd and started a garden club. She holds a B.S. in medical technology and serves her church as deaconess, women's ministries assistant, and flower arranger, and plays her accordion for special music. She especially enjoys prayer ministry. **Mar. 17.**

Suzanne French lives in Florida with her husband and enjoys attending church in Palmetto, where she is active in women's ministries. She is currently working, but looks forward to retirement within the next year. **Jan. 16.**

Edna Maye Gallington is part of the communication team at Southeastern California Conference of Seventh-day Adventists. She is a member of Toastmasters International and the Loma Linda Writing Guild. She enjoys freelance writing, music, gourmet cooking, entertaining, hiking, and racquetball. **Mar. 30, June 24, Dec. 25.**

Melinda Gladding has been active in church programs since she was 13. She works at the Samaritan Center in Collegedale, Tennessee. Her career has been motherhood, and she loves camping, hiking, drawing, reading her Bible, crafts, music, and delights in making people happy. **Dec. 19.**

Evelyn Glass enjoys her family and loves having her grandchildren live next door. She and her husband, Darrell, live in northern Minnesota on the farm where Darrell was born. Evelyn is active in her local church and her community, writing a weekly column for her local paper. She is women's ministries/family life director for the Mid-America Union of Seventh-day Adventists. **July 12, Sept. 22.**

Carrol Grady, a minister's wife with three grown sons and four granddaughters, lives in the beautiful Northwest. She is enjoying her long-anticipated retirement, with more time for reading, writing, quilting, music, and her latest interest, e-mail. She edits two newsletters and has authored a book, articles, and poems. **Jan. 23.**

Mary Jane Graves and her husband enjoy retirement in beautiful western North Carolina. They have two adult sons and two granddaughters, who are growing up too fast. Among other things, Mary Jane enjoys reading, gardening, family, and friends. **Feb. 25, Dec. 6.**

Carol Joy Greene is enjoying her golden years with her retired minister-husband in Florida. They have three adult children. She finds great pleasure in baby-sitting her young granddaughters whenever the opportunity arises. Carol Joy is an active participant in the women's prayer ministries in her church. **Jan. 13, Aug. 1, Dec. 4.**

Glenda-mae Greene is assistant vice president for student services at Andrews University. She delights in being the cherished aunt of three nieces and a nephew. Her contributions in this book are the end products of praying with a pen as she prepares for her speaking appointments with various women's and church groups. **Feb. 1, May 11, Aug. 4, Sept. 7, Oct. 31, Dec. 14.**

Gloria Gregory is a minister's wife, mother of two girls, and an associate professor of nursing at West Indies College, Mandeville, Jamaica. A graduate of Andrews University's Extension Program, with a Master of Education degree, her hobbies include handcrafts, playing word games, sewing, and gardening. **Feb. 3.**

Eshwari P. Halemane is a women's ministries director living in Belgaum, Karnataka, India. **June 5.**

Kathryn Hammond is retired but presently works as a pharmacy clerk. She enjoys meeting all the people who come for prescriptions. Her greatest joy, however, is her husband, son, and grandchildren who live nearby. **Aug. 23.**

Lynnetta Siagian Hamstra is the associate director of women's ministries for the General Conference. She was born and raised on the island of Borneo, in the state of Sabah, Malaysia. She inherits her love for music from her mom and traveling from her dad. She also enjoys reading and sewing. She lives in Maryland with her husband, Dan, and their dog, Abercrombie. **April 6.**

Dessa Weisz Hardin and her physician-husband spent four and a half months in China, working on the Loma Linda University project at the Sir Run Run Shaw Hospital. When home, she continues her community volunteer projects in the local library and in the public school reading program. **May 30, Oct. 21.**

Feryl E. Harris is a certified Bible instructor employed by the Mountain View Conference of Seventh-day Adventists in West Virginia as director of children's and women's ministries, trust services, and Sabbath school. She enjoys writing short articles, language study, singing, walking, and reading. **July 21.**

Peggy Harris is a local elder, board chair for WASH (Women and Men Against Sexual Harassment and Other Abuses), member of Kiwanis and Adventist-Laymen's Services and Industries, a writer, and a Bible hospitality seminar presenter. **June 18.**

Judith W. Hawkins is a county court judge in Tallahassee, Florida, where she lives with her husband, who is a college administrator. They have one adult son. A frequent speaker and presenter, Judith enjoys sharing her experiences with others. **Apr. 2, July 28, Oct. 4.**

Ann VanArsdell Hayward lives in a small town in Tennessee. After serving more than 30 years in the health-care industry, she actively works with senior citizens and her church and enjoys reading and travel. She says that it has been her privilege to be published in several editions of the devotional book after so many years of giving no thought to writing. **Dec. 13.**

Ursula M. Hedges is a retired secondary school teacher/administrator. Born to missionary parents in India, she and her Australian principal-husband have given 10 years of mission service in the Pacific, Australia, and New Zealand. **Jan. 29, Mar. 6, May 17.**

Roxy Hoehn writes from Kansas, the heart of America. She enjoys the adventure of travel and guided tours to learn about different parts of the world. She is active in women's ministries in the Kansas-Nebraska Conference of Seventh-day Adventists. **May 24.**

Karen Holford has written several books, including *Please, God, Make My Mummy Nice,* about how being a mother has taught her so much about God's love. She enjoys writing, crafts, being a mom to Bethany, Nathan, and Joel, and working with her husband, Bernie, in the Family Ministries Department of the South England Conference of Seventh-day Adventists. **Jan. 6, Feb. 14, Apr. 24, July 3, Oct. 20, Dec. 18.**

Helene Hubbard, M.D., Ph.D., is a pediatrician. She enjoys conducting the Palmetto Seventh-day Adventist Church orchestra and working in Sabbath school. She writes a health column for the Christian magazine *Women of Spirit.* **Mar. 9, Sept. 13, Dec. 21.**

Lorraine Hudgins is retired with her minister-husband in Loma Linda, California. She has worked at the Voice of Prophecy, Faith for Today, and the General Conference of Seventh-day Adventists. She has written two books, and her articles have appeared in various publications, including all nine women's devotional books. Her five children and 11 grandchildren are her joy. **Feb. 7, Mar. 29, May 25, July 13, Oct. 6, Nov. 3.**

Barbara Huff is the wife of a retired church administrator, a mother, and grandmother. She is a freelance writer and a serious amateur photographer. Her hobbies include bird-watching and shell collecting. **Sept. 26, Nov. 15.**

Viola Poey Hughes works in the marketing and development bureau at the Adventist Development and Relief Agency, and lives in Silver Spring, Maryland, with her husband, Chris, and two boys. Viola enjoys writing and research on international development issues. **July 29, Oct. 24.**

Bonnie C. Hunt is a retired nursing faculty member from Southern Adventist University in Tennessee. In her retirement she coordinates a learning assistance program for nursing at the university. The fact that her three grown children and five grandchildren live nearby is, she feels, one of God's greatest blessings to her. **Dec. 12.**

Christine Hwang, a family physician practicing in Toronto, Ontario, Canada, enjoys traveling and anything to do with food. She has traveled extensively on six continents, coordinates primary and junior Sabbath school programs, and is on her church board. She was a volunteer clinical adviser to an Adventist Development and Relief Agency project in Cambodia. **Apr. 22, Aug. 21.**

Aleah Iqbal, a freelance writer who lives with her family in Willimantic, Connecticut, home-schooled her children for 10 years. Her publishing credits include a book of poetry, original recipes for community cookbooks, and health store newsletters. In the past she hosted her own local cable television show. She is currently writing a children's book. **May 8, July 31, Oct. 18, Nov. 5, Dec. 24.**

Judy Haupt Jagitsch writes from central Illinois, where she and her husband live in retirement. They have five children and four grandchildren. Judy has worked at all levels of children's ministries in her local church and is presently church clerk. Her grandchildren are her greatest pleasure, followed by beautiful colors and vegetarian cooking. **Feb. 19.**

Lois E. Johannes retired from service for the Seventh-day Adventist Church in Southern Asia and the Far East. She lives near a daughter in Portland, Oregon. Lois enjoys community service involvement. **Apr. 4, July 14.**

Sushama Joseph is a women's ministries director living in Trichur, Kerala, India. She has two grown children. **Jan. 15.**

Anaudi Kanduluna lives in Nagabat, Assam, India. She helps in a children's Sabbath school and youth singing group. Her hobbies include reading, cooking, listening to music, forming a singing group, teaching, friendship, and associating with Christian leaders. **June 30.**

Marilyn King and her husband, Marvin, are retired and live by the beautiful Umpqua River in Oregon. Marilyn is a registered nurse with an M.B.A. degree and teaches music and Bible for her church. Her hobbies are family fun, nature, pets, and church activities. **Apr. 16, Nov. 21.**

Hepzibah G. Kore is Director for Women's Ministries, Shepherdess International, and Special Ministries for pastors' wives of the Southern Asia Division of Seventh-day Adventists. She and her husband have a son and daughter, a son-in-law, and two grandsons. Her hobbies are gardening, reading, and listening to music. She enjoys meeting with women of various cultures. **Sept. 10.**

Zodwa Kunene, a first-time contributor, is a pastor's wife and lecturer at Bethel College of Education in Butterworth, Eastern Cape, South Africa. She enjoys reading and sharing God's love through her hospitality and radiant disposition. **Sept. 25, Nov. 28.**

Mabel Kwei is the wife of the president of the Seventh-day Adventist Gambia

Mission Station in Africa, director of Gambia women's ministries, and lecturer at Gambia College. She works with her husband in pastoral work and loves reading. **Apr. 20.**

Nathalie Ladner-Bischoff and her husband, Marvin, live in Walla Walla, Washington. She is a retired nurse, and besides homemaking, she reads, writes, gardens, and skis. She's had several magazine stories published. Her most recent publication is *An Angel's Touch,* a book containing stories of miracles, answered prayers, and angel encounters. **Jan. 4, June 21, Oct. 27.**

Gina Lee is a freelance writer who has had more than 500 stories, articles, and poems published. She enjoys working at the local library, teaching a writing class, and caring for her four cats. **Jan. 9, Mar. 11, May 23, Aug. 17. Nov. 16, Dec. 23.**

Ludi Leito, a 25-year-old administrative assistant for the Youth Department of the General Conference of Seventh-day Adventists, has a degree in communications and biology and is currently working on her M.A. in communications. In her spare time Ludi enjoys writing poetry and short stories, but her greatest hobby is black-and-white photography and development. **Jan. 25.**

Ruth Lennox is a retired physician and is women's ministries director for the British Columbia Conference of Seventh-day Adventists in Canada. She and her husband have three married children and three little granddaughters. Ruth enjoys writing and producing monologues of Bible women, walking with her husband and her dog, and having a wonderful time with her granddaughters. **Mar. 28, Nov. 24.**

Karin Lepke is the wife of a graduate student. She has worked in Germany as a secretary with the Adventist Media Center and the criminal police. She and her husband are eager to reach resistant people groups with the gospel of Christ. Her hobbies include gardening, videotaping nature, reading, baking, and simply making contacts with people. **June 27.**

Cecelia Lewis writes from Huntsville, Alabama. She is a Bible instructor and teaches baptismal classes for adults, youth, and children at the Oakwood College Seventh-day Adventist Church. She enjoys tutoring at the elementary school, reading, writing, gardening, and being a member of the bell choir. **July 5.**

Bessie Siemens Lobsien is a retired librarian who has served in the United States and in several other countries. She has had articles and poems published. Bessie also serves her church as communication secretary. **Jan. 27, Mar. 14, Apr. 28, June 2, Aug. 18, Dec. 27.**

Alicia Márquez has been accountant for the Greater New York Conference of Seventh-day Adventists for 10 years and has worked for the Spanish telecast *Ayer, Hoy y Mañana.* She chairs the women's ministries committee, is treasurer of the women's prayer retreat, and an elder at Far Rockaway Spanish Seventh-day Adventist Church. Born in Uruguay, she came to the United States 29 years ago. **June 20, Oct. 7.**

Philippa Marshall is a retired nurse who is involved with her local church and voluntary work. She enjoys writer's holidays and meeting other writers. Philippa attends women's ministries retreats and visits friends and family. **Apr. 19, July 22.**

Peggy Mason lives in Wales with her husband and one of her two adult sons. She is a teacher of English and a writer whose hobbies include dried flower growing and arranging, cooking, sewing, gardening, and reading. She is a pianist/composer and enjoys working for her church and community. **Apr. 23.**

Mary Maxson is women's ministries director for the North American Division of Seventh-day Adventists. She and her pastor-husband, Ben, served in team ministry in Georgia, Carolina, and Missouri, and in mission service in Argentina and Uruguay. Certified in marriage enrichment and as a hospital chaplain associate, Mary has been an editorial and administrative assistant. **Nov. 4.**

Ellen E. Mayr has worked for the past 10 years as department director for women's ministries, children's ministries, and family ministries. She and her husband have two grown children, Siegward and Hearly. She enjoys reading, preparing materials, writing, and singing along with the piano. **Apr. 7.**

Maria G. McClean, originally from Barbados, lives with her husband, Wayne, and daughter, Kamila, in Toronto, Ontario, Canada. She is a member of the Toronto West Seventh-day Adventist Church, where she is involved in various ministries. She enjoys Bible study, music, and writing. **Jan. 14, Mar. 1, June 3, Aug. 11, Oct. 11, Dec. 2.**

Patsy Murdoch Meeker, of Virginia, enjoys writing, reading, photography, and occasional trips to visit her scattered family. **Dec. 9.**

Eunice Mafalda Michiles is a teacher. She was a member of the national legislature for 16 years and the first female senator in Brazil. She has four children and five grandchildren. She likes to work in social assistance in her church and in women's ministries. She also likes to cook for her family on the weekends, read, and listen to music. **June 10, Aug. 13.**

Susen Mattison Molé was born in India to missionary parents and spent most of her early life in the Far East. She is a full-time mother and teacher to two home-schooled daughters, but occasionally finds time for her hobbies: reading, trekking, and needlepoint. She is married to a naval officer and continues to travel the world. **Mar. 24, Aug. 10, Sept. 9.**

Marcia Mollenkopf, a retired schoolteacher, lives in Klamath Falls, Oregon. She is active in local church activities and has served in both adult and children's divisions. Her hobbies include reading, crafts, and birdwatching. **May 19, Sept. 12.**

Esperanza Aquino Mopera is a registered nurse in the Virginia Beach, Virginia, public schools. She is director of women's ministries and a Sabbath school teacher at the Tidewater Seventh-day Adventist Church. Her hobbies include gardening and watching backyard lake inhabitants. She also enjoys baby-sitting her grandchildren. **Apr. 11, Oct. 17.**

Bonnie Moyers lives with her husband and two cats in Staunton, Virginia. She is a certified nursing assistant, musician for two Methodist churches, and does painting and papering and freelance writing whenever she can fit them in. She is the mother of two adult children and has one granddaughter to enjoy. Her writings have been published in many magazines and books. **June 17, Oct. 30, Nov. 25.**

Lillian Musgrave and her family have made northern California their home for nearly 40 years. She enjoys music, writing (including poetry and songs), family activities, and church responsibilities. **June 25.**

Sibusisiwe Ncube-Ndhlovu is a prospective M.B.A. student who enjoys singing, swimming, watching soccer, cooking, visiting, and reading. **May 29, Nov. 26.**

Anne Elaine Nelson, a retired teacher who home-schools children, has written a book, *Puzzled Parents.* She helps her husband with his business in Michigan. They have four children and 11 grandchildren. Active with women's ministries, youth, and Sabbath school in her church, she says her favorite activities are sewing, music, photography, and creating memories with her grandchildren. **July 15.**

Vera Nelson is a retired secretary living in Hayden, Idaho. She serves in her church community services center and the church library. She enjoys reading, writing, and an occasional Maranatha project. She's trying to learn how her new computer works. **Apr. 30.**

Desmalee Nevins is a health education officer with a Master's degree in public health. She lives in Trelawny, Jamaica, with her husband, and five children. Her hobbies are singing, reading, and mentoring. She is active in music, youth, and family ministries in her church. **Mar. 13.**

Cynthia Alexander Nkana, M.D., is a missionary physician at Bella Vista Hospital in Mayaquez, Puerto Rico. Her husband, Sam, and their three children, Ethan, Enoh, and Emmanuel, all support mission service. **Sept. 3.**

Sheree Parris Nudd, F.A.H.P., an accomplished speaker and a published author, is a regional director for the Brook Grove Foundation in Montgomery County, Maryland. She has been involved in pioneering Internet ventures for nonprofit and online charity auctions. Sheree is a wife, mother, and career woman. **Sept. 30.**

Edna May Olsen and her husband moved from England to California the summer of 1999. Her hobbies are swimming, writing, hiking, church work, and spending time with their three daughters and three granddaughters. **Apr. 15, June 7, Aug. 28.**

Jemima D. Orillosa works as a secretary at the General Conference of Seventh-day Adventists in Silver Spring, Maryland. She has a loving husband and two teenage daughters she adores. She was a missionary in Africa for eight years and in Cyprus for two years. She loves to be with people. Writing, walking, and entertaining visitors and friends are some of her hobbies. **Feb. 6, Apr. 14, May 18, Aug. 29, Oct. 15.**

Hannele Ottschofski lives in Germany with her family. She is editor of the local Shepherdess newsletter and loves to read and write. She presents seminars at women's retreats and loves to play the piano and direct a choir in her local church. She has just completed her first handmade quilt for her grandson. **Mar. 16, July 24, Oct. 9, Dec. 16.**

Ofelia A. Pangan serves God with her minister-husband in central California. She loves reading, gardening, traveling, and playing Scrabble. Even more, she loves visiting her three grown-up children and her grandchildren. **July 1, Aug. 7, Oct. 12, Dec. 10.**

Revel Papaioannou is a pastor's wife in the biblical town of Berea (now Véroia, Greece). She has four married sons and six grandchildren. Her interests include church work, mountain walking, and collecting stamps, coins, and telephone cards. **July 2.**

Jill Warden Parchment, a retired physician's wife, is on several editorial committees and enjoys helping in church and civil projects. She and her husband do volunteer work around Loma Linda, California. **Nov. 30.**

Celia Parker writes from Nottingham, England. She is a retired care assistant for the elderly. She enjoys being on the lay preacher's team in her local church, writing letters of encouragement, walking, and singing. Her joy in life is her family, and she has two adult children and three grandchildren living in Northern Ireland. **May 6.**

Margie Penkala is manager of the Graphic Arts Department at St. Helena Hospital in California. She enjoys working with children at the church, where she and her husband are members. Her hobbies include traveling with her husband, researching family roots, spending time with their grandchildren, and editing the quarterly newsletter *SynapSez.* **Feb. 2.**

Ivy Petersen has retired after 34 years of being a teacher, lecturer, and principal from first-grade to college level. She and her lecturer-husband have both served as local elders and lay preachers. They now travel South Africa, promoting and establishing women's ministries. They have five children and 10 grandchildren at last count. **July 6, Nov. 13.**

Ahalya Bai Philips is the women's ministries director of South Karnataka Section of Seventh-day Adventists. She lives in Bangalore, India, where she enjoys reading, gardening, and writing. She has at various times worked as an office secretary and the dean of girls at a boarding school. **Feb. 4.**

Birdie Poddar is from northeastern India. She and her husband enjoy retirement but keep busy. She enjoys gardening, cooking, baking, sewing, reading, writing, and handcrafts. They have a daughter, a son, and four grandsons. **Feb. 28, Sept. 14, Dec. 5.**

Lanny Lydia Pongilatan, from Jakarta, Indonesia, works in the Sabbath School/Personal Ministries department at the General Conference of Seventh-day Adventists. A professional secretary, she was an English instructor in Indonesia. She enjoys playing the piano, listening to gospel songs, reading religious books, exercising, and swimming. **Feb. 24, Apr. 5, Nov. 29.**

Joshna Prakash is a teacher who lives in Bidar, Karnataka, India. She is actively involved in women's ministries in the villages around Bidar. **Apr. 26.**

Balkis Rajan is director of women's ministries, family and children's ministries of the

Upper Ganges Section of Seventh-day Adventists in Hapur, Uttar Pradesh, India. She has worked 22 years as a teacher. She is the mother of two children. **Jan. 12.**

Carolyn Rathbun Sutton, former editor of *Guide* and author of *Journey to Joy* and *No More Broken Places,* now lives in Grants Pass, Oregon. A wife and mother, Carolyn enjoys teaching a children's Bible class, volunteering at a wildlife rehabilitation center, doing freelance writing/public speaking, and learning how to drive a tractor. **Mar. 27, Sept. 15, Nov. 1.**

Judith Redman is a wife and a mother of two girls and lives in a village on the south coast of England. She works as a part-time secretary for a large multinational company. She enjoys caravaning, crafts, playing squash, and takes an active role in the running of her local church. **May 28.**

Jean Reiffenstein-Rothgeb lives with her husband in Utah, a state that offers every kind of outdoor activity there is. They are both employed by an orthopedic surgeon, though they should be retired. Their children, grandchildren, and great-grandchildren occupy their thoughts and prayers, but their many church offices are very important also. **Jan. 3.**

Charlotte Robinson, a third-generation Seventh-day Adventist, is a wife and the mother of three. She has had stories published in *Our Little Friend, Primary Treasure, Guide, Insight,* and the *Adventist Review.* Between taking her junior/earliteen-age children to school and cleaning two post offices, she likes to mow lawns, write letters, and do almost anything but clean house. **Feb. 13, July 27.**

Hilkka Rouhe has lived most of her life in Finland and Sweden. She has many skills, including knitting and handicrafts. She has knitted many beautiful baby jackets for an orphanage in Romania. She loves traveling to visit her children and grandchildren, who all live far away. **Mar. 25, Aug. 14, Nov. 23.**

Mercy Samson is director for women's ministries, Shepherdess International, children's ministries, and family ministries in the South Andhra Section of India. A graduate of Spicer College in Pune, India, she was a teacher in various Seventh-day Adventist schools for 26 years. She is a first-time contributor. **Feb. 5.**

Deborah Sanders has shared from her personal journal, *Dimensions of Love,* since the beginning of this devotional book series under the pen name Sonny's Mommy. She lives in Canada with Ron, her husband of 32 years. They have two blessed children, Andrea and Sonny. Sonny is severely mentally disabled with autism. Deborah enjoys trying to make others feel special. **Jan. 31, Apr. 12, Aug. 9, Sept. 28. Dec. 28.**

May Sandy enjoys being involved in her local church as the clerk and an elder. Women's ministries work keeps her mentally and spiritually challenged. During her long service leave this year she hopes to achieve two long-term goals: to use efficiently old and modern technology (a computer and treadle spinning wheel). **Sept. 21.**

Marie H. Seard, retired, is living in Washington, D.C., with her husband, who works at the world headquarters of the Seventh-day Adventist Church. She is a regional vice president of the Oakwood College Alumni Association. She has written several devotional pieces and enjoys traveling, reading, and writing. **Jan. 2, July 17.**

Trudy Severin is a contract medical technologist working in Lebanon, Pennsylvania. She enjoys traveling, singing, hiking, camping, exploring, swimming, snorkeling, meeting new people, and, most of all, encouraging young people to hold on to Jesus. She is married with one young child. **Apr. 9, Oct. 8.**

Donna Lee Sharp is active in her local church as organist, pianist, Sabbath school and Daniel seminar teacher, and worship committee member. She is involved in music for a senior center, convalescent homes, and Christian Women's Club. She enjoys bird-watching, reading, traveling, and visiting her five children and seven grandchildren. **June 13.**

Donna Sherrill works in a small country store close to Jefferson Adventist Academy in Texas. She is working toward making an album of songs she has written and is publicist for a Christian country recording artist. **Nov. 20.**

Carrol Johnson Shewmake and her pastor-husband are now retired but still active in prayer ministry. Carrol is the author of five books on prayer and often speaks at camp meetings, prayer conferences, women's retreats, and individual churches. She is the mother of four adult children and has eight grandchildren. **Jan. 17, June 26, Oct. 1.**

Rose Neff Sikora lives in the beautiful mountains of western North Carolina. A registered nurse for the past 20 years, she has interests that include camping in a travel trailer, writing, spending time with her three grandchildren, and helping others. She has had many articles and stories published in the local newspaper, magazines, and this series of devotional books. **Jan. 18, Mar. 20, June 22, Sept. 2, Nov. 27.**

Sandra Simanton is a licensed clinical social worker and works as a family therapist in Grand Forks, North Dakota. She lives with her husband and two children in nearby Buxton. She works with the children's ministry at her church and enjoys reading and sewing. **June 15, Dec. 3.**

Taramani Noreen Singh has been a teacher for 15 years and has served many years as a secretary in the mission offices where her husband worked. She presently lives in eastern Uttar Pradesh, India. **Mar. 22.**

Melinda Skau is a family practice physician who serves with her surgeon-husband in rural Nigeria. The highlights of her life are David, age 12 and Keri, age 10. She relaxes by reading and writing, and enjoys water sports and bird walks. **Feb. 11.**

Ethel Footman Smothers writes from Grand Rapids, Michigan. She is a published poet and children's book author. Ethel and her husband have four daughters and seven grandchildren. **Feb. 12, Apr. 1.**

Ginger Snarr graduated from Walla Walla College School of Nursing in 1960. Currently, she is a homemaker who lives in Vancouver, Washington, with her husband, Dudley. During the past few years she and her husband have made several trips to do humanitarian work, mostly in the former Soviet Union. **Feb. 20.**

L. Winsome Speck and her husband, now retired, spent 20 years as missionaries in New Guinea. A women's ministries leader, she has published three books, enjoys producing biblical drama, coordinating arts and crafts, demonstrating vegetarian cooking, conducting prayer and Bible study groups and seminars. She loves walking and spending time with her husband and family. **Feb. 8, May 3.**

Ardis Dick Stenbakken is director of women's ministries for the General Conference of Seventh-day Adventists in Silver Spring, Maryland. When not busy with women's ministries, this former English teacher likes to spend time with her husband and their two married children, of whom they are very proud. She also enjoys reading and spending time with friends. **Jan. 30, Mar. 19, May 7, July 25, Sept. 23, Oct. 23, Dec. 1.**

Iris L. Stovall, administrative secretary in women's ministries at the General Conference of Seventh-day Adventists in Silver Spring, Maryland, is also assistant editor of the department's monthly newsletter. Married, with three adult children, she is dreaming of writing a children's book. Singing, reading, videography, and beautiful sunsets are things she enjoys. **Jan. 24, Mar. 21, May 15, Aug. 5, Nov. 9, Dec. 30.**

Rubye Sue is a retired secretary, having worked at numerous denominational conference and educational facilities. She and her husband enjoy traveling and spend summers in Tennessee and winters in Florida, where he has a 700-tree citrus grove. **Oct. 13.**

Jean Sundaram enjoys cooking, gardening, tailoring, reading, and interacting with her two young adult children. Enoch is a medical doctor, and Synthia is a physiotherapist. Jean is the women's ministries director of the South Tamil Conference of Seventh-day Adventists in India. **Jan. 20.**

Loraine F. Sweetland is a retiree, church clerk, newsletter editor, school board chair, and Sabbath school teacher. She writes a weekly church article for the local newspaper in her hometown in Tennessee. Her hobbies are teaching nutrition classes and surfing the Internet. **Jan. 10, June 11, Oct. 10.**

Claudette L. M. Tang-Kwok, a member of the Burnt Mills Seventh-day Adventist Church in Maryland, has had three articles published in the *Adventist Review.* Claudette, a legal secretary at a Washington, D.C., law firm, has two adult daughters and lives in Beltsville, Maryland. **Apr. 18.**

Frieda Tanner, a retired registered nurse, now devotes her time to creating and sending Sabbath school material to needy children of the world. **May 20.**

Arlene Taylor, risk manager at St. Helena Hospital in California, is also founder/president of a nonprofit corporation which promotes brain-function research, provides resources, and helps individuals learn how to be more successful. A brain-function consultant, she enjoys traveling around the world, presenting seminars about personal and spiritual growth. **Jan. 19, May 4, July 10, Sept. 27.**

Stella Thomas works in the General Conference of Seventh-day Adventist Global Mission Office in Silver Spring, Maryland. She is a primary Sabbath school teacher at the Takoma Park Seventh-day Adventist Church in Maryland. She enjoys traveling and being a mother to her two children. **Aug. 6.**

Stella Thompson is a wife, mother, and writer. She is currently completing doctoral studies, and teaches college writing and adult literacy. She enjoys reading, writing, art, sewing, walking, and keeping in touch with friends. **Jan. 1, Feb. 27, June 28, Sept. 20.**

Ena Thorpe is the women's ministries leader in her church. She is married and has three grown children, two of whom are married. She is a retired registered nurse who enjoys doing the Lord's work, reading, crocheting, and playing Scrabble. **Mar. 2.**

Joan Ulloth has been teaching nursing at Kettering College of Medical Arts in Ohio since 1983. After earning her Ph.D. in educational leadership from Andrews University, Berrien Springs, Michigan, she married Lonnie Dorgan in October 1998. She has been involved in the handbell ministry of her church since 1984 as both a ringer and the director of the youth handbell choir. **Feb. 10.**

Nancy L. Van Pelt is a certified family life educator, best-selling author, internationally known speaker, author of more than 20 books, and has traversed the globe, teaching families how to really love each other. Her hobbies are getting organized, entertaining, having fun, and quilting. Nancy and her husband live in California and are the parents of three adult children. **Mar. 15, June 14, Aug. 19, Nov. 22.**

Nancy Cachero Vasquez is volunteers coordinator for the North American Division of Seventh-day Adventists. She is the mother of three adult daughters and wife of a vice president of the North American Division. She is coauthor of *God's 800-Number: P-R-A-Y-E-R,* and a former missionary who enjoys reading, writing, shopping, and spending time with her husband. **July 30, Nov. 10.**

Kelly Veilleux lives in Waterville, Maine. She is a wife and mother and works full-time as the CFO of a trucking company. She is the women's ministries director for the Northern New England Conference of Seventh-day Adventists and is head elder in her local church. She loves to work with women and young people. **Oct. 22.**

Vasti Viana is the wife of a pastor, José Viana, and mother of two adult children. Ricardo is married to Lisley, and Joyce to Hiroshi. Vasti was previously the women's ministries director in the South American Division of Seventh-day Adventists. She likes music, reading, and walking. **May 26, Nov. 14.**

Donna Meyer Voth is married and has an adult daughter. She is involved in planting a new church in Portage, Michigan. She gives Bible studies and enjoys leading women's study groups. She teaches part-time and volunteers for the American Cancer Society. **Feb. 22, Oct. 3.**

Nancy Jean Vyhmeister is a professor of mission, a missionary, and an editor. More important, she is a wife, mother, and grandmother (and though she lives there, is decidedly not a fan of Michigan winters!). **Jan. 22.**

Céleste perrino Walker is a professional writer/editor living in Rutland, Vermont, with her husband, Rob, and children, Joshua and Rachel. She teaches her son a bilingual kindergarten program and piano. She enjoys reading to her children, painting, photography, canoe camping, and portraying an eighteenth-century French woman at historical reenactments. **Apr. 21.**

Cora A. Walker lives in Queens, New York. She is a nurse and is an active member in a local Seventh-day Adventist church in Queens. Reading, writing, sewing, classical music, singing, and traveling fill her leisure time. She has one son. **May 9, June 4, July 20.**

Mae E. Wallenkampf is a homemaker and former music teacher. She likes to sing in a group, play the clarinet, cook, bake, entertain, and write. For more than 15 years she typed (and later used the computer) for her minister-teacher-author-husband. She enjoys her three children, five grandchildren, and two great-grandchildren. **July 16.**

Kimberly Palmer Washington is an international singer-evangelist and Bible instructor who travels all around the world, attending tent meetings, concerts, and workshops. She lives in Thomasville, Georgia, with her husband and daughter. Kimberly says she lives her life for the Lord and is waiting for Jesus to come. **July 18.**

Anna May Radke Waters is the mother of five and grandmother of seven. She dearly loves God and helping people to know of God's love for them. Playing Scrabble, traveling with her husband of 46 years, and doing counted cross-stitch, knitting, and crocheting are among her favorite pastimes whenever she finds time to relax. **Jan. 5, Mar. 4, May 16, Aug. 8, Oct. 16, Nov. 17.**

Ruth Watson has been a bookkeeper, elementary teacher, and office manager. Her most enjoyable job is her current one—grandmothering—even though it's unsalaried. She likes to improve her skills in writing, church activities, making scrapbooks, and garden painting (with flowers). **Jan. 8, Mar. 12, July 7, Sept. 19, Nov. 6, Dec. 17.**

Dorothy Eaton Watts is associate secretary of the Southern Asia Division of Seventh-day Adventists. She is also a freelance writer, editor, and speaker. She has been a missionary in India for 16 years, founded an orphanage, taught elementary school, and has written more than 20 books. Her hobbies include gardening, hiking, and birding (with more than 1,000 birds in her world total). **Jan. 21, Mar. 3, May 5, June 6, Sept. 4, Nov. 18.**

Penny Estes Wheeler had her first story published in *Guide* in 1969 and has been writing ever since. Now editor of *Women of Spirit,* she loves telling stories and frequently teaches or speaks for women's retreats. She and her husband enjoy the ever-widening worlds of their four adult children. **Feb. 21.**

Victoria L. Wickwire is a certified nurse-midwife and an assistant professor of nursing at Andrews University. She and her husband, Bruce, enjoy living in Michigan; they have three adult children. Vicki loves going on mission trips with her husband, teaching, working on her Ph.D., flower gardening, landscaping, interior decorating, and hiking. **Dec. 15.**

Vera Wiebe enjoys working with her husband as a partner in pastoral ministry. She has two adult sons, who are both married. She is a member of the women's ministry committee for the British Columbia Conference of Seventh-day Adventists. Playing the piano and sewing are two of her hobbies. Working with people brings her a lot of joy. **Aug. 20, Nov. 2.**

Mildred C. Williams and her husband live in California, where she works part-time as a physical therapist. She enjoys Bible study and teaching, writing, public speaking, sewing, and gardening. She has two daughters and one granddaughter. **July 26, Oct. 2, Dec. 29.**

Sharon Dalton Williams is a freelance writer from Laurel, Maryland. **Jan. 7, Apr. 10, Oct. 26.**

Patrice Williams-Gordon lectures in the natural science department at Northern Caribbean University in Mandeville, Jamaica. She enjoys reading, homemaking, speaking engagements, and family life. Her greatest ambition is to have an unswerving relationship with Christ. She and her pastor-husband have two daughters, Ashli and Rhondi. **Mar. 8, July 9, Sept. 11.**

Mary H. T. Wong is director of children's, family, and women's ministries in the Northern Asia-Pacific Division of Seventh-day Adventists, headquartered in Seoul, Korea. She and her husband have been involved in educational work in colleges in Singapore and Taiwan and in church leadership in Maryland for most of their working careers. **July 11.**

Prayer Requests

By the side of every soul
is an angel presence.
—This Day With God, *p. 332.*

Prayer Requests

Consecrate yourself to God in the morning;
make this your very first work.
—Steps to Christ, *p. 70.*

Prayer Requests

A heart of faith and love is dearer to God
than the most costly gift.
—Desire of Ages, *p. 615.*

Prayer Requests

Prayer is the opening of the heart
to God as to a friend.
—Steps to Christ, *p. 93.*

Prayer Requests

Prayer does not bring God down to us,
but brings us up to Him.
—Steps to Christ, *p. 93.*

Prayer Requests

God will do marvelous things
for those who trust in Him.
—Testimonies, *vol. 4, p. 163.*

Prayer Requests

The gates are open for every mother
who would lay her burdens at the Saviour's feet.
—Desire of Ages, *p. 512.*

Prayer Requests

Do not neglect secret prayer,
for it is the soul of religion.
—Testimonies, *vol. 1, p. 163.*

Prayer Requests

Prayer is the breath of the soul,
the channel of all blessings.
—Maranatha, *p. 85.*